Fundamentals
of Retiree Group Benefits

Dale H. Yamamoto

ACTEX Publications, Inc.
Winsted, CT
ActexMadRiver.com

Requests for permission should be addressed to
ACTEX Publications
P.O. Box 974
Winsted, CT 06098

Manufactured in the United States of America

10 9 8 7 6 5 4 3 2

Cover design by Christine Phelps

Library of Congress Cataloging-in-Publication Data

Yamamoto, Dale H., 1952-
  Fundamentals of retiree group benefits / Dale H. Yamamoto.
    p. cm.
  Includes bibliographical references and index.
  ISBN-13: 978-1-56698-586-4 (pbk. : alk. paper) 1. Retirees--United
States. 2. Postemployment benefits--United States. 3. Insurance,
Group--United States. I. Title.
  HQ1063.2.U6Y36 2006
  331.25'50973--dc22

                                          2006033452

ISBN: 978-1-56698-586-4

PREFACE

This book should have been first written 25 years ago. In 1980, several employers offered retiree group benefits to their employees in the U.S. because of the tax-effective benefit and relatively low current costs. With retirees representing a small percentage of the overall covered population, it was an inexpensive fringe benefit. Some employers even paid for the Medicare Part B premium for the retiree and spouse. A few employers provided free coverage to their retirees—absolutely no contribution requirement for the former employees. These benefits were at the top of their game at this time.

Besides the tax-effectiveness of the benefit back then, most employers did not understand what the long-term cost of this obligation was. Unlike pension plans that were subject to the newly required minimum funding rules of the Employee Retirement Income Security Act (ERISA), retiree group benefits were largely unfunded and accounted for on a pay-as-you-go basis. For companies who did want to prefund their obligations, they could find vehicles that allowed them to almost fund as much as they wanted, sheltered the investment earnings from taxes and paid tax-free benefits.

Life was simple with very few rules and relatively low cost. Tax legislation passed in 1984 that restricted prefunding retiree obligations and subjected the investment earnings to taxes for certain types of funds. The Financial Accounting Standards Board (FASB) adopted new accounting standards in 1990 that required companies to accrue for future retiree group benefit payments during an employee's working career—similar to pension plans. This new accounting requirement along with high medical cost trends in the late 1990s sparked a major revolution in the design and employer financing. Other influences on retiree group benefit design include court decisions, new legislation, overall retirement strategy changes, and the health care market in general.

Much has changed in 25 years. There is a great variety of designs and financing arrangements utilized by employers that are very different from three decades ago. Few employers can claim to just have one "plan." Most have different programs for salaried versus hourly employees; vary the plans by location, retirement date or employment date; have legacy plans due to prior mergers and acquisitions; and even have employees without a plan.

Retiree group benefits have earned a reputation for being difficult to understand. Half retirement benefit and half group insurance—few professionals have mastered both fields. In addition, complex finances blend the world of pension mathematics and health plan pricing.

This book attempts to provide a fundamental understanding of almost all of the elements that make up the world of retiree group benefits. Some things may have been missed and things will definitely change. I hope there is something of interest to everyone.

Because of the complex nature of the subject, I owe a great deal of gratitude to several friends who volunteered their time to review the drafts of this book. In alphabetical order, they are Paul Fronstin (Employee Benefit Research Institute), Randy Johnson (Motorola), Frank McArdle (Hewitt Associates), Tricia Neuman (Kaiser Family Foundation), Jeff Petertil (independent consultant), Adam Reese (Hay Group) and Allen Steinberg (Hewitt Associates). Each one of these reviewers is well-known in this field and provided invaluable input to make this a much better book.

I also want to thank Gail Hall of ACTEX for her encouragement to complete this project. This book was started four years ago as a collection of various articles and papers that I had authored over the years. Updating that material turned out to be more work than I had anticipated. And, there were several topics that I had never written about. Gail did what all great leaders do, she gave me a deadline. Material was further updated because of changes in the last four years and expanded with new text. And, this book is the result.

Finally, I thank my wife Louise and son Ben for sacrificing valuable vacation time so that I could write this book. It made for great conversation after taking two four week vacations, when most of the writing was done, to tell friends what I did on my time off of work. Typical response was, "are you nuts?" with a few just shaking their heads. Most days comprised of writing in the morning, doing something fun mid-day and back to writing in the evenings. So, the next vacations will include a lot more of the "fun" during the day.

Dale H. Yamamoto
October 2006

TABLE OF CONTENTS

1 INTRODUCTION

Retiree life and medical benefits were introduced to U.S. employee benefit programs in the late 1960s. The medical plans were first designed to supplement the Medicare program and were viewed as a "no cost" benefit. At the time, the benefits were very inexpensive because medical costs were relatively low and there were few retirees. Life insurance benefits for retirees were often added as a natural expansion of retiree benefits.

In recent years, some employers have expanded their post-employment offerings to include long-term care insurance and continuing-care retirement communities. These benefits are usually offered to employees at their own cost (i.e., employee-pay-all). Others include severance, dental, vision and hearing benefits.

In some respects, these benefits are similar to pension plans. They are provided to employees after they have contributed their services to their employer. Many times, the benefits are continued for the retirees' lifetime. Like pension plans, some plan designs even vary based on service. But, unlike pensions, these retiree group benefits are generally not extensively prefunded.

Retiree group benefits have gained much more attention since the early 1990s. The primary reason is the accounting rules that became effective for most companies in 1993, issued by the Financial Accounting Standards Board (FASB). These rules (FAS No. 106)[1] require employers to account for retiree group benefits while an employee is working rather than waiting until he or she is retired and the payments are made. A similar rule just released by the Governmental Accounting Standards Board (GASB) will have a similar effect on U.S. states and municipalities starting in 2006.

---

[1] Financial Statement of Accounting No. 106, *Employers' Accounting for Postretirement Benefits Other Than Pensions,* Financial Accounting Standards Board, December 1990.

Other factors have also forced attention on retiree group benefit plans. In 1960, when many employers were adopting retiree health care plans, the U.S. spent $28 billion on health care-related costs. This represented 5.2 percent of the gross domestic product (GDP). By 1980, the spending grew to $255 billion or 9.1 percent of the GDP and in 1990 $717 billion or 12.4 percent of GDP. Spending continued to grow in the 1990s, reaching $1 trillion in 1995 or 13.8 percent of GDP.[2] And health care spending is expected to reach $2 trillion in 2005 and $3 trillion by 2011.[3] Most executives are very aware of how their companies' medical plan costs have increased over the same period. Couple this with an increasing number of retirees due to maturing populations (in some cases exacerbated because of recent layoffs and early retirement incentive plans) and greater financial pressures. One can conclude very quickly that retiree medical plans cost REAL money!

The purpose of this book is to provide the reader a fundamental knowledge of the key issues with retiree group benefits. It is important to recognize how both pensions and health care interact with each other as well as differences in the delivery of the benefits. A secondary purpose of this book is to put under one cover, all of the disparate focuses of these complex benefit offerings, including the history of the benefits, Medicare, design strategies, funding options, legal considerations, accounting and actuarial calculation methods.

Employer-sponsored retiree group benefits continue to be an important source of coverage for Medicare-eligible retirees with 35 percent of Medicare beneficiaries covered under employer plans in 2002.

---

[2] Centers for Medicare & Medicaid Services, Office of the Actuary, Data from the National Health Statistics Group. February 2006.

[3] Borger, Smith, Truffer, Keehan, Sisko, Poisal, and Clemens, *Health Spending Projections Through 2015*, Health Affairs, February 22, 2006.

Supplemental Health Insurance of Medicare Beneficiaries, 2002

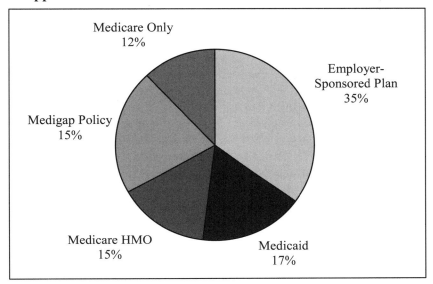

Source: Kaiser Family Foundation Analysis of the Medicare Current Beneficiary Survey 2002 Cost and Use File

Figure 1.1

MEDICARE

The Medicare program in the U.S. is usually the primary health insurance source for citizens and permanent legal residents age 65 and over. Unlike other industrialized countries, the U.S. does not have a socialized health care system for the majority of its population.

The U.S. has primarily an employment-based health care system. For persons covered under employer-provided health plans, the former employees and their family members are provided care in a private system that is reimbursed by the health plans. The form of reimbursement may go through the patient in a fee-for-service system. Under this approach, the provider (e.g., a physician, hospital, lab), typically provides the patient a bill, the bill is submitted to the health plan for payment and if the plan does not pay the full amount of the bill, the patient pays the remainder. Other forms of reimbursement may be that the providers are part of the health plan (i.e., physicians are paid a salary and on staff and the health plan owns the hospital). Under this type of system, the patient goes to the provider and generally pays a nominal copay to use the facility or see a physician. And, there are variations in between these two.

The Medicare system is more like a fee-for-service plan with some other options available. Most of the Medicare beneficiaries are over age 65, although 6 million disabled persons are also covered. Medicare is the primary provider of health coverage for the aged as long as the person is not covered as an active employee in an employer-provided health plan. This creates a very large difference in the employer plan costs when a retiree turns age 65. Typical employer plan costs per person are about $8,000 for a pre-65 retiree and $3,000 for a post-65 retiree in 2006.

The introduction of prescription drugs to the Medicare program in 2006 creates a new set of delivery models under the program and opportunities for employers to coordinate their programs around the new benefit.

The existence of Medicare at age 65 or prior disability creates a challenge in the design and valuation of the retiree medical plans. Employer plan costs per person prior to Medicare eligibility are two to four times higher which creates both a plan design challenge as well as a social responsibility question because without Medicare and employer-sponsored coverage, many retirees and disabled individuals will be uninsured. The challenge is exacerbated by the fact that the Medicare design is based on the typical employer-based design used in the 1960s. Employer designs have evolved and changed but Medicare has been slow to adapt.

Other governmental systems may have similar distinctions by age. For example, Canada's provincial plans do not cover certain prescription drugs after a person becomes age 65.

PLAN DESIGN CHANGES

The first plan design changes intended to reduce employers' future obligations started in the early 1980s and have continued through the mid-2000s. These historical changes concentrated on who pays what share of the premium cost of the medical benefits—the employer or the retiree. More recent changes have focused more on the control of health care spending.

Early Plan Changes

Most of the retiree medical plan changes made in the early 1980s when the FASB first started to review the accounting of the benefits were modest and consisted of:

- Introducing or slightly increasing the level of retiree contributions;

- Adopting policies of setting retiree contributions as a fixed percentage of plan cost; and

- Changing the method of coordinating benefits with Medicare.

More recently, companies have been reassessing the design of their plans by introducing features similar to pension plans, such as:

- Redefining eligibility requirements to be more stringent (e.g., requiring a person to be at least age 60 with 15 years of service versus age 55 with 5 or 10 years of service);

- Introducing service-related benefits (e.g., the employer portion of plan cost varies depending on the employee's years of service at retirement);

- Adjusting retiree contributions based on the employee's age at retirement (i.e., early retirement reductions);

- Setting the employer subsidy to the retiree medical plans as a fixed dollar amount and not a percentage of plan costs (e.g., the company will annually pay for up to $75 per year of service at retirement and the retiree pays the excess), and

- Providing an account-based employer subsidy for retiree group benefit plans (e.g., the employee "earns" $1,500 for each year of service that they work, so an employee with 20 years of service at retirement has $30,000 to use for purchase of employer plan options or for any other medical expense).

Future Plan Design Considerations

Most of the early plan design changes shifted the costs from the employer to retirees. It is likely that future changes will also continue to shift cost to retirees. But if retiree health plans are to remain an employer-provided benefit, future changes will need to result in reduced total costs in order to make the plans affordable.

The basic framework for these changes will be similar methods that employers have used to reduce health care costs for their active employees. These recent changes were seldom applied to retiree plans because of the thought that "retirees are different." This is especially true for those eligible for Medicare.

Retirees are different from active employees in many ways. It is harder to get communication to them because they do not come to work regularly. Many have family physicians that they have been seeing for a long time, making it uncomfortable and difficult to change. Some move away from where they worked, and it is difficult to physically meet for a company-sponsored event. Despite these obstacles, many health care management strategies used for active employee plans can work for retiree plans. However, they may have to be designed with a different emphasis for retirees.

Future efforts will be to change the value proposition of retiree healthcare including:

- Providing an account-based employer subsidy (generally non-funded accounts),

- Consumerism initiatives to encourage efficient care,

- Information and tools with which to make informed decisions,

- Overall total cost management, and

- Other methods to effectively coordinate the employer plan with Medicare.

Most of the plan design changes outlined above do not have the same dramatic accounting cost reductions achieved by some of the fixed dollar benefit designs introduced in the early 1990s. The overall retiree health care costs, however, will be controlled. If a fixed dollar benefit design has not been adopted, these changes will reduce future cost increases, justifying a lower accounting cost.

Controlling health care costs in this fashion may prevent the desire to increase other benefits (e.g., pension benefits) because the retiree's out-of-pocket health care costs are contained. More importantly, most of the changes will be a "win-win" for the company and its retirees.

In cases where cost control is not enough, some employers are making the hard decision that they can no longer afford to subsidize retiree group benefit coverage but are sensitive to the fact that without employer-sponsored coverage, some individuals may not be insurable. This will lead to more access-only retiree coverages, especially for pre-65 retirees. That is, retirees will be required to bear the full cost of the plans.

PREFUNDING

Although not often a popular notion for controlling retiree group benefit costs, a large number of major employers currently have some assets set aside for a portion of their FAS 106 obligations. Most employers will argue that their internal rates of return far outweigh returns they can achieve by prefunding retiree group benefit plans. The key impetus for prefunding will be more philosophical than financial.

Due to the rules on selecting a discount rate under the Governmental Accounting Standards Board (GASB) Statement No. 45, governmental entities may conclude that prefunding makes sense from a financial statement perspective.

LEGAL ISSUES

Retiree group benefits have been the subject of several court cases. Many involve collectively bargained contracts, although there have been many involving salaried employees. Early court cases tended to favor the plaintiffs, and employer plans were required to continue or maintain provisions in their plans indefinitely. After several of these cases were decided, employers began to include language in their communication of retiree group benefit plans that they have the right to amend or terminate the plans in the future. Since that time, courts have tended to favor the employers' side because of this type of language in their legal documents as well as plan description summaries provided to employees and retirees. In addition, courts have ruled on age discrimination issues within a retiree medical program and the level of prefunding an employer may set aside.

NATIONAL HEALTH CARE

The employer's role in the health care delivery system has an uncertain future. The Medicare program may be changed in the future and there could eventually be another major push for national health care. The framework of many of the design sections of this book will likely be included in any national program. Also, since many of these design changes are relatively simple to adopt (large case management, spousal initiatives, retiree education), it makes sense to adopt them now and reduce the short-term costs of retiree medical plans.

ACCOUNTING

The change in accounting treatment of retiree group benefits in the early 1990s had a dramatic impact on the designs of these programs. The Financial Accounting Standards Board introduction of Statement of Financial Accounting No. 106 (FAS 106) in 1992 increased many employers' retiree group benefit costs by factors of five to ten times their previously recognized costs. Although not changing the true nature or cost of retiree group benefit plans, the requirement to accrue the benefits similar to pension plan accounting generally accelerated the accounting recognition of the cost of the plans from tomorrow to today.

The accounting treatment is very similar to pension plan accounting concepts with some special additional assumptions such as probability of future participation in the plans and assumptions to anticipate the future costs of the program, including estimating the current year claim costs as well as future costs.

The GASB issued Statements 43 and 45 in 2004 to provide standards of accounting for retiree group benefit plans (and their trust funds) and for state and local governmental employers' financial statements, respectively. Patterned after FAS 106, it is expected to have similar impact on the delivery of retiree group benefits to these governmental entities as it is adopted over a three year period based on the size of the employer beginning in 2006 for GASB 43 and 2007 for GASB 45.[4]

---

[4] Statement No. 43, *Financial Reporting for Postemployment Benefit Plans Other Than Pension Plans*, [17]; and Statement No. 45, *Accounting and Financial Reporting by Employers for Postemployment Benefits Other Than Pensions*, [18]. Actual first effective for financial statements beginning after December 15, 2005 for GASB 43 and after December 15, 2006 for GASB 45.

And finally, as of the writing of this text, the accounting profession is attempting to establish international standards. By doing so, significant changes will occur that will require amendments to FAS 106. The primary change will be the reduction in the degree of smoothing of accounting costs in exchange for more transparency in current obligations.

ACTUARIAL METHODS AND ASSUMPTIONS

The projection of retiree group benefit payments blends the actuarial practices of pension and health actuaries. Pension actuaries have the background and knowledge to project long-term costs, and health actuaries have the expertise to estimate the current costs of health care and their likely costs in the short-term.

This textbook provides the fundamentals of plan design, accounting, funding and legal issues of these post-employment benefits. Although many references in this textbook focus on the U.S. medical system (i.e., no national health plan until age 65), the principles are applicable to other countries.

EROSION OF
2 RETIREE HEALTH BENEFITS

No matter what survey the reader is studying, the theme is always a downward slope of employers offering retiree health care benefits. The titles of two papers have used the term "erosion" of retiree health benefits.[1] Although written four years apart from each other, many of the same issues are shared by them. It is likely that these same issues will continue during the next several years. Each paper cites surveys from various sources, graphically showing this erosion.

Percentage of Large Firms (200+ Employees) Offering Health Insurance to Retirees, 1988-2005

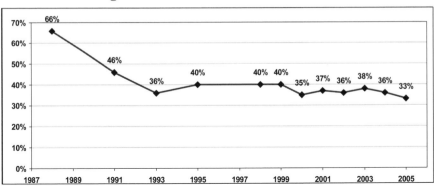

Source: Kaiser/HRET survey of employer-sponsored health benefits, 1999-2005; KPMG survey of employer-sponsored health benefits, 1991, 1993, 1995, 1998. The Health Insurance Association of America (HIAA), 1988.

Figure 2.1

---

[1] Paul Fronstin, *The Impact of the Erosion of Retiree Health Benefits on Workers and Retirees*, [15] and *Retiree Health Benefits: Employer-Sponsored Benefits May Be Vulnerable to Further Erosion*, [38].

11

Figure 2.1 shows the typical downward slope of retiree group benefit prevalence. The largest decline took place in the early 1990s when the then new accounting standard, FAS 106, became effective.

Figure 2.2 shows the prevalence of retiree health care benefits over a shorter time period but with a split between pre- and post-Medicare eligible retirees, and with both large and small employers included in the analysis.

**Percentage of Private-Sector Establishments
Offering Health Insurance to Retirees, 1997-2002**

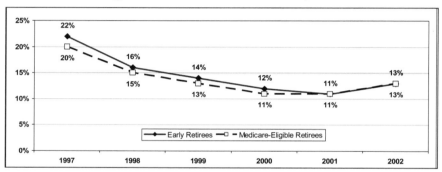

Source: EBRI from various tables at www.meps.ahcpr.gov/Data_Pub/IC_Tables.htm

Figure 2.2

The upward movement from 2001 to 2002 provides some hope. However, other survey data (including others referenced in this chapter) show a more continued downward slope including those from consulting firms (Hewitt Associates, Watson Wyatt, Mercer) and from policy organizations such as the Kaiser Family Foundation.

Figure 2.3 shows a similar graph only for large employers who have historically been more likely to provide retiree health care. The downward trend for this group is less dramatic than Figure 2.1, but continues beyond 2001. And, the gap between pre- and post-65 prevalence appears to be widening.

**Percentage of Large Employers Offering
Health Insurance to Retirees, 1991-2005**

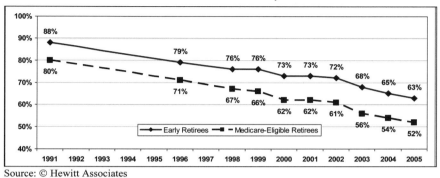

Source: © Hewitt Associates

Figure 2.3

The prevalence of retiree health care declines significantly by the size of employer. Figure 2.4 shows the differences in 2005.[2]

**Percentage of Employers Offering
Retiree Health Insurance Coverage by Size of Firm, 2005**

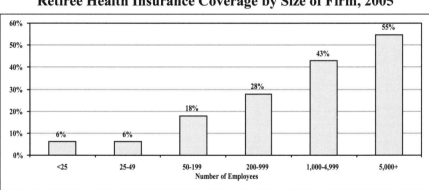

Source: 2005 Kaiser/HRET Employer Health Benefit Survey

Figure 2.4

The public sector data (Figures 2.5 and 2.6) does show some variation from the steep downward slope. Those local governments offering retiree health care are relatively stable during the six year observation period. State governments have been less likely to eliminate retiree health care coverage but have followed a similar trend as the private sector in terms

---

[2] Kaiser Family Foundation and Health Research and Educational Trust, *Employer Health Benefits 2005 Annual Survey*, September 2005.

of modifying the plan designs to require greater contributions and cost sharing by retirees.

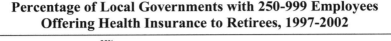

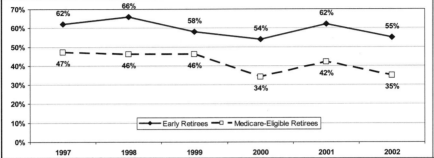

Source: EBRI from various tables at www.meps.ahcpr.gov/Data_Pub/IC_Tables.htm

Figure 2.5

Percentage of State Governments Offering Health Insurance to Retirees, 1997-2002

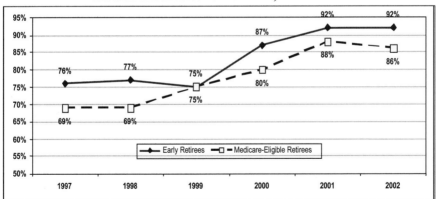

Source: EBRI from various tables at www.meps.ahcpr.gov/Data_Pub/IC_Tables.htm

Figure 2.6

Many observers will be watching the public sector offering of these benefits in light of new accounting standards going into effect from 2006-2009 for trust funds and government entity financial statements.[3]

---

[3] Statement No. 43, *Financial Reporting for Postemployment Benefit Plans Other Than Pension Plans*, [17] and Statement No. 45, *Accounting and Financial Reporting by Employers for Postemployment Benefits Other Than Pension Plans* [18].

These standards will require public sector employers to include the value of retiree health plan obligations on their financial statements on an accrual basis similar to the FAS 106 rules for private sector employers. FAS 106 is commonly "blamed" as the reason for the decline in employer-sponsored retiree health care benefits. Many have instead viewed the accounting standard as an "eye-opener" to the real current value of the benefits that were often considered nominal.

Figure 2.7 shows an interesting trend line – the number of retirees with employer-sponsored health benefits between 1994 and 1999 was relatively stable. This is over the same period of time where many surveys show dramatic reductions in the number of <u>employers</u> offering retiree health coverage. This phenomenon occurs because when employers change their plans and drop coverage, they almost always "grandfather" current retirees and some active employees so that their coverage is not completely eliminated.

Percentage of Retirees with Employer-Sponsored Health Benefits

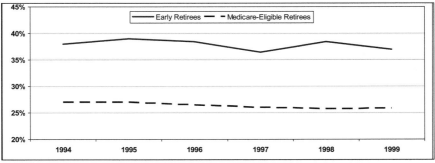

Source: GAO analysis of Current Population Survey, March Supplements 1995-2000

Figure 2.7

Besides the prevalence of employers offering retiree health care, both papers note that many other employers are reducing their benefits design by increasing various cost-sharing elements (e.g., increasing deductibles, out-of-pocket maximums and copays), restricting eligibility and increasing retiree contribution requirements. The common cost control method of placing caps on the employer obligation will continue to have a very big impact on the cost-shifting to retirees.

The introduction of the new Medicare prescription drug program may further entice employers to drop coverage—at least for Medicare-eligible retirees. Nine percent of respondents to the 2005 Kaiser/Hewitt survey of large private sector employers indicated that they plan to discontinue drug coverage in 2006.[4] However, with the government taking on more responsibility in financing health care for these retirees, it could delay much further action to reduce coverage, at least in the short-term. In the same survey, 91 percent of employers planned to continue their drug coverage, representing 98 percent of all retirees.

The GAO report cited the Hewitt study that estimated employers will have cost savings from the introduction of the Medicare drug benefit and would likely retain the employer coverage.[5]

The Congressional Budget Office (CBO) assumed in their estimates of the new program that 2.7 million Medicare beneficiaries would lose their employment-based benefits. Another CBO study concluded that 17 percent of Medicare Part B enrollees would lose their employer-sponsored plans.[6] And another study estimates that about a quarter of retirees (2.1 million) will lose their coverage.[7]

Estimates made by an EBRI analysis found that two to nine percent of current Medicare beneficiaries would lose their employee benefits because of the new Medicare benefit. They cite other factors that may also force employers to drop benefits such as business conditions, accounting, and cost trends. The GAO paper adds other factors such as the Erie County age discrimination case[8] and the aging baby boom generation as contributions to the decision to drop coverage.

---

[4] Kaiser Family Foundation and Hewitt Associates, *Prospects for Retiree Health Benefits as Medicare Prescription Drug Coverage Begins*, December 2005.

[5] Hewitt Associates, *The Implications of Medicare Prescription Drug Proposals for Employers and Retirees*, Kaiser Family Foundation, July 2000.

[6] Holt-Eakin, Douglas, CBO letter to Senate Budget Committee, November 20, 2003.

[7] Thorpe, Kenneth E., *Implications of a Medicare Prescription Drug Benefit for Retiree Health Care Coverage: An Update Based on the Medicare Conference Agreement*, Emory University, November 17, 2003.

[8] *Erie County Retirees Association v. County of Erie*, 220 F.3d 193 (3rd Cir. 2000) cert. denied, 69 U.S.L.W. 3409 (U.S. March 5, 2001) (No. 00-906). See Chapter 6.

**Baby Boom Generation Will Greatly Increase
the Elderly and Near-Elderly Population**

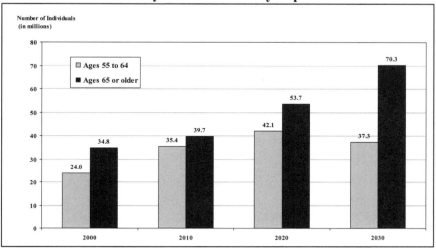

Source: GAO Report. U.S. Census Bureau, "Projections of the Total Resident Population by 5-Year Age Groups and Sex with Special Age Categories: Middle Series," selected years 2000 to 2030, January 2000

Figure 2.8

The post-65 population is expected to double between 2000 and 2030. This will put an increasingly severe strain on the health care system because the average cost of care is higher for this population than all others. Figure 2.9 provides a relative comparison of costs by age. Both male and female costs per capita continue to increase until age 75 and then begin to decline. Most clinical experts anecdotally believe that the observed decline is because individuals reaching these ages are healthier than average and there is less heroic medicine performed. A 75 year female costs 2.7 (2.4 ÷ 0.9) times a 40 year old female and a 75 year old male costs 4.1 (2.9 ÷ 0.7) times 40 year old male.

Total Costs by Age

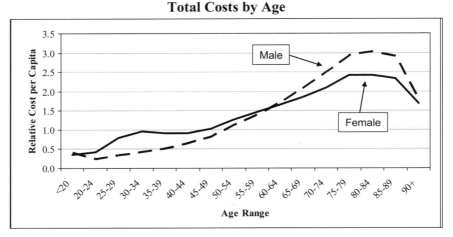

Source: © Hewitt Associates 2006 medical pricing model

Figure 2.9

IMPACT ON RETIREES

The impact of eroding coverage on individual retirees is varied and depends on a number of factors. EBRI compiled various statistics from the Survey of Income and Program Participation (SIPP) that show interesting characteristics of the currently covered retirees and how access to retiree coverage has changed between 1997 and 2002. The following table is an extract of some of the analysis.[9]

Key points in their analysis include:

- Early retirees lost coverage at a greater rate than Medicare-eligible retirees.

- Females had higher drop of coverage than males,

- Those with lower education levels saw higher erosion of coverage than those with advanced education.

---

[9] Extracted from Figures 14 and 15 from EBRI Issue Brief No. 279, March 2005 [15].

Table 2.1

Percentage of Retirees with
Employer-Sponsored Retiree Health Coverage

	Early Retirees (55-64)			Medicare-Eligible Retirees		
	1997	2002	Percentage Change	1997	2002	Percentage Change
Total	39.2%	28.7%	− 26.8%	28.1%	25.5%	− 9.1%
Gender						
Male	48.5	40.6	− 16.3	34.2	33.3	− 2.8
Female	29.0	18.5	− 36.2	21.6	18.4	− 14.7
Education						
>high school	18.3	12.1	− 33.7	18.6	16.2	− 13.1
High school	42.0	28.0	− 33.4	29.7	25.7	− 13.4
College	49.4	35.4	− 28.4	39.3	33.5	− 14.6
Post-college	63.1	53.6	− 15.1	48.6	46.1	− 5.1
Union status						
Union	57.1	49.9	− 12.5	42.6	37.9	− 11.1
Nonunion	32.1	21.8	− 32.1	22.8	21.4	− 6.1

Other characteristics analyzed include race/ethnicity, region of the country, age retired, industry, class of worker (i.e., private versus government), annual income and firm size.

In virtually all groups, early retirees lost more ground than Medicare-eligible retirees. Overall, the percentage of early retirees with coverage declined 26.8 percent compared to 9.1 percent for Medicare-eligible retirees. This is an interesting result when compared to the prevalence data in Figure 2.3 that shows that Medicare-eligible retirees lost more ground during the same period (about 7 percent reduction in early retiree coverage compared to 12 percent for Medicare-eligible retirees). This seems to imply that the drop in early retiree coverage occurred at small to medium sized employers in greater numbers than at larger employers.

This loss of coverage will affect retirees differently. Some may have other coverage available through their spouse or from another association program or public program for which they may be eligible. Some early retirees may use the health continuation coverage (COBRA) available from their former employer, but that coverage is generally only for 18 months. Some may be healthy enough to have individual health insurance available. Many retiring are, however, in poorer health and therefore will not be eligible for individual insurance coverage. The GAO paper shows the percentage of employed and retired individuals who reported their health to be fair or poor.[10] In general, these individuals are not likely to be eligible for individual medical policies. And without access to a nationalized program like Medicare, they enter the uninsured statistics.

	Percentage Reporting Fair or Poor Health	
Age	Employed	Retired
55 – 64	11.3	21.7
55 – 61	10.6	19.7
62 – 64	14.5	23.7
65+	17.7	35.3
65 – 74	17.0	30.0
75+	20.0	40.2

For those lucky enough to be eligible for coverage, they may be surprised at the rates that they will have to pay. The GAO requested rates from some carriers in a variety of states and include the following table of the differences in rate between a 30-year old and a 60-year old for illustrative purposes.

	Deductible (plan type)	Monthly Premium 30-Year Old	Monthly Premium 60-Year Old
Carrier A (Arizona)	$250 (indemnity)	$ 162	$ 512
Carrier B (Illinois)	$500 (PPO)	$ 116	$ 439
Carrier C (Colorado)	$0 (HMO)	$ 132	$ 324

Note that the GAO report was released in May 2001 so these rates need to be adjusted appropriately for cost trends between today and then. Even in 2001, for a retiree to have to pay $5,000 a year for health care coverage ($10,000 for a family of two), it is a very visible part of their budgets. Health care costs have increased 7 to 10 percent between 2001 and 2006 which makes the cost $7,000 to $8,000 per person!

---

[10] GAO analysis of the March 2000 Current Population Survey.

3   MEDICARE

Medicare is the federal health insurance program in the U.S. that provides benefits primarily to individuals age 65 and over, and to disabled workers.[1] Individuals with end-stage renal disease (ESRD) also qualify. Unlike many other countries, the federal government does not provide a universal health care program other than Medicare. The federal government provides financial subsidy for low-income health programs (Medicaid) that is operated and jointly financed by the states. The federal government also provides coverage for military and civilian federal retirees.

Individuals are entitled to Medicare as a result of paying into the Social Security system through payroll taxes while they work. There are also some premium requirements when a person enrolls in Medicare Parts B, C and D, as defined in the next section.

Since Medicare's inception in 1965, the program has provided insurance for hospital stays with some short-term skilled nursing home care and professional services. It was intended to provide relatively comprehensive health care coverage and was patterned after the common form of group insurance of the time—the Blue Cross and Blue Shield hospital and medical coverage design. In the 1980s, Medicare began offering managed care options from private insurers. And finally, the program began covering prescription drugs in 2006, which was the largest portion of health care spending that Medicare did not cover in the prior four decades.

ELIGIBILITY

There are two parts of the "original" Medicare program. Part A, or the Hospital Insurance (HI) program, covers inpatient hospitalization and limited skilled nursing facility care. Part B, or the Supplementary Medical Insurance (SMI) program, covers physician, outpatient services (i.e.,

---

[1] Title XVIII of the Social Security Act, designated *Health Insurance for the Aged and Disabled* established as part of the Social Security Amendments of 1965.

laboratory and x-ray services), certain home health visits and other medical services.

When a person attains age 65, they qualify for Medicare Part A (hospital coverage) if either they or their spouse paid into the Social Security or the Railroad Retirement system and earned at least 40 Social Security credits (or at least 10 years of Social Security covered work). Credits are based on the amount of earnings during the year. In 2006, an individual earned one credit for each $970 of earnings (up to four per year). The $970 earnings amount is indexed. There is no premium requirement for Part A since it is presumed paid from workers' payroll taxes. In reality, Medicare taxes paid in a current year are mostly used to pay current benefits. In other words, the Part A program works on an intergenerational transfer system. Today's employed generation pays the benefits for the retired generation in return for the "promise" that the future employed generation will pay their benefits when they are retired.

Individuals who did not work the required 10 years may purchase the Part A coverage ($393 per month if they have less than 30 credits of covered employment or $216 per month if they have 30 to 39 credits in 2006). They may also qualify based on their spouse's earnings history if the spouse is at least age 62 and has worked 40 calendar credits.

If a person is covered by Part A, they are eligible for Part B (other medical coverage). Part B coverage requires payment of a monthly premium, so the program is voluntary. In 2005, about 95 percent of older Americans enrolled in Part A were also enrolled in Part B coverage. This percentage has been slowly declining since 1984, when 98 percent of Part A enrollees also enrolled in Part B.

As demonstrated in Figure 3.1, overall enrollment in Medicare has increased significantly since its beginning in 1966. Part A enrollment has grown from 19.1 million in 1966 to 42.0 million in 2005 and Part B enrollment has grown from 17.7 to 39.7 million over the same time period.

HI and SMI Historical Enrollment

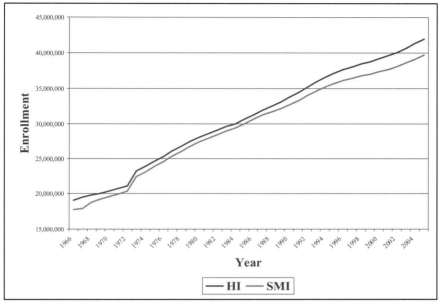

Source: 1966-2005 Medicare Enrollment Trends, Centers for Medicare & Medicaid Services, Office of the Actuary

Figure 3.1

Included in the enrollment numbers are disabled workers who have increased even more dramatically. Enrollment increased from 1.7 million in 1973 when they were first covered to 6.7 million in 2005 under HI (Part A). Over the same time period, enrollment increased from 1.6 to 6.0 million under SMI (Part B). To be eligible for coverage as a disabled worker, an individual under age 65 must have been entitled to Social Security or Railroad Retirement disability benefits for at least 24 consecutive months. Effectively, this means that a person needs to be disabled for 29 months (five-month elimination period plus 24 consecutive months of disability) before they can be covered by Medicare. For disabled persons with amyotrophic lateral sclerosis (ALS or Lou Gehrig's disease), they are eligible for Medicare the first month they get disability benefits.[2]

In addition, persons with end-stage renal disease (i.e., permanent kidney failure requiring ongoing dialysis or transplant) who have paid Medicare

---

[2] The Medicare, Medicaid, and SCHIP Benefits Improvement and Protection Act of 2000 (Pub. L. 106-554) waived the regular 24-month elimination period.

taxes for 40 credits (or their spouse has) also qualify for Medicare coverage.

The following table shows the enrollment split between aged and disabled eligibility for enrollees in either Part A or Part B.

Year	Total Enrolled	Aged Enrollees		Disabled Enrollees	
		Number	% Total	Number	%Total
1966	19,108,822	19,108,822	100%	—	
1970	20,490,908	20,490,908	100%	—	
1975	24,958,552	22,790,157	91%	2,168,395	9%
1980	28,478,245	25,515,070	90%	2,963,175	10%
1985	31,082,801	28,175,916	91%	2,906,885	9%
1990	34,203,383	30,948,376	90%	3,255,007	10%
1995	37,535,024	33,141,730	88%	4,394,294	12%
2000	39,619,986	34,252,835	86%	5,367,151	14%
2005	42,394,926	35,633,683	84%	6,708,551	16%

Source: Centers for Medicare and Medicaid Services, Office of the Actuary

The other two parts of Medicare, Part C (coordinated care plans) and Part D (prescription drug plans), base eligibility from the Parts A and B requirements. To be eligible for any Part C plan, the person must be entitled to Part A coverage and enrolled in Part B. To be eligible for a Part D plan, the person must be either entitled to Part A coverage or enrolled in Part B. Therefore, a person could enroll in a Part D plan if they didn't enroll in Part B but that same person could not enroll in a Part C plan without enrolling in Part B.

MEDICARE HEALTH PLANS

The Medicare program offers several alternative health plans. Beneficiaries have the option to elect either the "Original Plan" or one of the "Medicare Advantage" (MA) options. In addition, they can voluntarily enroll in a prescription drug plan either separately (a private PDP option) or through a MA plan that includes prescription drugs (MA-PD). Many experts have been concerned that the availability of these multiple choices has created confusion amongst the beneficiary population.

The following diagram illustrates how Medicare is organized.

Medicare Health Plan Diagram

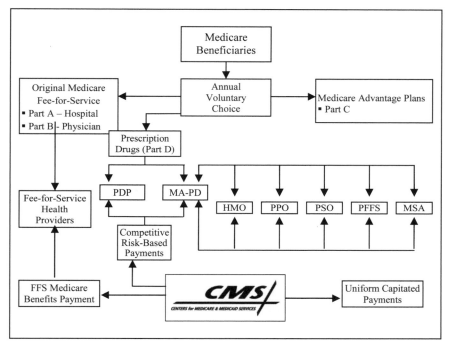

Figure 3.2

Briefly, Medicare beneficiaries annually "enroll" in either the Original Medicare program or one of the Medicare Advantage plans. If they are currently covered under the Original Medicare program (Parts A and B) and they wish to continue, they do not have to actively enroll. By doing nothing, they will continue their plan coverage (passive enrollment). If they enroll in an MA plan, they have to follow the rules of the MA plan and cannot utilize the Original Medicare plan. That is, if they join an HMO, they must use the providers of that HMO. If they use a provider outside of the network, they will have to pay the entire cost out-of-pocket. Separately, beneficiaries also voluntarily enroll in a private prescription drug plan. The Centers for Medicare & Medicaid Services (CMS) pay the fee-for-service health providers based on Medicare fee schedules under the Original Medicare plan, and pay the MA plans a uniform payment per covered beneficiary (capitated payment). The private prescription drug plans are paid a competitively bid amount based on their bid relative to the average bid in each market.

Original Medicare Plan

The Original Medicare Plan is basically the original fee-for-service plan that has been offered under the Medicare program from inception. The two parts of Medicare – Part A and Part B – were originally the plan design separation of the program between hospital and medical services. The two part financing of Medicare continues despite the introduction of the MA plans, where they are required to participate in both Parts A and B if they are enrolled in an MA plan. Most retirees are automatically covered by Part A by paying taxes on their pay while working. Part B is a voluntary program and requires the beneficiary to pay periodic premiums that cover about 25 percent of the total cost of the program (generally deducted from their Social Security checks).

Part A services include:

- Inpatient hospital care for up to 90 days per benefit period (a benefit period begins on the first day of admission through 60 days after discharge, if the beneficiary is not readmitted during that period) and 60 lifetime reserve days. Inpatient hospital care that is covered by Part A include the costs of a semi-private room, meals, regular nursing care, operating and recovery room charges, intensive care, inpatient prescription drugs, laboratory testing and radiology, psychiatric hospitals, inpatient rehabilitation and long-term care hospitalization when it is medically necessary, as well as other medically necessary services and supplies provided in the hospital.

- Skilled nursing facility (SNF) care for 100 days after an inpatient stay. SNF care is generally covered under Part A only if it follows within 30 days of an inpatient stay of three days or longer and is certified as medically necessary. The covered services are similar to the hospital stay and also include rehabilitation services and appliances.

- Home health care for 100 days after an inpatient stay of at least three days. Home health services are covered by both Parts A and B. Prior to 1998, home health care was entirely covered under Part A. The Balanced Budget Act of 1997 (BBA)[3] transferred home health services that were not associated with either a hospital or SNF stay to Part B. Part A covers the first 100 days after an inpatient stay. Part B covers the later visits.

---

[3] *Balanced Budget Act of 1997* (Pub. L. 105-33)

- Hospice care (excluding room and board) is provided to terminally ill persons with life expectancies of six months or less who forego the standard Medicare benefits for treatment of their illness and receive only the hospice care. Such care includes pain relief, supportive medical and social services, physical therapy, nursing services and symptom management.

- Inpatient psychiatric care for up to 190 days during a beneficiary's lifetime.

An important concept in the structure of the Part A services is the benefit period. The period starts when the beneficiary is first admitted to the hospital and ends when there is a break of at least 60 consecutive days where no inpatient hospital or SNF care is provided. For any benefit period, after 90 days and all reserve days are exhausted, the beneficiary must pay the full cost of care.

Part B services include:

- Physician services including office visits, surgical procedures and consultations. Some services provided by chiropractors, podiatrists, dentists and optometrists are also covered if medically necessary. Also covered are services by Medicare-approved practitioners such as certified registered nurse anesthetists, clinical psychologists, clinical social workers, physician assistants and nurse practitioners and clinical nurse specialists in collaboration with the physician.

- Durable medical equipment, lab and diagnostic x-rays, and screening tests.

- Outpatient hospital services such as the emergency room or outpatient clinic, same day surgical centers and ambulance services.

- Some home health care not covered by Part A.

- Laboratory testing, radiological services and certain preventive care screening tests.

- Outpatient behavioral health services.

- Most physical, occupational and speech therapy.

- Outpatient rehabilitation facility services and mental health care in partial hospitalization psychiatric program if the physician certifies that inpatient treatment would be required without such treatment.

- Radiation therapy, renal dialysis and some transplants (e.g., heart, lung, heart-lung, liver, pancreas, bone marrow and intestinal).

- Drugs and biologicals that cannot be self-administered, such as hepatitis B vaccines and immunosuppressive drugs (certain self-administered anticancer drugs are also covered).

- Preventive health services (e.g., annual mammograms, diabetes screening, annual pap smears for high-risk beneficiaries, colorectal cancer screening and prostate cancer screening).

In general, to be covered, all services must be either medically necessary or one of the several preventive benefits that are prescribed by law.

Key services not covered by Medicare are:

- First three pints of blood
- Some preventive health care
- Vision and hearing care equipment
- Dental care
- Long-term care

The benefits provided by the Original Medicare plan subject the covered expenses to a combination of deductibles and coinsurance.

Part A (Hospital) Design

Part A plan designs are generally based on fixed dollar deductibles and coinsurance that are subject to change each year based on historical cost changes. All dollar amounts shown below are for calendar year 2006.

- Initial deductible: $952 per benefit period

- Daily inpatient coinsurance: $238 (25 percent of initial deductible) per day for days 61 through 90 and $476 (50 percent of initial deductible) per day for reserve days (up to 60 lifetime days).

- Home health care provided without deductible for the first 100 visits after a 3-day hospital stay.

- Skilled nursing facility coinsurance: $119.00 (one-eighth of initial deductible) per day for days 21 through 100 if followed by a 3-day hospital stay.

Part B (Medical) Design

The medical design is similar to major medical plans with a deductible and coinsurance.

- Annual deductible: $124 (in 2006)

- Coinsurance: 20 percent of Medicare allowable charge (50 percent for outpatient behavioral health services and no coinsurance for home health care).

- Out-of-pocket maximum: None.

- Annual benefit maximum: Unlimited.

Starting in 2005, the deductible was set at $110 and then automatically indexed in the Medicare Modernization Act of 2003 (MMA)[4]. It had been $100 from 1991 through 2004. Note that the stated coinsurance of the Part B benefits is 20 percent. For certain outpatient services (e.g., diagnostic lab, x-ray and surgical facilities), however, beneficiaries may currently pay close to 50 percent of the Medicare based charge (i.e., the amount that Medicare allows to the providers). This methodology was changed in the BBA[5] so that ultimately, the beneficiaries' coinsurance will be based on the Medicare payment amount. This methodology is being phased in over a 20-year period.

Physicians may voluntarily agree with Medicare to accept the Medicare payment and the required beneficiary coinsurance as payment in full (participating physicians). Physicians who elect not to be part of the participating physician program are allowed to bill patients up to 15 percent more than the Medicare-approved amount in total. However, the Medicare-allowed charge for non-participating physicians is 95 percent of the allowed charge for participating physicians. For example, if a fee for a given service is $100 for a participating physician, it is $95 for a non-participating physician. Thus, the non-participating physician cannot bill more than $109.25 ($95 × 1.15) in total. CMS statistics show 91.5 percent of physicians billing Medicare were participating physicians in January 2003.[6] These percentages

---

[4] *Medicare Prescription Drug, Improvement, and Modernization Act of 2003* (Pub. L. 108-173) passed by Congress and signed by the President at the end of 2003.

[5] See page 32 for an explanation of BBA.

[6] CMS Data Compendium, 2003 Edition.

have historically varied by year and by specialty. The following table shows the historical participation percentages by specialty.

Table 3.1
Medicare Participating Physicians

	1990	1995	1998	1999	2000	2001	2002	2003
	Percent of Physicians Participating							
Physicians (M.D.s and D.O.s):								
General practice	39.7	59.9	71.1	73.7	80.2	79.0	80.2	84.3
General surgery	55.8	80.2	89.3	90.4	93.3	92.5	92.8	95.6
Otology, laryngology, rhinology	45.2	77.1	87.7	88.7	91.8	91.3	91.7	93.9
Anesthesiology	30.8	73.9	85.9	88.9	93.7	92.3	92.3	95.5
Cardiovascular disease	60.6	84.9	91.5	92.9	95.8	94.4	94.3	96.4
Dermatology	53.4	79.3	87.2	88.0	90.8	90.1	90.1	92.4
Family practice	47.2	74.5	85.9	86.9	90.8	90.3	90.8	93.2
Internal medicine	48.8	73.8	84.8	86.8	90.7	88.7	88.8	92.2
Nuerology	53.1	78.9	87.1	88.4	92.1	89.9	89.1	93.3
Obstetrics/gynecology	48.8	72.5	81.3	82.9	86.8	86.3	86.5	88.8
Ophthalmology	55.6	81.2	89.8	90.9	93.3	92.8	93.3	95.1
Orthopedic surgery	53.7	82.6	90.4	90.6	93.8	93.1	92.4	95.5
Pathology	53.4	78.9	86.6	89.8	93.6	92.2	92.0	95.4
Psychiatry	41.6	58.7	70.4	73.9	79.1	79.6	80.4	83.0
Radiology	55.6	82.8	88.3	91.6	95.3	91.9	91.6	95.7
Urology	49.6	83.0	90.6	91.5	94.6	93.8	93.6	96.0
Nephrology	66.5	87.0	91.3	93.0	95.1	93.6	93.6	95.5
Clinic or other group practice – not GPPP	68.7	79.4	90.1	89.2	91.6	92.7	93.5	93.4
Limited license practitioners (LLP):								
Chiropractor	26.2	42.6	54.3	56.3	59.4	63.0	64.4	65.2
Podiatry-surgical chiropody	54.0	79.2	87.9	88.4	90.7	91.6	92.1	92.3
Optometrist	54.0	66.9	74.7	76.0	78.4	80.0	80.6	82.4

Source: CMS Data Compendium, 2003 Edition

If a physician is not a participating physician, he or she may still accept Medicare assignment on a case-by-case basis. In 2002, when 89 percent of physicians were participating physicians, 98 percent of Medicare claims were assigned.

Payment Distribution by Major Service

The following figure shows the distribution of Medicare payments by major service.

**Percentage Distribution of 2004 Payments
From the HI and SMI Trust Funds**

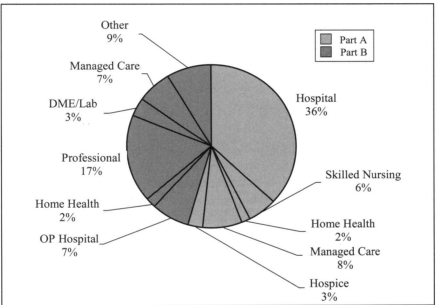

Source: 2006 Annual Report of the Medicare Trustees

Figure 3.3

Coverage Gaps

The gaps in coverage that are typically cited with the Medicare design of Parts A and B are:

- No coverage of drugs above $2,250 (indexed) until the catastrophic coverage limit is reached ($3,600, indexed, of out-of-pocket spending).
- No limit on beneficiary cost sharing (e.g., typical employer out-of-pocket maximum cost sharing is $2,500 per year).
- Limited long-term care benefits (especially if there is no hospital stay)

Coordinated Care Plans (Part C)

"Coordinated care" or managed care plans have their genesis in the "risk contract" programs first offered in 1982. The program paid managed care organizations (primarily risk HMOs) to provide at least the same coverage as the fee-for-service Medicare plan under their managed network systems. In return, the organizations were paid a fixed amount per covered beneficiary (capitation). The fixed amount was originally intended to pay about 95 percent of what Medicare was paying in their service area. The capitation amount was considered a fair amount since the managed care organizations could utilize their health management techniques to control costs and utilization. And, the Medicare program would benefit from paying 95 percent of what it would have paid. Congress made further modifications to the program in 1985 to attract more managed care organizations.

Medicare beneficiaries began to enroll in the risk HMOs because of the lower copay requirements and richer benefits. Many HMOs provided added services such as preventive care and prescription drugs that were not provided under the Medicare fee-for-service plan. By 1997, 70 percent of Medicare beneficiaries lived in areas where a risk plan was available to them and 5.2 million beneficiaries (13.5 percent of Medicare population) had enrolled in one of the plans.

Balanced Budget Act of 1997 (BBA)

Under the BBA, Congress expanded the risk contracting program to include other types of private plans. The resulting Medicare+Choice (*M+C*) program allowed for other organizations to offer plans under similar financial conditions as the risk contract program. These plans included preferred provider organizations (PPOs), provider service organizations (PSOs, primarily hospitals and large physician groups), private fee-for-service plans (PFFS) and medical savings accounts (MSAs). All plan offerings (except the MSA) must provide benefits that are at least equal to the Original Medicare plan design, excluding hospice benefits.

HMO

HMOs that continued under the *M+C* programs were primarily those that were previously risk contracts under the old program. They offer benefits that are similar to those offered to non-Medicare beneficiaries with relatively complete services and low copayments. For example, a plan may charge $15 per office visit, $250 per inpatient stay and 50 percent coinsurance on outpatient drugs. By the end of 2005, there were 187 organizations offering HMO options.

PPO

PPO plans (or preferred provider networks) offer both in-network as well as out-of-network benefits. Generally, if a beneficiary goes to a network provider, they have a lower cost sharing requirement than if they go to a non-network provider. At the end of 2001, there were two PPO plans available. In 2005, 82 organizations offered a PPO.

PSO

Provider service organizations (or PSOs) are generally more similar to HMOs than PPOs. They generally require a beneficiary to only use their facilities and panel of physicians. The sponsor of the PSO is usually a hospital system but could also be a large physician group. PSO plan designs are generally similar to an HMO. At the end of 2001, there was one PSO plan available, but six by the end of 2005.

PFFS

Private fee-for-service (PFFS) plans offer higher benefit levels than the Original Medicare plan while negotiating with physicians to accept slightly different payments than under Medicare. PFFS plans receive the same capitated payment as all other M+C plans so they will generally include a high degree of medical management that is common in HMOs. At the end of 2001, there was one PFFS plan but by the end of 2005 there were 16 PFFS plans, with three plans providing coverage in most states.

MSA

A medical savings account (MSA) plan is a combination high deductible fee-for-service plan and a savings account that is funded by Medicare. Beneficiaries can use the savings account to pay for amounts under the deductible or save it for future health care expenses. At the end of 2005, there were no MSA plans available.

The BBA also established new financing guidelines that had the effect of increasing the payment rates in rural areas and reducing the rates in urban areas. This was in an attempt to improve the access of these plans to more beneficiaries. An unintended result of this action was that because of the constraints on the payments to the existing plans in urban locations, many either cut back on the areas they served or completely abandoned some areas of the country. The result was that beneficiary access to *M+C* plans declined from a peak in 1998 (74 percent of beneficiaries had access) to a low in 2003 (59 percent access).

Unfortunately, the refinements made by Congress under the BBA did not address the majority of service areas where plans were receiving very low increases from year-to-year (the minimum 2 percent per year increase) and those plans had to increase copayments, reduce covered services and increase premiums. As a result, there was a significant amount of "disenrollment" in *M+C* plans beginning in 2000, through 2004.

The following chart shows managed care enrollment from 1991 through 2005 (including risk contract enrollment prior to 1999).

Number of Beneficiaries and HMO Plans in the M+C/MA Program

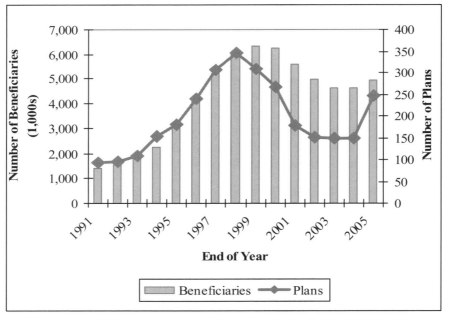

Source: Monthly Medicare Managed Care Reports, Centers for Medicare & Medicaid Services

Figure 3.4

Medicare Modernization Act

The MMA is best known for establishing the new prescription program, but it also included legislation to improve plan payments and reinvigorate the managed care options. Along with it came a new name – Medicare Advantage (MA) program. The primary change to the types of plan offerings was an incentive for PPOs to offer coverage on a regionwide basis beginning in 2006.

Beginning in 2006, the MMA established new regional PPOs that cover a geographic area broader than a few counties. In general, the regions are individual states, or groups of states in more rural areas. There are 26 regions in the country as shown in Figure 3.5.

Medicare Advantage Regions[7]

Figure 3.5

PPOs entering into the market in 2006 and 2007 must serve the whole region with the same level of benefits. These new plans will also enjoy risk sharing with the government to encourage their development. CMS will be able to draw on a $10 billion stabilization fund to promote regional PPOs.

---

[7] Centers for Medicare & Medicaid Services, December 2004

Prescription Drug Plans (Part D)

The MMA represented the most expansive changes to the Medicare program since its inception. The biggest part of the new legislation was the addition of a prescription drug benefit to the program beginning in 2006. The plans may be stand-alone prescription drug plans (PDPs) or plans added on to a managed care plan under Medicare Advantage (MA-PD). The prescription drug benefit is a voluntary benefit under the Medicare program and is provided by private insurance companies.

The MMA specifies a standard benefit design:

- $250 annual deductible;

- Benefit of 75 percent of the cost of eligible drugs from the $250 deductible up to an initial coverage limit of $2,250;

- Beneficiaries pay the full cost of drugs from $2,250 until they have paid $3,600 out of their own pockets (the next $2,850 in claims if they have no other coverage);

- After beneficiaries have paid the $3,600 out-of-pocket, a benefit with beneficiary copays equal to the greater of $2 for generics and preferred multiple source drugs and $5 for all other drugs, or 5 percent of the cost of the drug.

All of the above dollar amounts are for 2006 and are indexed in the future based the cost of the prescription drug program. The above is considered the "standard" benefit offering that a plan must provide. Plans can be designed with other features as long as it is actuarially equivalent to this standard design. Most of the designs first offered in 2006 varied from this standard design in some fashion (e.g., lower or no deductible, higher benefit for generics, and copay design instead of coinsurance). PDPs may also offer supplemental benefits to the standard benefit if they also offer a plan in the region that only provides the actuarial equivalent to the standard benefit.

Unlike the original Medicare program, the PDPs are private plans placing independent bids to cover Medicare beneficiaries. Plans must cover all eligible beneficiaries in a region for which the plan submits a bid. There are 34 PDP regions, which are either individual states or groups of states.

Many of the regions in the following figure are the same as the Medicare Advantage regions but a few are different. Each region must have at least two drug plans – at least one must be a standalone PDP, and the other can be either a PDP or a MA-PD plan. If two plans are not offered in a region, the government will be able to enter into a contract with a PDP sponsor to provide coverage in that region and the government will cap the risk borne by the plan. If the region still does not have the minimum two plans, the government will be able to contract with a PDP sponsor under whom the government pays for the actual cost of the benefits and management fees subject to administrative performance measures.

Medicare PDP Regions[8]

Figure 3.6

In order to protect Medicare beneficiaries, the MMA contains a number of rules for the PDP sponsors, including rules regarding the use of formularies, accessibility of drugs through retail pharmacies (versus mail order pharmacies), standards for electronic prescribing and participants' rights.

The MMA provides for financial assistance with premiums and cost sharing for low-income individuals. This assistance varies depending on income level and available resources as shown in the Table 3.2.

---

[8] Centers for Medicare & Medicaid Services, December 2004

Table 3.2

Low Income PDP Subsidies

Income level	Dual Eligible (Medicare and Medicaid)			Other Low Income Medicare Beneficiaries	
	Nursing home resident	Income less than 100% of FPL[9]	Income at or above 100% of FPL	Income less than 135% of FPL	Income less than 150% of FPL
Asset Test	None	None	None	Less than 3 times SSI asset test ($6,000 individual or $9,000 family)[10]	Less than $10,000 individual or $20,000 family[11]
Monthly premium	$0	$0	$0	$0	Sliding scale up to full amount
Annual deductible	$0	$0	$0	$50	$50
Copayments before out-of-pocket limit	None	$1 generic/ $3 brand	$2 generic/ $5 brand	$2 generic/ $5 brand	15%
Out-of-pocket limit	Not applicable	$3,600	$3,600	$3,600	$3,600
Copayments after out-of-pocket limit	None	None	None	None	$2 generic/ $5 brand

ENROLLMENT

Individuals entitled to Medicare are automatically enrolled in Part A when they turn age 65 if they are receiving Social Security or Railroad Retirement retirement benefits prior to age 65. Individuals who have been entitled to Social Security or Railroad Retirement disability benefits are automatically enrolled beginning in the 25th month of disability payments (the

---

[9] The federal poverty level (FPL) is updated annually. For 2006, it is $9,800 for an individual and $13,200 for a family of two.

[10] 2006 amount, future years indexed by CPI-U

[11] 2006 amount, future years indexed by CPI-U

first month if receiving disability benefits because of ALS). Part A benefits are also provided to insured workers with end stage renal disease (ESRD) and to insured workers' spouses and children with ESRD. Individuals can apply for Medicare as soon as they are diagnosed with ESRD. Coverage usually starts the fourth month of dialysis treatment or the month of receiving a kidney transplant.

For persons who have not filed for Social Security or Railroad Retirement benefits, they must apply for Part A coverage. Those who are not otherwise entitled to Medicare may enroll after age 65 and pay the full or partial cost of Part A coverage.

Individuals already receiving Social Security or Railroad Retirement benefits are automatically enrolled in Part B too. If a person does not want Part B, they will have to decline coverage. Individuals receiving disability benefits under Social Security or Railroad Retirement will also be automatically enrolled. For persons not receiving Social Security or Railroad Retirement benefits, they will have to enroll when they apply for retirement benefits or Part A.

For individuals who are automatically enrolled, they will receive initial enrollment packages three months prior to turning age 65 or three months prior to the 25th month of disability. Otherwise, eligible individuals may apply to enroll beginning three months prior to becoming age 65 to three months after. If they apply before turning age 65, they are eligible for benefits beginning the month that they turn age 65 (unless their birthday is on the 1st, then coverage begins the month before). If they apply to enroll after turning age 65, benefit eligibility is delayed. If enrolling in the month turning 65, eligibility begins the first of the next month. Enrolling the month after turning 65, eligibility begins the first of the second month after month enrolled. Enrolling two or three months after turning 65, eligibility begins three months after month enrolled.

Enrollment Example

John turns age 65 in June. If John applies to enroll in March, April or May (three months before the month he turns age 65), his Part B coverage will start June 1. If he enrolls later, his coverage start dates will depend on the month that he enrolls:

- June, his coverage starts July 1.
- July, his coverage starts September 1

- August, his coverage starts November 1.
- September, his coverage starts December 1.

General Enrollment Period

For those who do not enroll in Part B during an initial or special enroll-ment period, they can sign up during the general enrollment period from January through March each year. Their coverage will begin on July 1. A late enrollment penalty of 10 percent will apply for each full 12-month period that they could have enrolled with no penalty.

Special Enrollment Period

For persons continuing to work after age 65 and covered by a group health plan, they have a special enrollment period available to them. They can sign up for Part B while working or eight months following the earlier of the month the group health coverage ends or employment ends. As long as the person was covered by a group health plan since turning age 65, they will not be subject to the late enrollment penalty. The Part D plan requires a certificate of creditable coverage to demonstrate prior coverage to avoid its late enrollment penalty. Part B does not have an equivalent requirement.

Medicare Advantage Enrollment

Any person eligible to enroll in Medicare Parts A and B can also enroll in a Medicare Advantage plan during the same enrollment periods. A person can switch MA plans during open enrollment periods from No-vember 15 through December 31 every year. If a person enrolls in a dif-ferent MA plan during this period, their enrollment in the old plan will be terminated at the end of the year and coverage in the new plan begins January 1 of the next year. If a person is enrolled in an MA plan and moves out of the service area, the individual may join another MA plan that serves the area of their new home or return to Original Medicare when they move. Each plan will need to be notified of the timing of such a move to ensure continuous coverage.

Prescription Drug Plan Enrollment

Enrollment periods for PDP coverage are similar to the MA enrollment pe-riods. If an eligible beneficiary does not join a Medicare prescription drug plan during the initial enrollment period or upon becoming eligible for Medicare and does not have credible coverage from another source (e.g., employer or VA plan), he or she will be subject to a late enrollment penalty of one percent for every month that they do not have PDP coverage.

FINANCING

The Centers for Medicare & Medicaid Services (CMS) is the agency under the Department of Health and Human Services (HHS) responsible for the administration of the Medicare program. The program is financed through two trust funds—the Hospital Insurance (HI) Trust Fund covering Medicare Part A and the Supplementary Medical Insurance (SMI) Trust Fund covering Parts B and D.

Hospital Insurance Trust Fund

The HI program is financed the same way as Social Security—primarily through a mandatory payroll tax—and is intended to be self-supporting. The program should be funded entirely or almost entirely from the following sources:

- Payroll taxes

- Investment income from trust fund assets

- Premiums paid by beneficiaries who voluntarily participate in Part A

- A portion of the federal income taxes paid on Social Security benefits for high-income beneficiaries

In fiscal year 2005, about 95 percent of the HI trust fund revenue came from the first three sources above.[12] Almost all workers in the United States are covered by the HI program and pay taxes to support the cost of benefits for current Medicare beneficiaries. The current HI payroll tax rate is 1.45 percent of earnings – paid by both the employee and their employer for each employee. Self-employed persons pay the full amount, or 2.90 percent. Beginning in 1994, unlike the Social Security wage base, there is no annual limit on the earnings subject to tax for HI. Prior to 1994, the tax applied only up to a specified maximum amount of earn-

---

[12] The Board of Trustees, Federal Hospital Insurance and Federal Supplementary Medical Insurance Trust Funds, *2006 Annual Report of the Board of Trustees of the Federal Hospital Insurance and Federal Supplementary Insurance Trust Funds*, May 1, 2006, p. 48, Table III.B.4. [4]

ings. The HI tax rate is specified in the Social Security Act and cannot be changed without legislation.

The trust fund assets are invested in interest-bearing securities of the U.S. government. Interest payments and redemptions on these securities come from current federal revenues or issuance of additional federal debt.

Supplementary Medical Insurance Trust Fund

Unlike the HI program, the SMI program is not intended to be self-supporting. It relies heavily on general tax revenues. SMI is financed through beneficiary premium payments ($88.50 per beneficiary per month in 2006) and contributions from the general fund of the U.S. Treasury. Beneficiary premiums are set at a level that generally covers 25 percent of the average expenditures for aged beneficiaries, although premiums are higher for individuals with higher incomes, as a result of the MMA and the Deficit Reduction Act of 2005. Beneficiaries who enroll later than their first eligibility period and were not covered by an employer-provided health plan are required to pay higher premiums (an additional 10 percent for each full year of delay). The balance of the funding is from the general fund of the U.S. Treasury and is the largest source of SMI income. The SMI trust fund also receives income from interest earnings on its invested assets, as well as a small amount of miscellaneous income. Beneficiary premiums and general fund payments are determined annually by the CMS Office of the Actuary.

Year	Monthly SMI Premium Rate
2000 (actual)	45.50
2001	50.00
2002	54.00
2003	58.70
2004	66.60
2005	78.20
2006	88.50
2007 (projected)	98.20
2008	98.20
2009	98.30
2010	102.20

Note: The 2006 Trustees report

The 2006 Trustees report projected the 2007 through 2009 Part B rates to remain about $98 because of the physician payment system combined with the large increase required for the 2006 rates. The report goes on to mention that the level rates are unlikely to actually occur before legislative changes intervene. The reason for making such a statement is the precedent that has been set by Congress for increasing physician fees that were limited in prior years.

Low income beneficiaries (incomes below 135 percent of poverty level and limited resources) are eligible for subsidies that pay for some of or their entire Part B premium. In addition, the increase in Part B premium in any year for an individual cannot be greater than their cost of living adjustment in their Social Security check.

The SMI premium rate has never been based on earnings – all beneficiaries paid the same rate. Starting in 2007, the government subsidy to the premium will be less for higher income beneficiaries. This reduction in government subsidy will be phased in over three years and be fully effective in 2009.[13] The "band" of subsidy in which an individual is included will be based on their modified adjusted gross income from two taxable years prior to the premium year. For example, for the 2007 premium year, the income from 2005 will be used to determine the appropriate premium bracket. The following table shows the government subsidy percentages based on income bands to be used for 2007.

| Year | Income Bracket (inflation adjusted) | | | | |
	<$80,000	$80,000 to $100,000	$100,000 to $150,000	$150,000 to $200,000	$200,000+
2007	75%	$71\frac{2}{3}$ %	$66\frac{2}{3}$ %	$61\frac{2}{3}$ %	$56\frac{2}{3}$ %
2008	75%	$68\frac{1}{3}$ %	$58\frac{1}{3}$ %	$48\frac{1}{3}$ %	$38\frac{1}{3}$ %
2009+	75%	65%	50%	35%	20%

---

[13] The MMA phased the reduction in over five years (2007-2011). The Deficit Reduction Act of 2005 (Pub. L. 109-171) decreased the phase-in period to three years (2007-2009).

If the income-related premium rates were fully effective in 2006, the premium rates would look like the following:

Hypothetical 2006 SMI Rates

Income Bracket	SMI Premium Rate
<$80,000	$ 88.50
$80,000 to $100,000	$ 123.90
$100,000 to $150,000	$ 177.00
$150,000 to $200,000	$ 230.10
$200,000+	$ 283.20

Although high income beneficiaries would be paying close to $3,400 per year, the total estimated cost per Medicare beneficiary for Parts A and B is $8,853 ($4,618 for Part A and $4,235 for Part B) from the 2006 Trustees report. Their share of the total costs is 38 percent. Of course, they also paid the HI payroll tax while employed.

The projected costs are determined on an incurred basis and make provision for incurred but not reported (IBNR) claims. IBNR claims are for services that beneficiaries have already received during the year that have not been paid by Medicare because they have not been processed or even submitted to Medicare until after the end of the year.

Funds may accumulate in the SMI trust funds if projected contributions exceed cash disbursements. Most of these accumulated funds are earmarked for the IBNR reserves and the remainder is used as a contingency reserve.

The basic structure of this financing system can only be changed by an act of Congress.

Medicare Advantage

Medicare Advantage plan capitation payments are financed from the HI and the SMI trust funds in the same proportion as the fee-for-service plan for the two Parts. The pharmacy benefits for Medicare Advantage-Prescription Drug (MA-PD) plans are financed the same as stand-alone PDPs.

Prescription Drug Plans

The prescription drug benefits are financed by general revenues and beneficiary premiums – the same as Part B.

Overall Financing

The overall spending in the Medicare program is graphically shown in Figure 3.7. Total Medicare spending is projected to approach 14 percent of the gross domestic product by 2080, with a deficit in the HI trust fund accounting for close to 4 percent of GDP by the end of the 75-year projection period.

Sources of Medicare Income and Expenditures as Percent of GDP

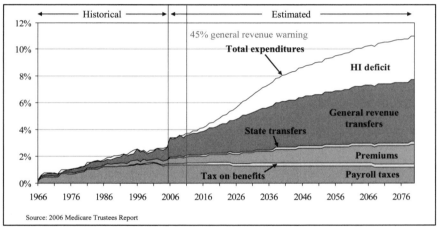

Source: 2006 Medicare Trustees Report

Figure 3.7

The MMA added a new financial early warning indicator to the annual Trustees report. If the percentage of Medicare spending in any of the next six years after the year of the report requires general revenue spending equal to 45 percent or greater, they must issue an "excessive general revenue Medicare funding" warning in its report. The 2006 Trustees report included the first such warning and it is expected that the 2007 report will also include the warning. If the Trustees report an excessive general revenue funding warning in two consecutive reports, the President is required to submit changes to the program to reduce the general revenue spending. This must be on an expedited basis with required Congressional action by the end of July.

PROVIDER PAYMENTS

Part A payments were originally made to providers on a reasonable cost basis. Medicare payments for most inpatient hospital services are now made under a reimbursement method called the prospective payment system (PPS). Under the PPS, a specific predetermined amount is paid to the provider for each inpatient hospital stay that is based on a diagnosis-related group (DRG) classification. In some cases the payment that the hospital receives under this system is less than the hospital's actual cost of providing the services and in other cases it is more. The hospital absorbs any of the loss or makes a profit. There are some payment adjustments for very high cost inpatient hospital stays. Payments for other Part A covered care (i.e., skilled nursing care, home health care, inpatient rehabilitation and psychiatric care) are made under separate prospective payment systems.

Prior to 1992, physicians were paid on the basis of reasonable charge. This amount was initially defined as the lesser of (1) the physician's actual charge; (2) the physician's customary charge; or (3) the prevailing charge for similar services in that area. Beginning in 1992, the allowed charges were defined as the lesser of (1) the submitted charges, or (2) the amount determined by a fee schedule that is based on a resource-based relative value scale (RBRVS). Payments for durable medical equipment (DME) and clinical laboratory services are also based on a fee schedule. Most hospital outpatient services are reimbursed on a prospective payment system, and home health care is reimbursed under the same prospective payment system as Part A.

If a Part B provider agrees to accept the Medicare-approved rate (i.e., takes assignment), then the Medicare payment provided to them (both the Medicare benefit payment and the beneficiaries' coinsurance payment) are considered as payment in full for that service. The provider may not request any additional payments (beyond the initial annual deductible and coinsurance) from the beneficiary or insurer. If the provider does not take assignment, the beneficiary may be charged for the excess. Limits now exist on the excess that doctors or suppliers can charge. Physicians are "participating physicians" if they agree before the beginning of the year to accept assignment for all Medicare services they furnish during the year. Since Medicare beneficiaries may select their doctors, they have the option to choose those who participate. As discussed earlier, non-participating physicians receive a lower payment from Medicare but can bill up to 15 percent more than the Medicare approved payment in total.

Medicare Advantage Plans

Medicare payments to Medicare Advantage plans are based on a blend of local and national capitated rates. Actual payments to plans are risk adjusted based on demographics and health status of individual beneficiaries.

Original Risk Plan Payment

The original payment rates to managed care plans were based on costs under the traditional fee-for-service plan. Rates by county were first calculated based on an adjusted average per capita cost (AAPCC) of fee-for-service Medicare. The rates were normalized by age, gender, Medicare eligibility (i.e., aged or disabled), Medicaid coverage and whether or not the individual is institutionalized.

The capitation rates paid to the plans were set at 95 percent of the AAPCC. These rates were determined in advance (i.e., projected) and participating plans were given these rates adjusted for age, gender, Medicare eligibility, Medicaid coverage and institutional status.

The AAPC rates varied significantly by county. For example, the 1997 capitation rate for both Parts A and B ranged from $220.92 per month in Arthur County, Nebraska to $767.35 in Richmond County, New York. Even some adjacent counties had variations greater than 20 percent.

The plans were required to provide at least the same level of benefits as the regular Medicare plan. For plans that could deliver health care at a cost less than the calculated payment rate, they were required to use the difference to provide additional benefits (e.g., prescription drugs or reduced cost sharing on other services) or return the excess to Medicare. Virtually all plans provided the additional benefits which created a major incentive for Medicare beneficiaries to enroll in the plans.

Balanced Budget Act (BBA) Payment Changes

The original risk plan payment method was criticized by many because payments were unpredictable, had large variations by county and did not adequately differentiate by the true risk characteristics of the covered population. In order to address these concerns, the BBA changed the base payment rate to be the greater of:

(a) a blend of the county rate and national rate (with the 1997 county rates calculated under the old method as a base),

(b) a minimum rate , and

(c) the prior year's rate increased by 2 percent.

The amounts in (a) and (b) above are increased based on historical Medicare fee-for-service experience and blended between the county rate and the national rate over a six-year period from 1998 through 2003. In 2003, the blended rate is 50/50 (i.e., 50 percent county rate and 50 percent national rate). The county rates reflect adjustments that are specified in the BBA. The national rates for each county are determined by adjusting the national rate by each county's Medicare hospital wage index and the geographic physician practice cost index.

Each of the components is designed for a specific reason. The blended county and national rate was to increase rates in lower cost counties and lower rates in higher cost counties to reduce the perceived disparity. The minimum rate was to serve as floor to accelerate the rate increase for the very lowest cost counties. The prior rate increased by 2 percent was intended to help protect the high cost counties.

Finally, after determining the highest of the above three rates, a budget neutrality adjustment is applied to calculate the final rates. This adjustment is made to assure that the total payments under this methodology was the same as if the area specific rates only were used to pay the $M+C$ plans. Only the blended payments rates could be adjusted to achieve budget neutrality.

The BBA set the minimum rate for 1997 and 1998 with a mandated index after 1998 based on the rate of growth of the overall Medicare program. In 2001, Congress set the minimum rate to two amounts—a high floor for counties in metropolitan areas with a population more than 250,000 and a low floor for other counties. In 2001, the high floor was set at $525 and the low floor was $475.

The above changes did not solve the issue of reflecting the true risk characteristics of the *M+C* population. Various studies had indicated that risk contract HMOs attracted a better than average risk group that is not fully recognized by the simple demographic adjustments made in the payment procedures.

A risk adjustment methodology was phased in to respond to this criticism. The initial methodology chosen was primarily based on inpatient claim data – called the Principal Inpatient Diagnostic Cost Group (PIP-DCG) method. Further study was conducted to determine alternative methods that consider other claims data. Ultimately, the risk adjustment method will drive the payment rate system and was originally intended to be phased in over a five-year period. By the end of this five-year period, a more comprehensive risk adjustment method was to be implemented.

Calendar Year	Demographic Method	Risk Adjustment Method
2000	90%	10%
2001	70%	30%
2002	45%	55%
2003	20%	80%
2004	0%	100%

The above schedule was modified legislatively to further delay the full effect of the risk adjustment method. From 2000 to 2003, the rates used 10 percent of the risk adjustment method in the rate development. The schedule was not followed because of concerns by many managed care organizations that the PIP-DCG methodology had major shortcomings because only hospital admissions were used to determine risk characteristics. For example, a plan that was able to reduce hospital admissions through their care management program would appear to have healthier enrollees than the average and therefore receive lower payments.

A new risk adjustment method was implemented in 2004 (pursuant to the Benefits and Improvements Protection Act of 2000[14]) that accounted for

---

[14] The Medicare, Medicaid, and SCHIP Benefits Improvement and Protection Act of 2000 (Public Law 106-554).

hospital outpatient and physician services. CMS evaluated several risk adjustment models including ambulatory care groups (ACGs), the chronic disease and disability payment system (CDPS), the clinical risk groups (CRGs), the clinically-detailed risk information system for cost (CD-RISC) and the diagnostic cost group/hierarchical condition categories (DCG/HCC) models. The DCG/HCC model was chosen primarily because of its transparency, ease of modification and consistency with clinical results. The developers of the model worked with CMS to modify it for Medicare's data limitations resulting in the CMS-HCC model.

Briefly, the DCG/HCC model uses the encounter data (similar to claims data including information about the services provided) received from plans and assigns each diagnosis code (there are over 15,000 ICD-9-CM codes) into about 800 diagnosis groups which then get translated into almost 200 condition categories. The CMS model utilizes a select number of the condition categories (about 70) that are derived from about 3,000 ICD-9-CM codes. The model then places the categories into a hierarchical scoring template to determine the risk score for each individual. Some individuals may have more than one condition category identified from the encounter data and the scores for their conditions will be combined into an aggregate risk score that may be more or less than the simple addition of the separate conditions.

This method was again to be phased in over a period of time.

Calendar Year	Demographic Method	Risk Adjustment Method
2004	70%	30%
2005	50%	50%
2006	25%	75%
2007	0%	100%

MMA Payment Changes

The payment adjustments made in the MMA are intended to improve the payment to MA plans and encourage more plans to enter the MA plan space. The three-part payment rate calculation is modified such that the minimum increase starting in 2004 is the greater of 2 percent or the projected per capita growth in Medicare spending instead of just 2 percent. Also, a fourth part is added that is equal to the projected per capita fee-for-service spending in the county. This amount must be determined at least every three years. In the interim, it is updated based on the same minimum increase (i.e., 2 percent or per capita Medicare spending growth). This payment rate is equal to the benchmark rate for the county. For most plans, the benchmark will be a weighted average of the county benchmarks for the plan's service area. For a regional PPO plan, the benchmark will be a blend of the county benchmarks and the regional bids. The blend of the bids will be the national percentage of beneficiaries enrolled in a MA plan (either local or regional).

Beginning in 2006, plans submit bids reflecting the payment per enrollee that they are willing to provide the Medicare covered benefits. Plans will get paid their bids (up to the benchmark rate) plus 75 percent of the amount that the benchmark rate exceeds their bids. Plans are required to provide additional benefits to beneficiaries or reduce their premiums in the amount of the additional 75 percent. For plans with bids above the benchmark, enrollees must pay the difference as an additional premium.

This new process is not radically different than it was pre-MMA. Prior to 2006, plans submitted an adjusted community rate (ACR) to provide the Medicare level of benefits. If their ACR was greater than the per capita payment, the plan could increase benefits (which most do) or return money to the enrollees. If they return money, 80 percent can go to the enrollee and 20 percent goes to Medicare.

Under the new payment system, a smaller portion goes back to the enrollee in the form of additional benefits (75 percent versus 100 percent under the old system) or premium rebate (75 percent versus 80 percent).

The MMA did not change the risk adjustment phase-in, so for 2006, 75 percent of the costs are based on risk adjustment and 25 percent on the demographic factors. In 2007, 100 percent of the costs will be adjusted by the risk model.

Prescription Drug Plans (PDPs)

Payments to PDPs are based on a combination of direct subsidy payments, catastrophic benefit reinsurance and risk sharing payments. In addition, Medicare will pay for the premium and cost-sharing assistance provided to low-income beneficiaries.

The payments to the PDPs are performed in several steps after all of the bids are submitted to CMS. Each PDP provides its expected costs for the standard benefit (i.e., the 75 percent benefit), the catastrophic benefit (i.e., the 95 percent benefit) and the expected reinsurance payment (i.e., 80 percent of all charges included in the catastrophic benefit calculation). The next step is to determine the beneficiaries' premium for the PDP's specific bid.

The beneficiaries' premium is equal to the bid for the standard benefit multiplied by the "beneficiary premium percentage." The percentage is equal to 25.5 percent divided by 100 percent minus the ratio of the total reinsurance payments reported divided by the sum of the total reinsurance payments plus the total payments for the standard bid. This percentage is then multiplied against the standard bid for the PDP and adjusted for the difference in PDP's bid and the geographically adjusted national average bid plus any additional amounts for supplemental benefits of the PDP. For a plan that has expected reinsurance payments and standard bid that are exactly equal to the national average, their total payment from CMS will be equal to the average 74.5 percent of the total.

For example, using an estimate of the average bids for 2006, with the total expected reinsurance payment per person of $34; and total payment for the standard bid equal to $92; the beneficiary premium percentage is developed as follows:

$$\frac{25.5\%}{100\% - \dfrac{\$34}{\$34 + \$92}} = 34.92\%.$$

And, the beneficiaries' premium, before adjustments, is equal to the $92 standard bid times 34.92 percent or $32.

The above amounts may be derived from the following components of the average bids.

Expected claims per month	$ 113
Administrative expenses	13
Total costs per month	$126
Expected reinsurance	(34)
Standard bid	$ 92

The direct subsidy payment is then equal to the PDP's total bid that is risk adjusted based on the enrollees of the plan less the calculated beneficiary premium. That is, the bid amount is risk adjusted and the beneficiary premium is not. Along with the reinsurance subsidy paid for claims exceeding enrollees' out-of-pocket limits, the total CMS payment will be about 75 percent of the total standard benefit bid. The direct subsidy amount will be paid to the PDP as a monthly capitated amount. The reinsurance payments are made for claims submitted equal to 80 percent of the total charges above the beneficiaries' out-of-pocket threshold ($3,600 for 2006).

There is a second level of risk adjustment based on the actual experience of the PDP relative to their original bid. If actual risk adjusted costs exceed the corridors around the standard bid, CMS will share in the higher or lower experience. For 2006 and 2007, the first corridor is plus and minus 2.5 percent of the target bid. If costs are either higher or lower than these corridors, CMS will receive adjusted payments. If actual experience is between 2.5 and 5.0 percent more than the target, they are at risk for 25 percent of the amount and Medicare will pay an additional 75 percent. If the actual experience exceeds the target by more than five percent, Medicare will pay an extra 75 percent for amounts between 2.5 and 5.0 percent and 80 percent for the amounts exceeding five percent. If actual experience is less than 2.5 percent lower than the target, the PDP refunds 75 percent of amounts between 2.5 and 5.0 percent below their target and 80 percent of amounts less than five percent below their target.

For 2008-11, the risk corridors are widened so that the first corridor is plus and minus 5.0 percent. The risk sharing would be 50 percent for amounts between 5.0 and 10.0 percent and 20 percent above 10.0 percent.

Employer Retiree Drug Subsidies

For employers who continue their group health plans that include prescription drugs, Medicare pays 28 percent of total costs between $250 and $5,000 (2006 and indexed thereafter). Employers are required to demonstrate that their plans are actuarially equivalent to the Medicare program in both total benefits delivered as well as the level of employer subsidy compared to the government subsidy of the standard Part D benefit design. The average subsidy payments have been estimated between $500 and $700 per person. The average reported by respondents to the Kaiser/Hewitt survey averaged $626. The total savings expected by these respondents was 7 percent of total retiree health care costs (including spending for both pre- and post-65 retirees).[15]

MEDICARE CLAIMS PROCESSING

Medicare's Parts A and B fee-for-service benefits are processed by non-government organizations or agencies that contract with CMS to serve as the fiscal agent between providers and the Federal Government. These claims processors are known as intermediaries and carriers. They apply the Medicare coverage rules to determine the appropriateness and amount of claims.

Medicare intermediaries process Part A claims. They also process outpatient hospital claims for Part B. Examples of intermediaries are Blue Cross and Blue Shield plans in various regions of the country and other commercial insurance companies. The intermediaries' responsibilities include the following:

- Determining costs and reimbursement amounts
- Maintaining records
- Establishing controls
- Safeguarding against fraud and abuse or excess use
- Conducting reviews and audits
- Making the payments to providers for services
- Assisting both providers and beneficiaries as needed

Medicare carriers handle most of the Part B claims. Examples of carriers are the Blue Shield plan in one state and various commercial insurance companies. The carriers' responsibilities include the following:

- Determining charges allowed by Medicare
- Maintaining quality-of-performance records
- Assisting in fraud and abuse investigations

---

[15] Kaiser Family Foundation and Hewitt Associates, *Prospects for Retiree Health Benefits as Medicare Prescription Drug Coverage Begins*, [28].

- Assisting both suppliers and beneficiaries as needed

- Making payments to physicians and suppliers for services that are covered under Part B

Peer review organizations (PROs) are groups of practicing health care professionals who are paid by the Federal Government to oversee the care provided to Medicare beneficiaries in each State and to improve the quality of services. PROs educate other health care professionals and assist in the effective, efficient, and economical delivery of health care services to the Medicare population.

ADMINISTRATION

The Department of Health and Human Services (DHHS) has the overall responsibility for administration of the Medicare program. Within DHHS, CMS has the responsibility for administering Medicare. The Social Security Administration (SSA) provides assistance by initially determining an individual's Medicare entitlement, by withholding Part B premiums from the beneficiaries' Social Security benefit checks, and by maintaining Medicare data on the master beneficiary record. The Internal Revenue Service in the Department of the Treasury collects the HI payroll taxes from workers and their employers.

A Board of Trustees, composed of two appointed members of the public (one from each party) and four members who serve by virtue of their positions in the Federal Government (the Secretaries of the Treasury, Labor, and Health and Human Services Departments, and the Commissioner of Social Security), oversees the financial operations of the HI and SMI trust funds. The Secretary of the Treasury is the managing trustee. The two members from the public are appointed by the president to four-year terms and are subject to Senate confirmation. The Board of Trustees annually reports to Congress on the financial and actuarial status of the Medicare trust funds on or about the first day of April.

State agencies (usually the state health departments under agreements with CMS) identify, survey, and inspect provider and supplier facilities and institutions that want to participate in the Medicare program. In consultation with CMS, these agencies certify the qualified facilities.

4   RETIREE BENEFIT DESIGN

The enactment of Medicare in 1965 influenced employers in the U.S. to offer retiree medical benefits to former employees. Other pieces of legislation also influenced the design of retiree medical benefits, but it wasn't until the Financial Accounting Standards Board (FASB) began to research the accounting treatment of these programs that employers truly understood the financial implication of their retiree group benefit obligations. In the years that preceded the adoption of Statement of Financial Accounting No. 106 (FAS 106) in 1990, benefits professionals and boardrooms were buzzing about what to do about these "expensive" benefits. FAS 106 did not change the value of these benefits – only how they were valued. It required companies to accrue, on a present-value basis, the future value of retiree life and health benefits. So companies had to reflect on their financial statements not only the current payments to retirees, but also an expense and liability for the payments to future retirees.

This change in accounting made some employers decide to terminate benefits and others to limit their future obligations. According to a Hewitt Associates database[1] with research on about 1,000 large employers, the percentage of companies offering health care benefits to Medicare-eligible retirees decreased from 80 percent in 1991 to 64 percent in 2005. The same research showed that about 27 percent of employers provided free medical coverage to Medicare-eligible retirees in 1991– in 2005, that figure dropped to 3 percent. These two statistics support the trend of employers passing more of the cost of medical plans to retirees and their families.

In a recent survey[2] of 300 large employers, 71 percent of respondents said they increased premium and 34 percent increased cost sharing for retirees under their medical program between 2004 and 2005. Eight percent of these employers said they imposed new caps on their contributions to the program.

---

[1] © Hewitt Associates 2005 SpecBook.

[2] Kaiser Family Foundation/Hewitt Associates, *Prospects for Retiree Health Benefits as Medicare Prescription Drug Coverage Begins*, [28].

The plans available to retirees in the 1970s and 1980s were generally continuations of active medical plans. Retirees generally paid the same premium for coverage as their active counterparts. Retirees eligible for Medicare had their benefits coordinated with the government program so that they would get all of their medical costs paid for by the combination of the two programs (i.e., standard coordination of benefits, discussed further below).

Most employers considered anyone eligible to receive a pension benefit as also eligible for the retiree medical plan. Typically, employees who were at least age 55 and had ten years of service at the time of retirement were allowed to participate in the program.

A basic difference in employer-sponsored medical benefits between pre- and post-65 retirees in the U.S. is the availability of the Medicare program. Therefore it is important to understand how plans coordinate with the government program. The same principles could potentially apply with social insurance programs in other countries.

TODAY'S TYPICAL RETIREE GROUP BENEFIT PROGRAM

The typical health plan for pre-65 retirees is a continuation of the same program available while they were working. It is generally a preferred provider option arrangement (PPO) with a $250 deductible, 80 to 90 benefit percentage and a $2,500 out-of-pocket maximum. The post-65 retirees convert to an indemnity plan using Medicare payment rates as the approved charge level. Dental coverage is generally terminated at retirement and life insurance benefits are reduced. The average employer subsidy is 60 percent of the total cost of the plan.

Appendix A provides more details on the prevalence of the various features offered to retirees.

WHY OFFER RETIREE GROUP BENEFITS?

A very basic question to ask before trying to decide what to do with an employer's retiree group benefit plan is to ask, why offer such a plan in the first place. Many reasons can be listed for either starting or maintaining a plan including:

- Retiree group benefits are a tax-effective means of providing retirement financial security.
- They are a valuable benefit for those currently receiving the coverage or who are soon to retire – particularly pre-65 retirees.
- The benefits can support workforce planning and growth opportunities for employees.
- Availability of ongoing health care coverage is a social responsibility of the employer.
- Retiree health care benefits help provide a competitive package of total compensation.
- The current cash costs are nominal relative to the total spending on benefits.
- Retiree benefits are often at the top of the list of union demands.

All very good reasons, but as the *Erosion* chapter indicates, the prevalence of employer-sponsored retiree group benefits has declined over the last decade and is seemingly still eroding. Several reasons were cited in that chapter as to why employers are dropping coverage. One way to establish the rationale to eliminate coverage is to provide a counterpoint to each of the reasons for maintaining a plan.

- Health care benefits are tax-effective but employers do not receive a full "credit" for providing the benefit because of the hidden costs of their subsidy to the plans.
- The benefits are valuable for a minority of active employees. It is not until employees begin to seriously consider retiring (around age 50) that the benefit becomes valuable in their eyes.
- Historical employment relationship (that focused on long-term career) may be diminishing.
- As workers assert their independence and their lack of loyalty to their employer, the sense of providing retiree health care as a social responsibility is quickly evaporating.
- Competition is more global and becoming more difficult to measure today, with employers competing for workers from not only their own industries but also from similar industries or local talent. As more of the competitors eliminate retiree health care coverage, it makes it easier to drop or reduce the benefit, especially as global competitors and newer industries tend not to provide these benefits.

- The cash cost of retiree health care is increasing faster than any other cash item for most companies. So for many, it is no longer a nominal financial commitment. Since most employers must produce financial statements in accordance with generally accepted accounting principles, the accrual cost required by FASB and GASB is a significant financial measure.

- Retiree benefits are definitely at the top of most union demands, but recent collective bargaining sessions have indicated some negotiating ability in this area. The value of these deferred benefits is traded for something more valuable to current workers. In addition, it has been recognized by both labor and management that the legacy costs resulting from prior bargaining of several industries have been increasingly difficult to maintain and have been partially responsible for the companies' financial difficulties.

Of course, the above reasons for and against providing retiree health benefits may have a different priority for each employer. The first step in deciding the nature and type of retiree group benefit to provide is to consider each of them and others as appropriate. The options should also be considered in conjunction with the goals and objectives of the retirement income programs, the overall benefits program and human resource philosophy.

For example, as an employer moves away from defined benefit pension plans to defined contribution plans, one way to maintain the higher reward for long service employees that is a characteristic of defined benefit plans is to maintain the retiree health plan. The plan would need to be structured to reward longer service and to create a pricing structure that is transparent enough for the retirees to understand its value.

If a retiree health plan were to be maintained, some other characteristics that are often considered when making a decision on the overall design are:

- Simplicity
- Ease of administration
- Ease of communication to retirees
- Predictability and stability of costs
- High perceived value of the benefit by a broad group of employees
- Consistency with other health plan offerings (e.g., for active employees)

MEDICARE INTEGRATION

Most retirees in the U.S. are covered under the Medicare program when they turn age 65. Social insurance programs of other countries have varying degrees of medical coverage. In the U.S. as well as most other countries, the government plan is the primary payer. That is, the government plan pays first and the secondary insurer (in this case the employer plan) pays next. When an employer provides continued medical coverage and other coverage is available, there are three basic methods to coordinate or integrate benefit plans. These methods are standard coordination of benefits (COB), exclusion or carveout. These coordination methods typically apply to Medicare Parts A and B. The coordinated care plans under Medicare Part C are paid directly by Medicare so no explicit coordination in design is necessary. There are several alternative strategies to coordinate employer plans with the Part D drug plans and are discussed in a later section. In the following examples, Medicare is the primary plan and the employer plan is the secondary plan.

Standard Coordination of Benefits (COB)

Standard COB usually results in full payment of the covered medical expense when the benefits of both the primary and secondary coverages are combined. Technically, the plan pays the lesser of the regular plan benefit (assuming it was the only plan) and the difference between covered expenses and the primary plan benefit payment. If C = covered expense (the medical charge that is covered by the plan), M = the Medicare payment and $\%$ represents the application of the employer's benefit provisions (i.e., accounting for any copays, deductibles, and coinsurance), the following formula represents the resulting standard COB payment.

$$\text{The lesser of } C \times \% \text{ or } C - M$$

Most times, the latter part of the formula is the result. Note that if $C - M$ is the resulting benefit, combining the above plan benefit and the Medicare benefit yields C, or the covered expense. The retiree has had his or her entire cost paid (assuming the entire service was a covered expense).

Exclusion

The exclusion method of integration first excludes any benefits paid from the primary plan and then applies the benefit formula of the secondary plan. The following formula describes this method.

$$(C - M) \times \%$$

Under this method, there is usually a benefit paid because Medicare will pay less than the covered expense.

Carveout

Of the three methods, the carveout method produces the smallest employer benefit. Under this method, the employer benefit is first determined assuming that Medicare did not exist, and then Medicare is subtracted from the result.

$$(C \times \%) - M$$

Variations

There are variations of the three methods above. For example, when coordinating with the U.S. Medicare program, it is common for plans to use the exclusion method with Part A (hospital) benefits and the carveout method with the Part B (supplemental medical) benefits. The reason is that for most hospital stays, the Medicare benefit is greater than the employer benefit, but for medical services, Medicare usually pays less than an employer plan. With this kind of scenario, the timing of claim submission of each of the bills can make a difference. This is best shown by an example.

Assume that the retiree has one hospital stay during the year along with various medical services. The hospital stay included total costs of $10,000, of which Medicare paid all but $952 (the Part A deductible in 2006). The medical services amounted to another $3,000, of which Medicare paid $2,185. The employer plan has a $250 deductible and pays 80 percent after the deductible with an out-of-pocket limit for the retiree of $2,000 (including the deductible).

There are several ways the retiree might submit claims during the year, especially if the $3,000 of medical services was not all incurred at the same time. The following are three different ways to submit claims. First, all bills are submitted together; second the hospital bills are submitted first and the medical bills later; third the medical bills are first, then hospital.

All Bills Submitted

	Exclusion	Carveout
Covered expenses	$ 13,000	$ 13,000
Medicare	(11,233)	--
Net expense	1,767	13,000
Deductible	(250)	(250)
Subject to coinsurance	1,517	12,750
Coinsurance	(303)	(1,750)
Benefit before Medicare	1,214	11,000
Medicare	--	(11,233)
Net benefit	1,214	0

Medical Services Submitted First

	Exclusion		Carveout	
	Medical	**Hospital**	**Medical**	**Hospital**
Covered expenses	$ 3,000	$ 10,000	$ 3,000	$10,000
Medicare	(2,185)	(9,048)	--	--
Net expense	815	952	3,000	10,000
Deductible	(250)	0	(250)	0
Subject to coinsurance	585	952	2,750	10,000
Coinsurance	(113)	(190)	(550)	(1,200)
Benefit before Medicare	452	762	2,200	8,800
Medicare	--	--	(2,185)	(9,048)
Net benefit	452	762	15	0
Total net benefit	1,214		15	

Hospital Services Submitted First

	Exclusion		Carveout	
	Hospital	**Medical**	**Hospital**	**Medical**
Covered expenses	10,000	$ 3,000	$ 10,000	$ 3,000
Medicare	(9,048)	(2,185)	--	--
Net expense	952	815	10,000	3,000
Deductible	(250)	0	(250)	0
Subject to coinsurance	702	815	9,750	3,000
Coinsurance	(140)	(163)	(1,750)	0
Benefit before Medicare	562	652	8,000	3,000
Medicare	--	--	(9,048)	(2,185)
Net benefit	562	652	0	815
Total net benefit	1,214		815	

Note that the exclusion method of integration produced the same benefit in all of the above calculations. Regardless of the order of claim submission, this will always be true. The carveout method, however, produced a different benefit amount in each.

All Bills Submitted

When all the bills are submitted at one time, no benefit is payable under carveout.

Medical Services Submitted First

If the medical services bills are submitted first, the carveout plan will pay $15. This is greater than if all bills are submitted, because the high hospital payment under Medicare is not recognized in the calculation of the medical services benefit. When all expenses are submitted in one claim, the plan can take advantage of the Medicare hospital payment. The plan could try to recoup the overpayment after the hospital bill is submitted, but plans generally do not ask the retiree for money back after he or she has been paid.

Hospital Services Submitted First

If the hospital bills are submitted first and this benefit is determined to be zero, and then medical services bills are submitted, there could be a larger benefit payable. Since the hospital bill has met the plan's out-of-pocket limit, all medical services charges are paid at 100 percent. In total, this results in $815 benefit. Many plans include a provision that if there are any "debits" in the benefit calculations during the year, they may be carried forward to subsequent claims. For example, the hospital benefit would have been $8,000 under the employer plan and Medicare paid $9,048, leaving a $1,048 debit that can be recouped from later claims. If there are no other later claims, the debit goes away at the end of the year. When this approach is used, the plan will not pay anything (the $815 benefit is reduced by any debit carry-forwards) and there will be a remaining $233 debit.

If a plan uses a debit approach, a retiree who does not submit the hospital claim will get a benefit from the plan that is equal to the example shown above when medical services are submitted first (i.e., $15).

An easy way to avoid this timing issue when coordinating with Medicare is to use the exclusion method for all hospital benefits and the carveout method for all other benefits. The timing problem arises when some services are paid at a higher amount than other services in the primary plan than in the secondary plan. Splitting the coordination method between the two services with different reimbursement methods will keep payments consistent regardless of claim submission timing.

Supplement

Another form of integration is to "supplement" the primary plan. A supplement plan pays for expenses that the primary plan does not pay (e.g., additional services, copays, deductibles, and coinsurance). This approach is possible only when the secondary plan has advance knowledge of the primary plan design, which is easy if the primary plan is a government plan. In non-U.S. countries with a national health plan, employer-based plans generally use this approach to coordinate benefits.

In the U.S., an example of a supplement plan to Medicare is one that pays for the Part A deductible ($952 in 2006), 50 percent of any coinsurance that Medicare does not pay (i.e., 50 percent of the 20 percent coinsurance), and for services not covered by Medicare (e.g., physician charges in excess of Medicare allowable fees and emergency care outside of the U.S.). These designs are commonly referred to as "Medigap" plans in the U.S. because they fill in the "gaps" that Medicare does not cover.

Individually-sold Medigap plans are regulated in the U.S. by state insurance laws. Ten specific plan designs (Plans A-J) were developed by the National Association of Insurance Commissioners (NAIC) as promulgated by federal law so that no other type of plan may be sold. Plans K and L were added in 2006 to provide lower cost plans with catastrophic protection. The following table summarizes the design requirements of the ten plans offered in most states[3].

Standard Medigap Plan Designs

Design Feature	A	B	C	D	E	F	G	H	I	J	K	L
Basic benefits	✓	✓	✓	✓	✓	✓	✓	✓	✓	✓	✓	✓
Part A deductible		✓	✓	✓	✓	✓	✓	✓	✓	✓	50%	75%
Skilled nursing facility			✓	✓	✓	✓	✓	✓	✓	✓	50%	75%
Foreign travel emergency care			✓	✓	✓	✓	✓	✓	✓	✓		
At-home recovery				✓			✓		✓	✓		
Part B excess charges						✓	✓		✓	✓		
Part B deductible			✓			✓				✓		
Preventive medical care					✓					✓	✓	✓

[3] Massachusetts, Minnesota and Wisconsin offer designs that are slightly different than above.

Basic benefits for Plans A through J include Part A coinsurance for in-patient care (excluding the initial deductible—$952 in 2006) for up to 150 days ($238 per day for days 61 through 90 and $476 for 60 lifetime reserve days in 2002), 100 percent of Medicare-eligible hospital care expenses after 150 days, Part B coinsurance (excluding the Part B deductible—$124 in 2006), and the first three pints of blood. ***The basic benefits for Plans K and L*** are slightly different and include the Part A coinsurance for both Plans K and L, 50 percent of Part B coinsurance for Plan K and 75 percent for Plan L, 100 percent of preventive services for both Plans K and L, 50 percent of the first three pints of blood for Plan K and 75 percent for Plan L, 50 percent for hospice care cost-sharing including respite care for Plan K and 75 percent for Plan L.

Part A deductible means 100 percent payment of the initial deductible for hospital stays ($952 in 2006).

Skilled nursing facility coverage pays 100 percent of the daily coinsurance for days 21 through 100 ($119.00 per day in 2006).

Foreign travel emergency care covers 80 percent of medically necessary care after deductible, $50,000 lifetime maximum.

At-home recovery care provides short-term assistance for people recovering from an illness, injury or surgery and who qualify for Medicare home health care. The plan pays up to $40 per visit for up to seven visits per week for up to eight weeks after Medicare covered home health care ends. The maximum annual benefit is $1,600.

Part B excess charges pay for physician charges in excess of Medicare allowable fees. Plan G pays 80 percent and Plans F, I and J pay 100 percent.

Part B deductible covers the $124 (in 2006, indexed) Part B deductible per year.

Preventive medical care coverage pays for basic preventive care such as routine physical exams, serum cholesterol and diabetes screenings, hearing and thyroid function test. Maximum benefit of $120 per year.

Prescription drugs coverage is generally not available unless a beneficiary had coverage before 2006. Enrollees with existing Medigap drug coverage had to decide in 2006 whether or not to continue in the Medigap drug plan with the knowledge that if they were to drop the coverage, they would likely have to pay late enrollment penalties because the Medigap plan was not as good as Medicare's standard benefit design. If the beneficiary decides to stay in the Medigap drug benefit, it pays 50 percent of cost of prescription drugs after a $250 deductible with a maximum benefit of $1,250 for Plans H and I and $3,000 for Plan J. For example, to reach the $1,250 benefit maximum under Plan H, you must have $2,750 in expenses ($250 + ($1,250 ÷ 0.50)).

Out of pocket limits protect the insured against high expenses under Plans K and L. Plan K has a $4,000 annual limit and Plan L has a $2,000 annual limit. Once the out of pocket limit is reached, the plan pays 100 percent of the covered charges for the rest of the calendar year.

Note that the plan designs described above represent the standard Medigap policies that an insurance company may offer to individuals. It does not restrict the designs that an employer may offer its retirees under an employer-sponsored group program.

Relative Costs

In general, the standard COB method of integration will be the highest cost alternative, followed by exclusion and carveout. The cost of a supplement plan can be low or high depending on what it covers. The following chart provides some rough national claim cost rates (single retiree rates for year 2006) for plans that coordinate with the U.S. Medicare program.[4]

Method of Integration	Average	Low	High
Standard COB	$ 1,350	$ 1,150	$ 1,550
Exclusion	1,000	800	1,200
Carveout	650	550	800
Supplement	1,250	950	1,500

Medical claim costs only (i.e., no prescription drugs or administrative expenses) for Medicare-eligible retirees.

[4] Based on Hewitt Associates' © 2006 Medical Pricing Model.

The above costs will vary by group depending on factors such as location, health status, demographics, and plan design. They are intended to represent medical claims only and do not include a provision for expenses or any other adjustments (e.g., premium tax, insurer profit and margin, risk) or costs for prescription drugs.

MEDICARE PRESCRIPTION DRUG COORDINATION[5]

The Medicare Modernization Act of 2003 (MMA) was signed by the President in December 2003 and CMS released final regulations in January 2005.

Congress recognized the importance of maintaining a viable employer-sponsored health insurance market when the debate about the new Medicare drug benefit began. As a result, there was careful deliberation in both houses on how to best achieve their goal of providing prescription drugs to the Medicare population as a whole and to assure continued employer involvement in the delivery of health care to retirees.

The key message delivered to employers when the MMA was released was that of flexibility. The Congress recognized the employers' important role and they were given a number of alternatives to consider—all of which will reduce their costs of providing a very important benefit to their former employees.

Included in both the MMA and regulations were a variety of alternatives for employers to use in order to take advantage of the new program. These include:

- Maintain their current employer-sponsored plan and receive a retiree drug subsidy from Medicare based on actual spending.

- Contract with a PDP or Medicare Advantage prescription drug (MA-PD) plan to provide pharmacy benefits to their Medicare-covered retirees (an individual must be enrolled in Medicare Part A and/or B to be eligible for Part D benefits);

---

[5] The material is taken from the article "What Comes After the Retiree Drug Subsidy," by Dale H. Yamamoto, which appeared in the 3rd Quarter 2006 *Benefits Quarterly*, (copyright) International Society of Certified Employee Benefit Specialists, Inc. [43].

- Contract with CMS directly to become a Medicare PDP or MA-PD for its own retirees; or

- Provide a separate prescription drug plan that coordinates or supplements the benefits of any available PDP.

Of course, an employer may also decide that Medicare-covered retirees now have access to many high quality prescription drug plans so their coverage is to some extent redundant.

Most employers elected to continue their prescription drug plan for 2006 (the first year of the Medicare prescription drug benefit) and accept the retiree drug subsidy. This was partially due to the lack of time to adequately study all of the alternatives but also because the alternatives had too many unknowns to make a thoughtful decision on their viability.

In a year-end 2005 survey by the Kaiser Family Foundation and Hewitt Associates[6], 79 percent of employers said they would accept the retiree drug subsidy in 2006. Of the remaining employers 10 percent said they would supplement the new Medicare program, 2 percent would sponsor their own Medicare prescription drug plan and 9 percent would discontinue their plans. An interesting statistic in the survey results are the corresponding results when measured as a percent of retirees affected by the decisions. As a percent of retirees, 89 percent were in a plan that accepted the retiree drug subsidy, 7 percent in plans that supplemented Medicare, 2 percent in employer-sponsored drug plans and 2 percent of retirees had their plans discontinued. The implication of these percentage differences is that a greater percentage of larger employers accepted the retiree drug subsidy while a relatively higher percentage of smaller employers discontinued their plans.

For the employers accepting the retiree drug subsidy for 2006, they were asked if they would continue accepting the subsidy in 2007 and 2010. 82 percent responded that they were somewhat or very likely to accept the subsidy in 2007 and the response rate dropped to 50 percent in 2010.

---

[6] McArdle, Neuman, Strollo, Atchison, Yamamoto; *Prospects for Retiree Health Benefits as Medicare Prescription Drug Coverage Begins*; Kaiser Family Foundation and Hewitt Associates; December 2005 [28].

Table 4.1

Likelihood to Continue Accepting Retiree Drug Subsidy

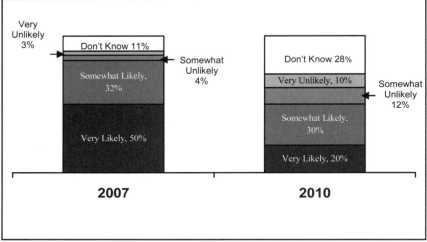

Source: Kaiser/Hewitt 2005 Survey on Retiree Health Benefits, December 2005

The course of events over the next three years that will drive the ultimate decision to continue accepting the federal subsidy will be many, and each employer will have a unique combination of factors that will drive the decision. A key consideration will likely be financial, but other factors will also enter the picture.

The Alternatives

The key to the success of any of these alternatives is the availability of providers willing to offer services to administer the programs. Each alternative has its own complexity and will require specialized treatment.

Retiree Drug Subsidy

Employers who maintain their prescription drug plan and meet certain requirements will receive a retiree drug subsidy from Medicare to encourage their maintenance of the plan. The primary requirement that they must meet is to certify that their plans are at least actuarially equivalent to the standard Medicare design (i.e., the $250 deductible, 75 percent benefit to $2,250 and 95 percent after $5,100 in 2006). This actuarial equivalence test is different than the one that PDPs must satisfy to offer alternative designs.

A plan sponsor (either an employer or union) must apply for the retiree drug subsidy every year. Included in the application is an attestation by a qualified actuary that their plan is at least actuarially equivalent to the Medicare Part D standard benefit. The procedure includes two tests—a gross value test and a net value test.

Gross Value Test

The gross value test compares the total employer plan value against the total value of the Medicare standard benefit. This test is based on the experience of the plan sponsor to the extent that there is credible data available. This determination is made by the actuary using the claims paid under the employer plan and an actuarial estimate of the Medicare benefit using the experience of the employer. The actuary may make adjustments for anticipated changes in utilization under the Medicare plan due to the differences in design.

In most situations, an employer will not have credible data to estimate the value of the Medicare benefit, especially due to the catastrophic benefit under Medicare. The use of normative data, adjusted for the level of employer costs, will therefore often be used to perform the test.

The following table illustrates the testing using an extract of the illustrative table provided by CMS in their April 2005 guidance on the actuarial equivalence standard.

Frequency	Average Charge	Employer	Basic Benefit	Catastrophic Benefit	Total Medicare
0.1106	$ 0	$ 0	$ 0	$ 0	$ 0
0.1975	670	503	315	0	315
0.2082	1,912	1,434	1,247	0	1,247
0.2068	3,121	2,341	1,500	0	1,500
0.1095	4,265	3,199	1,500	0	1,500
0.0916	5,534	4,151	1,500	412	1,912
0.0758	10,731	8,048	1,500	5,349	6,849
1.0000	2,963	2,223	1,047	443	1,491

The above table is based on an employer plan that pays a 75 percent bene-fit with an average cost of $2,223 per year for a single Medicare eligible person. The basic benefit is the 75 percent payable under Medicare be-tween the deductible of $250 and the first coverage limit of $2,250. The catastrophic benefit is the 95 percent after $3,600 out of pocket threshold that occurs after $5,100 in total spending $250 + ($3,600–$250).

Assume another employer with the same benefit design but with costs of $2,000 per person. The distribution could be adjusted to get a $2,000 cost in this case by multiplying the average cost by a factor equal to $2,000 ÷ $2,223 since the benefit is a multiple of the total charge.

Frequency	Average Charge	Employer	Basic Benefit	Catastrophic Benefit	Total Medicare
0.1106	$ 0	$ 0	$ 0	$ 0	$ 0
0.1975	603	452	265	0	265
0.2082	1,721	1,291	1,103	0	1,103
0.2068	2,809	2,107	1,500	0	1,500
0.1095	3,838	2,878	1,500	0	1,500
0.0916	4,980	3,735	1,500	0	1,500
0.0758	9,656	7,242	1,500	4,328	5,828
1.0000	2,667	2,000	1,008	328	1,336

In both of these cases, the gross value test is met. In the first, the total employer value is $2,223 and the calculated Medicare value is $1,491. Note that the Medicare value is based on a calculated number and is not a published amount or prescribed amount from CMS. The second case met the test because $2,000 is greater than the estimated Medicare value of $1,336.

Using the distribution in the first case, the employer design could be a 51 percent benefit and still meet the test.

If the benefit were a fixed-dollar copay design, the total charge would have to be adjusted, and an estimate of the value of the copay would need to be made, a demonstration of which is beyond the scope of this textbook.

Since most employer plans provide a benefit for virtually all drugs, ac-counting for different PDP formularies is generally not critical to include in the calculations. However, it may be necessary to account for some differences in drugs covered under either the employer plan or required under the standard Medicare design. For example, an employer plan may not cover lifestyle drugs and the standard Medicare design is required to cover some drugs in this category. Appropriate adjustments should be made in the testing.

Net Value Test

The net value test is performed by subtracting the retiree contribution rate from the gross value of the sponsor's plan. The net value of the Medicare benefit may be determined by subtracting the national average beneficiary premium as determined by CMS ($32.20 for 2006) or assuming that the value of the beneficiary contribution is 25.5 percent of the Medicare value.

The purpose of this test is to assure that the employer subsidizes their plan as much as the federal government subsidizes the standard PDP design. This is to assure that employers do not receive a "windfall" from the Medicare program if they require significant retiree contributions.

Using the values from the first case, the results of the net value test may be as follows, assuming that retiree pays 50 percent of the cost of the plan:

	Employer Net Value	Medicare Net Value Using National Beneficiary Premium	Medicare Net Value Using 25.5 Percent
Gross value	$ 2,223	$ 1,491	$ 1,491
Retiree contribution	1,111	386	380
Net value	1,112	1,105	1,111
Test result		Pass	Pass

If the retiree had to pay 60 percent, the net value would be $889 which is less than either of the two net Medicare values, and the plan would therefore fail the test.

If the employer is willing to provide supplemental coverage to Part D for any retiree who decides to enroll in an individual Part D plan, the net value of the standard Medicare coverage may also be adjusted to recognize the lower catastrophic coverage because of the effect of the true out-of-pocket definition.[7] This was alluded to in the discussion of the Medicare drug benefit in that the catastrophic benefit begins payment as soon as a beneficiary has $3,600 (in 2006) of true out-of-pocket (TrOOP) costs. Any employer payment that supplements a Medicare benefit does not count as part of the retiree's TrOOP.

Assuming that with a 75 percent benefit, no retiree receives a catastrophic benefit due to TrOOP, the net Medicare value can be reduced by the full value of the catastrophic benefit or $443.[8] This would result in the following, assuming retirees now must pay 60 percent of the cost.

	Employer Net Value	Medicare Net Value Using National Beneficiary Premium	Medicare Net Value Using 25.5 Percent
Gross value	$ 2,223	$ 1,047	$ 1,047
Retiree contribution	1,334	386	267
Net value	889	661	780
Test result		Pass	Pass

The plan now passes even though the retiree is paying 60 percent of the cost of the plan. The employer must, however, provide a supplemental benefit to Medicare for those electing a Part D plan. Two coordination methods will therefore need to be administered – the employer plan and a Medicare supplement plan.

Aggregation of Plans

The gross and net value tests must be performed according to the rules that CMS has published and there are definitions of plans and benefit options that they have constructed for these tests. Their definition of a plan is based on the same definition provided under the health care continuation rules under the COBRA.[9] This is a legal definition of plan and is dependent on the nature of available written contracts and government

---

[7] This "special adjustment" is addressed in more detail in CMS guidance released April 7, 2005 on the topic of actuarial equivalence under the retiree drug subsidy.

[8] A more complete claims distribution may show that some members actually would receive a catastrophic benefit but the assumption that nobody is affected simplifies this illustration.

[9] The Consolidated Omnibus Budget Reconciliation Act of 1986 required employer plans to continue coverage for certain covered members losing coverage. The MMA rules point to Treasury regulation 26 CFR §54.4980B-2 which is the COBRA definition of a group health plan.

filing. Within a "plan," the employer may also define "benefit options." Benefit options are any different benefit designs, category of benefits or cost-sharing arrangement offered with a plan. For example, a plan may have different benefit designs (i.e., different coinsurance or copays) for those retiring on different dates. The benefit option may be different for groups of retirees (e.g., salaried versus hourly, geographic location differences). Or the benefit option may have different retiree contribution requirements (e.g., by service at retirement, by plan location). The plan sponsor has the flexibility to define benefit options that make sense for their offerings.

In the end, the actuary will be attesting to the fact that each benefit option meets the gross value test and each plan or aggregation of benefit options meets the net value test. See Appendix E for the Academy Practice note on Actuarial Equivalence.

Subsidy Payment

For each "qualified retiree" under plans and benefit options that meet the tests, Medicare will pay a retiree drug subsidy during the year based on their actual spending. For all Part D covered drugs that are between $250 and $5,000, Medicare pays 28 percent of the total cost. This amount is further adjusted for any other rebates that the plan sponsor may receive. This payment may be received monthly, quarterly or annually from Medicare. The actual timing depends on the employer's application request and the frequency of their payment request to CMS.

The payments may be received during the year based on the plan sponsor's payment request where summarized claims data is reported. After the end of the plan year, the plan sponsor compiles a more detailed report to CMS that will reconcile all costs, including actual rebates received. Since rebates are often received three to six months after a claim is paid, this detailed reporting will be several months after the end of a plan year. The regulations state that this report must be within 15 months after the end of the plan year.

Note that the subsidy payment calculation is performed first by reflecting the spending by the participant with the $250 cost threshold and $5,000 cost limit (both 2006 amounts and indexed for the future) and then adjusting for any rebates. The following table illustrates this calculation for two retirees, assuming that the rebate is three percent of the total charge.

	Total Drug Costs for the Plan Year	Amount between $250 and $5,000	28% of Amount	Estimated Rebate	Retiree Drug Subsidy
Retiree 1	$ 800	$ 550	$ 154	$ 17	$ 137
Retiree 2	6,000	4,750	1,330	143	1,187
Total	6,800	5,300	1,484	160	1,324

Employer PDPs

An employer has several options to provide a PDP or a MA-PD to only its retirees. Most of the waivers discussed below are needed to provide one of these plans. CMS describes these alternatives as follows:

- Pay for enhanced coverage through a PDP or MA-PD plan to subsidize more of their retirees' cost-sharing and provide additional benefits (employer insured); or

- Offer their own PDP or MA-PD to their retirees (direct contract).[10]

A way to distinguish these two alternatives from each other is that the first one is generally an insured contract and the second is self-funded. In essence, they represent the two ends of the spectrum of typical employer financing arrangements. A hybrid of these two alternatives is to pay for the standard benefit coverage provided from a PDP on an insured basis and self-insure the enhanced coverage with the same PDP. This is similar to the suggested CMS alternative of supplementing the standard Part D coverage, but under a more controlled administrative environment where one PDP handles all benefit administration. If the PDP would allow the employer to act as a reinsurer of the coverage for their retirees, the two alternatives become identical in financial cost and risk for the employer.

Employer Waivers

Special treatment is given to these two alternatives in the form of waivers of certain Part D requirements. The uncertainty of these waivers was one of the reasons many employers elected to accept the retiree drug subsidy

---

[10] Note that CMS uses consistent terminology in its guidance and other material to refer to these two alternatives. The first alternative, referred to as "employer insured" in this text, is called an "Employer Group Waiver Plan" or "EGWP" by CMS. In some older CMS material, it is referred to as "800 Series Plans." The second alternative, "direct contract," is "Direct Contract Employer Group Waiver Plan."

for 2006. Since CMS and the providers will have had two years of experience, the use of employer waivers will be better understood for a 2008 implementation of these alternatives.

Most of the key waivers that employers (or the PDP or MA-PD) will want to receive have been automatically granted by CMS. CMS issued three guidance papers on waivers on February 11, 2005, March 9, 2005 and April 6, 2005[11].

The initial guidance dealt with the timing of applications and the entry requirements to become a PDP. The timing waivers only applied for 2005 and were intended to give employers more time to elect one of these options, but with all the uncertainties in providers' ability to administer the plans, few took advantage of the delays. The other waivers included in this guidance will pave the way for future employer initiatives. These include waiving the requirements that the PDP:

- be licensed in each state where the employer has retirees,

- accept all Medicare-eligible beneficiaries who reside in their service area,

- limit coverage to only beneficiaries who live in the PDP's service areas, and

- meet minimum enrollment standards.

In essence, the above waivers allow an employer to offer a PDP on a national basis not subject to state insurance licensing in each state and to restrict enrollment to just the employer's retirees.

The second guidance issued in March provided further waivers of many of the Part D requirements that would otherwise make it difficult for the employer to cover only its own retirees on a national basis. These waivers focus on operational aspects including:

- the requirement of the PDP to have a policy-making body with oversight and control of the PDP,

---

[11] *Part D Waiver Guidance for Employer/Union Retiree Coverage*, Centers for Medicare & Medicaid Services, February 11, 2005 (updated 01/04/06); *Additional Part D Waiver Guidance for Employer/Union Retiree Coverage*, Centers for Medicare & Medicaid Services, March 9, 2005 (updated 01/03/06); and *Additional Part D Waiver Guidance for Employer/Union Retiree Coverage*, Centers for Medicare & Medicaid Services, April 6, 2005 (updated 01/04/06).

- the strict definition of actuarial equivalence for a PDP where the design must be equivalent for each level of the standard benefit definition (however, the plan must still be actuarially equivalent in total, and the catastrophic benefit must be part of the design),
- the waiver of federal solvency requirements of PDPs on a case by case basis,
- pharmacy network access requirements,
- the content of marketing and communication materials standards and approval, and
- CMS beneficiary reporting requirements that can be modified to be consistent with existing employer benefit rules (e.g., ERISA and securities laws).

These waivers allow an employer to replace the policy-making body of the plan with its regular governance process and offer benefits more aligned with designs offered to pre-Medicare members.

The third set of waiver guidance clarified some of the earlier guidance and added some other waiver items. An important clarification was regarding the service areas for MA-PD plans and PDPs offering employer coverage. In this case, if the MA-PD plan or PDP offers non-group coverage in a region where the employer has most of its employees, that plan may offer nationwide coverage to that particular employer. If the plan does not offer non-group coverage in that populous employer region, they can only offer coverage in the region they have non-group coverage. For example, if an employer has most of its employees in the state of California, a PDP that offers regular PDP coverage in the state of California, may offer nationwide coverage to that employer. If the PDP only offers regular PDP coverage in Nevada, it can only offer coverage in the state of Nevada for that employer.

This guidance also clarified that employer-only Part D plans will be reimbursed based on the national average premium (adjusted for the health status of covered retirees), and the reinsurance payments will be made at the end of the year rather than monthly. The reinsurance payment should not be significant in most cases because little, if any, would be expected to be paid because it only kicks in after a retiree has had $3,600 in true out-of-pocket (TrOOP) costs[12], which will be very few under a typical

---

[12] The catastrophic benefits begin when a beneficiary has reached the true out-of-pocket (TrOOP) amount ($3,600 in 2006 and indexed thereafter). The TrOOP does not count any Part D plan costs that are paid by an outside source (e.g., an employer plan).

employer design. Given the low national average beneficiary premium (estimated to be $25 per month for 2006); the potentially higher employer costs will not be reimbursed.

Other waivers included in the guidance are:

- Allowance for variation from standard PDP uniform premium rule (all beneficiaries must be charged the same rate) within reasonable bounds (i.e., can vary by classes such as service, location, job category, exempt/non-exempt, etc.) but the full Medicare subsidy must be passed on to retirees.
- Modified rules for low income subsidy-eligible retirees regarding their premium charge and plan design;
- Waiver of the PDP requirement that premiums be allowed to be withheld from Social Security checks;
- Allowance for employer based plans (either direct contract with CMS or employer insured with PDP) to be on a non-calendar plan year with rules on what PDP provisions to use for the plan year; and
- Allowance for employer to enroll its retirees on a group basis instead of the required individual enrollment requirements for PDPs.

Other waiver requests will be reviewed on a case by case basis. With all of the uniform waivers published by CMS, few individual waivers will be needed. On January 25, 2006, CMS published the individual waivers that it granted for 2006. CMS indicated that such approved waivers apply to any similarly situated entity seeking to offer, sponsor, or administer an employer-sponsored group prescription drug plan that meets the conditions of the waiver. So, in addition to being able to request individual waivers, an employer should consider reviewing the existing waivers to see what can be approved under certain conditions. For example, CMS waived the Medicare appeals and coverage determination requirements, subject to certain requirements, and allowed a direct contract employer group prescription drug plan to follow the ERISA requirements for appeals and coverage determinations.

Common Characteristics

There are several common characteristics between the employer insured and direct contract arrangements. Most of the CMS waivers apply to both strategies, including the ability to:

- Offer coverage on a nationwide basis (as long as the employer insured PDP meets the coverage rules set out by the third waiver guidance);

- Provide flexible design construction to closely match non-Medicare coverage;

- Maintain custom pharmacy networks;

- Provide employer-specific communication material that can include other medical benefit information;

- Maintain non-calendar year plan provisions; and

- Enroll retirees on a group basis.

Although CMS has bent over backwards to allow employers to offer designs as close as possible to other coverage they provide, the Part D coverage has to provide for the same catastrophic level of benefits (retiree copayment equal to the greater of $2 generic/$5 brand or 5%) that all Part D plans must provide. So the employer will have to either maintain the same catastrophic limits as commercial PDPs follow or periodically update their own limit (at least $3,600 in 2006). Since most retirees will not reach the catastrophic limit, the employer will not have to change the limit every year. Setting the limit in the legal plan document equal to the Medicare limit will ease periodic plan amendments. It may, however, require communication to retirees each year as the limits are adjusted due to the indexing process.

For a PDP that pays for 75 percent of the cost of all drugs, only 1.2 percent of retirees[13] are expected to exceed the catastrophic limit for 2006. For those retirees, their benefit will be about 27 percent higher so the actual cost increase will be less than one percent. And, the government pays for much of this cost anyway through their reinsurance payment of 80 percent of the charges (i.e., the employer only pays about 15 percent) so the actual employer cost will be slightly lower.

---

[13] Hewitt Associates © 2005 pharmacy pricing model, national average utilization projected to 2006.

The Differences

The primary difference between the two alternatives is the financing. As mentioned above, "employer insured" is fully-insured and the "direct contracting" is self-insured. For employers acting as reinsurers under the direct contract approach, most of the employer insured comments will apply to them (i.e., risk tolerance, administrative expenses and cash flow). Inherent in this financing difference are the key considerations in deciding whether or not to insure or self-insure any health care benefit – risk tolerance, differences in administrative expenses, cash flow and design flexibility.

Risk Tolerance

Risk in healthcare comes from two sources – the risk of catastrophic claims (either individual or the whole group) and fiduciary/legal risk.

Pharmacy costs are more predictable than other health care costs. They are also lower in average costs compared to other health care services. The catastrophic claim risks are therefore lower than with overall health care claim risks. Beyond the scope of this textbook, an analysis should be conducted to determine the financial volatility for the retiree group being considered for self-insuring to decide whether the risk is acceptable.

If the contract is insured, at worst, the employer may share the risk of any lawsuit. An employer that self-insures will bear all of the fiduciary/legal risk. For a fee, an insurance company may agree to accept a portion of the risk as part of the general services provided in their administrative contracts as they do with regular health care contracts.

Administrative Expenses

In a typical self-insurance feasibility analysis, as much as one-third of the insurance company's expenses can be eliminated by self-insuring. Much of the savings, however, come from expenses that are not present in the PDP environment. Charges such as premium tax, commissions and conversion charges do not exist in an employer insured PDP. The primary source of potential savings between the employer insured PDP and the direct contract PDP will be the risk charge the insurance company assesses. This may be worth one to three percent of the cost of the plan.

The reason that the risk charge may be as high as three percent for these two contracts is that neither financing arrangement is protected by the risk sharing provisions that commercial PDPs get from their Medicare contracts. This is further leveraged because the CMS payment is based on the national average premium and not the expected costs of the employer group. Commercial PDPs are paid based on their bid so as experience evolves, their payments will be based on their experience.

Cash Flow
Medical claims generally have a four to six week lag time in payment, and self-insured plans enjoy the "float" created by this delay in payment. Prescription drug claims are paid faster due to electronic processing that usually starts at point of sale. There may be some further delay in CMS payment but this will likely be insignificant. In fact, it may be possible that insured contracts will receive faster payment due to their volume of transactions with CMS and its payment system.

Design Flexibility
The ultimate goal of most employers, from a design perspective, is to maintain the same plan design for pre- and post-65 retiree groups. For employers who have accepted the retiree drug subsidy, this is achieved by that alternative as long as the plan design meets the actuarial equivalence test. Few employer-sponsored prescription drug plans failed this test from an overall plan value basis (the gross test under the CMS procedures). The plans that failed tended to have limited benefits (e.g., $1,000 annual maximum) or very high coinsurance (e.g., 50%). Most of the plans that failed the RDS actuarial equivalence test did so because the employer subsidy was low (e.g., retiree access only plans).

As mentioned earlier, under either employer PDP alternative (employer insured or direct contract), the plan has to provide the catastrophic benefit. Since Medicare pays for most of this cost, this should not be a financial impediment in the decision process. There may be a philosophical reason for not wanting such high benefits (e.g., concern of over-utilization of the new biotech and other specialty drugs on the market today).

The employer may have more flexibility by becoming a direct contract PDP because the employer insured PDP may have limited design flexibility in their product line. For example, the employer insured PDP may have a different formulary list than the employer's other plans and not be able to make changes. The direct contract PDP will have much more flexibility to match the other pharmacy designs it provides the non-Medicare population.

Hybrid Employer PDP

The hybrid plan is in essence a variation of the supplement or wrap plan suggested by CMS. It consists of an umbrella employer plan that supplements a standard benefit PDP. The standard PDP is a regular Medicare PDP program. For most multi-state employers, a PDP with nationwide coverage would be required. Assuming the current ten national PDPs continue offering their product beyond 2007, this should be a viable alternative.

The employer will contract with one of the PDPs to provide the standard Part D benefit design that they offer. This part of the contract will be a fully-insured contract with premiums based on the rates in each region the PDP offers coverage. A uniform blended fully-insured rate may be negotiated based on the retiree census. A separate contract with the same PDP will be established for the umbrella employer coverage. The benefit paid from the umbrella contract will be equal to the employer's defined benefit formula less the standard Part D benefit. For prescriptions where the Part D benefit is greater, the umbrella plan will pay nothing. In some circumstances, the overall benefit under the hybrid plan may be greater than the regular pre-retirement benefit.

The extent that the hybrid plan will pay greater benefits than the underlying employer design will greatly depend on the value of the employer plan relative to the standard Part D plan. For example, many employer plans have relatively high fixed dollar copays for generic drugs (e.g., $10). With an average priced generic in 2006 expected to be about $22.50, the standard Part D plan would pay $16.88 ($22.50 × 75%) and the employer would pay $12.50 ($22.50 − $10.00). The net employer benefit under this supplement plan would therefore be zero because the standard benefit is greater than the employer design. In fact, for the average priced generic drug, any copay greater than $5.62 ($22.50 × 25%) would pay no benefit. Therefore, the total plan (the standard Part D plan plus the employer supplement) will have higher claim costs than the employer plan alone.

Although the benefit for generics may be higher, the cost savings from the overall Medicare reimbursement may overcome the higher net cost of the benefit. Financial analysis of the specific designs will need to be done prior to making a decision to use this approach.

This administrative approach works more efficiently than a more open supplement arrangement that is discussed in the next section because both the employer umbrella plan and the PDP are administered by the same vendor. The coordination of the true out-of-pocket (TrOOP) provisions of the MMA is therefore easily handled.

One potential confounding issue with this approach is that some national PDPs may offer coverage on a national basis but the plan design of their standard benefit offering varies by geography. Individual products will generally not be the preferred offering and the employer should take advantage of the CMS waiver to contract with the PDP to offer a uniform design nationwide.

The primary reason for using the hybrid plan approach is that it provides greater flexibility in design than the fully-insured approach and allows the employer to directly finance the supplemental benefits.

Medicare Advantage Plans

The above discussion of employer alternatives focused specifically on the prescription drug side of alternatives. Many Medicare Advantage plans offer combined medical and pharmacy plans (MA-PD) as well as stand-alone medical and pharmacy plans. And, there are more than the well-known HMO-type plans under the Medicare Advantage umbrella being offered for 2006. There are PPO plans (offering network and out-of-network benefits), provider-sponsored (PSO) plans and private fee-for-service (PFFS) plans. The PPO and PSO plans tend to be offered in more urban areas of the country where networks are easily established but PFFS plans are broadly offered.

All MA plans are reimbursed by CMS in a similar manner with fixed payments. These payments are based on the expected costs of those covered using factors such as age, gender and location but also whether they are disabled, and further modified by a risk adjustment methodology that uses claims information to determine expected cost levels.

A key advantage of considering an MA-PD or MA and PDP plan is the opportunity to integrate the overall care management of the Medicare-eligible retiree. The insurer covering the retiree can use its entire medical management infrastructure that is typically focused on non-Medicare participants because saving overall medical costs directly reduce the net plan costs. Under typical Medicare supplement plans, most reduction in overall medical costs help to reduce Medicare's costs with little benefit to the employer's net plan cost.

As implied above, these plans may be structured as an employer insured plan or a direct contract plan.

Supplement Plan

A key to success for a true supplement plan (or wrap plan) is the TrOOP facilitation. The TrOOP facilitator (one vendor was selected for nation-wide coverage) has two responsibilities: to serve as a resource to pharmacies for plan eligibility and to keep track of the TrOOP amount for each beneficiary. Pharmacies will be able to use their real time services to check both Part D plan benefit information as well as other insurance (e.g., employer-sponsored plans). The facilitator will keep track of the individuals' TrOOP balances so that the Part D plans can properly calculate the correct benefit amount. It is still the Part D plans' responsibility to track the TrOOP costs for their covered members but the facilitator allows for universal tracking of the amounts.

On the surface, this facilitation seems simple but it involves interactions between hundreds of Part D plans and potentially even more supplemental plans (e.g., employer plans and other individual plans). All of this is expected to occur while the retiree is waiting for their prescription at the drug store. Anything less will create frustration for retirees and complaints to Medicare and employers.

The key advantage to offering a supplement plan is that it is comparable to how the other medical benefits are currently handled and provides for a high level of design flexibility. The plan will also tend to continue under the same financial basis (insured or self-insured) as current and look the same as other covered groups (e.g., active employees).

The disadvantages begin to appear when considering the details. These will all be issues that will need to be resolved up front before proceeding. Assuming that the TrOOP facilitation works, the following plan design and administration features should be considered and finalized.

Formulary

All Part D plans have formularies or a preferred list of drugs. If the employer plan also has a formulary driven plan design, special communication will have to be provided to retirees. In general, this should not be a big issue for most retirees with spending less than the Part D plan initial coverage amounts (the 75% benefit). If their drug is on the preferred list of either the Part D plan or the employer plan, they will gain favorable benefit treatment under one plan or the other. It becomes more problematic when the retiree exceeds the initial coverage limit under the Part D plan ($2,250 in 2006), and the drug that they were taking was on the preferred list of the Part D plan but not on the preferred list of the employer plan. Then their copayment may change dramatically during the year.

For example, assume the Part D plan benefit is 85% for a preferred brand name drug and 65% for a non-preferred brand name drug and the employer plan has a similar benefit design. Then assume that the retiree is taking a drug that is included in the Part D formulary but not the employer's. For spending under the initial coverage limit, the retiree's benefit will be the 85% from the Part D plan and the employer plan pays nothing. When the spending exceeds the initial coverage limit, the Part D plan pays nothing and the employer plan will pay a 65% benefit. Now the retiree is placed in a dilemma – does he or she change to a preferred drug under the employer plan or stay with the original drug? If the retiree originally selected a drug on the employer's preferred list, the benefit payment would always be 85%. While under the Part D coverage limit, the Part D plan pays 65% of the cost and employer plan pays 20%. After the coverage limit, the employer plan pays the total 85%.

Worst case is when the Part D plan does not pay a benefit at all for a particular drug but it is covered by the employer plan. A hypothetical Part D payment may be imputed in these cases. This is similar to the practice when an individual does not enroll in Part B – the Part B benefit is estimated and reflected in the employer plan benefit payment. In addition, if the drug is not covered by the Part D plan, none of the retiree's out-of-pocket costs count toward the Part D plan's true out-of-pocket.

Drug Price

All plans have negotiated prices with pharmacies and they are all different. The benefit payment is "easy" to determine. Assuming the Medicare beneficiary is a retiree, the Part D plan pays first and the employer plan will pay what they would have paid if the Part D plan did not exist less what the Part D plan pays. For Drug X, the Part D plan has negotiated a price of $80 and the employer plan has negotiated a price of $100 for the same drug. If both plans pay a benefit of 75 percent of the cost, the Part D plan would first pay $60 ($80 × 75%) and the employer plan would pay $15 ($100 × 75% − $60). In total, a benefit of $75 will be paid by both plans. What is the retiree's responsibility now? $5 or $25? Or should both benefit payments be based on the same price? A common practice will emerge over time but this is an issue to be resolved in advance.

Part D Plan Enrollment

For employers supplementing Part D, do you allow retirees to elect any Part D plan? Or, do you limit the Part D plans with which the plan will coordinate? Although the MMA expressed a standard Part D design in the legislation, Part D plans were allowed to deviate from the standard design as long as they were actuarially equivalent. For 2006, most plans do deviate from the standard design by offering no deductible or lower deductibles than the standard $250, or varying benefit payments for preferred drugs or generics. By limiting the number of Part D plans with which the employer will coordinate, the administration of the supplement becomes a little more manageable and the costs will be more predictable.

Part D Premium

Part D coverage carries a premium based on the plan selected and the location of the retiree. The employer should determine how to account for this added premium requirement as a transition issue. One employer response may be that since retirees typically pay for their Part B premium, they should also pay for the Part D premium. Part D is a new Medicare benefit and by making them pay the new premium, the employer has just increased the total monthly premium requirements for retirees relative to employer premium requirements and Medicare (both Parts B and D).

If the employer wants to reimburse the retiree for the Part D premium, the fact that the rates will vary makes it difficult. If the employer reimburses the retiree with an amount that exceeds the actual Part D premium, the remaining amount of reimbursement technically is taxable. Making available a flat amount per retiree or reducing the employer premium by a flat amount would be one method to account for the new cost.

Eliminate Employer Coverage

Most employer plans pay, on average, 60 to 80 percent of the total cost of drugs as a benefit. On the other hand, the standard Part D benefit pays a little over 50 percent of the total cost. The premium subsidy provided by the employer varies widely as shown in Figure 4.1. The federal government subsidizes about 75 percent of the "premium" of the standard Part D benefit.

Distribution of Employers by Retiree Contribution Percentage

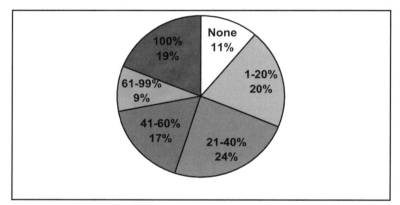

Source: Kaiser/Hewitt © 2005 Survey on Retiree Health Benefits, December 2005

Figure 4.2

In 2005, the average retiree contribution was 38 percent based on the 2005 Kaiser/Hewitt survey.[14]

One way to view the value of the prescription drug benefit is to combine both the plan design "value" and the employer subsidy "value." This can be accomplished by multiplying the percentage of benefit paid by the plan and the employer subsidy (the complement of the retiree contribution percentage). Assuming the standard Part D benefit pays 50 percent of the total cost and the government pays for 75 percent of the cost, the net value is 37.5 percent (50% × 75%). For the employer charging retirees the average 38 percent of cost, they will have to provide a plan that pays at least 60 percent

---

[14] McArdle, Neuman, Strollo, Atchison, Yamamoto; *Prospects for Retiree Health Benefits as Medicare Prescription Drug Coverage Begins*; Kaiser Family Foundation and Hewitt Associates; December 2005 [28].

(37.5% ÷ 62%). This benefit percentage can be determined either through actuarial modeling or by requesting data from the pharmacy claims payer that show what percent of total cost is being paid by the plan.

Similar calculations can be performed for different levels of benefit or contribution level. If the net employer value is less than the standard benefit net value of 37.5 percent, the employer's pharmacy benefit is re-dundant to the Part D benefit that all Medicare-eligible retirees have available to them and retirees may be better off enrolling in Part D.

Even if the net value of the employer plan is greater than the Part D net value, an employer might consider eliminating their coverage because there is access to an alternative, albeit less valuable, plan. An employer may consider providing the difference in value in another form such as reduced contributions to the other medical or life insurance coverage or by creating a special healthcare reimbursement account that would be available to pay for non-covered healthcare costs.

Financial Comparisons

One of the most attractive features of the retiree drug subsidy was the fact that it was tax free. But what if an employer isn't incurring tax because it is a non-profit entity or in a 0% tax bracket for the foreseeable future? The per-retiree drug subsidy for most employers is estimated to be between $500 and $600.[15] If the amount was taxable and the employer had a 35 percent marginal tax rate, the subsidy would have to be $770 to $920.

The following table provides estimates of potential savings per person on a tax-adjusted basis to keep the amounts comparable.

Alternative	2006 Tax-Adjusted Savings
Retiree drug subsidy	
— Non-taxable entity	$500 – $600
— 25% marginal tax rate	$670 – $800
— 35% marginal tax rate	$770 – $920
Employer PDP	$550 – $850
Supplemental PDP	$450 – $950
Eliminate	$1,000 – $2,500

[15] Hewitt Associates estimate based on actuarial attestations performed for the 2006 cal-endar year.

Unfortunately the estimates for the potential savings are broad because there are many factors that go into the calculations and it is difficult to generalize. For taxable employers, each alternative tends to produce roughly the same savings per person. For non-tax-paying employers, the employer PDP or supplemental PDP options are likely to produce greater savings than the retiree drug subsidy approach. No estimate is provided for the Medicare Advantage alternatives in the above table. Savings on the non-pharmacy portion of the retiree medical plan may be nominal to as much as 30 percent.

TODAY'S PLANS

Today's retiree medical plans were shaped during the 1980s and 1990s. Employers began to amend these plans during the early 1980s. Most of these changes were modest and consisted of:

- Introducing or slightly increasing the level of retiree contributions (today, employers pay 60 to 80 percent of the cost of the plan);
- Adopting policies of setting retiree contributions as a fixed percentage of cost; and
- Changing the method of coordinating benefits with Medicare—for example, from standard coordination of benefits to either the exclusion or the carveout method.

Retiree Contribution Levels

Employers typically introduced very modest changes in retiree contribution levels during the 1980s. Many who offered free coverage introduced modest retiree contributions equal to around five to ten percent of the cost of the plan. Those who required retiree contributions increased them slightly during the 1980s. Very few made dramatic changes.

Setting Retiree Contributions as Fixed Percentage

Some employers established policies of setting their contribution levels at a fixed percentage of total cost during the 1980s. This made retirees more aware of the cost of coverages or at least how much they are changing each year.

Medicare Coordination

In 1980, most retiree medical plans for Medicare-eligible retirees coordinated with Medicare using a standard coordination of benefits form of integration. Under this method, the plan pays the lesser of what the plan would have paid if Medicare did not exist or the amount that Medicare does not pay. The result was the plan usually paid the full amount that Medicare did not pay and the retiree paid nothing.

By the early 1990s, most plans changed their method of integration to either the exclusion method or the carveout method. Both paid less benefits than the standard coordination method but generally provided the same or better coverage for the retiree compared to what they had before becoming eligible for Medicare.

Changes Post-FAS 106

After the issuance of FAS 106 in 1990, employers began to introduce features to control their future obligations, such as:

- Redefining eligibility requirements to be more stringent than in their pension plans (e.g., requiring a person to be at least age 60 with 15 years of service versus age 55 with five years of service);

- Introducing service-related benefits (i.e., the employer portion of plan cost varies depending on the employee's service at retirement);

- Adjusting retiree contributions based on the employee's age at retirement (i.e., early retirement reductions); and

- Setting the employer subsidy of the retiree medical plans as a fixed dollar amount and not as a percentage of plan costs (e.g., the company will annually pay for up to $75 per year of service at retirement and the retiree pays the excess cost).

Redefine Eligibility

Traditionally, retiree group benefit plan eligibility was tied directly to the early retirement requirements for pension plans, which for most pension plans was when an employee turned age 55 and had at least 10 years of service. When pension vesting rules were liberalized in the late 1980s to a five-year rule, most pension plans reduced their early retirement eligibility rule to age 55 with five years of service. Without thinking, many also allowed retiree group benefit eligibility to be at the same 55 and 5. Since that time, many employers have moved away from providing an employer-provided subsidy to employees with such low service. Some have allowed low-service retirees to enroll in their group benefit plans but with no company subsidy.

Service-Related Benefits

In responding to the question, "should an employee retiring with 10 years of service receive the same level of retiree group benefits as a 30-year employee?" employers began to adopt service-related benefits. A few offer different benefit levels by service category. Since most of the cost of a medical plan is for a relatively small percentage of the covered population, it is difficult to design different plans that provide adequate coverage and reflect great enough differences in cost. Instead, retiree contribution levels differentiate the benefit levels. Schedules have been adopted, such as setting the employer-paid portion of the plan equal to 2.5 percent of cost times years of service or by service groupings such as:

Years of Service	Employer	Retiree
Under 10 years	0%	100%
10 to 14 years	20%	80%
15 to 19 years	40%	60%
20 to 24 years	60%	40%
25 to 29 years	80%	20%
30 and more years	100%	0%

Retirement Age Adjustment

In the U.S., medical benefits paid before Medicare-eligibility age are three to six times more expensive than benefits paid after Medicare-eligibility. This means that the cost of the benefit for an employee retiring at age 55 is significantly greater than for an employee retiring at age 65. The phenomenon occurs under group medical plans in other countries too but the differences generally will not be as great. Under a typical pension plan design, this is indirectly adjusted because the benefit is based on years of service and often pay at retirement, and directly adjusted by an early retirement reduction factor. The following graph provides a simple illustration of this.

**Ratio of Present Value of Retiree Medical Benefits
by Age to the Present Value at Age 65**

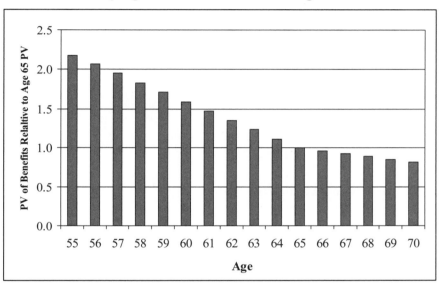

Figure 4.2

Assuming that an employer is targeting age 65 as the "normal" retirement age, they would have to reduce the age 55 benefit by 55 percent $(100 - 1.0 \div 2.2)$ or about 5.5 percent per year. By the same token, employees retiring after age 65 could be rewarded with higher subsidies $(1.0 \div 0.8 - 1.0 = 0.25,$ or 5.0 percent per year).

Caps on Subsidies

Fixed Dollar Subsidy (Cap)

The changes described earlier in this chapter alleviated some of the costs of providing benefits to retirees but none of them gave employers control over future cost increases. They all were subject to the underlying costs of the benefits driven by health care cost changes. Fixing the employer subsidy to the plans puts control over the net expenditure by an employer. These fixed subsidy strategies took on a variety of forms.

Most employers have implemented some type of cap on their program. Figure 4.3 shows the prevalence of caps for pre- and post-65 retirees.

Employer Caps on Obligation

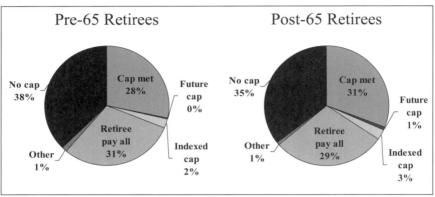

Source: © Hewitt Associates, 2005 SpecSummary

Figure 4.3

About two-thirds of these large, private-sector employers who provide coverage have some type of cap on their retiree medical obligations for both pre- and post-65 retirees. And, for those with caps, most have met the cap and retirees are paying the full cost of any rate increase each year. Only a very small percentage have caps that have not been met yet (0.3 percent and 0.8 percent for pre- and post-65 retirees, respectively). Caps are far less common among collectively bargained plans.

Total Expenditure Cap

Some employers stated their future obligation for the retiree health care plan as a total amount that they are willing to pay. For example, the company will not pay more than twice the amount they paid in 2000. Assuming they had 10,000 lives covered under their plan (pre- and post-65 retirees and their dependents), and the cost in 2000 was $3,000 per life, the company will not pay more than $60 million ($2 \times \$3,000 \times 10,000$) in any future year.

Defined Contribution Cap

Many employers state their cap as a fixed amount per person. For example, assume a plan costs $5,000 per life under age 65 and $2,000 per life over 65 and the employer pays 80 percent of the cost of plan. The future employer obligation may be stated as paying 80 percent of the cost of the plan but no more than $8,000 pre-age 65 and $3,200 post-age 65 or double the current amount.

Of more significance from an accounting perspective is the level of savings achievable. Companies that have adopted fixed dollar benefits have dramatically reduced their FAS 106 cost. Retirees, however, bear the brunt of the additional costs, as shown by Figure 4.4.

Figure 4.4 shows a projection of the above example. The employer pays 80 percent of the cost of the plan until $3,200 is reached. With the employer's obligation "fixed" at double today's levels and total costs increasing at 10 percent per year, the retiree will pay over $10,000 per year in just 20 years. All the inflationary costs after the eighth year are passed on to retirees.

Employer/Retiree Cost Sharing Projection

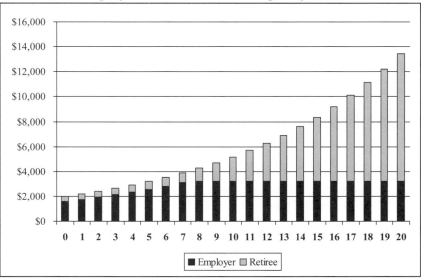

Figure 4.4

Account Balance Plan

An account balance plan sets the employer subsidy as a lump sum amount provided each year. For example, a plan may give an employee $1,000 for year of credited service. For an employee who retires with 20 years of service, he or she would have a $20,000 account balance that may be used to pay for retiree group benefit premiums. The amount may be used on an "as-needed" basis and withdrawn at the retiree's discretion each year. The withdrawal process could be similar to submitting claims to a flexible spending account. A retiree sees a doctor, receives a bill and submits it to the employer to be paid from the account balance. The retiree could also set up a monthly withdrawal to pay for all or a portion of the required retiree group benefit premium. As long as the account balance is positive, the retiree continues participation in the plan. As soon as the balance is depleted, the retiree no longer has employer money to pay for health care.

Alternatively, the plan may allow for an "annuitization" option. The lump sum is converted to a monthly annuity (or some other period). The annuity amount may be set differently for months before and after age 65 to allow for the change in retiree contribution requirements during the two age ranges. The annuity payment could then be used to provide for required retiree contributions or accumulate in another annual account to be used like a spending account.

The annual accrual could be developed in a variety of ways. The main steps are:

- Determine target retirement age (e.g., 62).

- Include spouse benefits in the present value or include only a partial present value of spouse benefits because not all retirees cover spouses.

- Determine maximum service period for counting in the plan or the service period where the company will pay the maximum benefit (e.g., 30 years of service).

- Determine key assumptions to develop present value. These may be the same assumptions used in the FAS 106 calculations. They should, however, be selected as the best estimate of future expectations, which may be different. For example, the trend rates may be selected as closer to recent experience than FAS 106 assumptions (e.g., 12 percent grading to 5 percent in ten years instead of 10 percent grading to 5 percent in five years).

- Determine target present value of benefits at the target retirement age (e.g., about $69,000 assuming male, target retirement age 62, 70 percent with spouse coverage, 8 percent discount rate, 12 percent to 5 percent in five years and 1983 Group Annuity Mortality (GAM) table).

- Divide the target present value by the maximum service period (e.g., $2,300 = $69,000 ÷ 30).

Generally, employees earn the same lump sum for each year of service regardless of whether or not they are expected to cover a spouse in retirement. This type of plan creates greater equity between retirees because it explicitly adjusts the employer subsidy to age and service at retirement and dependent coverage election. If the target assumptions selected above are set to provide today's retirees with the same average costs, there will be winners and losers. Winners are those who retire after the target retirement age, have long service and only elect single coverage. Losers are those retiring early with shorter service and elect family coverage.

Some plans may provide "interest" credit on account balances based on a specified index (e.g., medical CPI, overall company wage changes, a formula based on company profitability).

Managed Care

Some employers have looked at managed care programs to help reduce costs through provider discounts and better management of care. Pre-Medicare retirees can be enrolled in the same types of managed care plans as active employees—preferred provider options (PPO), point-of-service (POS) plans, and health maintenance organizations (HMO).

For Medicare-retirees, the most common managed care plans are HMOs. Survey data indicates that the number of large employers offering Medicare HMOs increased from 7 percent in 1993 to 40 percent in 1998.[16] In 2000, however, it dropped to 35 percent and remained stable through 2004 where it was offered by 37 percent of respondents. By 2004, a few large employers offered PPOs (10 percent).

Medicare managed care appealed to employers because of their ability to control health care costs. HMOs offered lower premium levels than under traditional indemnity plans, which reduced the employer's accounting costs. Retirees were attracted to HMOs because the benefits typically are better than those of an indemnity plan.

---

[16] Mercer, *National Survey of Employer-Sponsored Health Plans*, 1998 and 2004.

Most of the growth in Medicare managed care offerings by employers occurred between 1993 and 1996. Employer sponsorship of Medicare HMOs has slowed considerably since then and has decreased in the last two years. The primary reason for the slow down is the instability of the overall participation of HMOs in the Medicare program (now known as Medicare Advantage), including health plans dropping out of the program and reductions in service areas announced in 1998 and 1999. Additionally, the negative publicity around these announcements, the experience of affected retirees, and the backlash against managed care in general have likely caused greater reluctance among retirees with employer coverage to try HMOs.

A few employers have assumed that Medicare-eligible retirees have some viable plan options available to them through the Medicare Advantage program so that the employer plan is not necessary. Until 2006, most of these options had limited or no prescription drug benefits, so most employers have not eliminated their coverage. With the availability of the new Medicare Part D benefits, it could become a more viable alternative if the plans can demonstrate that they will be stable and sustainable.

The MMA's expansion of PPOs and private fee-for-service plans along with the prescription drug benefit, could offer intriguing alternatives for employers too. These alternatives are considered further in the next section on "Future Plan Design Considerations."

Current Retirees

Many employers in the U.S. adopted the above changes for future retirees, thus creating a "grandfathered" group of retirees with greater retiree benefit coverage. This grandfathered group may include employees who are close to retirement or eligible to retire when the plan change is announced as well as current retirees. The decision to grandfather any group of employees and retirees is often based on the extent of the legal obligation to continue the benefits unchanged.

Companies that adopt a combination of the above plan design changes, especially the fixed dollar benefit, create an employer commitment that is more like that of a pension plan. Retiree health benefits are largely unfunded and not qualified as a retirement plan under tax laws. An important feature of the health plan is that benefit payments are not taxable to the retiree.

This will create a future concern of managing retirees' new financial burden – increasing medical insurance costs. When faced with this dilemma, employers will have to decide whether the policy set today should be changed (i.e., increase the fixed dollar benefit) or other benefits (e.g., pensions) should be increased to compensate for the higher medical plan costs borne by the retirees. If the employer increases benefits in either form, accountants may ask whether further increases should be anticipated in the accounting cost.

FUTURE PLAN DESIGN CONSIDERATIONS

Most of the early plan design changes shifted the costs from the employer to retirees. If retiree health plans are to remain an employer-provided benefit, future changes will need to find ways to reduce total costs in order to make the plans affordable for both the employer and the retiree.

The basic framework for these changes will be similar methods that employers have used to reduce health care costs for their active employees. These recent changes were seldom applied to retiree plans because of the thought that "retirees are different," especially, Medicare-eligible retirees.

Retirees are different from active employees in many ways. It is harder to get communications to them because they do not come to work regularly. Most have family physicians that they have been seeing for a long time, making it uncomfortable and difficult to change. Some move away from where they worked, and it is difficult to physically meet for a company-sponsored event. Despite these obstacles, many health care management strategies used for active employee plans can work for retiree plans. They may, however, have to be designed with a different emphasis for retirees.

The following briefly summarizes some potential strategies and how they can apply to retirees.

Large Case Management

A minority of retirees, as is true for active employees, generate most of the claims. For a typical plan, 10 percent of the retirees are responsible for two-thirds of the claims paid. The claims payer will review all health care services being received by retirees that are considered "financially" significant. This type of "managed care" has generally been dismissed for Medicare-eligible retirees because it usually saves the government (i.e., Medicare) more than the plan. This is true, but potential savings for the plan may still be significant for extremely large claims.

Utilization Review

Utilization review (UR) is designed to evaluate the appropriateness of medical treatment before it is provided. Virtually all active medical plans use some form of utilization review. Limited UR is performed for Medicare-eligible retirees. Utilization review firms are now beginning to recognize the importance of early detection of many age-related conditions and have structured special review processes for retiree groups.

Medicare Balance Billing Limits

Physician Payment Reform (included in the 1989 tax legislation – the Omnibus Budget Reconciliation Act of 1989) created a limit on how much a physician could bill a patient above what Medicare bases its payment on. Since 1993, physicians cannot "balance bill" more than 115 percent of the Medicare Allowable Charge (MAC) less the Medicare reimbursement. For example, if Medicare's MAC is $1,000 and Medicare pays $800, the physician cannot bill the patient more than $350 ($1,150 – $800). In other words, the physician cannot receive total reimbursement over $1,150, even if his standard charge for the service exceeds that amount.

The effect of this balance billing limit is significant. In the past, if a physician billed the excess over Medicare, it was, on average, about 40 percent above the MAC according to Hewitt Associates estimates. This translates into an 18 percent reduction in physician charges [1.00 – (115 ÷ 140)] for retirees using doctors that do not accept Medicare payment as "payment in full." Even more dramatic is the reduction in cost to an employer's plan. For a MAC of $1,000, the current physician charge was, on average $1,400. If Medicare pays 80 percent of the MAC, the employer plan used to pay on covered expenses of $600 ($1,400 – $800). With balance billing limits, the covered expenses are $350 ($1,150 – $800). That is over a 40 percent reduction!

With the electronic processing between the physician offices, Medicare and the insurance companies, there is less likelihood today that a retiree would be overcharged. A retiree education program aimed at helping to catch these overcharges may save some money. A simple letter or article in a retiree newsletter, with illustrations, will allow retirees themselves to monitor the balance billing by physicians.

Reasonable and Customary Limits

Many claims payers use the "90th percentile" of costs as their reasonable and customary (R&C) charge level. Some claim payers have routinely reduced their R&C amount to the 75th or 80th percentile level. This may create retiree relations problems because it is viewed as a "back-door" way to shift costs. Because of Medicare's balance billing limits, this is seldom relevant for Medicare eligible retirees.

Spousal Initiatives

Most employer plans cover spouses of eligible retirees. An increasing number of retirees will have spouses who are eligible for other medical coverage. "Spousal initiatives" encourage spouses to accept their own plans. This may be accomplished in one of three ways:

(1) Introduce a surcharge to spousal coverage if the spouse has other available coverage;

(2) Pay the retiree a bonus for signing a spouse under the spouse's plan; or

(3) Make the spouse ineligible if other coverage is available.

The surcharge or bonus could be a fixed amount (say $25 to $100 per month) or a fixed percentage of plan cost. A provision could be included for ineligible spouses that they can become eligible if their own coverage is not available in the future.

Dynamic Provisions

The retiree plans should be changed periodically to reflect more dynamic plan provisions. Fixed dollar plan deductibles, out-of-pocket maximums, and other copays, contribute about 1 percent of annual cost increases for pre-65 retirees and about 3 percent for post-65 retirees. This is caused by a "leveraging" effect because the dollar amounts are fixed. The following shows the leveraging effect on the plan deductible.

Deductible Leveraging

	Year 1	Percent Increase	Year 2
Covered expense	$ 1,000	20.0%	$ 1,200
Plan deductible	$ 200	0.0%	$ 200
Subject to coinsurance	$ 800	25.0%	$ 1,000
Coinsurance	80%	0.0%	80%
Plan benefit	$ 640	25.0%	$ 800

The above table shows the total covered expense increasing at 20 percent, but the benefit paid by the plan increases by 25 percent. By indexing these fixed dollar deductibles and copays to the overall increase in health care costs, this "leveraging" effect is eliminated.

Another issue shown in the table is that in Year 1, the plan pays for 64 percent of the total. In Year 2, it increases to 67 percent. From a philosophical point of view, should the plan be providing an increasing level of benefits in the future?

Managed Prescription Drugs

Prescription drugs represent a significant portion of health care costs for retirees, even for employers receiving the retiree drug subsidy from Medicare. The typical plan covering Medicare-eligible retirees will still have 45 to 65 percent of the total cost from drugs. Depending on the type of provisions put in place, managed prescription drug programs can both reduce costs immediately and decrease the ongoing cost increases. Specific features of a managed retiree prescription drug plan include:

Negotiated reimbursement rates

Incentives to get retirees to buy their prescription drugs from a more limited number of pharmacies can yield reduced costs for both the employer and retirees.

Reduced administrative fees

If a limited number of pharmacies are included on the "preferred" list, efficiencies can be gained in the administrative area.

Real-time eligibility information

Increased sophistication with direct links to the claim administrator's eligibility data base will enhance the accuracy of claim payment and reduce paying for ineligible retirees. Making use of internet-based pharmacies could facilitate this process.

Utilization review

Concurrent, retrospective, and prospective utilization review can be used to improve the coordination of medication. This may include requirements such as prior authorization for certain prescriptions, therapeutic interchange for some therapeutic classes recognized as highest savings potential, step therapy edits to assure the best long-term treatment at the lowest cost, and physician profiling. The review process can also be used to monitor a patient's medication program. For example, a patient not taking high blood pressure medication daily has a higher chance of future cardiovascular disease. Monitoring this type of noncompliance can reduce the occurrence of larger claims down the road.

Mail-order plan

Many employers with mail-order drug plans have found that their costs are actually higher than they were without the plan. This is due to many factors but much of it is because only a small percentage of active employee drug claims is covered in a mail-order plan. A large portion of retiree prescriptions is for maintenance drugs. Because of this, a mail-order plan can save more money for retirees than for active employees.

Other plan design strategies

Other plan design strategies may be used to reduce costs by encouraging lower cost drug therapies. For example, lower copays can be introduced for generics (e.g., $3 or $5 per prescription), with coinsurance for brand name drugs (e.g., 25 or 30 percent). As more former "blockbuster" drugs lose their patent, the price variability of generics will increase which implies that coinsurance should also be used for generics. With generics priced at about 20 percent of brand names, this will produce a reasonable price incentive to use the generic option.

For certain therapeutic classes, the plan could pay at a defined maximum level (a therapeutic MAC or maximum allowable charge). This currently makes the most sense for anti-ulcer, cholesterol reducing and anti-arthritis therapeutic categories. The MAC could be set at a given "percentile" of a range of available drugs dispensed.

Medicare Coordination

The section on Medicare highlighted several different alternatives for employers to coordinate with the Medicare Part D program. Using the above strategies with some of the Part D coordination methods has the opportunity to create greater savings, especially where Medicare is providing a fixed amount (e.g., direct contract PDP).

Enhanced Quality

There are several ways employers are attempting to enhance the quality of services provided to employees that will also reduce costs. Similar programs can also be used for retirees and include:

> "Centers of Excellence" could be used in specific cases. The most common centers used are for very specialized areas such as transplants and cancer. Since these are potentially prevalent conditions for retirees, a center of excellence may be in the best position to deliver the highest quality and most cost-effective care.

> Health care coalitions are developing in many areas. They are formed by local employers to address issues involving the quality, affordability, and accessibility of health care services for their employees. An employer could consider supporting coalitions in areas where its retirees may live (e.g., Arizona and Florida).

> Outcome monitoring can be used to encourage retirees to use specific quality providers. In these programs, the actual results of certain medical care are monitored and attempts are made to influence or direct a patient to providers with the best quality results who also tend to be the most cost-effective.

Retiree education programs can help retirees understand the role of providers and become better consumers. Examples of retiree education programs are:

- Providing a checklist of questions to get the most out of physician office visits;

- Explaining Medicare balance billing limits discussed earlier;

- Explaining the provisions of Medicare and how the employer's plan coordinates benefits with Medicare so employees can decide when to retire if continued medical insurance is a key issue; and

- Providing information on local providers and referral services for specific needs. Many physicians accept Medicare payment in full. A list of these doctors can be obtained from the Centers for Medicare and Medicaid Services (CMS) or through their website at www.medicare.gov. As a service to retirees, a list of local physicians could be distributed annually with other retiree information.

Managed Health

More employers are looking to ways to encourage employees to change a behavior that may result in large claims in the future. Introducing similar managed health initiatives for retirees should yield the same result.

Lifestyle education is something that begins while employees are still active and carries on during their retirement years. For retirees, this could be in the form of monthly or quarterly newsletters, DVD/videotape library access (even available through the mail), internet or company intranet sites and informal meetings or formal courses. The primary purpose would be to provide information on how lifestyle affects their health.

Lifestyle-based contribution rates or employer contributions to a medical reimbursement account could be introduced to encourage healthy behaviors. For example, non-smokers could be charged a lower rate than smokers, or a $100 per year contribution to a medical reimbursement account could be made for those promising to wear seat belts.

Credits for healthy lifestyles while active could be provided to retirees. For example, if a retiree participated in at least two lifestyle-related programs in the last ten years of active employment, they receive a $100 annual contribution to a medical reimbursement account.

Adjusted benefit levels could be administered if the care is due to a lifestyle-related cause. For example, the plan might pay 60 percent versus 80 percent for an auto accident injury due to no seat belt, or cellphone use, or driving while intoxicated, or for any tobacco-related illness. It may even pay no benefits if the insured were convicted of an illegal activity such as "driving under the influence."

Consumer Awareness Initiatives

The latest initiatives employers have introduced to manage health care costs are a variety of consumer awareness programs. Different experts may refer to these in different ways but the intent is to deliver to employees enough information to make health care decisions on the basis of cost and quality of care. This is similar to how consumers purchase any other product, rather than today's health care world where there is a lack of economic need for employees to look for the best quality at the best price.

Decision-Making Tools

Employers provide employees and retirees with various tools to help them make the right decision in the choice of a health care plan, maintain appropriate healthy lifestyles, and select the appropriate physician. The tools may be as simple as having employees fill out a health risk questionnaire and then providing them with alternative health care options such as specialty care, information on certain chronic conditions, introduction to an appropriate disease management program, or immediate access to a health care advocate to answer questions. The questionnaire may be able to provide enough information to assist the employee in selecting the most appropriate health plan option and provide some insights into personal care.

Many employers include some type of incentive to use these tools, including basic educational material on their value, some monetary incentive (e.g., nominal cash, participation in a raffle for a larger prize, health coverage credits for a flexible benefit program), free visit to a financial planner, or a free month in the health club.

Some employers (55% in a recent survey[17]) believe that offering employees these types of tools has prompted employees to make health-related goals including dieting, exercising, chronic condition management and selecting high quality physicians.

---

[17] © Hewitt Associates, *Health Care Expectations: Future Strategy and Direction 2006,* March 2006.

Provider Information

Many health care experts are encouraging greater *transparency* in the delivery of services. The term transparency may be viewed in many different ways, so one must be careful in its interpretation. It could mean improved disclosure of the price of services upfront, before the services are performed and a discussion about viable alternatives. It could be at a higher level where an outside entity would evaluate providers (hospitals and physicians) on the quality and cost of their historical services and openly provide a score or grade for each of them. Or, it could be anything in between.

Today there is more complete and statistically valid data for hospitals, and many employers provide their employees and retirees access to information through an internet site or by phone. Fewer provide cost and quality information on physicians because of the lack of statistical rigor in today's data.

Personal Health Information

Most employers are now providing employees and retirees, through their health plans, access to their own health plan claims information. This makes it easier for members to understand their historical spending, creates greater awareness of the cost of health, and better helps them to plan for the future. In addition, some provide modeling tools for the members to make appropriate benefit option choices and to show the various other programs offered (condition and disease management programs, wellness programs, smoking cessation programs, etc.).

Health Information Technology

A higher degree of interest is being expressed in the expansion of the use of technology in the area of health care. This includes the greater use of remote care through connection with deep specialists via high-speed two-way video lines as well as the "simple" transfer of complete medical histories to treating providers.

Provider Payment

Some employers are encouraging health plans to change their payment levels to providers based on the quality of care delivered. This has taken on many forms including fee schedules set by an objective quality measuring index; pay-for-performance where providers may be eligible for periodic bonuses depending on quality scores; and alternative network schemes with providers that vary depending on quality.

Medicare Advantage PPO and PFFS

Both PPO and PFFS plans were available prior to the passage of the MMA but the changes made in the law for plan payment has increased the number of insurers offering those plan options. Employers now have the opportunity to work with the insurers to customize either option to fit their retiree medical program. Key reasons for considering one of these MA programs are the:

- Ability to have better control over total health care delivery;
- Potential financial savings;
- Coordination of medical and prescription drug plan vendors.

Delivery Control

All MA plans are paid a capitated amount from Medicare and are responsible for the total delivery of the health insurance benefit. The capitations are adjusted for the health risk of the enrollees, but an opportunity to control costs beyond the risk adjustment is still feasible. The risk adjustment model used by CMS is a reasonable model but no model can perfectly anticipate costs. One measure of any statistical fit of a theoretical model compared to actual results is the R^2 measure that compares the difference between actual results and predicted results. A score of 100 percent would be perfect prediction and a score of 0 percent means there is no correlation. The R^2 of the DCG/HCC model from which the CMS model (CMS/HCC) is derived was 11.2 percent compared to 6.2 percent for the old CMS model (the PIP-DCG model that only used inpatient data) and 1.0 percent using demographics alone.[18] For a variety of reasons, R^2 is probably not the best measure of a risk model but it does indicate that even though the CMS/HCC is significantly better than the other models, it's a long way from having a perfect prediction score of 100 percent. Admittedly, no risk method comes close to approaching 100 percent. But that is one reason that an employer could take advantage of the potential difference in actual experience versus the risk adjusted capitation amount.

[18] Pope, et al, *Risk Adjustment of Medicare Capitation Payments Using the CMS/HCC Model* [34].

For example, assume the national average per person cost is $10,000 for total health care. But, an employer has a healthier population that may cost only $8,000. It is likely that the risk adjustment model only gives credit for a fraction of the $2,000 difference. It is difficult to determine what the fraction is but it could very easily be 40 to 75 percent. Assume that it is 75 percent, the worst case. Then the capitation rate would be adjusted so that instead of a $10,000 expected cost, after risk adjusting, the cost is $8,500 ($10,000 − $2,000 × 0.75). That gives the employer $500 in excess of their actual costs.

Further savings can be achieved by managing chronic conditions better than the Medicare program does, since the risk adjustment factors are based on this. This could work even if the employer population is a higher risk group than the national average if the medical management of the higher cost risks can reduce costs more than the risk adjusters indicate. For example, if the risk adjusters estimate the high cost persons to be $20,000, if the employer can keep actual costs for those individuals under $20,000, the difference produces a lower net cost back to the employer.

Other Savings

Another source of potential savings is the mismatch between the Medicare reimbursement payments relative to costs by location. The changes that were adopted by the BBA and further adjusted by the MMA create some disparity between the payment rates and the actual costs by county. Figure 4.5 illustrates graphically this potential by county. The white areas of the map indicate no added savings from a disparity in payment rates to expected costs in the area. The darker the area is, the greater the expected savings because the MMA payment rate is greater than the expected costs for that location.

PFFS Payment Savings by County

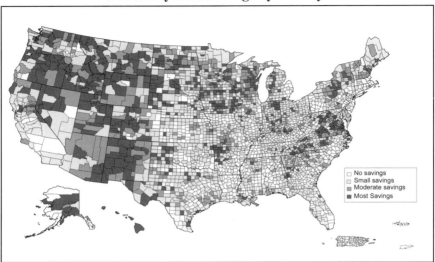

Figure 4.5

Medical and Drug Plan Coordination

The synergies of putting both the medical and the drug benefits with one carrier is the improvement in the ability for them to appropriately identify members that would benefit from some type of medical management. Using claims based health risk identifiers that use both medical and prescription drug claims data enhances both the speed and accuracy of chronic condition identification.

Also, since the plan is getting two different payments from Medicare—for Parts A and B and the Part D plan—the insurer can use the two to offset payment variations by location.

TRANSITION

When an employer contemplates making any changes to a retiree health plan, consideration must be given to the individual situations of current employees and retirees. Usually the best way to design a retiree health plan is to design it for the person the company will hire tomorrow. Inevitably if that message is not delivered up front, discussions get bogged down with personal issues. For example, "we can't reduce benefits for the XYZ plant because George was planning to retire next year." Or, "we can't eliminate coverage for the ABC division because Alice retired last year and was just diagnosed with cancer." By designing the plan for the unknown person starting work tomorrow, it makes it less personal. After the plan is finalized, everything else is "transition."

One way to "draw" the line between the new and old plans is to create a grid of employee and retiree headcounts by age and service for active employees. In many companies, there were distinct hiring patterns so that there are "bulges" in the count, so that natural cutoff criteria can be visually identified.

Another consideration is the perceived value of the benefit. As mentioned previously, this benefit is not perceived to be of any value until someone is close to retirement. This may be different by company but most of the time this cutoff is around age 45 or 50.

What types of communication have employees had in the past regarding the plan? Most employers continually send the message that this benefit may be terminated at any point in time. Thus, many younger employees in particular have little expectation of receiving this benefit or for that matter, Social Security and Medicare.

Some employees close to retirement are likely to be setting plans and deciding whether or not they can financially retire. An abrupt change will likely defer many of those decisions. This brings up the workforce management issues that must be considered.

Current retirees are generally not in a position to save more in the event of the loss of a benefit. In some situations, the employer-provided retirement package has been more than generous to current retirees so this may not be an issue for them. Or, there may be some retirees that retired under different programs that may not be as financially sufficient.

These and other considerations are made when establishing the transition policy. Some plan designs have built-in transitions. For example, providing retirees a lump sum at retirement that is equal to the current present value of benefits, keeps those retiring today whole but slowly provides a lesser benefit to those retiring later. This is because the lump sum required to pay for the same plan ten years from now for the same aged retiree will be about twice as much. So, if the plan provides the same dollar lump sum amount today and in all future years, the inflationary component of health care slowly erodes the value of the amount.

Common transition policies adopted by companies today are to leave both the current retirees (oftentimes with higher cost-sharing requirements) and older active employees in the existing plan, maybe with higher cost sharing requirements for the future retirees than what is provided to current retirees. The cut-off age for active employees is usually those eligible to retire at the time of the amendments (e.g., age 55 with 15 years of service) or would be eligible to retire within five years of the change.

SUMMARY

Most of the changes outlined above do not have the same dramatic accounting cost reductions seen by some of the fixed dollar benefit designs introduced in the early 1990s. The overall retiree health care costs growth will, however, be better controlled. And if a fixed dollar benefit design has not been adopted, these changes will reduce future cost increases, justifying a lower accounting cost.

Controlling health care costs in this fashion will prevent the need to increase other benefits (e.g., pension benefits). More importantly, most of the changes can be a "win-win" for the company and its retirees.

For further information on employer alternatives under Medicare Part D, see Appendix B.

Other Retiree Benefits

In addition to medical benefits, many employers offer other benefits to retirees, including the following:

- Dental
- Vision
- Hearing
- Death Benefits
- Medicare Part B premium reimbursement

DENTAL, VISION, AND HEARING

Dental, vision, and hearing benefits are sometimes continued for retirees. Many employers provide these benefits only to age 65. The following table shows the prevalence of these benefits.[19]

Other Retiree Benefits Offered by Employers	1998		2005	
	Pre-65 Retirees	Post-65 Retirees	Pre-65 Retirees	Post-65 Retirees
Dental plan only	22%	14%	12%	9%
Dental plan plus vision and/or hearing plan	8%	5%	16%	10%
Vision and/or hearing plan only	3%	2%	10%	7%
No dental, vision, or hearing plan	67%	79%	62%	74%
	100%	100%	100%	100%
	1,020 employers		*950 employers*	

Source: © Hewitt Associates SpecSummary

Plans that are continued for retirees generally have the same benefits that the active employee programs provide. Eligibility for the plans is usually tied to the same requirements as the medical plan.

Dental plan rates for retirees are usually about the same as for active employees. That is, a single retiree will, on average, cost about the same as a single active employee. The distribution of the types of costs will vary between the two, but the resulting cost will be the same. The active employee will have higher preventive and basic services, and the retiree will have higher major services.

Vision and hearing plan rates are usually about double the rate for active employees.

---

[19] 1998 and 2005 *SpecSummary*, based on complete plan-by-plan benefit specifications collected directly from participating plan sponsors included in the 1998 and 2005 Hewitt Associates SpecBooks™. SpecBook includes summaries of the principal benefit plans for salaried employees in 1998 and 2005 of 1,020 and 950 major U.S. employers, respectively © Hewitt Associates.

DEATH BENEFITS

Few employers are continuing some level of life insurance coverage for retirees. The following table shows the prevalence of death benefit coverage among large employers in 1998 and 2005.[20]

Type of Death Benefit		1998 Percent of Employers		2005 Percent of Employers
Death benefit continued		62%		39%
Amount does not reduce	35%		27%	
Amount reduces	25%		11%	
Amount ultimately reduces to $0	2%		1%	
Depends on plan selected by employee prior to or at time of retirement, age, service, or pay		2%		0%
No postretirement death benefit		36%		61%
		100%		100%
		1,020 employers		*950 employers*

Source: ©Hewitt Associates SpecSummary

Death benefit coverage has declined significantly in the last decade from 64 percent offering some level of coverage in 1998 to 39 percent in 2005. Generally, if the active coverage level is offered after retirement (e.g., one times pay), the amount will reduce to a lower level in the future based on a fixed schedule. Some schedules reduce from retirement, and others keep the benefit level for a period of time (e.g., level until age 65 or the first five years) and then begin to reduce. Some employers provide a lower fixed dollar death benefit (e.g., $2,000 to $10,000) after retirement. Most employers that provide amounts that do not reduce are providing the lower amount at retirement.

MEDICARE PART B PREMIUM REIMBURSEMENT

Most retiree medical plans require that the retiree be enrolled in both Medicare Parts A and B. Remember that Part A is mostly paid for

---

[20] 1998 and 2005 SpecSummary reports, © Hewitt Associates.

through payroll taxes while individuals are working. Part B coverage is generally paid for on a pay-as-you-go basis with the federal government paying about 75 percent of the cost and beneficiaries paying the other 25 percent. Some employers pay for all or a portion of this premium. However, the prevalence of employers reimbursing retirees for the Part B premium has declined rapidly.

The following table shows the change in prevalence of employers reimbursing the Part B premiums.

Group	1992	2004
Retiree only	13%	5%
Retiree and spouse	5%	2%
Active employee only	9%	1%
Active employee and spouse	4%	1%
Number of respondents	661	619

Source: Hay Group

Part B reimbursement policies have often been included in union demands during benefit negotiations. Salaried employees, though, generally have not had their premiums reimbursed. The following table shows the differences of Part B reimbursement policies between salaried and hourly employees in the U.S. in 2005.

Group	Salaried	Hourly
Retiree only	1.6%	8.2%
Retiree and spouse	0.5%	2.2%
Number of respondents	950	231

Source: Hewitt Associates

5   FUNDING

The *Erosion* chapter referred to many surveys asking for the prevalence of employers offering retiree health care coverage. Few surveys have dealt with prevalence of employers *funding* these benefits. One survey of large U.S. employers performed in 1992 indicated that 34 percent of the companies prefunded their retiree life and health programs.[1] Anecdotally, this statistic probably has not changed much in the last decade. Of those responding that they prefunded, most used a Voluntary Employees' Beneficiary Association (VEBA).

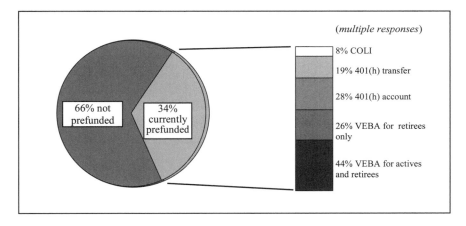

A Standard & Poor's review of 2005 year-end financial statements of their Fortune 500 found that the average funded ratio (assets to accounting liabilities) was 22 percent for retiree group benefits compared to 90 percent for pension plans. In their commentary, they cite that the lack of uniform information makes financial analysis and evaluation of limited value because the projections always include large disclaimers.

---

[1] 1992 © Hewitt Associates survey of 94 large U.S. employers.

They conclude that because companies are not required to prefund retiree group benefit obligations, the majority have chosen not to.[2]

Their survey data includes interesting results of the funded status for each company. Of the 500 employers, 295 record some level of FAS 106 obligation indicating that they offer retiree group benefits to some group of employees or former employees. Of the 295, there are 167 employers (57 percent) who show no assets backing up their obligation and only 9 employers (3 percent) with a funded ratio greater than 75 percent. The remaining employers mostly have funded ratios below 50 percent. The following table summarizes the results.

Funded Ratio	Number of Employers	Percentage of Total
None	167	57%
1-25%	65	22%
25-49%	37	13%
50-75%	17	6%
75-100%	9	3%
Total	295	100%

The issuance of new accounting standards around the world, recent court decisions, and legislative activity has increased public interest in retiree health benefits. This may, on the federal level in the U.S., lead to the legislation of these benefits. Such action would probably mean the introduction of vesting and funding requirements.

Retiree group benefits are often compared to retirement income pro-grams, defined benefit pension plans in particular, in the U.S. Both provide a benefit in retirement for an employee who has worked for a specified period of time for an employer. Both benefits are often viewed as lifetime benefits and the concepts of present value and measurement of a long-term benefit are shared by both. In most countries, however, and in particular the U.S., there are legislated funding requirements for pension plans and there are none for retiree group benefits. Pension plans also have rules regarding the ability for a plan sponsor to change the future benefits. In many cases, employers have a unilateral right to reduce and even terminate retiree group benefits. Exceptions to this may exist in some regulated industries and collectively bargained situations.

---

[2] Howard Silverblatt and Dave Guarino, *S&P 500 2005: Pensions and Other Post Employment Benefits,* Standard & Poor's Report, June 6, 2006 [37].

And, in the U.S., as discussed below, there are no fully tax-advantaged funding vehicles as there are for pension plans.

GENERAL BACKGROUND ON FUNDING VEHICLES

There are currently no requirements that retiree life and health benefits be funded in advance for most employers.[3] This leaves the employer with some basic prefunding decisions that are independent of an outside agency requiring the funding.

An ideal funding vehicle would provide:

- A current **company tax deduction** for contributions that adequately fund retiree health benefits;
- A **tax-free or tax-deferred savings** mechanism for employees;
- Investment earnings that accumulate in a **tax-sheltered** environment; and
- **Tax-free benefits** paid to retirees.

Some additional considerations are that:

- There is no impact on plan design provisions;
- Funds are counted as an asset under FAS 106; and
- Assets are revocable if the obligation to the plan changes.

Traditionally, two different investment vehicles have been used to prefund retiree life and health benefits:

- Welfare benefit funds, which is a very general term but commonly are either:
  — IRC §501(c)(9) trusts, often referred to as Voluntary Employees' Beneficiary Associations (VEBAs); or
  — Continuance funds held by insurance companies.
- IRC §401(h) funding in a qualified pension trust.

---

[3] There are some exceptions to this rule. Some public utility commissions require service providers to prefund any retiree group benefit obligation if they want to include the cost in their rate base charged to customers. Similarly, the federal government requires contractors to prefund if they want to include accrual costs in their contract price.

Recently, a few companies have begun to fund in less traditional vehicles such as:

- Incidental account under a profit sharing plan;
- Employee-purchased group annuities;
- §401(h) account with a money purchase plan (one company used an ESOP);
- Qualified retirement trust funds (e.g., pension plan or §401(k) profit sharing plan);
- Health Savings Accounts (HSA)

Only in limited situations do any of the above currently meet all of the requirements to be an ideal funding vehicle. (Two exceptions are VEBAs that are exempt from funding limitations due to collective bargaining and tax-exempt sponsor exemptions under the Code.)

The Deficit Reduction Act of 1984 (DEFRA) severely limited the use of welfare benefits funds (§501(c)(9) trusts/VEBAs) and insurance company reserves (continuance funds) to fund retiree life and health benefits. It places limits on deductible contributions and taxes some or all of the investment income earned by the trust. It also places limits on coverage amounts allowed to be funded for retiree life insurance benefits.

- Retiree health benefits funded in a pension plan (§401(h) fund) have limits on the amount that may be funded from both plan qualification and tax deductibility perspectives.
- Typical profit-sharing/savings plan arrangements can accumulate funds tax-effectively, but in general, retirees are taxed on benefits when they receive them. Profit-sharing/savings plans also have limits placed on the amount that can be contributed on a pre-tax basis.
- Employee contributions to purchase group annuity contracts are made with after-tax money. The IRS has not specifically addressed the taxability of benefits from these annuities, but there is an argument that they may be delivered tax-free.

The remainder of this section discusses considerations that should be made before prefunding, a description of the specific funding vehicles with current funding limitations imposed on each, and numerical examples comparing funding versus accounting costs for a specific company for a welfare benefit fund and a §401(h) account.

PREFUNDING CONSIDERATIONS

An employer thinking about prefunding must decide what is best for their particular circumstances from both a benefit perspective and an overall company financial management perspective.

Reasons to Fund

The following is a list of reasons to fund or advantages to prefunding:

- Funds contributed to a qualified trust receive tax advantages.

- Accrual expenses and/or contributions to prefund retiree health programs will more properly allocate costs between generations of stockholders.

- Investment earnings from prefunding reduce the annual FAS 106 cost.

- Funds built up in a qualified trust increase the security of the benefits to employees. Under the pay-as-you-go system of funding, the employee must depend on the continued willingness and ability of the employer to make benefit payments.

- Plan assets built up in an outside trust fund may be sheltered from corporate raiders.

- Funding provides cash-flow protection that allows management some latitude in how to use cash from year to year.

- A tax-deductible contribution to a fund may be worthwhile, even though the investment income may be taxed.

- For government contractors and certain regulated companies, amounts accrued for retiree life and health benefits may not be allowable charges unless they are funded.

Reasons Not to Fund

Among the reasons not to fund or disadvantages to prefunding are:

- An employer may be able to achieve a higher after-tax return by investing its capital in the ongoing development of the business rather than in a benefit trust.

- The existence of a trust fund with assets earmarked for retiree health benefits may imply that the plans are permanent, and may restrict the plan sponsor's flexibility in changing them in the future.

- The tax advantages of prefunding have been severely limited by DEFRA.

- §401(h) restrictions may be too limiting for effective funding.

- The presence of funding may be discounted by financial analysts and result in a decrease in corporate assets with a possible increase in corporate debt.

- New legislation may alter funding practices in the near future.

- The employer has less flexibility with the use of the cash than if the cash were retained in corporate assets.

- The reduction in FAS 106 cost is somewhat offset by a reduction in earnings elsewhere in the financial statement (e.g., reduced cash, increased borrowing).

WELFARE BENEFIT FUNDS

A "welfare benefit fund" is a term coined by the Deficit Reduction Act of 1984 (DEFRA). The term has created much confusion regarding what types of funds are included in its definition. Two types of funds that have been used to prefund retiree life and health benefits are clearly included in its definition. They are:

- §501(c)(9) trust funds (or VEBAs), and

- Insurance company continuance funds.

Before describing each of these funding vehicles, it is important to understand the general funding rules imposed on them by DEFRA.

DEFRA Limitations

Many commentators have viewed DEFRA as the first step in legislating restrictions on group life and health benefits. The Act established several limitations on life and health plans, including the funding of retiree life and health plans.

DEFRA also coined a new term—"qualified actuary." This is the expert who is required to provide actuarial certification that the reserves and liabilities held by benefit trusts are actuarially required. The actual qualification requirements are to be determined under future Treasury regulations (which, as of this writing over two decades later, have not been completed).

The level of benefits provided by the VEBA is not limited. DEFRA does, however, provide limits on the level of assets that may accumulate in the fund. Detailed discussion of the limits that are applied to benefits other than retiree life and health benefits are beyond the scope of this book.

Contributions Limited

A current deduction, up to DEFRA limits, is allowed for retiree life and health plan prefunding. The calculated contribution amount must be actuarially determined and **funded** during the tax year. In general, the actuarial calculation is limited to the current cost of the plan (i.e., no health care trend assumption allowed) and must be funded over the working lifetime of the covered employees. [IRC 419A(c)(2)] The funding definition under DEFRA is unclear for currently retired employees. Since retirees do not have a "working lifetime" remaining, the rules and regulations do not require any spreading of their costs. Informal conversations with the Internal Revenue Service have indicated that they believe some form of amortization should be used. The realized investment income on the retiree health portion funded after 1984 is taxed as unrelated business income tax with certain exceptions explained below. [IRC §512]

Tax-deductible funding for retiree life insurance was limited to face amounts of $50,000 or less. This change did not apply to employees age 55 or older and covered under a life insurance plan as of January 1, 1984 if they worked during 1983 or were retired before January 1, 1984. [IRC §419A(e)(d)]

Investment Income Taxed

Generally, welfare benefit funds have their investment income taxed for all amounts funded toward retiree health benefits. Unrelated business income tax (UBIT) must be applied on all realized investment income allocated to retiree health plan funds accumulated in a tax-exempt trust (e.g., a §501(c)(9) trust or VEBA). This tax is paid by the trust fund at regular trust fund rates.

Investment income on retiree life and health benefit accounts funded as of July 18, 1984 (preexisting reserves) are exempt from UBIT. All benefits paid are assumed to first come from these grandfathered amounts.

Unrelated business income is actually determined as the lesser of:

- The realized investment income of the trust fund (excluding income earned on retiree health liabilities contributed prior to 1984); and

- The excess, if any, of the trust fund's assets over the liabilities of the fund (excluding retiree health liabilities).

Deemed unrelated business income tax (DUBIT) is applied on investment income accumulated in a fund that is not tax-exempt (e.g., an insurance company continuance fund). This tax is determined by calculating the unrelated business income on the fund as if it were a tax-exempt trust, then including the fund's "deemed" unrelated business income in the employer's gross income. Therefore, the DUBIT of a non-exempt fund is taxed at the employer's marginal tax rate.

Continuation of Active Coverage

In concept, the plan funded in the trust fund must provide both active and retiree coverage. If the plan covers only retirees, it might be considered as providing nonqualified deferred income. If, however, the plan is a continuation of a plan maintained for active employees, it would not be considered deferred compensation. Informally, the Service has broadly interpreted continuation of an active plan. Although there is no official statement, if a requirement of eligibility in a retiree plan is that they had coverage under the active plan prior to retirement, the plan may be treated as a continuation of the active plan. Neither the actual funding vehicle (or insurer) or the plan provisions would have to be the same as the active plan. [DEFRA Blue Book][4]

Restricted Treatment for Key Employees

Contributions for key employees are applied against the Section 415 maximum dollar ($30,000, indexed, $44,000 in 2006) contribution limit calculations for defined contribution plans.

Key employees are defined in the top-heavy provisions in IRC §416. They are:

- Top 50 (or if less, the greater of three or 10 percent of employees) officers of the company earning more than $130,000 (indexed, $140,000 in 2006);
- 5 percent shareholders; or
- 1 percent shareholders of the company earning more than $150,000 from the company.

These contributions must be allocated to separate, individual accounts, and benefits paid from the trust may only be paid from these accounts. [IRC §419A(d)]

Employers generally exclude key employees when prefunding because of these added requirements. Note that once a key employee under these rules, they are always considered a key employee for this purpose.

Excise Tax

An employer would be assessed an excise tax equal to 100 percent on any of the following:

- The value of health benefits paid from the trust to retired key employees who are not paid from their separate accounts;
- The value of benefits paid to any retiree under a discriminatory plan funded through a §501(c)(9) trust; or
- Amounts reverting to an employer from a benefit fund. [IRC §4976]

---

[4] General Explanation of the Revenue Provisions of the Deficit Reduction Act of 1984, Staff of the Joint Committee on Taxation, December 31, 1984.

Exceptions to DEFRA Limitation Rules

Certain groups are exempt from many of the DEFRA limitations. These include:

- **Collectively Bargained Funds**. If 90 percent of the eligible employees covered under the VEBA are also covered under a collective bargaining agreement and if the benefits provided through the welfare benefit fund are subject to bargaining, the fund is not subject to the DEFRA deductible limits or UBIT. [IRC §419A(f)(5)(A)]

- **Employee-Pay-All Plans**. If the welfare benefit fund provides benefits that are solely funded by employee contributions, the fund is exempt from both tax deductible limits and UBIT. To be eligible, the fund must cover at least 50 employees, and employees cannot be entitled to any refund other than one based on the experience of the entire fund. [IRC §419A(f)(5)(B)]

- **Tax-Exempt Employer Funds**. If an employer who has been exempt from taxes for the last five tax years sponsors a welfare benefit fund, the fund is not subject to UBIT. Since the tax-exempt employer is not concerned with tax deductibility, tax deductible limits are not an issue. [IRC §512(a)(3)(E)(iii)]

- **10-or-More Employer Groups**. If a welfare benefit fund is established for a group of ten or more unrelated employers, the fund is not subject to the deduction limits, however it may be subject to UBIT.[5] To qualify, no employer may normally contribute more than 10 percent of the total contribution made by all employers and the fund may not experience rate the claims for individual employers. [IRC §419A(f)(6) and Reg. §1.512(a)-5T]

Contribution Strategies

In addition to the exemptions from DEFRA rules for specific groups, employers use different strategies to minimize the impact of the DEFRA restrictions. For example, to reduce the level of UBIT, a VEBA could invest in a life insurance or health insurance product with tax-free inside

---

[5] IRC §419A(f)(6) provides for exemption from the deduction limits for 10-or-more employers and Q&A 3 of reg. §1.512(a)-5T states that the account limits for VEBAs apply to 10-or-more employer plans in determining UBIT.

build-up of earnings. This trust-owned life insurance (TOLI) may be an individual or group issued policy. Trust-owned health insurance (TOHI) is a group contract with limited medical risk underwritten by an insurer to maintain affordable premiums. Alternatively, the VEBA could invest in tax-exempt securities to reduce its taxable income.

In addition, employers that are making relatively small prefunded contributions could utilize the funding limits available for other eligible benefits to provide tax-exempt buildups. For example, active and retiree medical claims could be paid through the trust allowing a claim liability for both groups to be accumulated in the fund at the end of the year. If this strategy is used, it does imply that the claim liabilities are not being funded in the trust and remain as book liabilities of the employer.

§501(c)(9) Trusts or VEBAs

IRC §501(c)(9) allows plan sponsors to establish a trust qualified under this section of the Code. It allows the plan sponsor to make tax-deductible contributions and accumulate tax-free investment earnings on funds for certain benefits other than deferred compensation and retirement benefits.

The general requirements of a VEBA are that the benefits be nondiscriminatory and provide for the payment of life, sick, accident, or other benefits to its members. The regulations provide for specific restrictions regarding membership to avoid discrimination. Basically, the trust should not discriminate in favor of officers, shareholders, or highly paid employees.

A VEBA is subject to all the limitations described above for welfare benefit funds.

In general, the primary advantages of using a VEBA for funding retiree life and health benefits are:

- A current federal income tax deduction is allowed, up to the DEFRA limits.

- Any contributions made in excess of the DEFRA limitations may be carried forward to future tax years.

- There apparently are no restrictions on the tax carry-forwards.

- Any excess contribution may eventually be taken as a tax deduction.

- Benefit payments to retirees are not taxable to the retiree.

- There is more flexibility in having access to funds than in other vehicles. Technically, a plan sponsor must use assets for the exclusive benefit of plan participants. Practically, however, the funds may be used up in a relatively short period of time by paying for active employee health costs.

- Advance funding should be considered prefunding for purposes of FAS 106, if the funds may only be used to pay retiree benefits.

- The existence of a fund would add benefit security for retirees.

The primary disadvantages are:

- Some or all of the realized investment income is taxed as unrelated business income tax.

- DEFRA limitations prevent "full accrual" of liabilities on a tax-deductible basis. This would prevent a plan sponsor from deducting the amount funded if that deposit represents the full accrual cost.

- Benefits provided under a VEBA are subject to nondiscrimination requirements and may not favor highly compensated employees. If the benefits are subject to any other specific nondiscrimination rules (e.g., cafeteria plan or self-insured medical plan rules), the general VEBA rules do not apply.

For benefits not subject to nondiscrimination rules (e.g., insured benefits), this would be an added consideration.

- No reversion from the trust fund back to the plan sponsor is allowed until all liabilities are satisfied. There is a 100 percent excise tax on any reversion. However, it is relatively easy to draw down assets in the trust by paying health benefits to active employees.

- Separate accounts need to be established for key employees (as defined by the top-heavy rules of IRC §416). This may be circumvented by not prefunding retiree health benefits for key employees.

- Trust assets must be used for the exclusive benefit of plan participants and are not available to the plan sponsor.

- If the employer is not currently paying federal income tax, the tax deductibility of the contribution has no value.

- The presence of a fund may restrict the employer's rights to terminate the benefits.

Insurance Company Continuance Funds

Under DEFRA, insurance company continuance funds are considered a welfare benefit fund and subject to all of its limitations and restrictions. These funds are accounts established by an insurance company for funding certain future benefit payments. They have more commonly been used to prefund retiree life insurance benefits but may also be used for retiree health plan payments. The funds are usually credited with a net "new money" interest rate earned by the insurance company. The net rate includes a small income tax charge based on the insurer's tax applicable to these reserves.

A current income tax deduction, up to DEFRA limits, is allowed if the funded amount is actuarially determined. The net investment income earned on the fund may be taxed to the plan sponsor as Deemed Unrelated Business Income Tax (DUBIT). As mentioned above, DUBIT is determined in the same manner as UBIT.

The same advantages and disadvantages addressed above for VEBAs apply to insurance company continuance funds. Some additional considerations that should be made for these funds are:

- The need to establish a trust is avoided.

- The plan sponsor may lose control over the long-term investment strategy of the funded assets.

- Insurers generally will keep the continuance fund only if they have the active employee business.

- Insurers own the reserve, and adequate termination provisions must be negotiated when establishing the contract.

QUALIFIED RETIREMENT PLAN (IRC §401(H) ACCOUNT)

IRC §401(h) was adopted in 1962 with regulations issued in 1964. The provision allows plan sponsors to fund certain retiree health benefits in the same trust fund as a pension plan. In essence, it would make the retiree health plan a part of the pension plan. The Omnibus Reconciliation Act of 1989 modified the Code to clarify that the plan sponsor must compare actual contributions to the trust fund under the subordination test discussed below. There was a short period of time where the IRS allowed plan sponsors to meet the subordination test even though they made no pension contribution by comparing medical contributions to the pension plan's normal cost.

The provisions of the pension plan must meet the following requirements:

- The pension plan document must specify the health benefits available and describe how they are determined;

- The health benefits provided under the pension plan must be "subordinate" to the retirement benefit;

- A separate account must be established and maintained for the health benefits;

- The employer contributions must be "reasonable and ascertainable";

- Amounts in the 401(h) account cannot be used for anything but medical benefits until all of the liabilities are satisfied. Any amounts allocated to the separate accounts must be returned to the employer after all liabilities for the benefits have been liquidated;

- A separate account must be established for each key employee and all benefits for these key employees (including their covered dependents) must be paid from these accounts (same requirement as for welfare benefit funds);

- A retiree must be eligible to receive pension benefits from the plan in order to also be eligible to receive health benefits; and

- Benefits must not discriminate in favor of officers, shareholders, supervisory employees, or those highly paid with respect to benefits, contributions, or coverage. [Reg. §1.401-14(c)]

"Subordinate" is defined in the regulations to mean that the cumulative actual contribution to the health benefit accounts, plus contributions to fund any retiree life insurance, may not exceed 25 percent of the total actual contributions to the plan from the date that health benefits have been provided. In other words, actual contributions for life and health benefits cannot exceed one-third (25% ÷ 75%) of the actual contributions for retirement benefits, excluding prior service costs. [Reg. §1.401-14(c)(1)]

The IRS has been consistent in its interpretation of the start date of the subordination test. They have used the rule that it is the later of the adoption date of the plan amendment adding the §401(h) account or the effective date of the plan amendment. [PLR 9652021, PLR 9834037, PLR 200550043]

A separate account does not require separate trust funds but there must be separate accounting of the medical and pension assets. If assets can be used to pay for pension benefits, it will not satisfy this requirement.

For the plan's employer contributions to be reasonable and ascertainable, the document must describe exactly what benefits are paid from the pension trust versus other sources such as general assets or a welfare benefit fund. Specifically, there should be documentation on the amount, the priority of payment and the time period that the benefits are paid from each source.

A key employee is defined by the Top Heavy provision in IRC §416(i) and once a key employee under this definition, they will always be considered a key employee for this purpose. Also, any contributions made to the key employees' individual accounts are counted toward their defined contribution limits. [IRC §415(l)]

A current federal income tax deduction is allowed, if the contribution is actuarially determined. The amount is subject to a maximum contribution equal to the greater of:

- The amount necessary to fund the remaining unfunded costs of past and current service credits over the future service of current employees, either as a level amount or a level percentage of pay; or

- 10 percent of the cost to completely fund or purchase the medical benefits. [Reg. §1.404(a)-3(f)(2)]

There is some disagreement as to what the two requirements mean. Some argue that they are very similar to the old pension plan maximum tax deductible requirements which traditionally were interpreted as the greater of an aggregate normal cost or normal cost (using any immediate gain actuarial method) plus 10 percent of the unfunded actuarial liability. Others take a literal interpretation of the greater of an aggregate normal cost or the unfunded amount times 10 percent.

These contributions do not affect the maximum deductible contribution limit for the retirement benefit portion of the plan. [Reg. §1.404(a)-3(f)(1)] The §401(h) account contributions are also not subject to any minimum required contribution amount as pension plans are. [Reg. §1.412(c)(3)-1(f)(5)]

The 25 percent limitation could restrict the **full accrual** of liabilities because of the funded status of the pension plan benefits. If a pension plan has been funded for many years, it has built up a substantial amount of assets to back up its liabilities. The retiree life and health plans have not. Therefore, the retiree life and health plans will need relatively greater future funding than the pension plan to meet their liabilities.

Also, if a pension plan should have its contributions limited by the full funding rules of ERISA, the tax-deductible contribution will be affected because of the §401(h) rules limiting retiree life and health contributions to 25 percent of total actual contributions to the pension plan trust. If the pension plan contributions are limited to zero, the retiree life and health contributions will also be limited to zero. In addition, if the retiree health plan is very rich and the pension plan is not, the 25 percent limit will restrict funding.

Few companies have taken advantage of §401(h). The major reasons are:

- Until DEFRA, §501(c)(9) trusts were more flexible in funding retiree life and health benefits.

- Plan sponsors were unsure how the inclusion of the retiree health plan in a pension plan affects their ability to change the health plan.

- Employers preferred funding on a pay-as-you-go basis.

There has been more interest in §401(h) recently because of the DEFRA restrictions on §501(c)(9) trusts, adoption within a money purchase pension plan and the availability of pension surplus transfers (described at the end of this section).

The primary advantages of using §401(h) for funding retiree health benefits are:

- The plan sponsor may be allowed a higher tax-deductible contribution under §401(h) limits than with other funding vehicles.

- Investment income in the §401(h) account is tax-free.

- Benefit payments to retirees are tax-free.

- Advance funding should be considered prefunding for purposes of FAS No. 106.

The primary disadvantages are:

- There has been little utilization of this provision to fund retiree health benefits so an employer could be placed under greater IRS scrutiny.

- The 25 percent of total contribution limitation restricts the funding of these retiree health liabilities where there are fully funded pension plans.

- Nondiscrimination requirements are not as well-defined as they are in other life and health plan funding vehicles, raising compliance questions.

- §401(h) defines benefit entitlements to retirees, not premiums paid. There could be difficulty in coordinating this definition when employees can choose between fee-for-service plans and HMOs.

- Although health benefits are not part of the **accrued** benefit for ERISA purposes and therefore presumably not subject to the anti-cutback rules that apply to pensions, there still may be problems connected with revisions that reduce health benefits to retirees.

- Separate accounts need to be established for key employees. This additional administration may be avoided by not prefunding benefits for key employees.

PENSION SURPLUS TRANSFERS

As mentioned above, §401(h) funding of retiree health plans has also drawn limited interest because of the ability to transfer pension surplus to the retiree health account under IRC §420. This section of the Code was added in the 1990 tax bill and amended four times – in late 1994, 1999, 2004 and 2006. Although the ability to transfer pension surplus is not specifically a prefunding transaction, it is important from the perspective that a few employers have utilized the provision and may encourage use of the accounts for future funding.

Employers with over-funded pension plans may transfer, on a limited basis, excess pension assets on a year-by-year basis. Excess assets are equal to the lesser of the actuarial or fair market value of assets, minus the greater of the actuarial accrued liability or 125 percent[6] of the current liability.

Annual transfers can be made for any year before 2013 (amended in 2004) up to the amount "reasonably estimated" to be paid by the employer during the tax year. However, a number of conditions must be met to make the transfer:

- All employees must be fully vested in their retirement benefits (including employees who left one year before the transfer is made);

- Employees must be notified before the transfer is made (and provided a calculation of their accrued benefit) at least 60 days in advance; and

- The employer may not reduce the per capita cost of the retiree medical plan during the five years after the transfer for pre-1996 transfers. For transfers made from 1996 through 1999, the "maintenance of cost" rule was changed to a "maintenance of benefit" rule such that the employer must maintain the same level of **benefits** during the maintenance period. Beginning in 2000, the maintenance-of-cost rule was reinstated.

---

[6] Transfers prior to 2004 also included a limit of the actuarial liability component equal to 170 percent of current liability that was repealed for years beginning after 2003 but under general sunset provision of EGTRRA, the limit is reinstated for years after 2010.

The maintenance of cost rule requires that the cost per capita not be reduced for the five taxable years, including the year of transfer, compared to the average per capita in the prior two years before the transfer.[7] Assume a transfer is made in 2006. The employer would calculate an annual per capita cost by taking the incurred claims and expenses for 2004 and 2005 and dividing by the average number of retirees covered during 2004 and 2005, respectively. The cost that must be maintained is the greater of these two rates. The per capita costs may not be less than this amount in 2006 through 2010. Each year of calculation refers to the employer's tax year. The per capita costs may be determined by different groups of retirees (e.g., pre- and post-65 retirees, salaried and hourly).

In addition to the above, beginning in 2002 an employer cannot significantly reduce its coverage during the cost maintenance period. For each year, the employer must calculate an "employer-initiated reduction percentage" and that amount cannot be greater than 10 percent in any one year or 20 percent for all years during the period.[8] The percentage is determined by dividing the number of retirees who lost coverage during the year due to an employer action (e.g., termination of coverage) by the total number of retirees at the beginning of the year. [Reg. §1.420-1]

For an employer who has prefunded retiree health obligations prior to the transfer, the qualified transfer amount must be reduced by the value of benefits not funded by the assets. Assets from §401(h) accounts and VEBAs must be included in the calculation. For example, if the there has been $500,000 prefunded in a VEBA and the present value of retiree benefits is $2 million, 25 percent of the current year payments must come from the VEBA and the other 75 percent can be transferred. [IRC §420(e)(1)(B)]

The Pension Protection Act of 2006 added the ability to transfer up to ten years of retiree medical obligations [new paragraph (f) under §420]. This

---

[7] IRC §420(c)(3)(E) allows some reduction in benefit for employers with liabilities at least five percent of gross receipts of the employer that are within the same percentage amounts as the reduction in covered retirees and are coordinated with each other. For example, if benefits are reduced 6 percent in one year, no more than 4 percent of retirees could lose coverage because of the employer's actions in that same year.

[8] The regulation was published in the Federal Register on June 19, 2001. The 10 percent test applied to a taxable year beginning on or after February 5, 2001. The 20 percent cumulative test applied retroactively to any transfer made on or after December 18, 1999. The regulation allowed for prospective correction to any action that contributed to the failure of the cumulative test prior to 2002.

may be done as a "qualified future transfer" or a "collectively bargained transfer." These transfers may be made if plan assets exceed the greater of the actuarial liability or 120 percent of the current liability. During the transfer period, the plan's excess funded status must be maintained at this level. If the status is not maintained, the employer must either make contributions to the plan to meet the minimum level or an amount required to meet the minimum level must be transferred from the §401(h) account. The transfer period must for at least two consecutive years to utilize these special rules.

The amount that can be transferred is the same as the qualified one year transfer plus up to nine more years equal to the present value of the benefits to be paid (determined under guidance to be issued by the Secretary). The minimum cost requirement is modified such that the employer could elect to continue applying the one year transfer test (i.e., costs maintained for the current year of transfer plus the next four years) or they must meet the same requirement for each year during the transfer period and the four subsequent years. A plan sponsor may also elect to use the old "maintenance of benefit" rule where they do not reduce the plan design or increase retiree contributions as a percentage of costs during the maintenance period. For a collectively bargained transfer, the test is met if the cost is not less than the amount specified in the collectively bargained agreement.

In addition, collectively bargained transfers can be made only if (1) the employer provided retiree medical benefits for the 2005 tax year and (2) the aggregate cost of benefits for that year was at least five percent of the employer's gross receipts. The provision also applies to any successor of these employers. Before the transfer is made, the employer must tell each union, in writing, that the transfer being made is a collectively bargained transfer.

Because of these conditions, few employers have taken advantage of this transfer provision.

PROFIT SHARING PLAN "INCIDENTAL" ACCOUNT

In general, profit sharing plans are only allowed to provide retirement income or deferred compensation. However, by Treasury regulations and a 1961 IRS revenue ruling, profit sharing plans are also allowed to provide "incidental life or accident or health insurance." Many experts have interpreted these rules to allow the establishment of separate profit sharing accounts to provide for retiree health benefits.

The IRS has provided little guidance on the structure and nature of these accounts. A number of revenue rulings require that contributions to the non-retirement account must be **incidental** to the retirement contributions. The incidental requirement is generally satisfied if contributions to the health care account do not exceed 25 percent of the total contribution made for each participant. Revenue Ruling 61-164 states that after a period of time (the later of two years after contributions are made, or the occurrence of a specified event such as five years of service), 100 percent of the account could be allocated to provide health benefits. However, these rules predate the adoption of §401(h) accounts, which have had subsequent interpretations. Because of the similarities, a strong argument can be made that these profit sharing accounts should have similar treatment as their counterpart pension accounts.

The **grayest** area for these incidental accounts is the taxability of benefits paid to retirees. Based on general rules regarding the taxation of medical benefits, an argument can be made that profit sharing plan distributions in the form of health insurance premiums are nontaxable to the retiree. A conservative interpretation of the rules would limit payments to premiums only and would not include health care benefits paid directly by the employer.

The primary advantages of using an incidental profit sharing account are:

- Communication of concept is relatively easy and "sellable" to employees.
- Employer contributions to the trust are tax deductible as paid.
- Investment income accumulating in profit sharing plan is tax-free.
- Medical insurance premiums paid from the account may be tax free to retirees.
- The profit sharing plan may already be established.
- Advance funding (provided the account is restricted and segregated for retiree medical benefits) should be considered an asset under FAS 106.

The primary disadvantages are:

- Few companies have adopted such programs. However, several accounting firms and investment management companies are promoting the concept.

- For most companies, the 25 percent incidental limit will restrict the "full accrual" of costs.

- Certain qualified plan rules are uncertain (e.g., minimum vesting, minimum distribution, and nondiscrimination rules).

- There is uncertainty regarding the taxability of distributions and whether they must be in the form of insurance premiums, or can be direct benefit payments.

EMPLOYEE-PURCHASED GROUP ANNUITIES

This approach has been adopted by at least one company when they eliminated their regular retiree medical plan. Under this approach, the employee uses after-tax pay to purchase an insurance company annuity contract. The annuity product guarantees the principal and offers interest guarantees each year. The employee owns the annuity, and the earnings are tax sheltered. At retirement, the employee may elect to receive cash (which is taxed under regular annuity payout rules) or a reimbursement to pay for medical benefits. Under IRS regulations originally issued in 1960, it could be argued that these medical benefits should be treated as payments under a health insurance policy and are not taxable to the retiree.

The primary advantages of using group annuities for employee-pay-all programs are:

- Investments may be tax sheltered but are at least tax deferred.

- Benefits may be paid tax-free.

- Employees may elect at retirement to use funds for either retirement or medical payments.

- Discrimination requirements are avoided since product is insured.

The primary disadvantage is the legal uncertainty of all the advantages mentioned above, in particular the tax-free nature of the benefit payments.

MONEY PURCHASE PLAN

As discussed earlier, a qualified pension plan may include a medical account to pay for retiree health care services. Under the Code, a money purchase plan is considered a pension plan. For employers already sponsoring profit-sharing plans (e.g., §401(k) plans), a portion of the plan may be converted to a money purchase plan.

One employer converted their Employee Stock Option Plan (ESOP) to a combination ESOP and §401(h) account. The employer has received a determination letter for their plan, but the IRS has stopped issuing determination letters for other HSOPs to give them more time to study the plan design. Although employers will not be able to receive determination letters on HSOPs in the near future, an employer may want to adopt a similar plan because it meets their particular objectives and needs.

The following steps may be followed to create a plan:

- Create a money purchase pension plan;
- Establish a §401(h) account within the new money purchase pension plan

In addition, the following steps were needed to create the HSOP:

- Establish an ESOP within the money purchase pension plan; and
- Leverage the ESOP and §401(h) account by borrowing cash to purchase company shares.

Each step outlined above is done for a specific purpose. The following provides a brief description of the rationale for each step.

Create Money Purchase Pension Plan

A money purchase pension plan is a defined contribution plan that qualfies as a **pension** plan under ERISA. Most pension plans are defined benefit plans, and defined contribution plans are typically considered savings or profit sharing plans under ERISA (e.g., §401(k) plans).

Under a money purchase plan, the plan sponsor must make a commitment to provide annual contributions to the plan that are based on a fixed formula. There are also restrictions on employee withdrawals to ensure that the money is used for retirement purposes. Employee contributions to the plan are made with after-tax money.

The creation of the money purchase plan retained the defined contribution nature of the employer's current retirement income philosophy. The employer's prior retirement program originally consisted solely of a profit sharing plan. The employer's contribution to that plan was based on a profit-driven formula.

Establish §401(h) Account

As discussed above, a separate medical account (§401(h) account) may be established for a pension plan. Typically, §401(h) accounts have been added to defined benefit pension plans, but the same rules apply to money purchase pension plans. A medical account may be added to a money purchase pension plan as long as the benefits provided by the account are **subordinate** to the retirement benefits. Again, the subordinate rule is satisfied as long as the annual cash contributions to the medical account do not exceed 25 percent of the total contributions to the pension plan.

The establishment of the §401(h) account now allows the plan to provide for some subsidy of retiree medical benefits at retirement on a tax-favored basis.

The contributions to the §401(h) account must be subordinate to the retirement benefit in aggregate. They do not have to be allocated to individuals on the same basis as the retirement contributions. For example, if average pay is $50,000 and retirement contributions are 6% of pay, the §401(h) contribution may be a flat $1,000 per employee instead of 2% of pay, which would allocate more to higher paid employees.

Establish ESOP within Money Purchase Pension Plan

A stock bonus plan was added to the money purchase pension plan that constitutes an ESOP. This allows the plan to invest a higher percentage in company stock. ERISA prohibits investment of more than 10 percent of the fair value of assets in employer securities for standard money purchase pension plans.

Leverage ESOP and §401(h) Account

The plan was then **leveraged** using two separate borrowings. The borrowing was for a 30-year term. The first borrowing was used to purchase convertible preferred stock that was put into a suspense account to be distributed over time to the plan participants. The amount distributed from this borrowing would go into the money purchase plan and is based on the same profit-driven formula of the old profit-sharing plan.

The second borrowing was used to acquire additional convertible preferred stock to fund the retiree medical account. These are individual accounts maintained for each distribution as opposed to pooled accounts that would be typical in a defined benefit plan. The original borrowing was intended to allow future distributions that were within the 25 percent subordinate limit; however, if the distribution does exceed that limit in a particular year, the excess would go into the stock bonus portion of the ESOP in that year only.

Comment on HSOP

The last two steps were used to create the HSOP. As mentioned, this type of plan will not be recognized by the IRS and due to tax law changes, leveraged ESOPs are no longer practical. It has been included in this textbook because it has been done and received considerable attention by the industry at the time.

Distribution at Retirement

Distribution from the retirement income portion of the plan would be the same as any conventional defined contribution plan. The money from the §401(h) account is distributed from the individual accounts as needed to provide funds to pay medical expenses to the extent covered by the company. After the funds from the account are exhausted, the company continues to provide for medical coverage from general assets.

The primary advantages of using a money purchase plan are:

- Contributions to the plans are tax deductible.
- Investment earnings are tax-free.
- Benefit payments to retirees are not taxable to the retiree.
- The prefunding of the retiree medical obligation adds benefit security for the retiree.
- The prefunded assets would be counted as assets under FAS 106.

The primary disadvantages are:

- The 25 percent subordinate limit generally will prevent "full accrual" of liabilities on a tax-favored basis.
- Individual retiree medical accounts (as opposed to pooled) are probably required.
- The IRS will not issue a determination letter on HSOPs.

SUPPLEMENTAL PENSION AND/OR RETIREMENT ACCOUNTS

Under this funding alternative, the plan sponsor would establish a supplemental pension and/or defined contribution account and communicate to employees that this account is to be used for retiree life and health benefits. Under the tax code, this is merely another profit sharing/money purchase plan that would have to meet all requirements for plan qualification.

This approach is commonly used when the direct employer subsidy to the retiree medical plan is reduced. When plan participants are told the company is reducing its subsidy to the retiree medical plan, they are also told that the "lost" subsidy is being offset by an increase in pension benefits. Of course, pension benefits are not subject to the same level of "cost of living increases" that medical plans are.

Companies who have adopted this form of "prefunding" have increased retirement benefits in a variety of forms. Examples include eliminating Social Security integration, adding a flat dollar benefit to the pension plan to match the lost subsidy in the retiree medical plan, and establishing or increasing a matching contribution to the savings plan.

The primary advantages to using a qualified retirement program to prefund retiree life and health benefits are:

- Subject to regular qualified plan limits, the employer contributions are tax deductible.

- For a very well-funded pension plan, it may be the best way to use up the surplus assets.

- Depending on communication, "funding" may shift some of the inflationary cost to retirees.

- Investment income is tax-free.

The primary disadvantages are:

- The new plan creates another set of vested retirement benefits.

- Since the plan is just another retirement plan, the retiree will receive his or her monthly benefit check, and any required retiree life and health premiums will be paid with after-tax dollars.

- There is no guarantee that the benefit will be used for life and health benefits.

- IRC Section 415 maximum benefit/contribution limits would make this plan ineffective for some employees.

- If funded in a pension-type benefit plan, the plan liabilities have to be accounted for under Financial Accounting Standards Board Statement No. 87.

A hybrid of the above in a total retirement scheme is to provide employees choice between retirement income benefits (e.g., a supplement to the pension plan) or additional employer subsidy (whether funded or not) to the retiree group benefit plan. This approach has generally not been supported by the IRS.

HEALTH SAVINGS ACCOUNTS

Health Savings Accounts (HSAs) that were established by the Medicare Modernization Act has oftentimes been referred to as a potential funding vehicle for retiree group benefits. An employee may participate in an HSA if they are enrolled in a high deductible health plan – a health plan with a deductible from $1,000 to $2,600 for an individual (2006 and indexed thereafter) or $2,000 to $5,150 for family coverage. HSAs are truly tax-effective in that contributions are tax-deductible, earnings are tax-sheltered, and distributions are tax-free (as long as they are used for medical expenses).

However, most analysis indicates that very few individuals will actually be able to save enough money in their HSAs. Many will require using the funds prior to retirement to help pay for out-of-pocket expenses while working. And, there are constraints on adequate funding for most individuals because the contributions are limited to the value of the deductible.

ILLUSTRATION OF FUNDING LIMITS ON PLAN COSTS

The following section illustrates how the funding limits discussed above operate. The examples show the basic calculations necessary under the various funding limit regulations. It does not consider special grandfathering provisions available or any other provision that may relate to a specific circumstance. The illustrations do provide an understanding of the typical funding situation for retiree health plans. The values are actual amounts for a large, mature manufacturing company with high benefits before 65 and relatively low benefits after 65.

Basic Data (all amounts in $1,000s)

	With Health Inflation	Without Health Inflation
(1) Normal cost	$ 33,300	$ 13,300
(2) Active liability	$ 491,700	$ 270,400
(3) Retired liability	$ 145,800	$ 109,400
(4) Total liability	$ 637,500	$ 379,800
(5) Benefit payments	$ 29,800	$ 29,800
Economic assumptions		
Interest rate	6.50%	3.90%
Health care trend *(15-year select period)*		
— Pre-age 65	10.0% - 5.00%	0.00%
— Post-age 65	12.0% - 5.00%	0.00%

A post-age 65 increase assumption that is less than the pre-age 65 long-term health care trend assumption was used to account for the expected slower Medicare increases in the future. The trends disclosed are based on covered expenses. Plan deductible and out-of-pocket maximum are assumed to be indexed with total health care cost increases. An interest assumption of 3.9 percent for the no-health care-inflation scenario was used to account for the fact, that under DEFRA, investment income is subject to the unrelated business income tax. Note that a 40 percent tax rate was assumed here. The current after-tax interest rate may be adjusted for a lower tax rate.

Best Estimate Plan Cost

The following calculation provides the **Best Estimate** accrual cost for the plan. The calculations include the assumption that health plan benefits will increase in the future (i.e., includes an inflation assumption).

(1) Normal cost	$ 33,300
(2) 20-Year amortization	54,300
(3) Plan cost: (1) + (2)	87,600
(4) Pay-as-you-go cost	29,800

Note that the plan cost is almost three times the pay-as-you-go cost. This relationship is typical for mature plans that are not currently prefunded. It is common to see plan costs six to ten times the pay-as-you-go costs.

Assuming the normal cost (service cost under FAS 106) and the liability (accumulated postretirement benefit obligation (APBO)) were determined in accordance with FAS 106, the following accounting cost may be determined:

(1) Service cost	$ 33,300
(2) Interest cost	42,600
(3) Amortization of APBO	31,900
(4) FAS 106 cost	107,800
(5) Pay-as-you-go cost	29,800

The FAS 106 cost is higher than the "best estimate" cost because of the difference in amortization methods. The FAS 106 approach has a "front-loaded" method.[9] Therefore, if no gains and losses occur, the "best estimate" cost will be lower than the FAS 106 cost in many future years.

DEFRA Limit for Welfare Benefit Funds

The following calculation provides the plan cost, as limited under DEFRA, for funded life and health plans. Since DEFRA precludes the use of a health care inflation assumption in developing the liabilities, the normal cost and actuarial liability used below are based on the values without health care inflation.

(1) Normal cost	$ 13,300
(2) 20-Year amortization	26,700
(3) Funded amount: (1) + (2)	40,000
(4) Pay-as-you-go cost	29,800

The accrual cost under the no-health care-inflation scenario still provides for a higher cost than the pay-as-you-go approach, but only about one-third more. The best estimate accrual cost is more than twice the amount allowed to be funded under DEFRA. A DEFRA plan cost that is one-third to one-half of the actuarially adequate funding level is common.

§401(h) Account Funding Limit

As described above, IRC §401(h) limits the contribution to fund the retiree health plan to one-third of the pension contribution to the trust

---

[9] Under FAS 106, the initial obligation is amortized as a straight line over 20 years plus interest. The "best estimate" amortization was based on a mortgage type method over 20 years including principal and interest.

fund. The following illustrates how the contribution limit is determined. It is assumed that the pension plan normal cost is $131,300.

(1) Normal cost	$ 33,300
(2) 20-Year amortization	54,300
(3) Plan cost: (1) + (2)	87,600
(4) §401(h) limit:	
(a) Pension normal cost:	131,300
(b) Limit: (a) ÷ 3	43,800
(5) §401(h) plan cost:	
lesser of (3) or (4)(b)	43,800
(4) Pay-as-you-go cost	29,800

Comments on Illustrations

As the illustrations show, limitations imposed under §501(c)(9) and §401(h) significantly reduce tax-deductible contributions (both by over half in this case). §501(c)(9) tax-deductible funding is reduced by 54 percent from the full accrual cost (1 − $40,000 ÷ $87,600). §401(h) funding is reduced by 50 percent (1 − $43,800 ÷ $87,600).

The §401(h) plan cost provides a higher permissible funding cost than either §501(c)(9) trust or insurance company funding in this case. However, if the employer's pension plan could not make contributions to its trust fund in a year because of tax limits, the §401(h) plan cost will also be zero. In that case, the §501(c)(9)/insurance company funding would be more advantageous. Conversely, if the pension plan provides higher benefits than the above example, the §401(h) plan limit will also be higher. Each plan sponsor's circumstances will warrant different conclusions.

CONCLUSIONS

There currently is no clearly preferable tax-effective funding vehicle available.

Depending on the funded status of a company's pension plan, §401(h) may be the best of the four alternatives from a current company tax standpoint. It allows the inclusion of a health care inflation assumption and the investment income is tax-exempt. §501(c)(9) funding can also be a good alternative.

Establishing a continuance fund with the insurance company of the active plan is easy to do. Since substantial funds will accumulate, more flexible investment options should be explored before a permanent policy is adopted. Also, DEFRA's funding limitations are imposed on these funds as well as on §501(c)(9) trusts.

Some companies have concluded that in order to fund at their desired level, they have to use two or more vehicles. This may include the use of separate VEBAs for their salaried and union employees to take advantage of the collectively bargained exemptions for the union employees. An alternative is a combination VEBA and §401(h) account to prefund different benefits (e.g., a VEBA for current retirees and a §401(h) account for future retirees). If a combination of trust funds is used, it is very important that the legal documents carefully define what benefits are paid from each fund.

Few companies have used the more leading edge funding vehicles (e.g., HSOP, employee group annuities, and incidental profit sharing accounts) since there are no clear IRS guidelines for any of the vehicles and in some cases, negative signals from the IRS.

The main disadvantage of funding within a qualified retirement plan is the lack of flexibility. Benefits, once established, are subject to all of the qualified pension plan rules. Benefits may, of course, be increased to account for health care inflation, but they cannot be reduced because of ERISA's anti-cutback rules. Although the benefits are subject to these anti-cutback rules, they may be changed prospectively. Benefits provided to retirees are taxable.

Funding Vehicle Summary

The following table provides a quick reference tool showing how each U.S. funding vehicle rates compared to the ideal characteristics.

Characteristic	VEBA	Insurance Fund	§401(h)[10]	Incidental Profit Sharing	Employee Group Annuity	Health Stock Option	Quali-fied Plan
Tax deductible employer contribution	😐	😐	😐	😐	😐	☹	☺
Tax-free or tax-deferred employee contribution	☹	☹	☹	☺	☹	😐	😐
Tax-sheltered investment	😐	😐	☺	☺	☺	☺	☺
Tax-free benefit payments	☺	☺	☺	😐	😐	☺	☹
No plan design impact	☺	☺	😐	☺	☹	😐	☺
FAS 106 asset	☺	☺	☺	☺	😐	☺	☹
Revocable assets	☹	☹	☹	☹	☹	☹	☹

☺ Favorable

😐 Unclear or restricted

☹ Not favorable

---

[10] Applicable 410(h) account in either a defined benefit plan or a money purchase defined contribution plan.

6   LEGAL ISSUES

Much of today's legal framework of health and welfare plans, including retiree benefits, is centered on the Employee Retirement Income Security Act of 1974 (ERISA). That law was intended to be an all encompassing statute covering all employee benefit plans. The greatest detail in all of these rules, however, was focused on retirement plans. Originally, only the disclosure and reporting rules, trust and fiduciary requirements applied to welfare plans. Later, other substantive rules that provided legal rights for participants were added (e.g., health care continuation and coverage rules). ERISA also established several governmental agencies to enforce the rules.

ERISA established a quasi-government pension guaranty insurance company, vesting rules, minimum participation requirements and funding standards for pension plans. In the years that followed, these rules have been expanded and detailed even further. Some rules were established for welfare plans but most were very general in nature with very little specificity. In a U.S. Supreme Court case[1], the discussion actually commented that "ERISA imposes on pension plans a variety of substantive requirements relating to participation, funding, and vesting.... It does not regulate the substantive content of welfare-benefit plans."

With the lack of detailed rules, courts have done their best in interpreting the law. And their decisions have formed the basic construct of employee benefit design. In the area of retiree group benefit plans, there are three areas that have dominated the court dockets:

- Termination and modification of benefits;
- Tax deductibility of funding; and
- Discrimination of benefit design.

Other legal issues involving retiree group benefits include the continuation of health insurance coverage, and privacy and protection rules (including pre-existing coverage rules).

---

[1] *Metropolitan Life Insurance Co. v. Massachusetts*, 471 U.S. 724, 732 (1985)

TERMINATION/MODIFICATION

Most of the court cases involving retiree group benefits have been in the area of the legality of terminating or modifying the programs. As mentioned above, ERISA provides significant detail on the ability of a plan sponsor to terminate or modify a retirement plan. However, since there are no rules on vesting or design constraints for retiree group benefits in ERISA, courts have historically looked to contract, trust and labor law for guidance.

One key concept under ERISA is its broad preemption of state law. This provision makes it clear that the intent of Congress was that federal law would apply exclusively to the regulation of employee benefits. This, coupled with the paucity of rules under ERISA, forced courts to create a body of federal common law.

Pre-ERISA Cases

Most of the court cases involving retiree group benefits were decided after the passage of ERISA but the few cases that were decided earlier, created the foundation of the common law decisions post-ERISA. Typically, the courts did not distinguish between pension and retiree insurance rights because there were no vesting and funding requirements for either benefit. In general, they held the belief that benefit provisions represented a component of a contract between employees and employers where employees accepted lower wages in return for benefits after retirement. Pension and insurance were both subject to this contract approach of benefit rights.

Most cases involving collectively bargained employees relied on labor law[2] which meant that federal law rather than state law was applicable. Nonunion employees brought cases to court under state contract law. Courts tended to view both types of cases similarly, so the state and federal distinction in interpretation is not significant.

Courts treated retirement benefits as lifetime, nonforfeitable benefits unless there was compelling evidence that contradicted that interpretation. Most companies at this time tended to be very paternalistic and courts fueled that behavior by imputing that responsibility to employers through their decisions.

---

[2] Section 301 of the Labor Management Relations Act (LMRA).

Courts utilized two overlapping theories in deciding these early cases – the deferred compensation theory that was applied to union retirees and the unilateral contract theory applied to nonunion employees. These two theories usually produced similar results, which upheld the lifetime nature of the benefits.

Deferred Compensation Theory

The basic premise of this theory is that employees earn their retirement benefits while working and accepting lower pay. If the court allowed retirement benefits to be terminated, it would mean that employees would lose what they had already earned.

A first step in advancing this theory for union employees is to conclude that benefits for retirees can be subject to bargaining. In the Inland Steel case, the court clearly concluded retirement plans were wages as contemplated by the National Labor Relations Board (NLRB) and are therefore subject to collective bargaining. The rationale was that the union was giving up current wages or other forms of pay in return for these retirement benefits.[3]

Courts made it clear in their decisions that they did not favor the concept of benefit forfeiture. This made most of these early cases very one-sided in favoring the retirees. All decisions stated that unless employers provided clear and unambiguous language stating their right to change or terminate benefits, it could not be done after retirement. In many cases, courts went out of their way to search for ambiguous contract language. For example, in one case the court found one clause in a collectively bargained agreement that limited the insurance plan for active employees to the duration of the contract. Another paragraph covering retiree life insurance stated that the company "will continue to cover such eligible retired employees with $2,000 life insurance." Since that paragraph did not mention a limit of such coverage, the court reasoned that it must be for the life of the retiree. Otherwise, the document would have included a comment in that paragraph limiting the benefit as it did for the active coverage.[4]

Not all cases tried under this contract theory favored the retirees. One case involved an agreement that clearly stated the retiree life insurance

---

[3] *Inland Steel v. NLRB*, 170 F2d 247 (7ᵗʰ Cir. 1948), *cert denied* 336 U.S. 960 (1948)

[4] *Upholsters' Int'l Union v. American Pad & Textile Co.*, 372 F.2d 427 (6ᵗʰ Cir. 1967).

benefit would only have to be maintained for the duration of the agreement. The court did not reach beyond the limits of the agreement and decided that the company could legally terminate these benefits when the agreement expired.[5]

Unilateral Contract Theory

This theory was often used for salaried employee cases. Remember, union contracts are considered "bilateral" so this theory would not be available under collectively bargained cases. When an employer establishes a benefit program (a retiree life insurance benefit, for example), and communicates the existence of the benefit to its employees, the employee accepts the benefit and satisfies the requirements to earn the benefit, the benefit then becomes vested and nonforfeitable. In these cases, even with clear language that allows the employer to terminate or amend the benefit, the employer may not be able to make changes.

In one case, even though the employer reserved the right to terminate retiree life insurance coverage, the court refused to enforce the clause and required the employer to continue coverage. The reasoning was that the employer could not deprive retirees of *vested rights* under the program.[6]

Post-ERISA Cases

The number of cases involving retiree group benefits exploded after the passage of ERISA in 1974. Some of the key retiree group benefit cases will be mentioned in this section and a brief summary of these and other cases are included in Appendix D.

It would be natural to extend the ERISA concept of vesting to retiree group benefits. The courts have taken that view despite the fact that Congress did not legislate such a requirement. In one case, the court concluded that even though ERISA does not require vesting for retiree group benefits, it didn't forbid it either.

---

[5] *United Rubber Workers v. Lee Nat'l Corp.*, 323 F. Supp. 1181 (S.D.N.Y. 1971).
[6] *In re Erie Lackawanna Ry.*, 548 F.2d 621 (6th Cir. 1977).

> The exemption from ERISA's vesting requirements does not prohibit an employer from extending benefits beyond the expiration of the collective bargaining agreement. Rather, the exemption allows the parties to determine the duration of the welfare benefits. Thus, the issue is "simply one of contract interpretation."[7]

Similar to pre-ERISA cases, courts treated union and non-union retirees differently. It is therefore worth looking at these two retiree groups separately.

Collectively Bargained Retirees

The most frequently cited retiree group benefit case involved a collectively bargained plan. In the Sixth Circuit landmark case, Yard-Man[8], the court characterized retirement benefits as "status" benefits and that they must be continued as long as the covered person retains that status—in this case, retired status. Once this status has been attained, an employer could not unilaterally eliminate the benefit and the union could not negotiate the benefit for the retirees because they are no longer covered by the collective bargaining agreement. The rationalization of the court was that they are benefits provided for past services rendered (similar to pre-ERISA cases) and retired workers, unlike active workers, have very little protection. It was therefore concluded that retiree insurance benefits were intended to be lifetime because active employees would only be willing to give up wages while working in exchange for these benefits.

In *Yard-Man*, the court thoroughly analyzed the collective bargaining agreement to come to its conclusion that the parties intended the retiree medical and life insurance benefits to be lifetime. The agreement stated that the company will continue to provide insurance benefits to employees in retirement. They cited ambiguity because it was unclear whether this statement was intended to stand on its own or be read in conjunction with the limiting duration of the agreement. Unfortunately for the employer, there was language regarding terminating benefits for active employees but not in the section on retiree benefits. The court reasoned that the parties would have included a termination clause for retiree benefits

---

[7] *Anderson v. Alpha Portland Industries, Inc.* 836 F.2d 1512, 1516 (8th Cir. 1988).

[8] *International Union, United Automobile, Aerospace and Agricultural Implementation Workers of America v. Yard-Man*, 716 F.2d 1476 (6th Cir. 1983).

if that was their intention, the same as they did for the active benefits. The court also found that there was limiting language for surviving dependent coverage with no limit on the overall program. And, it included language explaining that retirees must pay for coverage until age 65 and thereafter it is non-contributory which the court saw as a meaningless provision if the insurance expired at the end of the collectively bargained agreement. Finally, the court concluded that the general duration clause of the agreement (that all terms of agreement end at the end of the contracted period) did not extend to retiree group benefit coverage. The court summarized its view on the ambiguity of termination language as follows:

> Where ambiguities exist, the court may look to other words and phrases in the collective bargaining agreement for guidance. Variations in language used in other durational provisions of the agreement may, for example, provide inferences of intent useful in clarifying a provision whose intended duration is ambiguous.

Courts have also looked at other evidence to understand the intent of all parties including summary plan descriptions (SPD), other benefit summary booklets or human resource material, oral statements made to retiring employees by HR personnel, and the conduct of the parties (e.g., a history of continuing benefits past the expiration of an agreement or prior curtailment of retiree benefits without retiree complaint).

In *Cadillac Malleable* and *Bunker Hill*, the companies continued retiree insurance benefits during strikes. In both of those cases, the courts reasoned that if the parties intended retiree benefits to only last through the duration of the contract period, they would have discontinued the benefits during a strike. In addition, in retirement counseling, personnel staff made no distinction between pension and other retirement benefits in discussing their coverages in retirement. In *Cadillac Malleable,* letters had been sent from the employer to retirees announcing improvements in the benefits which the court interpreted as suggesting that they were lifetime benefits. In *Bunker Hill*, the SPD contained several paragraphs that gave retirees the impression that they had lifetime benefits.[9]

---

[9] *International Union, UAW v. Cadillac Malleable Iron*, 728 F.2d 807, 809 (6th Cir. 1984); *Bower v. Bunker Hill Co.*, 725 F.2d 1221, 1224 (9th Cir. 1984).

Courts have also looked to the extent a company has reserved their right to modify or terminate benefits. In *Morrell*, the court held that health benefits were non-vested benefits and the employer could modify or terminate.[10]

Nonunion Retirees

Plaintiffs and courts have cycled through several different theories, post-ERISA, in arguing that retiree group benefits cannot be terminated.

The district court in *Hansen* concluded that an employer could not terminate retiree group benefits as a matter of federal common law.[11] The district court considered its decision the "modern view," that such benefits vest at retirement saying,

> During the past 30 years, however, more and more courts have accepted "the modern view that the promise of a pension constitutes an offer which, upon performance of the required service by the employee, becomes a binding obligation."

The Sixth Circuit rejected this view and reversed this aspect of the district court's decision. They were careful, however, to preserve its view that although the status of being a retiree in itself does not create vesting, they favor the continuation of retiree benefits unless there is clear language to the contrary.

Subsequent cases have continued to recognize that ERISA does not require any form of automatic vesting of retiree group benefits. A plaintiff must show other reasons for why the promised benefits have to be continued. In Sprague, the Sixth Circuit stated, "an employer's commitment to vest such benefits is not to be inferred lightly; the intent to vest must be found in plan documents and must be stated in clear and express language."[12]

As mentioned earlier, ERISA's preemption of state law means that a retiree's only recourse in court in nonunion cases is under federal law. A key

---

[10] *John Morrell & Co. v. United Food & Commercial Workers International Union*, 37 F.3d 1302 (8th Cir. 1994).

[11] *Hansen v. White Farm Equipment Co.*, 2130, (N.D. Ohio, 1984), reversed 788 F.2d 1186 (6th Cir. 1986).

[12] *Sprague v. General Motors Corp.*, 133 F.3d 388, 400 (6th Cir. 1998).

issue that courts must then decide is whether or not Congress intended federal courts to create federal common law under ERISA. Under ERISA, Congress clearly stated that the regulation of employee benefit plans was a federal concern. And, there was a clear distinction in rules between pension and welfare benefit plans. There is express exemption from ERISA's participation, vesting and funding standards. The legislative history indicated that Congress was concerned that by adding vesting and funding requirements to welfare plans that it would create unnecessary costs and administrative complexity. So, by documenting its concern in the legislative history, was Congress trying to tell the courts that they should not create any form of common law around the concept of vesting?

Employers have always argued that ERISA never intended for vesting requirements to apply to group insurance plans and that courts should not be trying to create such requirements through the judicial system.

ERISA does require that employers precisely state the scope of the benefits to be provided under their plans. The plan document must specify the funding vehicle to be used, define the operational and administrative responsibilities, and state how the benefit payments will be made from the plan. If the plan document does not include specific language limiting the benefits, then courts may find them to be ambiguous and lifetime benefits might be inferred. The fact that ERISA does include many requirements yet not vesting, leaves some experts open to the idea that perhaps courts could create such a requirement under federal common law. They have argued that such a concept is consistent with the basic purpose of ERISA which is to promote and protect employee benefits. As such, if an employer creates lifetime benefits through the legal plan document, employees and retirees will have the right to enforce such promises.

The 1980s and 1990s saw most plan sponsors of retiree group benefits amending plans and including a reservation of rights clause. The clause gives the plan sponsor the right, among other things, to amend the plan. Courts have ruled in favor of the employer who includes such clauses in the documents. In *Moore*[13] and *Musto*[14], retirees challenged the employers' imposition of contribution requirements and increases in cost sharing plan provisions, maintaining that they were promised lifetime benefits at

---

[13] *Moore v. Metropolitan Life Insurance Co.*, 856 F.2d 488 (2nd Cir. 1988).

[14] *Musto v. American General Corp.*, 861 F.2d 897 (6th Cir. 1988) *cert. denied*, 490 U.S. 1020 (1989).

no cost. In *Moore*, the court went further by not allowing the fact that some retirees received oral promises of no cost because they received unambiguous written communication.

In *Sprague*, the District Court upheld a group of early retirees arguing that the employer's early retirement agreements promised to provide a certain level of coverage. The retirees argued that these agreements were separate documents and superseded the reservation of rights clause in the plan document. The decision was reversed by the appeals court because the documents' promises of lifetime benefits did not contradict with the employer's clear reserved right to amend or terminate the plan. They termed the employer's promise of lifetime benefits to be a qualified promise provided that the company decides not to terminate the plans. [15]

An indirect result of many employers who did not previously have a reservation of rights clause is a bifurcation of the retiree groups—those that did not have a reservation of rights clause in their communication prior to retirement and those that did. That is why it is very common to see different plans and contribution arrangements available to those who retired prior to a certain date (e.g., January 1, 1993) and after when reviewing the details of retiree group benefit designs.

In *Varity*, the Supreme Court ruled that the company violated its fiduciary duty by knowingly transferring the benefit obligations of one of its divisions (Massey-Ferguson) to a new corporate entity that subsequently went bankrupt. The Court could not conclude that a vested right existed and took an alternative route. They concluded that providing communication that ultimately proved to be untrue constitutes a breach of fiduciary duty. The Court viewed the transaction as harming the beneficiaries through deliberate deception and violated an ERISA-imposed fiduciary obligation to administer the benefit plans in the sole interest of participants. [16]

Summary

Clear and concise communication is the key to successfully retaining the ability to amend, modify and terminate a retiree group benefit program. Evidence of consistent communication of the same message, from all

---

[15] *Sprague v. General Motors Corp.*, 92 F.3d. 1425 (6th Cir. 1996).

[16] *Varity Corp. v. Howe*, 516 U.S. 489 (S.Ct. 1996)

sources, is also important. Cases have revolved around either arguing that retiree group benefit plans are earned or "vested" after attaining retirement status or that the employer has made "promises" of lifetime benefits. Lessons learned from prior court cases are that the more the plan sponsor has consistently delivered the message that they can change the plan and that there has not been any overt promises made, the more likely their position will be upheld in court.

BANKRUPTCY

Many experts thought the reorganization of LTV Corp. in 1986 would spur Congress to enact pension-type rules on retiree group benefit plans. No such legislation was enacted but it was the primary driver for the clarification of the bankruptcy code's treatment of the benefits.

On the very same day that LTV filed for bankruptcy, it notified their retirees that it intended to terminate all of their life and health insurance coverage. Reacting to the likely backlash of over 66,000 retirees losing their coverage, Congress quickly enacted legislation blocking LTV's intended plan termination.[17] In 1988, Congress amended the Bankruptcy Code by including specific rules governing insurance benefits for retired employees. These rules were modeled after the termination of collective bargaining agreements in Code Section 11.[18]

This new section prohibits a debtor (the employer) in reorganization from terminating their health and life insurance programs for retirees and their dependents without first negotiating the proposed modifications with representatives of the retirees, and seeking and receiving court approval to make the changes. If the debtor and the retirees cannot come to terms regarding the modifications and the debtor believes that the changes are necessary to permit reorganization, the bankruptcy court may allow the changes subject to statutory guidelines. In essence, the debtor and retiree representatives must have negotiated the benefits in good faith and the court must find that the proposed modifications are necessary to permit the debtor to reorganize and assure that all creditors, the debtor and all affected parties are treated fairly and equitably. This generally will require that the debtor must continue retiree health and life

---

[17] P.L. 99-591, §608 (1986); P.L. 99-656 (1986); P.L. 100-41 (1987)
[18] New code section 11 U.S.C. §1114, *Payment of insurance benefits to retired employees.*

insurance coverage while undergoing Chapter 11 reorganization. It may be possible to lower benefit levels and even terminate the plans if they negotiate it with the retirees' representatives or receive permission from the bankruptcy court. Payments that are made under reorganization are given high priority administrative expense status.

The Bankruptcy Abuse Prevention and Consumer Protection Act (BAP-CPA) added a provision in 11 U.S.C. §1114 to prevent last minute changes to retiree group benefits just prior to filing.[19] If the debtor, while insolvent, modifies its program within 180 days of filing, the court may reinstate the benefits unless there is other support for the change.

If an employer ultimately liquidates, the retirees' claims for lost insurance coverage become unsecured claims. The bankruptcy rules set active employee benefit payments to fourth and fifth priority expenses. This higher status does not apply to retirees. Interestingly, when Congress passed the rules on retiree benefits during reorganization, it did not address the status of the claims at liquidation. Any retirees with insurance claims at liquidation become one of the unsecured creditors of the debtor.

AGE DISCRIMINATION

Since the passage of the Age Discrimination in Employment Act of 1967 (ADEA), it was understood in the benefits community that retiree medical benefit design could differ between retirees under age 65 and those age 65 and over because of the presence of the Medicare program. ADEA prohibits discrimination against workers over age 40 in the workplace.

The Supreme Court decided in 1989 that ADEA did not apply to discrimination in employee benefits such as health insurance.[20] This was subsequently modified by legislation. However, the legislative history of the Older Workers Benefit Protection Act of 1990 that amended ADEA to specifically include employee benefits suggested that the prevalent practice of coordinating an employer health plan with the Medicare program would not violate the law.

---

[19] P.L. 109-8 (2005)

[20] *Public Employees Retirement System of Ohio v. Betts*, 492 U.S. 158, 109 S. Ct. 2854, 106 L. Ed. 2d 134 (1989)

In 2000, a U. S. District Court in Pennsylvania ruled that Erie County, Pennsylvania violated the ADEA when it provided its post-65 retirees with medical benefits that were "inferior" to those provided to its pre-65 retirees.[21] The court's ruling applied ADEA as interpreted by the Third Circuit Court of Appeals, which held in the prior year that ADEA applies to employer-sponsored retiree medical programs, and that employers cannot treat post-65 retirees differently than pre-65 retirees unless such differences are justified by the equal benefits/equal cost rule. In its decision, the court deliberately ignored legislative history that permitted benefit differences due to Medicare because it was not included in the written statute.

The *Erie County* decision increased the pressure on employers to examine their retiree medical programs to determine if there is a liability risk under Erie and to assess alternative plan designs. Six years later, the case is still under appeal and the Equal Employment Opportunity Commission (EEOC), who has administrative oversight of ADEA, has attempted to remedy the situation.

Erie County Case Background
The suit was brought by a group of Medicare-eligible retirees formerly employed by Erie County. Prior to 1997, Erie County offered all retirees a traditional indemnity insurance plan. In 1997, Erie County offered post-age 65 retirees health care coverage in a Medicare HMO, instead of the indemnity insurance they had before. The plan was a traditional HMO that only paid for services authorized by a primary care physician. To enroll in the plan, retirees had to live in the service area and pay the Medicare Part B premium. The HMO premium was zero until 1999 when it began to charge $47 per month that was paid by Erie County.

For retirees who were not Medicare-eligible, Erie County offered coverage under the traditional indemnity plan until the end of 1998 when it changed coverage to a point-of-service plan (POS). To enroll in the POS plan, a pre-65 retiree had to live in the service area and be ineligible for Medicare. Pre-65 retirees paid $12 per month under the indemnity plan if they did not live in the service area and nothing for POS coverage. Erie County paid $298 per month for indemnity insurance and $285 per month for POS plan.

---

[21] *Erie County Retirees Association v. The County of Erie Pennsylvania*, 220 F.3d. 193 (3rd Cir. 2000).

Under ADEA, an employer can avoid liability for age discrimination if it satisfies the equal benefits/equal cost rule. The equal benefits/equal cost rule permits an employer to establish that the actual amount of payment made or cost incurred on behalf of an older worker is no less than that made or incurred on behalf of a younger worker. The district court analyzed the equal benefits rule and found that Erie County could not meet this exception for the following reasons:

- **Post-65 retirees paid a greater proportion of the total premium cost (employer and employee-paid) than pre-65 retirees.** The court stated that the Medicare Part B premium represented a greater proportion of the total cost of the HMO than the pre-65 retirees' monthly contribution toward the cost of the indemnity plan or POS plan.

- **The HMO restricted post-65 retirees to the plan's hospitals and doctors.** Under the POS plan, however, pre-65 retirees could choose higher coverage levels available in-network or lower coverage levels out-of-network on an as-needed basis.

- **The HMO offered post-65 retirees prescription drug coverage through a closed formulary that had higher copayments than the drug coverage under pre-65 POS plan that did not have a formulary.** In addition, pre-65 retirees under the POS plan received the same drug benefit even if they chose the indemnity option for their medical services.

The district court then turned to the equal cost rule analysis but quickly disposed of it because it was undisputed that Erie County incurred a lesser cost for the post-65 HMO than for either the indemnity or POS plans. The court concluded that since Erie County could not meet the equal benefits/equal cost rule, its retiree medical plan was age discriminatory.

Another important aspect of this case is that the court found that retirees can sue under the ADEA even though they are no longer active employees. An associated claim in the case that retirees were treated less favorably than active employees was withdrawn before the appeal and the 3rd Circuit did not address it in their opinion.

A flurry of activity followed the appeals court's decision.

Employer Actions Resulting from Erie County Case

Employers met the decision with mixed reactions. In most cases, they have taken a "wait and see" attitude toward action. Now that some time has passed and there has been back and forth with court action, industry response and regulatory response; few employers have made changes to their plans as a direct result of the *Erie* decision.

Despite the general nonchalant employer reaction, employers with retiree medical plans should examine their designs post-*Erie,* in preparation for final decisions. In particular, employers that meet any of the following criteria appear to be most at risk because of differences in the retiree medical benefits offered to pre-65 retirees and post-65 retirees:

- Employers that operate in Pennsylvania, New Jersey or Delaware – or that have retiree populations in those areas;

- Employers that provide only pre-65 retiree medical coverage or reduce retiree medical coverage after age 65;

- Employers with lower caps for post-65 retirees;

- Employers with different options for pre-65 retirees and post-65 retirees (especially employers that offer fewer options to post-65 retirees); and

- Employers engaged in redesigning retiree medical plans without considering *Erie.*

Regulatory Action

The EEOC issued a revised Compliance Manual that adopted the court's position a few months after the 3rd Circuit decision. It required that employers could only provide different retiree health benefits to pre- and post-Medicare retirees if they can demonstrate that the benefits are equal or the costs for each group are the same.[22]

Less than one year later, the EEOC rescinded the provisions in the compliance manual pertaining to retiree health benefits. It announced that they wanted to further study the relationship of the ADEA and employer-sponsored retiree health plans.[23]

---

[22] Amended chapter on *Employee Benefits* adopted by the EEOC on October 3, 2000.

[23] EEOC formally rescinds the retiree health portions of the Compliance Manual on August 20, 2001.

In 2003, the EEOC concluded that the majority of existing retiree health plans did not comply with the equal benefits/equal cost rule and that making it a requirement will accelerate the trend of declining employer-sponsored retiree health benefits. They cited that section 9 of ADEA gives the EEOC the authority to establish reasonable exemptions to its rules when it is necessary in the best interests of the public. The EEOC released a proposed rule that allows employers to alter, reduce or eliminate employer-sponsored retiree health benefits when a retiree becomes eligible for Medicare and such design will not violate ADEA. This exemption was proposed to "ensure that the application of ADEA does not discourage employers from providing health benefits to their retirees."[24]

In the spring of 2004, the EEOC Commissioners approved a proposed final rule that would allow employers to coordinate their retiree health plans with the Medicare program.[25] The AARP sued the EEOC on behalf of six of its members in early 2005 in the U.S. District Court for eastern Pennsylvania. The suit claims that the plaintiffs and other Medicare-eligible retirees will suffer irreparable harm if the rule is allowed to be finalized. In March 2005, the Court stopped the EEOC from publishing its final rule. In the meantime, the Supreme Court ruled that government agencies may issue rules under its authority if they are reasonable. With this new ruling in hand, the district court judge reversed her decision and granted judgment to the EEOC but allowed the AARP to exhaust all its appeal rights before the EEOC can publish its final rule.

Court Action

Subsequent court action has been inextricably intertwined with the regulatory actions—one making a move that influences the other—so that it became difficult to talk about the two separately. After the 3rd Circuit found that ADEA should apply to this case, they remanded the case to the trial court to apply the equal benefits/equal cost rule. In March 2001, the Supreme Court refused to hear the case and in April 2001, the U.S. District Court[26] found that Erie County's retiree medical plan could not meet the test and therefore ruled in favor of the retirees.

---

[24] EEOC proposed rule published in Federal Register July 14, 2003, page 41542.

[25] EEOC press release, April 22, 2004.

[26] U.S. District Court for the Western District of Pennsylvania, No. 98-CV-272 (W.D. Pa.)

In July 2005, the Supreme Court ruled that a federal court is required to defer to an agency's rulemaking authority even if it differs from what the court believes to be the best interpretation of the statute is within the agency's jurisdiction.[27] In light of this ruling, the District Court requested the case be remanded back the court for reconsideration. In September 2005, the court granted judgment to the EEOC but retained the injunction on its release until the AARP exhausted all of its appeals.

The AARP formally filed their appeal to the 3rd Circuit in October 2005.

Erie County Reaction

Erie County has resolved the lawsuit by complying with the court by charging pre-65 retirees a premium comparable to the Medicare Part B premium rate, eliminating the indemnity plan for pre-65 retirees and offering only an HMO (i.e., no out-of-network benefits), and changing the pre-65 prescription drug plan to be comparable to the post-65 plan. In other words, the plan for the pre-65 retirees was reduced to the level of the post-65 retirees.

Erie Summary

In the end, the EEOC's right to enforce its proposed rule for retiree health plans rests in the courts—the 3rd Circuit and possibly the U.S. Supreme Court.

Reverse Discrimination

Although the U.S. Supreme Court refused to hear the appeal of the *Erie County* case, it did hear another age discrimination case involving retiree health care benefits.[28] Prior to July 1997, General Dynamics provided full health benefits to employees who retired after 30 years of service under a collective bargaining agreement. The company negotiated a new agreement where only employees who were age 50 or older with 30 years of service were provided full health care benefits on retirement. A group of employees between the ages of 40 and 50 sued General Dynamics on the grounds that they are being discriminated against in violation of ADEA.

---

[27] *National Cable and Telecommunication Association v. Brand X Internet Services*, 125 S. Ct. 2688, 162 L. Ed. 2d 820 (2005)

[28] *General Dynamics Land System, Inc. v. Cline*, 124 S.Ct. 1236 (2004).

The district court dismissed the case holding that ADEA does not prohibit an employer from discriminating against the protected class (i.e., employees age 40 and over) who are younger than the favored employees. The Sixth Circuit reversed that decision upholding the younger workers right to sue for the denial of the benefits. The court found that the ADEA prohibited discrimination against any individual in the protected class on the basis of age.

The Supreme Court reversed the Sixth Circuit decision citing that ADEA was enacted to prevent employers from favoring younger workers. It does not prohibit an employer from favoring an older employee over a younger one. The Court also rejected the EEOC regulatory position that a decision between hiring two individuals within the protected class be made on factors other than age. This ruling seems to give implied consent to the practice of "grandfathering" older workers when redesigning benefit packages. This ruling did not address whether or not older workers (or retirees) could be disadvantaged in their benefit package as addressed in the *Erie County* case and the EEOC final rules.

COURT CASES ON FUNDING

There are limited federal court cases involving prefunding retiree group benefit plans. There are four notable cases where three are similar to each other and all involve funding in a VEBA.

The similar cases involved many tax-related issues of funding but came down to claiming a tax deduction for retiree group benefits in a year for a portion of funding and subsequently using the money for other benefits. The courts viewed the funding as not made for the intended purpose when retrospectively observing how the monies were actually used and disallowed the tax deduction.[29]

The fourth case is more involved. The Wells Fargo case involved funding their VEBA more aggressively than the IRS national office considered reasonable.[30] As discussed in the chapter on funding, a VEBA may

---

[29] *General Signal Corp. & Subs v. Commissioner*, 103 T.C. 216, 232 (1994); *Parker-Hannifin Corp. v. Commissioner*, 139 F.3d 1090, 1094 (6th Cir. 1998); *Square D Company and Subs v. Commissioner*, 109 T.C. 200, 203 (1997).

[30] *Wells Fargo & Company (f.k.a. Norwest Corporation) and Subs v. Commissioner*, 120 T.C. 5 (2003).

be funded over the working lifetime of employees (along with some other constraints).

For tax years 1991 through 1994, the company contributed to a VEBA. The initial contribution made in 1991 was based on two components—active obligations and retiree obligations. For the active employees, the company funded about $3 million, which was an estimated $14 million obligation spread over the working lifetime of the employees. The company funded the full $28 million obligation attributed to the retirees. The total 1991 contribution was $31 million that they claimed was fully deductible under IRC §419A(c)(2).

Prior to 1991, the company had a VEBA that was established to pay for its medical and long term disability benefits. That VEBA was amended and restated effective January 1, 1991 to no longer pay for retiree medical benefits. A new VEBA was created in December 1991 to be used for the retiree medical benefits.

In the court's opinion, they stated that IRC §§419 and 419A provide the framework for funding. IRC §419(a)(2) permits the deduction subject to the limits of IRC §419(b). IRC §419(b) limits the deduction to the "qualified cost" that is equal to the "qualified direct cost" plus additions to a "qualified asset account." IRC §419A(a) defines a qualified asset account; §419(b) allows additions up to an "account limit;" and §419A(c) defines the limit as claims incurred but not reported and an "additional reserve funded over the working lives of the covered employees and actuarially determined on a level basis" for retiree life and health plans. The court identified the additional reserve as the issue of the case.

Included in the opinion are discussions of actuarial methods and expert opinion on the merits of each of them. Wells Fargo argued that the entry age normal cost method is the most appropriate because it directly allocates costs to an employee's working lifetime.

The IRS argued that the company's position is inconsistent with IRC §419A(c)(2); judicial precedent, Congressional intent, the accepted interpretation with pension plans, the law in effect at enactment of IRC §419, and principles of actuarial practice.

The court supported Wells Fargo with only minor challenge of the discount rates used during the tax years in question. The IRS has stated that it will not appeal this case but will likely challenge other tax payers adopting similar funding strategies.

OTHER LEGAL ISSUES

Retiree group benefit plans are also subject to other legal requirements of other welfare plans. As mentioned earlier, ERISA includes reporting and disclosure provisions for the protection of employees. Any time the plan sponsor changes the benefits, ERISA requires communication in the form of a summary plan description (SPD) or summary of material modifications (SMM). A SPD must be updated every five years for changes even if a SMM is distributed. Generally, any change must be communicated to participants no later than 210 days after the end of the plan year in which the change was adopted. If a change results in a material reduction in either covered services or benefits, then the revised SPD or SMM must be furnished to participants no later than 60 days after the date of the adoption of the modification or change.

Active health plans must allow for a continuation of coverage for a limited time when a participant loses coverage (often referred to as COBRA coverage because this rule was created by the Consolidated Omnibus Budget Reconciliation Act of 1986)[31]. Generally, termination of retiree medical coverage does not trigger COBRA coverage. If, however, there is a reduction in coverage within 18 months following termination or retirement or the employer files for bankruptcy, the retirees and dependents may be eligible for COBRA continuation benefits.

Spouses of covered retirees become eligible for COBRA if they lose coverage because the covered retiree dies or they divorce. Dependent children become eligible for continuation coverage if they lose coverage because the parent retiree dies, the parents become divorced or legally separated, or the child loses eligibility for coverage (e.g., due to age limits.)

In general, when Medicare coverage begins, COBRA coverage terminates. Timing, however, is important in these cases. If a participant first

---

[31] P.L. 99-272 (1986)

elects COBRA coverage and then enrolls in Medicare, an employer may terminate the COBRA continuation coverage. If a participant is already enrolled in Medicare when COBRA is offered, the participant may elect COBRA and the COBRA coverage cannot be terminated because he or she is enrolled in Medicare.[32]

Retiree health plans that are provided through fully-insured contracts are not subject to any form of non-discrimination rules, but self-funded plans are covered by the rules in IRC §105. In general, the plan is not allowed to discriminate in favor of highly compensated individuals in either eligibility or benefits. The plan must benefit 70 percent or more of all employees, or 80 percent or more of all the employees who are eligible for the plan if 70 percent or more are eligible to participate in the plan. Or the plan could be set up in a structure that can be deemed to be nondiscriminatory. If a plan is discriminatory, the benefits in excess of what the rank and file employees receive are taxable to the highly paid individual.

---

[32] Treasury regulation §54.4980B-7, Q&A-3.

7

ACCOUNTING UNDER FAS 106

In December 1990, the Financial Accounting Standards Board (FASB) released the long-awaited accounting standard for postretirement benefits other than pensions—Financial Accounting Standard No. 106 (FAS 106). The Board started this project in 1979 as part of its work on pension plan accounting. In 1984, the Board split out retiree life and health accounting as a separate project.

As an interim step, the Board released FAS 81, *Disclosure of Postretirement Health Care and Life Insurance Benefits*, which required employers to disclose in their financial statements both the existence of a plan and the annual cost. At the time, annual costs were typically accounted for on a "pay-as-you-go" or cash basis. As another interim step, the Board issued FASB Technical Bulletin No. 87-1, *Accounting for a Change in Method of Accounting for Certain Postretirement Benefits*. This bulletin discussed how an employer should handle an accounting change for retiree life and health plans. It included a brief explanation of how to change from a pay-as-you-go accounting method to an accrual method; including full recognition of the past service liability in the year of change.

The Board issued the Exposure Draft (ED) of proposed new accounting rules for retiree life and health plans in February 1989. In general, the ED mirrored many of the requirements found in the pension standards included in FAS 87 and 88[1]. The primary reason for the similarity is that the Board found the two types of benefits alike in several respects, and felt that different accounting should be prescribed only when there is compelling reason for it.

---

[1] Statement of Financial Accounting Standards No. 87, *Employers' Accounting for Pensions*, Financial Accounting Standards Board, December 1985 and Statement of Financial Accounting Standards No. 88, *Employers' Accounting for Settlements and Curtailments of Defined Benefit Pension Plans and for Termination Benefits*, Financial Accounting Standards Board, December 1985

SCOPE OF FAS 106

FAS 106 applies to any program, whether written or unwritten, that provides benefits to a former employee after he or she has retired. The statement applies primarily to retiree health benefits, but also covers other retiree group benefits, such as life insurance, tuition assistance, day care, legal services, and housing subsidies. If material, it would also include other benefits such as merchandise discounts, reduced fee services (e.g., reduced utility fees) and other benefits given to retirees. FAS 106 does not cover pensions (which are accounted for under FAS 87 and 88) or preretirement disability benefits (covered under FAS 112).

FAS 106 does, however, cover group benefits provided to disabled employees who have met the eligibility requirements of the retiree group benefit plan. For example, if eligibility for the retiree medical plan is age 55 with 10 years of service and eligible for an immediate pension benefit, any disabled employee meeting the 55 and 10 requirement who is not expected to return to work may be considered retired and covered under the retiree medical plan at that time, but not before.

Otherwise, continuation of medical coverage for disabled employees is not covered in this standard. Therefore, for FAS 106 purposes, disabled employees who are not actually retired, but continue to accrue pension benefits while disabled, will **not** be considered on disability retirement. They should be considered in any FAS 112 calculations.

However, for disabled employees expected to remain disabled until they meet the retiree medical eligibility requirements, deferred benefits **should be** included.

In order to avoid being required to value benefits paid to all disabled employees under FAS 106, the retiree group benefit plan should explicitly include disabled employees only after they are eligible to receive or actually begin receiving benefits from a retirement plan.

FAS 106 requires that **disability retirements** be considered in the cost calculations, including rates of disability. However, costs should only include the benefits deemed to be covered under the postretirement plan. For example, there may be 0.2 percent chance of disability at age 35, but benefits will not be paid until age 65 under the plan.

EFFECTIVE DATES

FAS 106 was effective for fiscal years beginning after December 15, 1992. The effective date was deferred for two years for small employers and non-U.S. plans. As with any new standard, the FASB encouraged early adoption of the rules.

IMPLICATIONS

The change in accounting rules had a major impact on employers' financial statements. Employers had to decide how this cost would be measured and whether they should adopt FAS 106 before 1993. Many employers, concluding that the accounting cost was too great, redefined their benefits commitment in order to reduce their cost.

PROPOSED AMENDMENTS TO FAS 106

The FASB is continually updating its standards to meet current accounting and disclosure needs. There have been several small amendments to FAS 106 since its issuance, with the most notable one being the FAS 132 that changed the disclosure requirements from the original statement.

In early 2006, the FASB issued a proposed statement that it expects to adopt by the end of the year that will primarily change the treatment of the unrecognized amounts on the balance sheet. *Employers' Accounting for Defined Benefit Pension and Other Postretirement Plans – an amendment of FASB Statements No. 87, 88, 106, and 132(R)* includes discussion of the balance sheet change and some other minor amendments to FAS 106. This is discussed in more detail at the end of this chapter.

PROFIT AND LOSS STATEMENT TREATMENT

The introduction of FAS 106 had a significant effect on employers' profit and loss (P&L) statements (a.k.a., income statement). The primary reason was the change from pay-as-you-go accounting to full accrual accounting.

Assumptions

FAS 106 requires employers to use the best information and estimates available in developing actuarial assumptions. The statement emphasizes the need for explicit (i.e., "stand-alone") assumptions, including the use of age-related health care costs.

In its discussion on assumptions, the Statement specifically includes discount rates, per capita claims cost by age, administrative costs, health care cost trend rates, Medicare reimbursement rates, salary progression (if applicable), turnover, retirement ages, participation rates, dependency status, and mortality. Additional factors may be assumed, but not those that anticipate future legislative or regulatory events. For example, it is not acceptable to assume that legislation will change Medicare reimbursement rates in the future.

It would be appropriate to recognize that the trend for Medicare-eligible retirees will differ from the trend for other medical plan participants. Current Medicare reimbursement rules will slow the cost increases of Medicare payments relative to other health care trends. Because of limitations on how much a provider can bill Medicare patients, Medicare-covered expenses paid by employer plans should trend lower than for non-Medicare retirees. However, the actuary also needs to consider the impact of Medicare reimbursement methods on the employer plan costs, especially the impact of prescription drug trends and Medicare HMO costs.

FAS 106 explicitly states that administrative expenses should be included in the projection of future costs.

The statement allows estimates, averages and other shortcuts that reduce the cost of calculating the required values as long as no material differences result.

For example, an employer sponsors 20 different HMOs and contributes the same amount to each. A detailed application of the rules would develop employer- and employee-provided claim costs for the 20 HMOs and then apply the provisions of the standard. A simplified approach may assume that all HMO participants are covered under one plan with an employer contribution equal to the average employer-provided claim cost.

Attribution Method

FAS 106 requires the expected future benefit payments to be accrued over each participant's working lifetime. The amount that is attributed to a financial accounting period is called the net periodic postretirement benefit cost (cost). As in FAS 87, it is based on the projected unit credit (**PUC**) actuarial cost method (see Chapter 9 for description of method).

To calculate the cost for each participant, an "expected postretirement benefit obligation" (EPBO) is determined as of the measurement date. The EPBO is the actuarial present value of all future expected postretirement benefit payments for that individual. Probabilities of termination, death, and retirement, as well as anticipated increases in plan costs, are taken into consideration in calculating the EPBO. The EPBO is then allocated between an amount attributable to service before the measurement date, service in the current year and future service, based on how the benefits accrue (benefit per years of service approach). The amount attributable to service before the measurement date is called the "accumulated postretirement benefit obligation" (APBO), and the amount attributed to the current year is the "service cost."

The measurement date mentioned above is the date to which all values are discounted. It will generally be the date of the financial statements (usually the end of the fiscal year). However, the standard will allow a measurement date that is within three months prior to the financial statement date.

Note that all components of plan costs are handled using the above method, including total health care plan costs, Medicare reimbursements, administration costs, retiree contributions, and contributions made by active employees while they are working.

In order to determine the service cost and the APBO, an "attribution period" has to be defined. This period generally begins at an employee's date of hire unless the plan actually specifies a later date when benefits begin to accrue. This is similar to pension plan accounting under FAS 87. The attribution period ends when the participant has "full eligibility." Full eligibility is "the date at which an employee has rendered all the service necessary to have earned the right to receive all of the benefits expected to be received by that employee (including any beneficiaries and covered dependents)." Full eligibility is earned by meeting age and/or service requirements.

Example 1: A plan provides benefits to employees who have 20 years of service and retire from active employment with the company; early retirement under the pension plan is age 55 with 10 years of service. The full eligibility date is the first date when the employee has 20 years of service **and** has attained age 55 with 10 years of service. In other words, the full eligibility requirement in this case is attainment of age 55 with 20 years of service. Employees hired before age 35 have full eligibility when they attain age 55 because they have more than 20 years of service by that age. Employees hired after age 35 have full eligibility when they have 20 years of service (they will all be past age 55 on that date).

Attributing benefits from hire age to full eligibility age may be significantly shorter than the FAS 87 period from hire age to retirement age.

The full eligibility date may be delayed beyond the normal "full eligibility" age and/or service requirements of the plan if increases in salary affect the ultimate benefit and the increases are not "trivial."

Example 2: A plan provides a life insurance benefit equal to 10 percent of annual pay at retirement. The earliest retirement age is 55, and the expected retirement age is 60 with pay increases at 6 percent per year from age 55 to age 60. In this case, an individual employee's insurance amount would increase 34 percent in the last 5 years of service. Based on the age and service requirements of the plan, the full eligibility date would be the earliest retirement date. However, because salary increases under this plan change the ultimate life insurance amount by more than a trivial amount, the full eligibility date is the expected retirement date.

The full eligibility date cannot be later than the expected retirement or disability date. For example, employees who are expected to become disabled at age 45 and remain disabled until age 65, have a full eligibility date of age 45, even though under the terms of the plan these employees will not be eligible for retiree group benefits until they are age 65 and begin to receive pension payments. Similarly, an employee who is hired at age 45, accrues an employer contribution of 5 percent of the cost for each year of service, and is expected to retire at age 62, has a full eligibility date of age 62. The employee has accrued a benefit with an 85 percent employer contribution, the highest benefit this particular employee will earn.

In general, an equal amount of the benefit obligation is allocated to each year of the attribution period. For plans that have an accrual formula (the minority of plans) **and** the formula is "front-loaded" (i.e., employees accrue more of their benefits in their early years of service), the allocation should be based on the benefit formula.

> **Example 3:** A participant earns an employer-provided life insurance benefit of $20,000 for each of the first 10 years of service and $5,000 for each of the next 10 years ($250,000 total life insurance after 20 years). Benefits accrue at the rate of 8 percent of the total benefit for each of the first 10 years and 2 percent for the next 10 years. This formula is probably front-loaded and should attribute benefits based on the accrual pattern. After 20 years, the participant would have earned the full benefit, thus reaching his or her full eligibility date.

By the time an employee reaches his or her full eligibility date, the actuarial present value of benefits is fully accrued. This does not mean that it is assumed that everyone retires at that date; it only means that the present value of the benefits expected to be paid (i.e., the EPBO) is fully accrued by that date (i.e., the APBO equals the EPBO). This approach is consistent with the FAS 87 pension accounting rules for benefit elements with a cliff effect, such as early retirement subsidies at 30 years of service and lump sum death benefits.

A plan could define the beginning of the attribution period as a date after an employee's hire date. For example, if the eligibility requirement for full benefits under the plan is defined as retirement after age 55 with at least 20 years of service performed after age 35, the attribution period begins when the employee attains age 35. If, however, the credited service period under the plan is nominal relative to the employee's total service at his or her full eligibility date, the plan formula is ignored and the attribution period will begin at the date of hire.

There is no clear definition of "nominal," although paragraph 409 uses the "20-years of service after age 35" illustration, implying that such a schedule is **not** nominal. Also, paragraph 410 indicates that one year of service is nominal in relation to an average 20-year service period for all active plan participants.

In general, benefits are deemed to accrue:

- Uniformly from the date of hire to the date the participant is first eligible to receive full benefits (attribution period): or
- In accordance with the plan if the accrual is defined and the benefit formula is front-loaded.

Components of Cost

The "net periodic postretirement benefit cost" represents the cost of providing postretirement benefits attributed to the current accounting period. It consists of the current year's cost plus other amounts recognized on a delayed or amortized basis. The components of the cost that must be included in the footnote disclosures are:

- Service cost. The cost of benefits that accrue for the period covered by the P&L statement.
- Interest cost. Interest on both the APBO (the analogue of the PBO under FAS 87), the service cost, and benefit payments using the discount rate assumptions. The interest cost attributable to the service cost may be included with the service cost.
- Expected return on plan assets. For funded plans, this is the expected return on the fair value of the plan assets for the plan year. The expected return is based on an after-tax rate of return to the trust fund.
- Amortization of the transition obligation (or, theoretically, transition asset, although this would be extremely rare). Many employers elected, at initial adoption of FAS 106, to recognize the transition obligation/asset for all "defined benefit" postretirement plans. Some delayed recognition by amortizing this amount.
- Net amortization and deferral. This component includes the amortization of prior service costs (i.e., plan amendments) and gains/losses.

These cost components may be positive or negative, depending on the facts.

The net benefit cost calculation is determined at the beginning of the fiscal year using an expected return on assets. This cost amount is fixed as of this calculation unless there are material changes during the year (e.g., a curtailment of benefits).

As in FAS 87, the net periodic postretirement benefit cost may be either expensed immediately in the P&L statement, or, if the employer is a manufacturer of goods, allocated to the cost of goods produced and implicitly expensed when the goods are sold or depreciated.

> **Example 4**: The net periodic postretirement benefit cost may be shown as follows:
>
> | (1) | Service cost | $ 25,000 |
> |-----|--------------|----------|
> | (2) | Interest cost | 30,000 |
> | (3) | Expected return on plan assets | (4,000) |
> | (4) | Amortization of transition obligation | 20,000 |
> | (5) | Net amortization and deferral | 5,000 |
> | (6) | Net periodic postretirement benefit cost | $ 76,000 |

Each of the components above will be discussed in detail below, including how the numbers were calculated.

Service Cost

The service cost is the portion of the EPBO attributed to employees' service during the current accounting period. It is generally determined as of the measurement date. In the example above, the service cost as of the beginning of the year was $25,000. The service cost may be shown as of the beginning of the year or the end of the year. If it is shown as of the beginning of the year, interest on the service cost must be included in the interest cost.

Interest Cost

Interest charged on the APBO is based on the discount rate. In general, the discount rate should be based on the rates of return on high-quality fixed-income securities available at the measurement date. Interest cost may also include interest on the service cost if it is not shown as an end-of-year amount. The discount rate should also reflect the timing of benefit payments under the plan.

In FAS 87, the discount rate is based on "the rates at which the pension benefits could be effectively settled." The Board intended the term "effectively settled" to mean the underlying interest rate used by the insurance company in establishing annuity rates, excluding any risk factor.

These underlying interest rates are typically very close to rates on high quality, long-term fixed income securities. Therefore, the discount rates used for FAS 106 purposes should not be too different from the FAS 87 discount rates.

These will be pre-tax rates, and FAS 106 prohibits the use of a lower after-tax rate for this purpose. In addition, basing the discount rate on the employer's internal rate of return is expressly prohibited.

> **Example 5**: In Example 4, the APBO was $480,000 and expected benefit payments during the year totaled $10,000. The discount rate was 6 percent. The interest cost calculation is as follows:
>
> $$\text{Interest cost} = (\$480,000 + \$25,000) \times 0.06 - \$10,000 \times 0.06 \times \tfrac{1}{2}$$
> $$= \$30,000$$

Since the $25,000 service cost was determined as of the beginning of the fiscal year, interest for one year must be included in the interest cost. Benefit payments are assumed to be paid uniformly during the year: therefore, a half-year of interest on benefit payments is also included in the calculation. It would be equivalent to calculate the service cost as $26,500 (valued at the end of the year) and the interest cost as $28,500. Note that the illustrations in the FAS 106 statement assume the service cost is valued at the end of the year.

Expected Return on Plan Assets

Calculating the expected return on plan assets requires an assumption about what plan assets will earn. Because plan assets may be held in both taxable and nontaxable trusts, FAS 106 provides that this rate of return will be the net of taxes expected to be paid by the trust. If the assets are held in a fund that is taxable to the **employer**, however, the Statement provides that the expected rate of return on plan assets is to be a pre-tax rate. This is because, in that case, the taxes will be included in the employer's provision for income taxes under FAS 109, and use of an after-tax rate would lead to double-counting the tax cost.

In the U.S., earnings on plan assets are taxable to the employer in limited circumstances. This can occur, for example, with excess assets under an insurance policy. The deemed unrelated business income is then taxable to the employer. Certain irrevocable trusts can be taxable to the employer if the employer retains a sufficiently large reversionary interest or the right to control income. The U.S. tax code calls these "grantor trusts."

FAS 106 recognizes as plan assets only funds that are segregated and restricted for the sole purpose of providing postretirement group benefits except for surplus recapture after existing obligations are settled.

An employer may invest in corporate-owned life insurance for the purpose of providing future retiree medical obligations. But because these assets are not for the exclusive use of the retiree medical plan, they cannot be used as plan assets. Likewise, assets in a §501(c)(9) trust may be intended to fund retiree medical benefits, but if those assets can legally be used to pay for other benefits, they cannot be counted as plan assets.

> **Example 6**: In Example 4, the market-related value of assets at the beginning of the year was equal to $110,000; the current year's contribution will be made at the end of the year; and the expected rate of return is 8 percent. The expected return on assets is determined as follows:
>
> $$\text{Expected Return} = \$55,000 \times 0.08 - \$10,000 \times 0.08 \times \tfrac{1}{2}$$
> $$= \$4,000$$

If contributions are expected to be made before year-end, the calculation should be adjusted to reflect the appropriate expected return.

Amortization of Net Transition Obligation or Asset

The net transition obligation (or, in rare cases, the net transition asset) is the difference between the APBO and plan assets (including as assets any existing accruals for these liabilities, and subtracting any existing asset for prepaid postretirement health care costs) when FAS 106 was first adopted. At adoption, the employer had the choice to immediately recognize the amount (with adjustments) or delay recognition to future periods (i.e., amortize). The decision between immediate or delayed recognition had to be applied to all plans.

The choice between immediate or delayed recognition was an "all or nothing" election. An employer could not immediately recognize a portion of the transition obligation and delay the remainder.

An employer that elected immediate recognition had to adjust the transition amount recognized for certain transactions that took place before they adopted the standard. The following two situations required adjustment:

- Plan initiation or benefit improvements adopted after December 21, 1990
- Business combinations completed after December 21, 1990.

For plan initiation or benefit improvements, the transition amount was adjusted to take out the effect of any changes. For example, if a new plan was adopted, the APBO and associated assets for that plan are excluded from the transition amount that will be immediately recognized. The portion of the transition amount attributed to the new plan was amortized in the future as discussed below.

For business combinations, the purchase accounting for these combinations had to be adjusted, as of the transition date, to include recognition of the APBO and assets as described in paragraphs 86 to 88 of the statement.

The amortization of any prior service cost not immediately recognized and the cumulative effect on past income of any retroactive adjustment of the purchase price allocation had to be recognized as part of the effect of the accounting change to adopt FAS 106.

The following example illustrates these concepts:

- Assume Company A adopted FAS 106 on 1/1/93. On 1/1/91 the company acquired Company B and used the purchase method of accounting, but did not recognize a postretirement benefit liability at the time of acquisition. On 7/1/92 the company adopted a new life insurance plan. Basic data is as follows:

Total APBO at 1/1/93	=	$ 2,000,000
Company B's APBO at 1/1/91	=	800,000
Life insurance APBO at 7/1/92	=	250,000
Average future service to full eligibility	=	25 years

- Recognition of the new plan would have been amortized in a straight-line over 25 years beginning 7/1/92. As of 1/1/93, $245,000 remains to be recognized [$5,000 (½ × $250,000 ÷ 25) would have been recognized in 1992].

- The $800,000 retiree group benefit plan APBO would have been an additional amount attributed to goodwill as of 1/1/91 for the purchase of Company B. Under the company's accounting policy, $40,000 (two years of 40-year amortization) would have been amortized during 1991 and 1992, leaving $760,000.

- On adoption of FAS 106 on 1/1/93, Company A wants to immediately recognize the transition obligation. Because there have been plan amendments and business combinations since December 21, 1990, however, only a portion may be immediately recognized. The following were recognized in the 1993 income statement:

Immediate recognition of transition obligation	$ 950,000
Amortization of prior service cost for prior plan amendments	5,000
Amortization of goodwill for prior purchase business combinations	40,000
Effect of accounting change	$ 995,000

- Because of the plan amendments and business combinations, only $950,000 ($2,000,000 minus $250,000 for the plan amendment minus $800,000 for the business combination) could be immediately recognized. The remaining $760,000 in goodwill from the 1991 acquisition was added to assets in 1993, and there was a $245,000 unrecognized prior service cost from the 1992 plan amendment. The net effect on the balance sheet may be illustrated as follows:

Increase in goodwill	$ 760,000	Increase in accrued cost	$ 1,755,000
		Decrease in equity	(995,000)
Net change	$ 760,000	Net change	$ 760,000

- The reconciliation of the funded status of the plan and the balance sheet as of January 1, 1993 is as follows:

Accumulated postretirement benefit obligation	$ (2,000,000)
Plan assets at fair value	0
Funded status	(2,000,000)
Unrecognized prior service cost	245,000
Accrued postretirement benefit cost	$ (1,755,000)

FAS 87 did not allow immediate recognition for pension plans. Employers most interested in immediate recognition were companies with very high or low earnings in the year of adoption that wanted to absorb them in a good year or report it as a nonrecurring item in a bad year. Most employers that could use immediate recognition did so primarily because it could be reported as a nonrecurring item, and future income statements would not be affected.

If delayed recognition was elected, the net transition obligation (or asset) was amortized on a straight-line basis over the remaining service to the date of expected retirement (**not** over service to full eligibility date) of active employees expected to receive benefits under the plan. This is a different amortization period from that used for prior service costs, but it is the same as that used for gains and losses. Note that the absence of vesting causes the average future service period to be longer than is normally the case in a pension plan. If the amortization period, as calculated above, is less than 20 years, 20 years can be used. If all or most of the plan participants are inactive, life expectancy is to be used in place of service.

The 20-year alternative does not apply if all or most of the participants are inactive and life expectancy is used.

Under Example 4, if the transition obligation is amortized over a 20-year period and the company had an APBO of $400,000 as of the date of adoption and no other accrued costs, the amortization is $20,000 ($400,000 ÷ 20).

For employers amortizing the transition obligation, there is a special test to assure that the net postretirement benefit cost under the new standard is greater than the pay-as-you-go cost. If the cumulative net postretirement benefit cost, at any time, is less than the cumulative pay-as-you-go cost for all participants after the transition date, a special additional amortization of the transition obligation is required. The additional amount will be equal to the difference between the two cumulative costs.

Example 7: The following example illustrates how this test operates:

Transition Obligation	=	$ 14,750
Service cost as of 1/1/2000	=	250
Interest cost for 2000	=	1,500
2000 benefit payments	=	3,000

The 2000 net periodic postretirement benefit cost is equal to:

Service cost	$ 250
+ Interest cost	1,500
+ Amortization of transition obligation (20 years)	740
= Net periodic postretirement benefit cost	$ 2,490

The cumulative benefit costs as of 12/31/2000 equal $2,490. Because this is less than the cumulative benefit payments of $3,000, an additional amortization of the transition obligation in the amount of $510 ($3,000 – $2,490) must be recognized in the 2000 cost. Thus, the total 2000 net periodic postretirement benefit cost is $3,000. The amortization amount is increased by $510 to $1,250 to satisfy the requirement.

This pay-as-you-go limit ensures that employers cannot lower their overall costs by adopting the Statement. Only employers with a very high proportion of retirees to actives will be affected by this limit.

Benefit payments made under a settlement are included in the cumulative amounts above. In addition, if there are any plan assets or accrued postretirement benefit expenses when the statement is adopted, subsequent benefit payments are first used to reduce these amounts or accruals, and then counted as cumulative benefit payments.

This is favorable to employers because it reduces the amount of any extra amortization that may be required.

Net Amortization and Deferral

Gains and losses due to differences between expected and actual experience and changes in assumptions are amortized over future years. Changes in obligations due to plan amendments (otherwise known as prior service costs) are also amortized over future years.

Gains and Losses

As in FAS 87, gains and losses are defined as the change in the APBO or in plan assets that results from experience that is different from assumptions or from a change in assumptions. Gains and losses do not have to be recognized until the unrecognized net gain or loss exceeds 10 percent of the greater of the APBO or the market-related (i.e., actuarial) value of plan assets. If net gains or losses fall outside of the 10 percent "corridor," the minimum amortization base to be included as a component of the plan costs is the excess of the net cumulative unrecognized gain or loss over 10 percent of the greater of net assets or the APBO (all as of the beginning of the plan year). The amortization is equal to this base divided by the average remaining service to the date of expected retirement of those active employees expected to receive benefits under the plan. This may be expressed as follows:

$$\frac{\text{Excess of the net cumulative unrecognized gain or loss over 10 percent of the greater of net assets or the APBO}}{\text{The average remaining service to the date of expected retirement of those active employees expected to receive benefits under the plan}}$$

If all or most plan participants are eligible to retire and receive benefits or are inactive, average remaining life expectancy is to be substituted for average remaining service.

Employers can use any other systematic method of amortizing gains and losses as long as the method:

- Provides amortization greater than or equal to the minimum method;

- Is applied consistently and to both gains and losses; and

- Is disclosed.

An employer may also elect to recognize gains and losses immediately. However, gains must first be used to reduce any remaining unrecognized transition obligation. Similarly, in the unlikely event that there is a transition net asset, losses would have to be applied first to the unrecognized portion of that asset.

As discussed above, measurement and disclosure items are determined based on the provisions of the substantive plan. In some situations, an employer may "forgive" a certain element of the cost-sharing provision of the plan (i.e., deviate from the substantive plan and create a gain or loss). For example, the substantive plan may dictate that retirees pay 25 percent of the cost of the plan. If the employer decides that 25 percent of the cost is too burdensome for retirees in a particular year and reduces their cost to 20 percent for that year only, that reduction in retiree cost is a deviation from the substantive plan. The deviation creates a gain or loss that must be recognized immediately in the current year.

In general, such deviations from the substantive plan will be small in relation to the total plan costs and may be considered immaterial.

The gain and loss component of the net periodic postretirement benefit cost is the sum of:

- The amortization of the unrecognized gains or losses (including assumption changes) based on the employer's policy; and

- The immediate recognition of any one-time deviation from the substantive plan.

Example 8: The prior year's discount rate was 9%. Continuing Example 4, assuming the prior year's values were: APBO = $400,000, service cost = $22,000, and benefit payment = $7,000, the experience gain or loss is determined as follows:

Actual APBO   = $480,000

Expected APBO   = ($400,000+$22,000)×1.09

      − $7,000×(1+0.09×½)

      = $452,665

(Gain)/loss   = $480,000 − $452,665

      = $27,335

Assuming the prior year's cumulative (gain)/loss was $25,000, the current year's cumulative (gain)/loss is $52,335. The 10 percent corridor is equal to $48,000 (10 percent of the greater of $55,000 or $480,000). Because the cumulative loss is greater than the corridor, the excess amount is recognized as a component of expense. Assuming the average future service is 15 years, the amortization amount would be $289 (($52,335 − $48,000) ÷ 15). Note, however, that the actual APBO is used to calculate the interest cost component.

Prior Service Cost (*Plan Amendment*)

Prior service cost is defined as the "cost of benefit improvements attributable to plan participants' prior service pursuant to a plan amendment or a plan initiation that provides benefits in exchange for plan participants' prior service." For an existing plan, a plan amendment always creates a prior service cost. If a plan is adopted that grants increased benefits only for future years of service, it does not create a prior service cost and costs should be attributed only to future years' service. For example, a new plan that provides an additional $25 per year benefit for each future year of service would not have a prior service cost at adoption.

The prior service cost is the portion of the benefits that is considered already accrued by virtue of the participants' prior service. Prior service cost is the change in the APBO due to a plan amendment or to the establishment of a plan. Note that a decrease in benefits results in a negative prior service cost.

Prior service cost is to be amortized over the expected future service to the full eligibility date of active employees expected to receive benefits under the plan. This is similar to FAS 87, and results in a schedule in which the amortization is higher in the early years, and then drops off in later years as employees are expected to terminate employment. If most or all of the participants are eligible to retire and receive benefits or are inactive, life expectancy is to be used in place of service.

To simplify administration of this rule, an employer may adopt an alternative method that results in more rapid amortization, such as straight-line amortization over the average years of future service to full eligibility for active employees expected to receive benefits under the plan.

If prior service cost is negative, it must first be offset against any existing unrecognized prior service cost, and then against any unrecognized net transition obligation. The balance is amortized as provided above. Immediate recognition of the balance is not allowed.

> **Example 9**: The following example illustrates the standard rule and the straight-line alternative. There are only three participants in the plan; one will become fully eligible in one year, one in two years, and one in three years. If the employer adopts an amendment increasing the APBO by $10,000, the prior service cost is $10,000. This would be amortized as follows under the two methods:

Year	Years of Service During Year	Amortization Standard Method	Amortization Alternative Method
1	3	5,000	5,000
2	2	3,333	5,000
3	1	1,667	0
Total	6	10,000	10,000

> (Average Future Service = 6 ÷ 3 = 2)

> The example does not include any prior service cost from previous amendments.

BALANCE SHEET CONSIDERATIONS

Accrued/Prepaid Expense

Most retiree health plans are not currently funded. Thus, when an amount is expensed (or added to the cost of a manufactured asset) that does not involve a cash outlay, a liability is created. This balance sheet liability is called the "accrued expense for postretirement benefits." Similarly, if cash outlays (for funding or for benefit payments) exceed costs recognized during an accounting period, any existing liability for such benefits is reduced on the balance sheet for the end of that accounting period; if there is still an excess, an asset is created. This asset is called "prepaid expense for postretirement benefits."

The liability for accrued expense will grow based on the difference between the expense and the cash disbursements.

Example 10: The accrued cost at the beginning of the year is $100,000:

	Accrued postretirement benefit cost at 12/31/Z	$ 100,000
+	Net periodic postretirement benefit cost	76,000
−	Contribution (benefit payment)	10,000
=	Accrued postretirement benefit cost at 12/31/Z+1	$ 166,000

Note that all prior service costs and net transition obligation will eventually flow through costs recognized on P&L statements and will consequently become part of the balance sheet liability for accrued expenses. The balance sheet amount will be the cumulative amount expensed less the amount funded (including benefit payments). This will ultimately approximate the APBO.

Minimum Liability

Under FAS 87, there is a minimum liability that must be recognized on the balance sheet. There is no comparable requirement in this Statement.

FOOTNOTE DISCLOSURE

Although accounting for postretirement benefits is done on a plan-by-plan basis, footnote disclosures may be aggregated in most circumstances. All postretirement health plans can be aggregated with all other types of postretirement benefits. Disclosures may be combined for U.S. and non-U.S. plans unless non-U.S. plans are a significant part of the APBO and those plans use significantly different assumptions.

The footnote disclosures include the following:

- A reconciliation of the beginning and ending balances of the APBO that shows, separately, the effects during the year of service cost, interest cost, contributions by plan participants, gains and losses, foreign currency exchange rate changes, benefits paid, plan changes, business combinations, divestitures, curtailments, settlements, and special termination benefits.

- A reconciliation of the beginning and ending fair value of assets showing the effects of actual return on assets, foreign currency exchange rate changes, contributions by the employer and plan participants, benefits paid, business combinations, divestitures and settlements.

- A schedule reconciling the funded status of the plan(s) with amounts shown on the financials. This will include the unrecognized prior service cost, net unrecognized gain or loss, unrecognized transition obligation or asset, and the total recognized accrued or prepaid expense.

- A breakdown, by component, of the net periodic postretirement benefit cost.

- The weighted average of the discount rate, the salary increase rate, and the assumed rate of return on plan assets.

- The assumed health care trend for the next year and a general description of the direction and pattern of future trend rates, together with the ultimate rate and when that rate begins.

- For health care benefits, the effect of a one-percentage point increase and decrease in the health care cost trend rate on the accumulated benefit obligation and the sum of service and interest cost, holding all other assumptions constant.

- The amounts and types of any employer securities included in plan assets, any amount of future benefits covered by insurance contracts issued by the employer, and any significant transactions between the employer and plan during the year.

- A description of any alternative amortization methods used.

- A description of any substantive commitment, such as past practices and history of regular benefit increases.

- The cost of providing any special or contractual termination benefits, and description of the nature of such events.

- An explanation of any significant changes in the benefit obligation that are not obvious from other disclosures.

The health care trend rate to be disclosed is the expected increase of the underlying covered expenses of the plan, **not** the claim costs. To illustrate, the actual valuation may anticipate that plan costs will increase at 8 percent per year, but the plan sponsor would disclose a 7 percent health care trend because the additional 1 percent is due to plan-specific reasons (e.g., frozen deductibles and out-of-pocket limits).

Nonpublic Entities

A "nonpublic entity" is an employer that (a) does not have their stock or securities traded in a public market (e.g., the New York Stock Exchange), (b) does not file with any regulatory agency in preparation for selling their stock or securities in a public market, or (c) is not controlled by any employer covered under (a) or (b).

Instead of using the standard set of disclosures outlined above, a nonpublic entity may elect to disclose an abbreviated list of disclosures.

- The APBO, fair value of assets, and the funded status of the plan(s).
- Employer contributions, participant contributions and benefits paid.
- The total recognized accrued or prepaid expense.
- The net periodic postretirement benefit cost.
- The weighted average of the discount rate, the salary increase rate, and the assumed rate of return on plan assets.
- The assumed health care trend for the next year and a general description of the direction and pattern of future trend rates, together with the ultimate rate and when that rate begins.
- The amounts and types of any employer securities included in plan assets, the amount of future benefits covered by insurance contracts issued by the employer, and any significant transactions between the employer and plan during the year.
- An explanation of any significant nonroutine events, such as plan changes, combinations, divestitures, curtailments, and settlements.

Defined Contribution Plans

A true "defined contribution" plan is one in which the employer's contributions are made during an employee's working career, and the employee has an account at retirement that is used to pay for his or her retiree health plan coverage. The employer contributions are accounted for on a "pay-as-you-go" basis; that is, the expense is equal to contributions to the plan.

If the employer provides any subsidy of the plan after the employee retires or terminates, those subsidies need to be accounted for like a regular retiree medical plan and accrued under the FAS 106 rules.

The disclosure of the contribution must be separate from any other retiree plan and must include a description of any significant change during the year that affects comparability such as a change in the rate of employer contributions, a business combination, or a divestiture.

COVERED PLANS

In comparison to FAS 87, what constitutes a "plan" under FAS 106 is not as clear. FAS 106 applies to all retiree group benefit plans that offer employer-provided benefits to current and future retirees, including their dependents. A retiree group benefit plan may be part of a larger plan that also provides benefits to current active employees. In this case, the benefits paid to active and retired employees will have to be accounted for separately.

The Statement focuses primarily on accounting for single-employer, defined benefit postretirement plans. A single-employer plan is a plan sponsored by one employer for a group of employees, retirees, and their dependents. A defined benefit postretirement plan is a plan that defines the retiree benefits in terms of (1) monetary amounts (e.g., $10,000 of life insurance) or (2) benefit coverage (e.g., $200 per day in the hospital, 80 percent of physician charges).

Substantive Plan

The concept of the "substantive plan" forms the basis of accounting under FAS 106. The substantive plan includes the current and future terms of the plan and the understanding of these terms between both the employer and the plan participants. The substantive plan typically includes the written plan (in the form of plan documents, insurance contracts, and summary plan descriptions). It may also include a "past practice" such as, maintaining a consistent level of cost-sharing between the employer and plan participants or increasing a fixed employer subsidy by medical CPI. Cost-sharing provisions include retiree contributions and plan coinsurance percentages, deductibles, copays, and out-of-pocket limits.

A consistent past practice of increasing or reducing cost-sharing provisions that follows an established policy may be reflected in the substantive plan. However, if these past changes were also accompanied by offsetting changes in other benefits, they **cannot** be considered. For example, if an employer has periodically increased retiree medical plan contribution rates but at the same time increased pension plan benefits, the pattern of future retiree medical contribution rates cannot be considered part of the substantive plan.

An employer's intent to change future cost-sharing provisions may also be part of the substantive plan. In order to include any future changes, there must be evidence that the employer has the ability and the intent to make such changes, and descriptions of the changes are communicated to participants. In assessing whether or not an employer has the ability to change the plan, the auditor will have to consider (1) the plan participants' willingness to accept the change without adverse reaction (such as a strike) and (2) whether or not the plan change will necessitate other offsetting changes (e.g., increasing pension plan benefits) to gain participants' acceptance of the change.

The substantive plan allows the employer to properly reflect its intended cost-sharing policies in the valuation process. This provides partial relief from otherwise assuming that health care costs will increase in the future but plan provisions, such as retiree contribution levels, do not change.

Aggregation of Plans

Many employers have more than one retiree group benefit plan. Some have multiple medical plans, several group benefit plans (e.g., life insurance, dental, vision, and hearing), as well as plans covering different groups of retirees. FAS 106 allows employers to aggregate these plans to some extent for both measurement (plan cost calculations) and disclosure (information disclosed in the footnotes of financial statements) purposes. For measurement purposes, funded plan costs must be calculated separately. Therefore, aggregation is not allowed for any plan that has "assets" under the FAS 106 definition of assets (i.e., restricted and segregated). Unfunded retiree health plans may be aggregated under two conditions:

(1) The plans provide different benefits (e.g., medical, dental; comprehensive, base/major medical) to the same group of employees; or

(2) The plans provide the same benefit to different groups of employees (e.g., identical retiree medical plans provided to union and salaried employees).

For example, a company that provides medical, dental, and vision care benefits to all retirees may aggregate the three plans when calculating the net postretirement benefit cost. This aggregation simplifies the accounting process.

The "same benefit" requirement under condition (2) may be interpreted as a benefit that is substantially the same. That is, a medical plan with a $100 deductible and another medical plan with a $200 deductible may be considered the same – and can be aggregated – because they provide close to the same benefit.

Other retiree group benefits (i.e., non-health benefit plans) may be aggregated under circumstances similar to those described under the health benefit rules. That is, plans providing different benefits to the same employees or the same benefits to different employees may be aggregated.

For disclosure purposes, FAS 106 gives even broader latitude for plan aggregation. In general, all plans may be aggregated for disclosure purposes. However, U.S. plans and non-U.S. plans must be shown separately if the APBO for non-U.S. plans is a significant portion of the total APBO and they use significantly different assumptions.

In addition, an employer that has some plans with assets in excess of the APBO and other plans with assets less than the APBO, may aggregate the plans for disclosure. However, an employer that combines these disclosures must:

- Disclose the aggregate APBO and the aggregate fair value of assets for all of the plans where the APBO is greater than the assets; and
- Disclose the prepaid and accrued costs separately in the financials.

An employer may elect to not aggregate plans in order to provide more useful information.

For most employers, all plans will be aggregated for the footnote disclosures. Note that one of the disclosure items is a detailed description of the net periodic postretirement benefit cost, showing each component separately. Although each component is actually calculated on a plan-by-plan basis, with some aggregation, this disclosure item accumulates each component for each plan. In general, this would not be the same as calculating the total net periodic cost by summing the service costs and APBOs and then applying the provisions of the statement. This is primarily because each plan may have different amortization periods (i.e., different average future working lifetimes) and different gains and losses that may or may not be amortized (due to the "corridor" approach of amortization).

Multiemployer Plans

True multiemployer plans are accounted for on a pay-as-you-go basis. The Statement defines a multiemployer plan as a plan that is usually subject to one or more collective bargaining agreements and to which two or more unrelated employers contribute. Assets are not allocated or restricted to separate employers. In fact, assets contributed by one employer may be used to provide benefits to employees of another employer. A key requirement is that the employer's only obligation is to make contributions to the trust based on hours worked or some other negotiated formula.

The net periodic postretirement benefit cost recognized for multiemployer plans is equal to the required contribution for the year. An employer may disclose the total contribution to a trust (both pension and postretirement). The disclosures should also include a description of any changes that affect comparability, such as a change in the rate of employer contributions, a business combination, or a divestiture.

Multiple Employer Plans

These are groups of single-employer plans that are combined primarily for purposes of broader risk distribution and reduced administrative costs. FAS 106 views this type of arrangement as the same as a single-employer plan—subject to all of the requirements of the statement.

Individual Contracts

The definition of a plan does not include true individual contracts. If the employer has multiple individual contracts with identical terms, however, a plan may be implied, and the Statement will apply.

True individual contracts providing retiree group benefits are accrued individually as deferred compensation, following the terms of the contract. Employers may apply some of the principles of this Statement to the accounting for these contracts.

Non-U.S. Plans

Except for the two-year delayed effective date, there are no special provisions for plans outside the United States. If an employer sponsors a retiree group benefit plan in their non-U.S. subsidiaries, they are subject to all of the provisions of the standard. As a practical matter, retiree group benefit plans are common only in the U.S. and Canada.

BUSINESS COMBINATIONS

If one company acquires another and the accounting is done on a purchase basis, the liability for these benefits will be considered part of the purchase price as in FAS 87.

If the acquisition is reflected under the pooling-of-interests method, there are no special adjustments; in effect, the two balance sheets are simply added together. The pooling-of-interests method is available only in common stock-for-common stock transactions; thus the purchase method is more often applicable.

In accounting under the purchase method, the liability for the benefits of the acquired corporation will be measured as the unfunded APBO for all participants in the acquired company's plans. After the acquisition, this is recognized on the acquiring company's balance sheet as an additional liability (i.e., additional accrued expense for postretirement medical benefits). Note that in this situation there is automatically an additional asset recognized. Because the liability is incurred as part of the purchase price, the assets of the company are written up as well. If this write-up would cause the assets to exceed fair market value, the assets are written up only to fair market value, and the balance is added to goodwill. Consequently, the acquisition of a company with a large unrecognized liability for these benefits will not cause the acquiring company's book net worth to decline, although it may create a large amount of goodwill as an asset, which may eventually have to be written off.

After the acquisition, all of the acquired company's unrecognized bases (i.e., gains and losses, prior service cost, transition obligation) simply disappear under the purchase method. Further, because it is the acquiring company's financials that are relevant, the amount of liabilities or assets the acquired company had previously recognized is no longer important.

Example 11: Assume the Example 4 company is acquired by another company. The funded status of the company's plan would be reconciled with the financials before and after the business combination as follows:

	Before Combination	After Combination
Accumulated postretirement benefit obligation	$ (480,000)	$ (480,000)
Plan assets	55,000	55,000
Funded status	(425,000)	(425,000)
Unrecognized transition obligation	320,000	0
Unrecognized loss	5,000	0
Accrued postretirement benefit cost	$ (104,000)	$ (425,000)

Looking at the retiree medical plan's financial effect in isolation, there appears to be a $321,000 increase in liabilities. Overall, however, there should be an offsetting asset either in the real value of the purchased company or in goodwill that will offset this liability increase.

If the postretirement benefit plan is amended as a condition of the business combination, the total APBO, including the effect of the plan amendment, should be accounted for as a business combination. Otherwise, the accounting will be treated in a two step process: (1) the APBO, before including the effect of the amendment, is accounted for as a business combination, and (2) the change in APBO due to the plan amendment is treated the same as any other plan amendment.

SETTLEMENTS AND CURTAILMENTS

Settlements

As in FAS 88, a settlement is an irrevocable transaction that relieves the employer of the primary obligation to provide the benefits, only if significant risk is eliminated. In FAS 88, the typical settlement involves the purchase of an annuity contract to provide all or a portion of the pension benefits. Settlements will be uncommon for retiree health plans, but they can occur for retiree life insurance plans, where insurance is readily available.

A settlement generally results in a gain or a loss. The maximum gain or loss recognized in such a situation is the unrecognized net gain or loss, plus any remaining unrecognized transition asset. Any unrecognized transition obligation is recognized under the pay-as-you-go minimum cost limits for amortization described above.

The maximum amount of gain or loss is prorated, depending on the fraction of the APBO settled. The net amount is then accounted for as follows: If it's a gain, it is first used to reduce any unrecognized transition obligation. Any amount remaining is taken into earnings. If the net amount is a loss, it is taken into earnings.

As with FAS 88, if the cost of all settlements during the year is less than or equal to the sum of the service cost and interest cost components of the net periodic postretirement benefit cost, gain or loss from the settlements can be ignored. Such a policy must be applied consistently from year to year.

Curtailments

A curtailment is an event that significantly reduces the expected years of service of active plan participants, or eliminates future defined benefit accruals for a significant number of active plan participants. Under FAS 106, prior service costs are amortized on the basis of future service under the theory that these costs are attributable to this future service. This theory ceases to have validity in a curtailment.

FAS 106 provides that all or a portion of prior service cost and unrecognized transition obligation is to be treated as a special loss in the event of a curtailment. If the curtailment results from the termination of a significant number of employees, the loss is the portion of the unrecognized prior service cost attributable to future years of service in the attribution period of the terminated participants (i.e., the amount of prior service cost that would have been amortized over their future service had they stayed in the employ of the employer), plus the portion of any unrecognized transition obligation attributable to remaining service of the terminated employees who were participants on the date of transition (i.e., the amount of the transition obligation that would have been amortized over their service in the future).

If the curtailment is due to the cessation of benefit accruals for a substantial number of employees, the loss is calculated in the same manner, treating employees who have lost benefit accruals as if they had been terminated.

Termination of a large number of employees generally creates a gain, because turnover is higher than anticipated. A curtailment may, however, create either a gain or loss and is measured by the change in the APBO. Special termination benefits are excluded from this calculation—the gain or loss associated with them is accounted for differently (see discussion below). If the gain exceeds any previously unrecognized net loss, it is a curtailment gain. If it is a loss, then to the extent it exceeds any previously unrecognized net gain, it is a curtailment loss.

For purposes of the preceding paragraph, any remaining unrecognized transition asset is treated as an unrecognized net gain.

The loss resulting from earlier amortization of unrecognized past service cost and unrecognized transition obligation and any curtailment gain or loss are then recognized in income. The timing of that recognition is as follows:

- If the net amount is a gain, it is delayed until the employees are actually terminated or the plan amendment ceasing accruals is actually adopted.

- If it is a loss, however, it is taken into income as soon as it is probable that a curtailment will occur and the effect can be reasonably estimated.

SPECIAL TERMINATION PROGRAMS

Postretirement benefits offered as a special or contractual termination benefit (e.g., enhanced retiree medical coverage under an early retirement incentive program) are to be accounted for under paragraph 15 of FAS 88. In other words, the entire cost of these benefits—or the entire increased cost if a portion has already been accrued for the terminating employees—is considered a loss when the employees accept the offer and that amount can be reasonably estimated.

The amount attributable to partially accrued benefits is determined by calculating the APBO after the acceptance of the offer, and subtracting from it a special APBO calculated under the terms of the plan prior to the offer of special benefits, but assuming that the affected employees would terminate at their full eligibility date (or, if already fully eligible, immediately). A special termination program may also result in a curtailment. This would be accounted for as described in the curtailment section above.

Effective Dates

FAS 106 was effective for fiscal years beginning after December 15, 1992 (i.e., starting with the 1993 calendar year for most employers). There was a two-year delay for application to non-U.S. plans and for private employers with 500 or fewer plan participants in all plans (i.e., to calendar year 1995).

> **Comment:** Postretirement health and life insurance benefits are not common in foreign countries other than Canada.

PROPOSED REFORMS TO FAS 106

The FASB believes that the current standards do not provide complete enough information about these benefits. For example, they cite that the standard allows an employer to recognize an asset or liability in its balance sheet that is almost always different than its funded status. The current standard does require disclosure of the funded status of the plans in the notes to the financial statements. The reason for the difference in the balance sheet and the notes is that the standard allows for delayed recognition of certain changes in the obligations and plan assets.

The FASB is recommending at least a two phased project to "correct" the deficiencies in the current FAS 106 standard. The first phase is to be effective in 2006 and 2007. The second phase is under study.

The first phase exposure draft was released in March 2006. It requires employers to move the funded status of the plans from the notes to the balance sheet. This requirement is effective for fiscal years ending after December 15, 2006. A second requirement is that employers may no longer use a measurement date other than the actual fiscal year end. This requirement is effective for fiscal years beginning after December 15,

2006. This will create the need for two measurements for plans currently using non-fiscal year end measurement dates—one for the year end funded status (the fiscal year end) and the other for the plan expense for the next year. For example, for a calendar year fiscal year and September 30 measurement date, the year end 2006 disclosure will be based on the September 30 measurement date. But the 2007 expense must be based on a beginning of year measurement or December 31, 2006. Therefore two valuations will be required at the end of 2006. From a practical perspective, actuarial standards allow a "roll-forward" of valuations for up to three years. Most actuaries will take advantage of a roll-forward methodology for the transition to the new measurement date.

The second phase of the project will focus on:

- Better recognition and display of the elements of benefits in earnings and other comprehensive income

- Better measure of the obligation

- More guidance on assumptions

- Consolidation of trust statements with the plan sponsor's statements

GLOSSARY OF TERMS USED IN FAS 106

Accumulated postretirement benefit obligation (APBO). The present value of benefits expected to be paid based upon benefits accrued to date. This includes the full present value of the expected benefit obligation for retired employees and active employees eligible to retire (or fully eligibility for the benefits, if different), and a pro-rata portion of the present value of the expected benefit obligation for other actives. The pro-rata portion will be based on the ratio of (a) service from date of hire to the valuation date to (b) service from the date of hire to the earliest retirement date, except for those plans that allocate benefits to specific years of service and are "front-loaded." Such plans will follow the allocation formula in the plan. This is the actuarial accrued liability using the projected unit credit cost method. It is equivalent to the projected benefit obligation (PBO) of FAS 87.

Attribution method. The method (a.k.a., actuarial cost method) for assigning postretirement benefits or costs to accounting periods of an employee's service. The method used in this Statement is the projected unit credit cost method, benefit prorate, typically from date of hire to the date an employee receives the greatest employer-provided value (generally earliest retirement age).

Attribution period. The portion of an employee's service over which the EPBO for that employee is allocated. The beginning of the attribution period will generally be the date of hire unless the plan specifically grants benefit credit at a later date. In that case, the beginning will be the date credit begins. The end of the attribution period is the date the employee attains full eligibility.

Cost-sharing provisions. These include any substantive plan provisions that describe how overall benefit costs are shared between the employer and plan participants, such as the level of retiree contributions, plan deductibles, coinsurance percentages, out-of-pocket limits and caps on employer costs.

Curtailment. See *Plan curtailment*.

Discount rate. The interest rate used to determine the present value of future cash flows.

Expected postretirement benefit obligation (EPBO). FAS 106 defines the EPBO as "the actuarial present value as of a particular date of the benefits expected to be paid to or for an employee, the employee's beneficiaries, and any covered dependents pursuant to the terms of the plan." This translates to the actuarial present value as of the measurement date of benefits expected to be paid, based on the expected retirement date for those not yet retired, and as of the measurement date for those who are retired. In other words, the actuarial present value of <u>all</u> future benefit payments.

Full eligibility. The status of an employee after he or she has satisfied all requirements (typically age and/or service) necessary to have earned the right to receive the largest employer-provided benefit the individual will accrue.

Health care cost trend rate. The anticipated rate of future increases in health care costs due to inflation, increased utilization, technological advances, changes in health status of participants, etc. The trend rate to be disclosed in the financial statement is the rate at which the underlying covered expenses of the plan are expected to increase, not the rate at which incurred claims are expected to increase.

Market-related value of assets. The amount of plan assets used to calculate the expected return on plan assets; it is equivalent to the actuarial value of assets. The amount can be either the fair value of assets or a smoothed value that recognizes fair value in a systematic and rational manner over not more than five years.

Measurement date. The valuation date of all values (i.e., service cost, APBO). Generally the date of financial statements, but it may be a date up to three months prior to that date, if used consistently from year to year.

Net transition obligation or asset. The difference between the accumulated benefit obligation as of the date of initial application of the Statement and the amount previously recognized (funded or book reserved).

Per capita health care cost. The expected cost of the health care plan, including claims and administrative expenses. It is intended to be the best estimate of the employer's future experience. Therefore, it will not necessarily be the same as the costs used for the current year's pay-as-you-go budget rates. The statement strongly suggests that costs should be based on age.

Plan. An arrangement that provides for benefits to retirees. It may be written or implied from the practice of paying benefits.

Plan assets. Assets that have been segregated and restricted (usually in a trust) to provide postretirement benefits.

Plan curtailment. An event that either reduces the expected years of future service of active participants or eliminates the accrual of future benefits.

Prior service cost. The increase or decrease in the accumulated benefit obligation due to plan amendment or plan initiation that is attributable to prior service periods.

Service cost. The portion of the EPBO assigned to the current plan year under the attribution method.

Settlement. An irrevocable action that relieves the employer of the primary responsibility for future benefit obligations and eliminates significant risk related to these obligations.

Substantive plan. The defined plan plus written or unwritten past practices and/or future intentions that modify the defined plan. For example, a consistent past practice of increasing retiree contributions or other cost-sharing provisions may reflect a substantive plan. Any intent to change the substantive plan may be anticipated only if there is evidence that the change is feasible, is likely to occur, and that the intent and manner of the change are communicated to plan participants.

Termination benefits. Additional benefits provided by an employer in connection with the termination of employment of a group of employees.

TECHNICAL COMMENTS

FAS 106 valuations utilize some unique calculations. This section provides some more technical detail behind the valuations.

Amortization

Traditional actuarial amortization methods are based on mortgage-type schedules. That is, both principal and interest are included in the calculations. In FAS 106, the amortization of the two components are done separately. The interest component is part of the interest cost in the net periodic postretirement benefit cost formula. The amortization of the principal amount is generally over the average remaining service period of active employees expected to receive a benefit. There are two different periods defined in FAS 106. Gains and losses and the net transition obligation amortization period are to the expected retirement date. Plan amendments are amortized to the full eligibility date.

Average Expected Future Service

The average expected future service is calculated using the following formula.

$$\frac{\displaystyle\sum_{t=0}^{u-x-1}\left\{\sum_{s=t}^{r-x-1}\left[{}_sp_x^{(T)}\sum_d q_{x+s}^{(d)}\times E_{x+s}^{(d)}\right]\right\}}{\displaystyle\sum_{t=0}^{r-x-1}\left\{\sum_d {}_tp_x^{(T)}\times q_{x+t}^{(d)}\times E_{x+t}^{(d)}\right\}}$$

*for all decrements **d**, where*:

x	=	attained age
r	=	age when probability of retirement is 1.00
u	=	retirement age (full eligibility age for amortizing plan amendments)
$E_{x+s}^{(d)}$	=	1.00, if a positive employer-provided benefit is projected to be payable based on termination of employment by decrement d at age $x+s$
	=	0.00 otherwise
${}_sp_x^{(T)}$	=	probability of survival from age x to $x+s$
$q_{x+s}^{(d)}$	=	probability of decrement d at age $x+s$

Note in the denominator that all employees who have reached the ultimate retirement age expectation (the age when the probability of retirement is equal to 1.0, or r as defined above) are not included in the calculation. In addition, for the calculation of average service for plan amendment amortizations, employees who reached their full eligibility age are also excluded.

FAS 106 prescribes that plan amendments are amortized at a percentage for the year derived from the ratio of the expected future service to be worked in that year to the expected future service to be worked in all years from the date of the amendment. To calculate this ratio, the actuary will have to calculate subtotals for each value of t. Due to its complexity, this calculation is seldom performed. Instead, the alternative of a straight-line amortization over the average projected future working lifetime to full eligibility date is almost always used.

The following example illustrates the calculation of the average remaining service. It is taken from the original Actuarial Compliance Guideline No. 3 (ACG No. 3) that has since been repealed.

Amortization Period Examples

The purpose of these simplified examples is to show the calculation of the average remaining service of those expected to receive benefits. They also show the calculation of the number of participants in the current active population.

Age at full eligibility is 55. Single assumed retirement age is 60. No pre-retirement benefit payable, e.g., disability

			To Full Eligibility		To Retirement	
Current Age	No. of Employees	No. Expected to Survive to Retirement[1]	Years to Full Retirement	Service Years	Years to Retirement	Service Years
50	100	80	5	400	10	800
35	100	15	20	300	25	375
25	100	5	30	150	35	175
Total	300	100		850		1,350

Average remaining service to full eligibility
    Total service years   850
    # expected to receive benefits   100
    Average service   8.5
Average remaining service to retirement
    Total service years   1,350
    # expected to receive benefits   100
    Average service   13.5

[1]Number Expected to Survive to Retirement are the active participants as defined in SFAS No. 106.

Attribution Period

The attribution period concept under FAS 106 is somewhat unique in its definition of the accrual period. Traditional actuarial methods calculate the accrual period from date of hire to date of retirement. FAS 106 defines it as generally date of hire to date that the employee earns the right to receive their full benefit. There is some subjectivity to this definition but it is generally a shorter period than the traditional accrual period used in pension valuations. The following chart from the repealed ACG No. 3 illustrates these calculations.

Attribution Examples

In all examples, PVB is defined as the present value of a benefit 100% paid by the employer, i.e., requiring no contributions from retirees.

Example 1

Employer plan provides a noncontributory retiree health care benefit to employees retiring on or after age 50 with at least 20 years of service.

	Employee			
	A	**B**	**C**	**D**
Age at Hire	30	30	25	40
Attained Age	52	40	45	50
Current Service	22	10	20	10
Assumed Age at Retirement	55	55	55	60
Age at Full Eligibility	50	50	50	60
Value of EPBO	PVB	PVB	PVB	PVB
APBO	EPBO	EPBO×(10÷20)	EPBO×(20÷25)	EPBO×(10÷20)
Service Cost	0	EPBO×(1÷20)	EPBO×(1÷25)	EPBO×(1÷20)

Example 2

Employer plan provides a contributory health care benefit to employees retiring on or after age 55 with at least 20 years of service. Although benefits accrue somewhat more quickly in the first 20 years than thereafter, this is not considered disproportionately front-loaded, and attribution is linear.

The values shown for employees A, B, C, and D demonstrate the effect of changing the assumed retirement age for a single employee (or the effect of retirement decrements at those same ages), as do sets E and F, G and H, and I, J, and K.

The employer-provided benefit as a percentage of the cost of coverage is as follows:

Years of Service	Employer-Provided Benefit
20 - 29	50%
30+	70%

Employee	Age at Hire	Attained Age	Current Service	Assumed Age at Retirement	Age at Full Eligibility	Value of EPBO	APBO	Service Cost
A	30	40	10	55	55	PVB×50%	EPBO×(10÷25)	EPBO×(1÷25)
B	30	40	10	57	55	PVB×50%	EPBO×(10÷25)	EPBO×(1÷25)
C	30	40	10	60	60	PVB×70%	EPBO×(10÷30)	EPBO×(1÷30)
D	30	40	10	62	60	PVB×70%	EPBO×(10÷30)	EPBO×(1÷30)
E	30	55	25	55	55	PVB×50%	EPBO	0
F	30	55	25	62	60	PVB×70%	EPBO×(25÷30)	EPBO×(1÷30)
G	20	35	15	55	55	PVB×70%	EPBO×(15÷35)	EPBO×(1÷35)
H	20	35	15	57	55	PVB×70%	EPBO×(15÷35)	EPBO×(1÷35)
I	40	55	15	60	60	PVB×50%	EPBO×(15÷20)	EPBO×(1÷20)
J	40	55	15	62	60	PVB×50%	EPBO×(15÷20)	EPBO×(1÷20)
K	40	55	15	70	70	PVB×70%	EPBO×(15÷30)	EPBO×(1÷30)

Termination Benefits
Special enhanced benefits at termination are frequently a part of an over-all early retirement incentive program (a.k.a., early retirement window, ERW). The plan may allow some employees to retire with retiree group benefits that they were not eligible for prior to the incentive program. The following is an example from the repealed ACG No. 3.

The plan sponsor has a postretirement benefit program that allows participants to receive benefits if they retire from active employment with at least 15 years of service and are age 55 or older. The sponsor's ERW allows participants to receive benefits if they retire from active employment with at least 15 years of service and are age 50 or older. The ERW also reduces the participant contributions to postretirement benefits by $200 a year for the first 5 years of retirement.

Participant A is 50 years of age and has 15 years of service when he accepts the ERW.

Participant B is 55 years of age and has 20 years of service when he accepts the ERW (he is fully eligible).

An assumed retirement age of 60 is used in these examples.

Items	Participant A	Participant B
[1] Age	50	55
[2] Service	15	22
Prior to the ERW		
[3] EPBO[1]	$70,141	$70,347
[4] APBO[1]	52,605	70,347
[5] APBO assuming retirement at elibigility[2]	71,447	95,543
After the ERW		
[6] APBO for postretirement benefit	127,624	95,543
[7] APBO for reduced contributions	810	798
[8] Total APBO under ERW	128,434	96,341
Effect of ERQ under SFAS NO. 106		
[9] Loss on account of termination benefit (current cost [9] = [8] minus [5])	56,987	798
[10] Loss (gain) which is part of normal amortized gain/loss [10]=[5] minus [4]	18,842	25,196

[1]Based on benefit for which participant is eligible, assuming retirement at the expected retirement date.

[2]For Participant A, APBO is based on the benefit for which A is eligible, assuming retirement at the full eligibility date (age 55); for Participant B, APBO is based on the benefit for which B is eligible if retiring immediately without the ERW.

8 OTHER ACCOUNTING

The world of accounting is slowly converging to one global standard – governed by the International Accounting Standards Board (IASB). The IASB historically has been heavily influenced by the accounting in the United Kingdom but the FASB has been working with the IASB recently to seek convergence of standards.

There are also a handful of other accounting standards that currently require some knowledge because they provide a different view than the U.S.-based FAS 106 model.

The IASB statement (IAS 19) on Employee Benefits prescribes the accounting and disclosure rules to be used by employers for their financial statements.

In 1999, the Canadian Institute of Chartered Accountants (CICA) issued their rules for accounting for employee benefits.

In the U.S., state and local government employers must comply with accounting standards established by the Government Accounting Standards Board (GASB). And the federal government follows the Federal Accounting Standards Advisory Board (FASAB) rules.

IASB RULES[1]

This section explains the language and principles of accounting for employee benefits. It is intended to give (financial) executives and other interested parties without an actuarial background an understanding of the impact, on the balance sheet and on the income statement, of applying International Accounting Standard 19 – Employee Benefits (IAS 19) (revised). IAS 19 prescribes the accounting and disclosure by companies

---

[1] The section on the IASB rules is modified from a white paper from Hewitt Associates, *Accounting for Employee Benefits Under IAS 19*, February 2005.

for their employee benefit programs. The section also discusses the parameters and mechanisms that drive the asset or liability recognized on the company balance sheet in connection with an employee benefit program and the benefit expense recognized in the income statement.

It is important to note that IAS 19 (revised) does not address the funding of an employee benefit program – that is, the determination of the cash contributions payable towards an employee benefit program. Funding or cash contributions are often driven by local country funding rules and/or tax legislation.

IAS 19 prescribes how companies should account for their employee benefit programs. An employee benefit program can be established under a formal agreement between a company and its employees (or their representatives), but it may also be an informal practice that gives rise to a constructive obligation to provide the benefits. In addition, local legislation may require that employers provide certain benefits for their employees.

IAS 19 identifies four categories of employee benefit programs:

(1) Short-term employee benefits, for example salaries, paid leave, bonuses (if payable within twelve months of the end of the period) and non-monetary benefits (e.g. medical care, cars) for current employees;

(2) Post-employment benefits, for example retirement benefits and post-employment medical care;

(3) Other long-term employee benefits, for example jubilee benefits, sabbatical leave, long-term disability benefits and bonuses (if payable twelve months or more after the end of the period); and

(4) Termination benefits.

Accounting for short-term employee benefits is generally straightforward, as no actuarial assumptions need to be determined or actuarial valuations performed. Generally, the benefit expense equals the cash payment. There is no specific disclosure requirement for this type of benefit. Short-term employee benefits will not be covered further in this textbook.

For the purpose of accounting under IAS 19 it is important to first understand the nature of an employee benefit program in order to define the category of the employee benefit program and the accounting treatment that applies. This sometimes proves to be a challenge.

Aspects of Accounting for Employee Benefit Programs

IAS 19 addresses three aspects of accounting for employee benefit programs:

- Determination of the amount reflected in the current income statement.

- Determination of the amount recognized on the company balance sheet.

- Description of the information required in the financial footnotes to the corporate financial reports. The disclosure requirements are designed to assist readers of annual reports in accurately assessing the financial position of a company. The required disclosures include expense and liability items, as well as the assumptions used in deriving the results.

All of these aspects will be discussed in more detail in the following sections.

The Role of the Actuary

Although IAS 19 gives substantial guidance, determination of the proper accounting values requires careful planning.

The actuary will be involved in several tasks for determining the benefit expense. The next section will describe the different areas in more detail for the employee benefit programs that have been categorized as (defined benefit) post-employment benefits:

- First, the benefits expected to be paid to each employee are allocated to past and expected future years of employment.

- Second, assumptions are made about future expected experience in areas such as economics and demographics. These are used to project forward an estimate of the benefits to be paid – the future cash flow of the plan – and then to discount these projected benefits to give their present value at the company balance sheet date. IAS 19 provides guidance in the selection of these assumptions, but considerable flexibility is available. For retirement plans, demographic assumptions will generally be the same as those used in the actuarial valuation prepared for funding purposes, while economic assumptions may be quite different. Although the actuary can provide input, the choice of the assumptions remains a company responsibility.

- Third, actuarial valuations are performed to calculate actuarial amounts called the service cost and the defined benefit obligation (DBO). The service cost and the DBO underlie the benefit expense (or income), which impacts the company's profit and loss, and the net liability (or asset). The actuary will also determine the impact on the benefit expense and the net liability of any special events that happen during the year and trigger a settlement or curtailment.

- Fourth, the actuary will prepare all information needed by the company for the IAS 19 footnote disclosures.

Because of the magnitude of the values involved and the flexibility available in setting assumptions, management and the actuary typically communicate closely and on an ongoing basis during this process.

More and more companies appoint a global actuary to help them develop a governance and accounting policy. The global actuary would also coordinate the whole IAS 19 accounting process for all the company's employee benefit programs around the world. This not only tends to provide better quality and consistency in the total IAS 19 reporting of the company, but it also provides valuable information on the employee benefit programs that can help the company manage their employee benefit programs and align them with their business strategy.

Post-Employment Benefits

A post-employment benefit plan can be classified as either a defined contribution or a defined benefit plan. For the purpose of the accounting under IAS 19, it is important to first understand the classification of the benefit plan:

- A defined contribution plan is a post-employment plan under which the company pays fixed contributions. The company will have no legal or constructive obligation to pay further contributions if the fund falls short of providing employee benefits relating to employee service in the current and prior periods, i.e. all actuarial or investment risk lies with the employee.

- A defined benefit plan is a post-employment benefit plan that is not a defined contribution plan.

Any guarantee relating to the benefits provided by what would otherwise be a defined contribution plan, or a practice of topping up the benefits in a particular pattern, may mean that the plan's accounting has to be on a defined benefit basis.

In some cases it will be a challenge for the company to determine whether the post-employment benefit plan should be classified as defined benefit or defined contribution for accounting purposes. This can be a particular issue where some or all of the benefits are insured. The company's participation in some so called "multi-employer plans" or state plans, even if they are defined benefit in nature, will be accounted on a defined contribution basis if the company cannot do defined benefit accounting.

For post-employment defined contribution plans, the accounting is straightforward, as the benefit expense equals the cash contribution payable by the company in respect of the period. The company will have no liability or asset to record on its balance sheet, other than any contributions owed at the year end. A company should disclose the amount recognized as an expense for its defined contribution plans.

For post-employment defined benefit plans, actuarial valuations will need to be performed to determine the benefit expense and the liability or asset to record on the balance sheet. In addition, specific footnote disclosures are required. The following sections describe the accounting process in more detail.

Allocating Benefits to Years of Employment

The cost of the benefits expected to be paid (i.e. the projected benefit) to each plan participant must be allocated to company accounting years. For former employees (retirees and those with vested benefits), this is easy – their benefits at the company balance sheet date are all treated as being in respect of years before that balance sheet date. The expected benefits with respect to a current employee, however, must be attributed to his past and expected future years of employment.

Often, the allocation follows the plan description. For example, if a pension plan provides a pension at retirement of 1% of final pay for each year of employment, IAS 19 will generally allocate the cost of a pension of 1% of final pay to each year of employment. However, there are specific rules as to how expected benefits are allocated to years of employment in some circumstances.

Benefits are allocated over the period from when employment first generates benefits under the plan to when further employment no longer increases the benefit. The allocation follows the plan further unless the formula assigns higher benefits to later periods of service, in which case the benefits are instead allocated on a straight-line basis.

The following examples illustrate this.

(1) A plan provides a pension at retirement of 1% of final pay for each of the first 10 years of employment, and 2% of final pay for each subsequent year. For an employee who commenced employment at age 40 and is expected to retire at age 60, the pension is expensed on the basis of a pension of 1.5% of final pay with respect to each year of employment.

(2) If employment before age 25 does not count towards benefits, IAS 19 similarly attributes no benefit to periods before age 25.

(3) If the plan provides a pension of 1% of final pay for each year of employment, to a maximum of 20% of final pay, the pension is expensed over the first 20 years of employment.

Making Assumptions About the Future

The company will have to set actuarial assumptions which will be used to calculate the variables that underlie the benefit expense. These actuarial assumptions comprise financial (economic) assumptions and demographic assumptions (relating to details of current and former employees).

The actuarial assumptions should be the company's best estimate and should be consistent with each other. IAS 19 provides guidance on how the assumptions must be chosen by the company. In particular, financial assumptions should be based on the market expectations at the balance sheet date as described below.

Discount Rate

In order to measure the liability, the projected benefit must be discounted to a net present value as of the current balance sheet date, using an interest assumption (called the discount rate under IAS 19).

The discount rate should be determined on the company's balance sheet date by reference to market yields on high quality corporate bonds (except where there is no deep market in such bonds, in which case the discount rate should be based on market yields on government bonds). The discount rate should reflect the duration of the liabilities of the benefit program. Fixed-income securities that receive a rating of AA or higher from Standard & Poor's (or Aa or higher from Moody's Investors Service) are generally considered to be a reasonable benchmark to set the discount rate.

Since IAS 19 requires the choice of a rate that reflects market conditions on the company's balance sheet date, it is anticipated that these rates will change regularly—usually every year. If the benefit expense needs to be calculated more than once a year (e.g., if the plan is amended or a significant workforce change occurs midyear), the rate may be changed even more often than annually.

Expected Rate of Return on Assets

When benefits are pre-funded, assets accumulate gradually over the working lifetime of each employee. These assets begin earning returns on the date of the first contribution and continue earning returns until the date of the last benefit payment. Earnings include interest, dividends, capital gains and losses, etc. The effect of these earnings on plan expense can be direct and dramatic. Only the expected return during the year, not the actual return, is considered when determining the current year's benefit expense. IAS 19 requires that this expected return represent expectations at the balance sheet date as to long-term investment returns at the beginning of each year.

The calculation of the plan surplus or deficit at the balance sheet date, and of the expected return for the following year, are based on the fair (market) value of the plan assets at that date.

Salary Increases and Benefit Increases

In order to then predict the plan's benefit stream, it is necessary to make an estimate of the benefit expected to be paid to each individual. In a defined benefit pension plan for example, a typical benefit is based on pay (e.g. 1% of final five-year-average pay for each year of service). IAS 19 requires pension expense for such plans to be based on projected final pay, rather than on current pay. Therefore, pay that the employee will be earning when the benefit comes into payment must be estimated. The effect of the salary increase assumption is direct. The higher the projected salary, the larger the projected benefits which, in turn, produce a higher liability and employer expense.

Salary increase assumptions tend to reflect three underlying components: inflation, merit increases, and promotions. Inflationary increases generally apply uniformly across the workforce. The level of anticipated inflation can vary widely among companies (primarily depending on whether the company focuses on current rates or longer term expected rates).

Increases attributed to individual development are usually larger, as a percent of pay, for younger employees than for older employees. Salary increase assumptions often reflect this declining pattern by age; however, uniform salary scales are also common – in part, because the relatively high termination rates among younger employees reduce the impact of a more refined salary increase assumption.

Benefits payable as an annuity, such as pension benefits, are sometimes linked to inflation or otherwise indexed after they come into payment. For benefits of this type, an assumption must be made about benefit increases after the employee has left employment.

If a plan formula considers only service (e.g. a flat amount payable when the employee completes 10 years of service), the benefit amount is easily projected for each employee reaching a specific age or amount of service. Typically, expense for this kind of plan is based on current benefit levels, so there is no need to develop an actuarial assumption to anticipate future benefit changes. If, however, there has been a clear pattern of changes or a clear commitment to make changes (e.g. if the benefit is indexed), IAS 19 requires recognition of these changes, and a specific assumption may be necessary.

Retiree medical benefits generally do not depend on service or salary. The rate at which the benefits increase depends on the structure of the benefits. For a plan that reimburses medical claims the rate could be equal to the health care cost trend rate, but some plans only provide a flat amount for each retiree, that may or may not be linked to inflation.

Pre-retirement Mortality

Some employees will die before reaching retirement. Mortality rates within the workforce are generally low, particularly in developed countries, and in most employment categories only weakly related to the type of employment. In addition, even large employers rarely have sufficient experience on which to estimate future employee mortality.

As a result, mortality rates are typically derived from standard tables based on nationwide experience rather than employer experience.

While deaths of active employees reduce the expense for benefits payable to (former) employees, that reduction may be offset in part by the cost of benefits payable to survivors.

Termination

People who leave their jobs far outnumber those who die while employed. Few employees hired at age 25 or 30 are likely to remain with the same employer for their full careers. The impact of turnover on plan costs can range from modest to enormous.

Assumptions regarding termination rates are usually based on an employer's own history (especially for large plans), as well as industry norms (more common for smaller plans). Rates vary widely among employers and industries, and they fluctuate over time.

In any organization, economic and personal factors influence whether an employee leaves or stays. Generally, younger employees are much more likely to leave than older employees, second-income wage earners leave before primary wage earners, and short-service employees leave more frequently than long-service employees.

Vesting strongly influences the financial effect of turnover. While uncommon in most types of employee benefits, vesting is a common pension provision in some countries. Upon vesting, an employee acquires a non-forfeitable right to a pension even if the employee leaves before reaching retirement age.

Even though higher turnover results in a reduction in the number of employees reaching retirement age, the resulting cost savings are partially offset by the vested benefits provided to some former employees. When pension plan benefits are based on final average pay, however, the benefit available to a former employee with vested benefits generally will be based on much lower pay than for the employee who stays until retirement.

Disability

Disability is another reason employees leave the active workforce before reaching retirement. This factor generally has a relatively modest impact on cost, because few employees leave work due to permanent disabilities. In addition, disabilities are more frequent among older employees, who often have worked long enough to earn most of their retirement benefits. As with mortality, few employers have adequate experience on which to base disability assumptions, and standard tables are generally used.

Retirement

Since benefit payments under retirement programs begin when an employee retires, and the employee's active service ends on this date as well, an assumption has to be made about the age at which employees are expected to retire. Since earlier retirement means more years of benefit receipt and less years of active service, the retirement age directly influences the cost of the plan. And of course, death, termination, and disability prevent employees from reaching retirement.

If a retirement plan provides early retirement benefits, retirement experience is often influenced by the provisions of the plan, including eligibility for early retirement and the reductions imposed. If benefits are low, employees tend to remain on the active payroll until normal retirement age or beyond. If the plan provides relatively rich benefits for early retirees, more are encouraged to leave early.

The employer who goes even further by providing medical care and survivor benefits to early retirees is likely to experience a somewhat higher incidence of early retirements than if such coverages are not available.

In addition, the financial condition of the individual, the opportunity for full- or part-time employment after retirement, and the availability of social security benefits at an earlier retirement age play key roles in the individual's retirement decision.

The plan's actuary and the employer should agree on an assumption regarding retirement age, or a series of retirement ages, that takes all these factors into account.

The larger the proportion of the active workforce that reaches the age at which retirement is subsidized, the greater the expense the employer must bear to provide those benefits.

Duration of Benefit Payments

Based on the assumptions discussed to this point, the actuary is able to estimate the number of employees who will reach decrement age and the size of the benefits they will be paid. Benefit may be paid as a lump sum, but also as an annuity, as is common for retirement benefits. For the latter the expected duration of benefit payments needs to be determined, based on a mortality assumption.

In the case of retirement benefits, post-retirement mortality is often based on the same table used to predict pre-retirement mortality. Using different tables for pre- and post-retirement mortality might make sense in some cases – for example, in industries where there are unusually high on-the-job risks.

Calculation of Benefit Expense (or Income)

The benefit expense is usually calculated as of the first day of the company's fiscal year, using the assumptions that were selected as of the last day of the prior fiscal year for year-end disclosure. Experience that evolves during the year does not affect the current-year expense; the experience affects results in subsequent years. The expense for the year may change if the plan is amended during the year or if a one-time employer event, such as an early retirement window, occurs. If an amendment or event is recognized midyear, expense is recalculated at that time, and the new calculation is used for the rest of the year.

The total benefit expense for a post-employment defined benefit plan is the sum—positive or negative—of the following components:

Service Cost

The service cost for a plan participant is the present value of the projected benefit treated as earned by an employee over the year, discounted to the balance sheet date, less any contributions payable by the employee. The service cost for the plan is the sum of the service costs for all the participants. This cost is dependent on the age of each participant, since the present value of a unit of benefit increases as the likelihood of remaining with the employer until retirement increases and the time to payment (years of discounting) decreases with each year of age.

The total of all past years' service costs is the past service liability. This liability is referred to as the defined benefit obligation or DBO. If the plan covers only inactive participants, the benefit obligation is the same as the present value of all future expected benefit payments.

The DBO is therefore the discounted value of the projected benefit that has been allocated to the participants' active employment before the balance sheet date. For an active employee, the service cost is the discounted value of the projected benefit that has been allocated to one year of service.

Interest Cost

Because all of the liabilities involved are present values, they grow with the passage of time. The interest cost reflects the expected growth in past service liabilities that will occur over the course of the next year. It is calculated by multiplying the DBO by the discount rate.

Expected Return on Assets

If a plan has assets, these assets are expected to grow with investment earnings, and those earnings are an offset to the other cost components of the plan. If a plan is sufficiently well-funded, the expected return might completely offset all other costs, resulting in a negative plan cost (an income). Since the actual earnings on the fund are not known at the time expense is determined, these earnings are estimated. The estimate is calculated by applying the expected rate of return on assets assumption to the fair value of assets, adjusted for contributions and benefit payments made during the year. The expected return and, therefore, the benefit expense are not subsequently adjusted when the actual return on assets is known at the end of the year. Instead, the difference between estimated and actual return becomes a gain or loss to be recognized in a subsequent period.

Amortization of Past Service Costs

If a benefit plan is amended to increase or decrease the benefits allocated to service that has already been rendered, an additional liability (or credit) is created that will not be accounted for in future service costs. IAS 19 requires this additional liability to be separately amortized over the average period until the benefits become vested. Consequently, if the benefits vest immediately following the plan amendment, the past service cost (or credit) should be recognized immediately.

Amortization of Gains and Losses

When experience differs from assumptions, an adjustment needs to be made. Gains and losses arise from a number of sources. These include pay or claims increases different from those assumed, higher or lower turnover than assumed, or a return on assets other than the rate assumed. An additional source of gains and losses arises when there is a change in assumptions, most notably a change in the discount rate, which often happens annually.

Due to the degree of uncertainty in the measurement of postemployment benefit plans, such as retirement plans, there may be substantial volatility in gains and losses arising from those plans. Therefore, for post-employment defined benefit plans, IAS 19 allows plans to amortize only unrecognized gains and losses that exceed 10% of the greater of the defined benefit obligation or the fair value of assets. The unrecognized gains or losses are the aggregate of all the gains or losses that occurred in the past less the amounts already amortized.

This does not mean that increases or decreases in the values of assets and liabilities are totally ignored – the interest cost will reflect the new liability value and the expected return on assets will reflect the new asset value. The amortization of gains and losses is re-determined each year by dividing the unrecognized amount of gain or loss (after recognition of the 10% corridor, if so chosen) by the average future working lives of the population.

Faster amortization of gains and losses is permitted but must be done on a consistent basis each year.

Amendments to IAS 19 in December 2004 introduced an additional option. If they prefer, companies can instead recognize gains and losses immediately, but through a second performance statement called the *Statement of Recognised Income and Expense* rather than through the profit and loss account.

Other Components of the Expense

Other items also included in the expense might be:

- The effect of any curtailment or settlement;

- Effect of any unrecognized asset due to the asset ceiling[2];

- Expected return on any reimbursement right recognized as an asset.

Net Liability (or Asset)

The net liability (or asset) is the amount a company has to recognize on its balance sheet.

The net liability (or asset) can be derived in two ways.

Reconciliation of the Funded Status

The funded status of the plan is the defined benefit obligation (DBO) reduced by the plan assets, where the plan assets are measured at fair value.

The net asset or liability on the balance sheet date is then determined as the difference between the funded status and any unrecognized amounts on the balance sheet date.

The following example illustrated the reconciliation of the funded status for a funded and for an unfunded plan for a company with balance sheet date December 31, 2004.

---

[2] A notable (and complex) feature of IAS 19 is the asset ceiling. If the amount to be recognized in the balance sheet is an asset, IAS 19 requires that this asset is limited to the total of cumulative unrecognized losses and past service costs together with the present value of economic benefits available, either in the form of refunds or reductions in future plan contributions.

	Funded Plan 31.12.2004	Unfunded Plan 31.12.2004
Defined benefit obligation	€ (1,500)	€ (1,500)
Fair value of plan assets	800	0
Funded status	(700)	(1,500)
Unrecognized past service cost	150	150
Unrecognized (gain) or loss	200	(200)
Net Asset or (liability)	€ (350)	€ (1,550)

Reconciliation of the Net Liability (or Asset)

The net liability (or asset) on the balance sheet date is also determined as the net liability (or asset) on the previous fiscal year's balance sheet, increased with this fiscal year's benefit expense (including any expense for curtailments or settlements) and reduced by the company contribution to the plan paid during the fiscal year. If the plan is unfunded then the company contributions are equal to the benefit payments made by the company.

Settlements and Curtailments

Certain events may occur that result in a disruption of normal patterns of exit and retirement of employees and the continuing accruals of plan benefits for employees. IAS 19 requires that events like settlements, curtailments, and the provision of certain termination benefits are reflected separately.

What is a Settlement?

A settlement occurs when an employer enters into a transaction that eliminates all further legal or constructive obligation for part or all of the benefits provided under a defined benefit plan. It occurs most frequently in pension situations. Two examples are:

- The employer pays a lump sum to a participant in lieu of continuing monthly benefits.

- The employer purchases non-participating annuities from an insurance company.

Expensing for Settlements

IAS 19 requires accelerated recognition of any unrecognized gains or losses, including any gains or losses created by the settlement. For example, the payment of a lump sum from a pension plan could result in a loss to the plan, if the amount of the lump sum exceeds the discounted present value of the pension otherwise payable.

If the entire benefit obligation is settled, all remaining unrecognized gains or losses are recognized immediately. If only a portion of the benefit obligation is settled, then typically that same percentage of the previously unrecognized gains or losses is recognized immediately, in addition to the gain or loss arising from the settlement.

For example, assume a plan has a €60,000 unrecognized loss prior to a settlement, and this loss is being recognized at the rate of €4,000 per year for the next 15 years (assuming the company has decided not to operate a 10% corridor). As a result of an annuity purchase, half of the plan's benefit obligation is settled, and the plan also incurs an additional €15,000 loss (because the annuities cost more than the present value of the pensions discounted at the interest rate used under IAS 19). Then, €45,000 would be expensed immediately as a settlement loss (i.e., the loss arising from the settlement of €15,000 plus half of the previously unrecognized loss of €60,000 or €30,000). The remaining unrecognized loss of €30,000 would be recognized in expense as €2,000 per year for the next 15 years.

What is a Curtailment?

A curtailment occurs when an employer either:

- Is demonstrably committed to make a material reduction in the number of employees covered by a benefit plan; or
- Amends the terms of a defined benefit plan such that a material element of future service by current employees will no longer qualify for benefits, or will only qualify for reduced benefits.

Curtailments are often linked with a restructuring exercise and an employer will therefore account for a curtailment at the same time as for a related restructuring. Two examples of a curtailment are:

- An employer terminates a large number of employees, for instance by closing a plant or offering an early retirement window.

- An employer terminates or freezes the plan, and no future benefit credits are earned.

A curtailment and a settlement may occur together or separately. For example:

- An employer buys annuities for all vested benefits—this is a settlement, but not a curtailment.

- An employer shuts down a plant, but maintains the benefit plan for all employees, including those terminated due to the plant shutdown—this is a curtailment, but not a settlement.

- A plan is terminated and annuities are purchased for all participants—this is both a settlement and a curtailment.

Expensing for Curtailments

Under IAS 19, recognition of certain costs is spread over the expected future working lifetimes of the active participants. If those working lifetimes are suddenly cut short, the deferred costs associated with those years—both unrecognized past service costs and unrecognized gains or losses—must be recognized immediately.

As for a settlement, if the curtailment only affects some of the employees covered by the plan, IAS 19 requires recognition of a proportionate share of the previously unrecognized past service costs and gains or losses to be recognized immediately—in addition to any gain or loss arising from the curtailment. However, it is not always clear how this proportionate share should be calculated. Typically the portion of the unrecognized amounts that is recognized immediately is based on the percentage reduction in the defined benefit obligation.

A gain (i.e. a reduction in the defined benefit obligation) may arise if, for example, a number of employees are terminated prior to vesting. A loss (i.e. an increase in the defined benefit obligation) may arise if the terminated employees receive benefits at an earlier age than was expected in a plan that subsidizes early retirement. (Not included here are termination benefits, which are discussed below.)

Gains or losses resulting from a curtailment or settlement should be recognized when the curtailment or settlement occurs.

Impact on Ongoing Expense

Because settlements and curtailments cause immediate recognition of previously deferred amounts, the amounts included in ongoing expense with respect to past service costs and recognition of gains or losses will change. In addition, changes in the size of the workforce are likely to reduce the ongoing service cost component of expense.

Footnote Disclosure Under IAS 19

One of the IASB's objectives is to provide disclosures that allow users of a company's financial statements to understand the extent and effect of an employer's provision for employee benefits. To accomplish this, IAS 19 requires extensive disclosure in the footnotes of a company's financial statements.

Disclosure information is determined at the end of the company's fiscal year. Assumptions are chosen that are appropriate as of that date, and these assumptions may be different from the assumptions that were chosen at the beginning of the fiscal year and used to determine expense. In particular, certain economic assumptions such as the discount rate will likely change annually.

Frequently, employers will not wish to (or will not have time to) calculate the liabilities based on year-end employee census data. IAS 19 allows reasonable approximations based on earlier data.

Required disclosures include the following:

- A reconciliation of the assets and liabilities (DBO) of the plan to the amount of the net liability (or asset) recorded on the employer's balance sheet.
    - The net liability (or asset) recorded on the balance sheet represents the difference between the amounts previously expensed and cumulative cash contributions. For example, if the company has cumulatively expensed more than it has cumulatively contributed, the balance sheet will show a net liability.

— The difference between the surplus or shortfall of assets over liabilities in the plan and the asset or liability recorded on the company balance sheet represents amounts that will be recognized through the plan's expense in future accounting periods. These amounts include the cost of plan amendments and actuarial gains and losses.

- A reconciliation showing the movements during the period in the net liability (or asset) recognized in the balance sheet. Amendments to IAS 19 issued in December 2004 will extend this from 2006 to require reconciliations showing the movements of both assets and liabilities, rather than just the net liability.

- The amount of expense for the fiscal year, along with all the components of benefit expense as well as the effect of curtailments and settlements.

- The assumed discount rate, salary increase assumption, expected long-term rate of return on plan assets and increases in benefits in deferment or in payment.

- For plans providing health care benefits to retirees: medical cost trend rates.

- Amendments to IAS 19 issued in December 2004 will also require from 2006 a breakdown of the asset value between asset classes, and a description of how the expected return on assets was determined.

Other Long-term Employee Benefits

Other long-term employee benefits include for example jubilee benefits (special awards at anniversary dates in Europe), sabbatical leave, long-term disability benefits and bonuses (if payable twelve months or more after the end of the period). The accounting under IAS 19 for long-term employee benefits is similar to that for postemployment benefit programs. However, a number of differences exist. The main differences are:

- Past service costs concerning long-term employee benefits are always recognized immediately.

- The measurement of long-term employee benefits is usually not subject to the same degree of uncertainty as the measurement of postemployment benefits. Therefore, gains and losses arising from other long-term employee benefits are recognized immediately.

Termination Benefits

Termination benefits are dealt with separately in IAS 19 because the event that gives rise to an obligation is the termination itself rather than employee service.

Termination benefits are recognized when (and only when) an employer is demonstrably committed to either:

- Terminate the employment of an employee or group of employees before normal retirement date; or

- Provide termination benefits as a result of an offer made in order to encourage voluntary redundancy.

An employer is demonstrably committed to a termination when (and only when) a detailed formal plan exists for the termination, without a realistic possibility of withdrawal.

It is worth noting that some employee benefits are payable regardless of the reason for the employee's departure. The payment of such benefits is certain (subject to vesting or minimum service requirements) but the timing of their payments is uncertain. These benefits are sometimes described as termination indemnities or gratuities, but under IAS 19 they are treated as postemployment benefits rather than termination benefits.

As termination benefits do not provide an employer with future economic benefits (i.e. active service of employees), the entire present value of termination benefits is recognized immediately as an expense.

CICA Rules[3]

The Canadian Institute of Chartered Accountants (CICA) introduced its accounting treatment for postretirement and postemployment benefits when it adopted Section 3461 of its Handbook. The new rules, effective for fiscal years beginning on or after January 1, 2000, requires employers to charge the cost of all postretirement benefits and certain postemployment benefits against income over the working lifetime of employees.

---

[3] The section on the CICA rules is modified from a client bulletin from Hewitt Associates issued June 15, 1999 entitled, "*CICA Issues New Accounting Rules for Postretirement and Postemployment Benefits.*"

Under the prior accounting rules, employers only needed to charge the cost of pension plans over the employees' working lifetime.

For most employers, the new rules will mean:

- A dramatic increase in the expense for postretirement benefits other than pensions (generally referred to as "other postretirement benefits"); and

- A more volatile pension expense, and likely a higher pension expense in the short-term.

Section 3461 modifies existing rules for defined benefit pension accounting and leads to more volatility in the annual pension expense. In the short-term, this added volatility is likely to translate into a somewhat higher pension expense. Changes may be even more dramatic for postretirement benefits such as health care for retirees, unless the employer has already been applying existing U.S. reporting standards. (Most Canadian employers were expensing these benefit costs only when the benefits are paid, which is after the employees retire. This is no longer acceptable.)

The new standards also apply to postemployment benefits—benefits that are paid after employment but before retirement. Examples include self-insured long-term disability plans, supplemental unemployment benefits, and continuation of health care to survivors on the death of an employee. For many employers, the additional expense associated with these benefits will be negligible.

Overview of the Rules

The new standards harmonize Canadian accounting practice with U.S. Financial Accounting Standards Board (FASB) requirements. The major changes reflected in Section 3461 are:

Employers will be required to charge the cost of other postretirement benefits over the working lifetime of the employees. Prior to Section 3461, there was no Canadian accounting standard for postretirement benefits other than pension plans, so current-claims-basis accounting was the norm. The new Canadian standard for other postretirement benefits mirrors U.S. FAS 106.

The expense calculation takes into account expected future medical costs, not just the cost of benefits today. It also includes an accrual for all active employees, reflecting the benefits they are expected to receive in retirement based on the likelihood they will stay employed until eligible for postretirement benefits. The combination of projected medical cost increases and inclusion of the entire workforce produces a much larger expense than determined under the current practice of expensing only current claims of current retirees.

Similarly, prior to Section 3461, there was no Canadian accounting standard for postemployment benefits such as health care after termination of employment (but before retirement) and compensated absences. The new rules for postemployment benefits mirror U.S. FAS 112, whereby the accounting treatment depends on whether the benefit vests or accumulates. (In the U.S., few employers followed this accounting treatment because they determined that the costs were not material.)

Benefits that vest or accumulate, such as sick days that are paid out at termination, or termination allowances paid to all employees, will be charged over the employees' working lifetime in a similar fashion as postretirement benefits. Terminal accounting (recognizing the full cost when the event occurs) can be used for postemployment benefits that do not vest or accumulate. Examples include self-insured long-term disability plans, paid parental leave, and survivor health care benefits.

Section 3461 modifies Canadian pension accounting standards to mirror U.S. standards. In particular, the basis for selecting the discount rate will be current settlement rates instead of a stable long-term discount rate assumption. Also, there will be a separate assumption required for expected return on assets. (The current standard does not address the use of a different expected rate of return on assets.)

The reported pension expense figure will be more volatile under the new rules than under the current reporting standard because the discount rate will be re-evaluated each year based on market interest rates at the measurement date.

Many employers currently use a higher discount rate for Canadian pension accounting purposes than could be justified based on current interest rates for high-quality bonds. These employers are likely to see an increase in pension expense in the short-term.

Section 3461 provides explicit guidance that the accounting costs of a benefit plan must reflect the substantive plan as well as the written plan. For example, a regular pattern of ad-hoc pension indexing provided every three to four years could require the employer to recognize the cost of future increases in advance. Similarly, a written or oral commitment regarding future plan changes should also be reflected. Regular negotiated pension increases, however, are not considered part of a plan's terms until such increases are negotiated and agreed to by the employer and its employees. Because of this, employers will need to be very clear in communicating benefit plans and managing employee expectations.

More detailed disclosure will be required, particularly for other postretirement and postemployment benefits, since there has been no guidance and no disclosure requirement for these benefits in the past.

Canadian employers who have been reporting figures for U.S. financial statements will find that Section 3461 is very similar to the U.S. rules. Many employers that have been preparing figures for U.S. reporting purposes have already been applying U.S. accounting rules for other postretirement and postemployment benefits for Canadian financial statement purposes. These organizations will see little change under the new rules.

Transition Rules

When the new standards were adopted, there was a difference between the accrued benefit obligation and the fair value of assets. This amount, less any amount already recognized on the balance sheet under the old accounting standards, was treated as a Transition Obligation (or Transition Asset, if the fair value of assets exceeds the accrued benefit obligation and any previously recognized accrued benefit asset). Employers who have been accounting for postretirement benefits on a current-claims basis likely had a large Transition Obligation for postretirement benefits.

The transition rules are very flexible. However, the same transition treatment must be used for all benefit plans (pension, other postretirement and postemployment benefits). The three transition options are:

- **Prospective Application**. The Transition Obligation (or Asset) is amortized over the expected average remaining service lifetime of the employee group. Any previously unamortized amounts under the old accounting standards are incorporated into the new transition amount. Hence, any old amortization schedules no longer apply.

- **Retroactive Application**. The Transition Obligation (or Asset) was taken as a one-time charge to the opening retained earnings. Restatement of financial statements for prior periods was encouraged but was not required.

Retroactive application was very attractive if the employer had a large Transition Obligation. Because the Transition Obligation can be charged against opening retained earnings, and not against current year expense, reported earnings was not affected. Future expense will be lower if the Transition Obligation was recognized as a one-time charge against opening retained earnings.

- **Match U.S. Figures**. The transition rules allow the initial Canadian recognized and unamortized values to be set equal to the U.S. values if the employer has been using different figures under FAS rules for U.S. accounting purposes. This option allows employers to use one set of accounting figures for both Canadian and U.S. purposes.

The ability to apply the new standards retroactively or adjust the opening balances to match figures used for U.S. reporting purposes was very attractive. Because the transition treatment must be consistent for all benefit plans, employers needed to evaluate all benefit plans before January 1, 2000 to determine the most advantageous transition treatment.

Early adoption for postretirement benefits provided more flexibility in transition. When U.S. companies adopted FAS 106, most used the retroactive adoption process. Some companies that adopted this approach, and then later reduced postretirement benefits, found that the rules allowed them to record a very low level of ongoing cost—the old, rich plan had been charged to prior earnings, and the reduction in benefits was then amortized as a benefit to future earnings.

Section 3461 Compared to U.S. Standards

Since a primary objective of adopting Section 3461 was to harmonize Canadian and U.S. accounting standards, there are very few remaining differences between accounting treatment in the two countries. However, two significant differences still exist:

- Canadian standards place a limit on the accrued pension asset that can be recognized on the balance sheet. This is not a change from current Canadian practice; it means that there is a limit on how much income can be generated by a pension plan in a surplus position. This limit is based on the present value of future accruals plus the amount of surplus that the entity has a legal right to withdraw. In the U.S., FAS 87 (the pension accounting standard) does not place any limit on the prepaid pension asset.

- Canadian standards do not prescribe an additional minimum liability calculation. U.S. rules under FAS 87 require plan sponsors with poorly funded pension plans to recognize a minimum liability on the balance sheet which, in some cases, may impact the reporting of comprehensive income.

Aside from these two significant differences, and a number of less significant differences (such as technical differences in curtailment accounting rules), Section 3461 is largely successful in harmonizing Canadian standards with the equivalent U.S. standards. Employers who are subject to both Canadian and U.S. standards may be able to reconcile the remaining differences with their auditors to produce one set of figures for both countries.

GASB Rules[4]

In June 2004, the Governmental Accounting Standards Board (GASB) approved the final set of accounting standards applicable to "other postemployment benefits" (OPEBs), which are non-pension benefits provided after a person leaves employment, such as retiree health care. The final standards are explained in two statements:[5]

- Statement No. 43, *Financial Reporting for Postemployment Benefit Plans Other Than Pension Plans*, and

- Statement No. 45, *Accounting and Financial Reporting by Employers for Postemployment Benefits Other Than Pensions*.

---

[4] The section on the GASB rules is reprinted with permission from copyrighted material submitted by Gabriel, Roeder, Smith and Company (GRS). It is derived from a briefing paper written by Paul Zorn, issued August 2004 [16] and from another paper written by James J. Rizzo for the Florida Governmental Finance Officers Association Newsletter, October/November 2005 [36].

[5] This briefing paper summarizes accounting standards published by the Governmental Accounting Standards Board. While it offers information about key aspects of the standards, it is not intended as a comprehensive description. Statements Nos. 43 and 45 may be ordered from the GASB's web site (www.gasb.org) or by calling 800-748-0659.

The GASB is a seven member Board selected from individuals knowledgeable about state and local governmental accounting issues. The Board establishes standards for measuring and reporting information presented in the financial reports of state and local governments, in essence setting generally accepted accounting principles. If a state or local government does not follow the GASB's standards, this will be noted in the audit letter that accompanies the government's annual financial report and may affect the government's credit rating.

Statements Nos. 43 and 45 provided detailed descriptions of the approved standards for the "measurement, recognition and display" of OPEB-related expenses/expenditures,[6] liabilities, assets, note disclosures, and other financial information published in the government's annual financial report. Statement No. 45 applies to governmental employers or other sponsors of OPEB benefits. Statement No. 43 applies to OPEB plans through which the benefits are provided. Although the statements do not require that the benefits be prefunded, they do define a financial framework for assessing the costs, design, and sustainability of OPEBs offered by state and local governments.

The GASB's standards apply to all forms of other postemployment benefits, but apply differently depending on whether the benefit is provided through a defined benefit OPEB plan or a defined contribution OPEB plan. In a defined benefit OPEB plan, the plan pays specific benefits to members after employment in a manner that does not depend solely on assets held in individual accounts. For example, the plan may pay 50 percent of the retiree's monthly health insurance premiums over the life of the retiree. In a defined contribution OPEB plan, the benefits are based solely on amounts held in individual accounts.

For benefits provided through defined benefit OPEB plans, the GASB's primary requirement is that the long-term cost of retiree health care and other OPEBs be measured and reported on an accrual basis using actuarial methods and assumptions applied in essentially the same way they are applied to state and local government pension plans. Most of the OPEB standards are written for this form of OPEB benefit.

---

[6] Whether a cost is recognized as an expense or expenditure depends on the underlying accounting basis of the financial statement in which it is displayed. If the financial statement reflects the full accrual accounting basis, the cost is recognized as an expense. If the financial statement reflects the modified accrual basis, the cost is recognized as an expenditure.

For benefits provided through defined contribution OPEB plans, the GASB requires the cost of the benefits be measured and reported as the employer's required contributions to the individual accounts. In essence, the accounting and reporting rules that apply to defined contribution OPEB plans are the same as apply to defined contribution retirement plans, as presented in GASB Statements Nos. 25 and 27.

Other Postemployment Benefits

The GASB defines other postemployment benefits as:

- Postemployment Health Care Benefits such as medical, dental, vision, hearing, and other health-related benefits whether or not provided separately from a defined benefit pension plan, and

- Other Postemployment Non-Pension Benefits such as life insurance, disability, and long-term care, but only if provided separately from a defined benefit pension plan. If provided through a defined benefit pension plan, the accounting rules related to defined benefit pension plans apply.

The GASB specifically excludes "termination offers" from the OPEB definition. Termination offers include benefits provided to employees as inducements to terminate employment (e.g., severance pay and early retirement incentives).[7] If such offers affect an existing OPEB plan, (e.g., by increasing the costs of retiree health care due to retirements that are earlier than would otherwise occur), the additional plan costs are recognized in accordance with the OPEB standards.

The GASB includes "implicit rate subsidies" in their OPEB definition, when annual health care premiums are based on a blended rate for both active employees and retirees. This is particularly relevant in situations where employers provide retirees with access to health care and charge them premiums based on a blended rate for both active employees and retirees. Although it may seem that the retirees are paying the full cost of

---

[7] The GASB's definition of OPEB also excludes the conversion of a terminating employee's unused sick leave credits to an individual account for payment of postemployment benefits. Instead, this conversion is treated as a "termination payment" and handled under GASB Statement No. 16. If the unused sick leave is used to provide for or enhance a defined benefit form of OPEB, however, (e.g., by converting it to service credit for retiree health care benefits) the resulting benefit is subject to the OPEB standards.

coverage, it is likely the blended premium will be less than the premium for retirees alone.

The GASB originally proposed excluding the implicit rate subsidy from the OPEB standards in situations where retirees pay 100 percent of the blended premium. In the final standards, however, the Board reversed this decision and now requires the subsidy to be included as a benefit subject to the OPEB standards, regardless of whether retirees pay 100 percent of the blended premium.

Government Retiree Health Care

The largest component of OPEB is retiree health care. Several surveys indicate that the majority of state and local governments provide some form of health care benefits for retirees. According to the Government Finance Officers Association's 1998 publication, *Prefunding Retiree Health Benefits*, 74 percent of state governments and 57 percent of local governments provide health benefits to retirees over age 65. Approximately the same percent provide health benefits to retirees under age 65.

Many of the arrangements were developed at a time when employers could sponsor retiree health care programs at a relatively low cost, often only a few tenths of a percent of active member payroll. Currently, however, many retiree health care sponsors pay 5 percent to 10 percent (or more) of payroll for these benefits. Moreover, health care costs for employers and retirees are likely to continue increasing due to an aging population, ongoing medical cost inflation, increased utilization of medical services, and other factors.

The GASB's General Framework

Currently, most governmental employers report OPEB costs as current expenses/expenditures and finance them on a pay-as-you-go basis. The GASB has long been concerned that this approach does not accurately reflect the magnitude of these costs or their long-term nature. The GASB sees OPEB benefits as similar to pension benefits in that they are accrued while the employee is working and paid after the employee leaves service or retires. Consequently, it argues that the costs of the promised benefits should be recognized when the employer receives the services (i.e., when the benefits accrue), rather than years later when the benefits are paid. The GASB has also been concerned that the employers' financial statements do not provide information about the accrued OPEB liabilities and the extent to which these liabilities are funded.

Because of the apparent similarities between pensions and OPEB, the GASB modeled the OPEB standards on its standards for pensions, as presented in GASB Statements Nos. 25 and 27. This is intended to make the standards easier to implement and interpret, since the OPEB standards will involve similar procedures, measurements, and financial reporting requirements.

Actuarial Valuations and Parameters

The GASB's primary requirement is that the long-term cost of retiree health care and other OPEB benefits be determined on an actuarial basis using methods and assumptions that are constrained in the ways described below. For OPEB plans with 100 or more total members,[8] an actuarial valuation would be done to calculate the employers' "annual required contribution" (ARC) associated with the benefit promise, as well as the actuarial accrued liability, actuarial value of assets, and other related information using the following parameters:

- **Substantive Plan** – this is the basis for determining the benefits to be included in the valuation. It is the terms of the plan as understood by the employer and members at the time of the valuation, as evidenced by written documents and communications, and including established patterns of cost sharing between the employer and members.[9] Changes in plan terms may be included to the extent they have been made and communicated to employees. Legal or contractual limits ("caps") on the employer's share of the benefits may also be included, if the limits are assumed to be effective given their record of enforcement and other relevant circumstances.

- **Valuation Frequency** – valuations must be done at least every two years for OPEB plans with 200 or more total members (including

---

[8] OPEB plans with fewer than 100 total members are allowed to use an alternative method for determining required contributions and accrued liabilities, as explained later.

[9] In some cases, plan documents may be out-of-date, poorly worded, or not defined in all situations. Consequently, professional judgment may be required to determine the substantive plan based not only on written documents but also on other communications and administrative practices. Clarification may require formal action by elected officials, may take time, and would need to be communicated with plan members. This process is best started as soon as possible.

active employees, terminated vested members, and retirees), and at least every three years for plans with fewer than 200 total members.

- **Actuarial Methods** – six actuarial methods are allowed: entry age, attained age, frozen entry age, frozen attained age, projected unit credit, and aggregate.[10] If the aggregate method is used to determine the contribution, the entry age method must be used to determine the actuarial accrued liability and unfunded liability that is reported in the notes to the employer's financial statements.

- **Actuarial Assumptions** – as guided by the Actuarial Standards Board, the assumptions should be based on the experience of the covered group (to the extent data are available) and reflect long-term future trends. Moreover, retiree benefit projections should be based on claims costs or on age-adjusted premiums.

- **Investment Return Assumption** – should reflect the long-term yield on investments expected to fund the benefits, considering the nature and mix of the expected investments. Both the investment return assumption and other economic assumptions should reflect the same inflation assumption.

- **Amortization Period** – the maximum period allowed for amortizing the unfunded actuarial accrued liability is 30 years. If a significant decrease in the actuarial liability results from a change in the actuarial cost method or method used to value assets, a minimum 10-year period is used to amortize the decrease in actuarial liability.

- **Actuarial Value of Assets** – must be a market-related measure (i.e., current market or a market-smoothing method).

A key point is that the investment return assumption should reflect the long-term yield on the investments that are expected to be used to finance the benefits. In this regard, the assumption is based on:

(1) **Plan assets** where the employer's funding policy is to consistently contribute amounts at least equal to the ARC and the assets are held in a trust or equivalent arrangement;

(2) **Employer assets** where the employer is funding on a pay-as-you-go basis, or where the assets are not held in a trust or equivalent arrangement; or

---

[10] See Chapter 9 for descriptions of each of these methods.

(3) **A proportionate blend** of plan and employer assets where the employer is contributing an amount greater that the pay-as-you-go rate but less than the ARC.

An "equivalent arrangement" is one in which employer contributions are irrevocable, dedicated to providing plan benefits, and legally protected from creditors of the employer(s) or plan administrator. Monies earmarked in the general fund or in another fund without these protections would not be considered plan assets held in a trust or equivalent arrangement.

Plan assets will generally consist of diversified equity and long-term fixed income securities, whereas employer assets are often restricted to short-term, fixed income securities. Consequently, the standards allow a significantly higher investment return assumption to be applied to funded OPEB plans where the assets are held in a trust or equivalent arrangement than to unfunded plans or those where the assets are not held in trust. Use of the higher investment return assumption would result in significantly lower actuarial liabilities and annual required contributions.

Standards for Employers Sponsoring or Participating in OPEB Plans

The GASB draws a distinction between the standards that apply to employers that sponsor or participate in OPEB plans and the standards that apply to the plans themselves. Essentially, employers must measure and report the long-term costs of the benefits and the extent to which the employer has contributed to meet those costs. OPEB plans must report the amount of assets that have accumulated to provide benefits, annual inflows and outflows, and the funded status of the plan. Generally, for these purposes, the same actuarial methods and assumptions are required for both the plan and its participating employer(s).

The standards for employers depend, in turn, on whether the OPEB plan that they participate in is a single-employer plan, agent multiple-employer plan ("agent plan"), or cost-sharing multiple-employer plan ("cost-sharing plan"). A single-employer plan is a plan that serves one employer. An agent plan is a plan that serves multiple employers, under which separate actuarial valuations are performed to determine the required contributions of each participating employer. A cost-sharing plan is a plan that serves multiple employers, under which a single actuarial valuation is performed for all employers combined. Under a cost-sharing plan, a single annual contribution rate is billed to all participating employers.

Employers in Single and Agent OPEB Plans

For governmental employers participating in single and agent OPEB plans, two key OPEB measures are calculated and included in the employer's financial statements:

- **The OPEB Cost** is the annual required contribution (ARC) determined by an actuarial valuation conforming to the GASB's parameters, with certain adjustments described below. The OPEB Cost is the basis for determining the employer's annual OPEB expense/expenditure shown in the employer's financial statements.

- **The Net OPEB Obligation** is the difference between the OPEB Cost and actual annual employer contributions to the OPEB plan, accumulated from the effective date of the OPEB standards.[11] The Net OPEB Obligation is the basis for determining the OPEB liability (or asset) shown in the employer's financial statements.

If the employer has a Net OPEB Obligation, the OPEB Cost must be adjusted annually to reflect interest accrued on the Net OPEB Obligation from the start of the year (with some additional adjustments). Unlike the GASB's pension standards, under which employers had to calculate and report a Net Pension Obligation for the 10-year period prior to the standard's effective date, the GASB does not require employers to calculate a prior Net OPEB Obligation, although an employer may elect to retroactively compute the Net OPEB Obligation.

In addition to requiring that government employers measure and report the long-term costs of retiree health care and other OPEBs in their financial statements, the OPEB standards also require other disclosures in the employer's annual financial report, including:

- **Notes to the Financial Statements** – summarizing plan provisions, authority for plan changes, significant accounting policies, contributions, reserves, investment concentrations, funded status, funding progress, actuarial methods, and actuarial assumptions.

---

[11] In order to count against the Net OPEB Obligation, employer contributions must be made to a trust (or equivalent arrangement) or used to pay benefits or premiums.

- **Schedule of Funding Progress** – showing actuarial accrued liabilities, actuarial value of assets, unfunded accrued liabilities, funded ratio, covered payroll, and unfunded liabilities as a percent of covered payroll for the three most recent actuarial valuations.

- **Schedule of Employer Contributions** – showing annual required contributions and employer contributions as a percent of the ARC for the three most recent actuarial valuations.

Employers in Cost-Sharing OPEB Plans

As noted earlier, a cost-sharing plan is a plan that serves multiple employers, under which a single actuarial valuation is performed for all employers combined. As a result, the benefits promised by individual employers are not valued separately. Instead, a single contribution rate is billed to all employers participating in the plan.

Instead of requiring employers in cost-sharing plans to individually value their OPEB Costs, the standards provide that these employers recognize their contractually required contribution to the cost-sharing plan as their OPEB expense/expenditure. Moreover, the employer's OPEB liability is the difference between the contractually required contributions and contributions actually made, rather than the Net OPEB Obligation.

However, if the assets of the cost-sharing plan are not held in a trust or equivalent arrangement, the OPEB rules for employers participating in an agent plan would apply to each participating employer. As a result, individual actuarial valuations would be required, and each employer would have to calculate and report its OPEB Cost and Net OPEB Obligation.

Standards for OPEB Plans

GASB's standards describe an "OPEB plan" as the trust or equivalent arrangement through which assets are accumulated to finance other postemployment benefits, and benefits are paid as they come due. Assets that are not irrevocably set aside in a trust or equivalent arrangement are considered employer assets, rather than plan assets.[12]

---

[12] OPEB plans that are not administered as trusts (or equivalent arrangements) should be reported as agency funds. Employer contributions to agency funds do not count against the employer's Net OPEB Obligation.

The standards apply to all types of defined benefit OPEB plans, including single employer, agent, and cost-sharing OPEB plans. If the OPEB plan is administered and funded solely by the employer, then the financial statements for the OPEB plan would be included in the employer's financial statements. If the OPEB plan is administered and funded through an entity outside the employer, then the OPEB plan would be reported in the outside entity's financial statements, to which the employer could refer in its own financial statements.

The standards require the following to be included in the OPEB plan's financial report:

- **Statement of Net Plan Assets** – showing the OPEB plan's assets, liabilities, and net assets. Investments are reported at fair value. Liabilities only include current liabilities and not unfunded actuarial accrued liabilities. (Note: unfunded actuarial accrued liabilities are shown in a separate schedule of funding progress, discussed below.)

- **Statement of Changes in Net Plan Assets** – showing additions to and deductions from assets, as well as the net change in assets. Additions include employer and employee contributions, investment income, and other additions. Deductions include benefit payments and administrative expenses. Investment expenses are shown separately as a reduction to income.

- **Notes to the Financial Statements** – summarizing plan provisions, authority for plan changes, significant accounting policies, contributions, reserves, investment concentrations, funded status, funding progress, actuarial methods, and actuarial assumptions.

- **Schedule of Funding Progress** – showing actuarial accrued liabilities, actuarial value of assets, unfunded accrued liabilities, funded ratio, covered payroll, and unfunded liabilities as a percent of covered payroll for the three most recent actuarial valuations.

- **Schedule of Employer Contributions** – showing annual required contributions and employer contributions as a percent of the ARC for the three most recent actuarial valuations.

Alternative Measurement Method for Small OPEB Plans

Employers in single-employer plans with fewer than 100 OPEB plan members (including active employees, terminated vested members, and retirees) may choose to use an alternative method for measuring annual required contributions and related OPEB liabilities. This was intended to ease the cost of complying with the standards for very small plans. Employers that use the alternative method must disclose its use in the notes to their financial statements along with the basis for all significant assumptions. Appendices in the GASB statements illustrate the calculations and assumptions to be used under the alternative method.

Implications

The GASB's OPEB project will likely have a significant impact on retiree health care plan design, sponsorship, and funding by governmental employers and plans. Because the standards require the calculation and display of the plans' annual required contributions and Net OPEB Obligations, a greater portion of OPEB plans will probably be prefunded. Also, because the standards allow a higher interest rate to be assumed for assets held in a trust or equivalent arrangement, it is likely that employers will hold their retiree health care assets in trust and invest them in a diversified mix of securities. It is also likely, however, that rapidly increasing retiree health care costs and their disclosure in governmental financial statements will cause employers to reevaluate the design of their OPEB plans.

Effective Dates

The OPEB standards will be phased-in, with the effective dates determined by the total annual revenues of the participating employer, as follows:

Total annual revenue of the sole or largest participating employer in the plan in the first fiscal year ending after ending after June 15, 1999	OPEB Statement will be effective for that employer for periods beginning after	OPEB Statement will be effective for that plan for periods beginning after
Phase 1 Governments – $100 million or more	December 15, 2006	December 15, 2005
Phase 2 Governments – $10 million or more, but less than $100 million	December 15, 2007	December 15, 2006
Phase 3 Governments – Less than $10 million	December 15, 2008	December 15, 2007

For example, a participating employer with a July 1 to June 30 fiscal year and total annual revenues of $75 million for the fiscal year ending June 30, 1999, would need to incorporate the OPEB employer standards into its financial statements for the fiscal year starting July 1, 2008, and ending June 30, 2009. The GASB's standards pertaining to OPEB plans would have to be incorporated into the OPEB plan's financial statements one year earlier – for the fiscal year starting July 1, 2007, and ending June 30, 2008.

Implementation Guide

The Implementation Guide issued by the GASB in the summer of 2005 includes 258 questions and answers and nine appendices (238 pages in all). The following are some of the key issues addressed in the Implementation Guide.

Some pension plans provide a health insurance supplement. If a pension plan makes or promises such payments without any proof of insurance expense or claims, then it is subject to the Pension Statements No. 25 and 27, not the OPEB Statements No. 43 and 54, regardless of being called a health insurance subsidy. If, however, such payments require some proof that the member has incurred some expense (e.g., to gain a tax advantage), then the employer contributions and accumulated assets used for that purpose must be separated from pension purposes and treated as OPEB for accounting purposes. [Q&A 7, 10-13, 15-18]

There are several subtleties in the guide's section on Timing and Frequency of Actuarial Valuations and the section on Benefits to Be Included. As one example, in practice, an actuary performs an actuarial valuation "as of" a given date, say October 1, 2005, called the valuation date. The resulting expense and disclosure information may be applicable to the employer's financial statements for the year ending September 30, 2006 or 2007. So the employee/retiree census data and plan asset values, if any, are determined as of the valuation date and the actuarial present values and actuarial accrued liabilities for the projected benefits are calculated as of the valuation date October 1, 2005.

Due to a lag in engagement and data collection, the actual work may not be undertaken until some time after the valuation date, say during February 2006. The Implementation Guide makes it clear that the OPEB plan provisions (who is eligible for coverage, at what level, for what premium, etc.) which are to be valued by the actuary are not those in effect on the valuation date but those plan provisions adopted and communicated by the employer at the time the actuary is doing the work, February 2006 in this case. So, if the employer adopts and communicates a change to the plan provisions after the valuation date but prior to the time when the actuary is doing the work (say January 1, 2006), then that change must be recognized in the actuarial calculations. This may become important when scheduling changes to the plan provisions. [Q&A 49]

There is an interesting clarification in the Guide concerning what is an "employer contribution in relation to the ARC," especially for unfunded plans. The old news is that the "Annual OPEB Cost" is the amount that is expensed on the employer's books, and is mostly made up of the "Annual Required Contribution" (ARC). It is also old news that the "employer contribution" in relation to the ARC offsets that expense. The clarification is that this is defined as the amount of the employer's subsidy for the current year's retirees for the current year. That portion of the annual OPEB cost that is not offset by the employer contribution in relation to the ARC flows down directly into the Statement of Net Assets. At that point, it is called a net OPEB obligation.

Prefunding

Naturally, if the OPEB plan is prefunded with a trust into which the employer makes deposits (as is done with a pension trust), then the employer's cash deposit into the trust is the employer contribution in relation to the ARC and has the effect of offsetting the annual OPEB cost. If the funding policy calls for a large enough deposit into such a trust, then it may completely offset the expense.

When the OPEB plan is unfunded, however, (i.e., when there is no trust fund to build up assets for the payment of future employer subsidies) determining the employer contribution was unclear to some. There had been some discussion and responses from GASB's OPEB Advisory Committee as to what actually is credited against the expense for an unfunded plan.

Statement No. 45 says that in such a case, the employer contribution includes "…payment of benefits directly to or on behalf of a retiree or beneficiary…" The news in the Implementation Guide is that the employer contribution (which offsets the expense) for an unfunded OPEB medical plan, for example, is:

- The age-adjusted premium paid for the year for all covered retirees and their dependents reduced by the actual retiree contributions charged for the year (or the employer-provided expected per capita cost), whenever a fully insured health plan is used to provide the benefits, or

- The actual claims paid for the year to or on behalf of retirees and their dependents reduced by the actual retiree contributions (and presumably reduced by any retiree/dependent stop loss reimbursements) on an accrual basis, whenever a "risk retention" health plan is used to provide the benefits. This includes health plans that are typically called self-insured, partially self-insured and even certain other types of insured contracts.

This is just one more reason to separate medical and prescription drug claims records for retirees and their dependents from those records for active employees for reporting purposes. [Q&A 60 and 61]

GASB chose not to answer how to account for the receipt of the Federal Prescription Drug Subsidy under Medicare Part D in the original Statement. FASB had already provided guidance on that topic. But due to the uniqueness of governmental accounting, GASB chose to defer guidance until the matter is studied further.

Small Groups

For some governments, a non-actuarial estimate can be useful for measuring the magnitude of the OPEB liability before implementation. A fully compliant actuarial valuation can seem expensive if an employer just wants a general idea of the size of the expense and liability numbers. It is possible that use of the alternate method will result in reduced actuarial fees and increased audit fees. Whether or not there would be a net reduction in fees is not yet known.

So an estimate (based on actuarial principles) can be very useful to management prior to actual implementation. Prime candidates for such an estimate are those employers who provide just the so-called "implicit rate subsidy," and no more. These employers permit retiring employees to continue medical coverage but charge them the blended or group rate.

GASB Statement No. 47

In June 2005, the GASB adopted an accounting standard that must be considered in connection with any program intended to provide incentives to retire or otherwise terminate employment early (sometimes called Early Retirement Incentive Plans or Early Retirement Windows). It also must be considered in connection with any program of severance pay or other such compensation for involuntary termination. These are called "termination benefits" and are governed by the new Statement No. 47. But at times, it can be unclear whether, for accounting purposes, the benefit is a pension benefit (No. 27), an OPEB (No. 45) or a termination benefit (No. 47).

The first determination that should be made is "for what purpose" the benefit is given. The issue turns on whether the benefits are provided as part of an employee's total compensation for prior services or as an inducement to hasten the termination of their employment. If, as compensation for prior service, the value should be allocated to prior years as under No. 27 (for pensions) or No. 45 for (OPEBs). But if the benefits are provided to employees as an inducement to termination, then the value should be addressed under No. 47 (Termination Benefits), and recognized in the financial statement for the period in which the termination offer is accepted.

For involuntary terminations, such as certain privatizing transactions or closures or individual employee situations, the value of the termination benefits should be recognized in the financial statements for the period in which the employer becomes obligated to provide the benefits to terminated employees.

There is an exception to all this when the termination benefits constitute an enhancement to an existing pension or OPEB program. In those cases, they should be reflected under Statements No. 27 or 45, respectively. For example, an early retirement incentive plan offered to employees over age 50 with 25 years of service might provide free medical coverage for a five-year period following the election to retire under the plan.

But if there is already a retiree medical program that charges retirees a specified premium for continued coverage, then this feature of the incentive plan is merely an enhancement to the existing OPEB and should be addressed under Statement No. 45. On the other hand, a lump sum incentive payment made out of general assets of the employer would probably qualify as a termination benefit and be governed by Statement No. 47.

FASAB RULES[13]

The Chief Financial Officer's Act of 1990 requires that federal governmental agencies produce financial statements. Among other things, the financial statements must account for the assets and liabilities of pension and other retirement-related benefits. The Federal Accounting Standards Advisory Board (FASAB) was created to consider and recommend accounting principles for the federal government.

FASAB No. 5 establishes the required actuarial cost method and assumptions for measuring and reporting the accrual cost of these benefits. The standard requires the use of the aggregate entry age level cost method and requires immediate recognition of plan amendments and actuarial gains and losses.

---

[13] Statement of Federal Financial Accounting Standards No. 5, *Accounting for Liabilities of the Federal Government*, Federal Accounting Standards Advisory Board, September 1995.

9 ACTUARIAL METHODS AND ASSUMPTIONS

The purpose of this chapter is to provide a basic understanding of actuarial methods and assumptions that may be used to value retiree group benefit plans for accounting and funding purposes. As background, it provides a brief review of actuarial methods and assumptions used in pension valuations. These are then compared to those used in group benefit plan valuations. The chapter will also explore additional assumptions that the actuary should consider in valuing retiree group benefit plans.

The methods and assumptions described in this chapter provide the basic framework for developing retiree group benefit obligations. Different approaches may be necessary to develop funding versus expense values due to legal or accounting constraints. The accounting and funding chapters describe these specific constraints.

To gain a greater understanding of the actuarial mathematics involved, other material on pension mathematics should be studied.[1] Many principles discussed in that material may be applied to retiree group benefit valuations.

GENERAL BACKGROUND

The valuation of retiree group benefit plans combines the actuarial principles of pension and group benefit mathematics. The projection and allocation techniques used to value pension plans are used, combined with group benefit plan forecasting procedures.

Pension actuaries have probably done the most work in this area. This was a natural evolution because of the similarities in technique between the two types of valuations. Group actuaries have more recently become involved because of the potential impact on the design and financing of these plans after the valuation work is complete. With increasing atten-

---

[1] See, for example, *Pension Mathematics for Actuaries* by Arthur Anderson [3].

tion to retiree group benefit plans by the accounting and legal professions, it is becoming more important to select assumptions that correctly reflect expectations for both the short- and long-term.

Group actuaries are better qualified to forecast the short-term financials of these plans and pension actuaries can provide valuable input regarding long-term expectations. The result of this cross-discipline valuation is an increasing need to utilize a team of pension and group actuaries in retiree group benefit projects.

This chapter is divided into the following sections:

- Actuarial assumptions for pension plans
- Actuarial assumptions for life and health plans
- Actuarial methods for pension plans
- Actuarial methods for life and health plans
- Selection of actuarial assumptions
- Selection of actuarial methods
- Experience gains and losses
- Summary

ACTUARIAL ASSUMPTIONS FOR PENSION PLANS

There are several assumptions that are shared between pension plan and retiree group benefit plan valuations. This section provides a brief discussion of the typical pension plan assumptions. The next section discusses how these assumptions impact retiree group benefit plan valuations as well as describes other assumptions that are unique to retiree group benefit plans.

Pension plan benefits are generally paid over a period that may extend 30-50 years in the future. As a result, assumptions must be chosen that reflect what the actuary expects to happen during the entire time-period. Pension actuaries have been making these assumptions for over seventy years now. These assumptions are usually divided between two basic sets: (1) economic and (2) demographic or personnel-related assumptions.

Economic assumptions for pension plans may include the following:

- inflation,
- investment earnings rate or funding discount rate,
- salary increase, and
- Social Security increase.

Demographic assumptions include:

- termination/turnover,
- mortality,
- disability, and
- retirement incidence.

The remainder of this section briefly discusses each assumption and its purpose within the pension valuation framework.

Inflation

The inflation assumption provides the base for all other economic assumptions. After the inflation assumption is chosen, the other economic assumptions will be considered as two components—inflation plus the real rate of return. General inflation over the last 50 years has averaged about 3.0 to 3.5 percent. Many economists expect that future long-term inflation will be higher than that level, often citing rates in the 4 to 5 percentage point range. The actuary should select an inflation rate that he or she feels most comfortable with, and base all other assumptions on this rate. Currently, inflation assumptions of 3 percent to 4 percent are common.

Discount Rate

This is the interest assumption used to discount all future benefit payments in any present value calculation. In a pension valuation for funding purposes, it represents the investment return expected from monies put into a trust fund over the next 30 to 50 years. As discussed above, it can be thought of as consisting of inflation plus real rate of return components. Different types of investments would dictate different levels of real rates of return. For example, a portfolio of stocks would have a different real rate than a portfolio of short-term government securities. Most pension plan valuations assume real rates of return between 1 percent and 5 percent.

For financial statement accounting, a discount rate similar to the above is selected for determining present values. This rate, however, is based on high quality fixed income investments that are currently available rather than the actual expected return of the plan's portfolio. This rate may be subject to change annually whereas, the funding discount rate assumption is only changed occasionally (perhaps only reviewed every three to six years). Accounting discount rates have been between 2 and 4 percentage points above the inflation rate.

Salary Increase

The salary increase assumption is used to project benefits at retirement for pension plans that base the benefit calculation on pay. If a pension plan is not based on pay, a salary increase assumption would generally not be used. Some actuarial cost methods use the salary increase assumption to allocate costs to different accounting periods. This assumption is very dependent on the participants included in the pension plan. Real salary increase assumptions in the range of 0 percent to 3 percent are common. In addition, for a salaried workforce, the increase assumption usually varies by age – decreasing with age as the effects of experience and promotion decline.

Social Security Increase

Many pension plans provide some form of integration with government benefits (e.g., Social Security in the U.S. and the Canada Pension Plan in Canada). This integration may be a direct offset of actual government benefits or different benefit accruals over and under government benefit earnings levels. Estimates are therefore needed for general inflation and wage increases because that is how government benefits are generally determined. The general inflation rate should be the same as the inflation assumption already chosen. General wage increases are different than the salary increase assumption of the employer. These wage increases are an average of increase for the entire national workforce. The valuation salary increase assumption is based on an individual employee's progression from hire date to retirement. The general wage increase assumption is usually in the range of 0 percent to 2 percent in addition to inflation.

Termination/Turnover

This assumption is for current employees who are expected to leave their employer before reaching retirement age. They may or may not have earned a vested benefit under the plan. This assumption is very dependent upon the type of workforce included in the valuation. Since younger and shorter service employees tend to change jobs more frequently, termination assumptions are often related to age and service. Termination rates of 30 percent to 50 percent are common for young employees with short service. Likewise, termination rates of zero are typical for older employees with long service. Rates also vary by employment conditions. For example, retail stores and fast food operations have much higher turnover that a typical salaried workforce.

Mortality

This assumption has its greatest impact after an individual retires. Before retirement, it produces little impact on the present value calculations because the rates are very low. General industry mortality tables are usually used in pension plan valuations because few employers have enough participants to develop their own mortality tables. The RP-2000 Mortality table is the most commonly used table today. The documentation accompanying these tables provides for alternatives, including blue collar/white collar splits, variation in pension amount and mortality projections. Some valuations are still using a version of the 1983 Group Annuity Mortality Table (1983 GAM), primarily with projection of mortality improvement.

Disability

Some pension plans provide a special benefit if an employee becomes disabled while covered under the plan. This requires an assumption of disability incidence and an assumption regarding recovery from disability. Disability rates under pension plans are typically low because of their restrictive definition of disability which usually requires a person to be totally and permanently disabled. The definition under a typical long-term disability plan is usually more lenient in requiring a person to be unable to perform duties of their own job for a short period of time (usually two years) and then unable to perform the duties of any work. Rates are usually developed through employer experience for large plans. Industry tables such as the Railroad Retirement Disability tables are used when experience is not available. The RP-2000 Mortality Table also includes disabled mortality rates.

Retirement Incidence

This represents the probability that an individual will retire during a given year. This rate is generally dependent on age and, sometimes, service. The assumption is usually developed based on the employer's own experience. Retirement incidence rates are generally low from the initial age of retirement eligibility (1 percent to 5 percent) through age 61. Rates at age 62 usually jump to 30 percent to 50 percent, because this is the first age a person can retire under social security in many countries (including the U.S. and Canada). Rates at 63 and 64 are lower, and rates increase dramatically again at age 65 and over. An "average" retirement age assumption is often satisfactory for pension plans, especially if no "subsidies" are given for early retirement. Some pension plans provide subsidies for early retirement in the form of reductions from normal retirement age that are less than an actuarial equivalent, others provide free supplemental benefit payments. If the plan includes one of these forms of subsidy, extra care is required by the actuary to select appropriate assumptions to reflect the increased cost of this benefit. If an early retirement subsidy is changed, it is likely that the retirement assumptions should be changed to reflect a different pattern of retirement.

ACTUARIAL ASSUMPTIONS FOR LIFE AND HEALTH PLANS

Retiree group benefits, just like pensions, are paid 30 to 50 years in the future. Therefore, these assumptions also must be chosen to reflect what the actuary expects to happen over the long-term. In general, a retiree group benefit plan valuation will use assumptions consistent with the pension valuation. There are also some very important additional assumptions required because of the nature of group benefits.

The economic assumptions used for pension plans that are also used for retiree group benefit plans are:

- inflation,

- discount rate, and

- salary increase.

Demographic assumptions include:

- termination/turnover,

- mortality,

- disability, and

- retirement incidence.

In general these assumptions are used in the same manner as in a pension plan valuation. For retiree group benefit valuations, however, each of the above assumptions may play a different role, in terms of significance, than in pension valuations. Therefore, it is very important that the actuary understands the impact each assumption will have on the retiree group benefit plan valuation. Rules of thumb traditionally used by pension actuaries may not produce accurate results if applied to retiree group benefit plan valuations. The following explains the differences, if any, of these assumptions in a retiree group benefit valuation.

Inflation

General inflation (not including health care inflation) plays the same role in a retiree group benefit valuation. Used in terms of these valuations, the inflation only represents the general inflation increases in the future. It does not include additional general medical inflation or any other increases due to health care utilization, technology or cost-shifting.

Discount Rate

Again, this is generally the same as in pension plans. An exception is made if the valuation is intended for determining the funding requirements of a retiree health plan. Limitations imposed by the Deficit Reduction Act of 1984 (DEFRA) subject certain retiree health funds to taxation. In these cases an actuary would use an after-tax rate of return instead of the customary before-tax rate used in pension plan valuations.
For FAS 106 purposes, the discount rate used in the actuarial present value calculations (obligations in FAS 106 terminology) should represent the rate available on current, high quality, fixed income securities. Common measures that are tracked are 30-year Treasury bills, Moody's AA bonds and PBGC immediate annuity rates.

Salary Increase

The only use for the salary increase assumption in retiree health valuations might be to allocate plan costs to different periods for prefunding purposes. This type of allocation by pay is discussed in the section on actuarial methods. If a retiree life insurance plan has benefits based on pay, the salary increase assumption used in the valuation should be consistent with the assumption used in the pension valuation.

Termination/Turnover

This assumption is generally the same as the pension plan. Since an individual who terminates from employment before retirement generally does not get any retiree group benefit plan benefits, it is important that this assumption closely represent actual terminations.

For cases where the pension plan turnover assumption is based on a liability weighted experience analysis, care should be taken that the results are valid for a retiree group benefit plan valuation. A reason that the table may not be valid is that, if it is an age-related table, the high turnover during an employee's early years may not be properly reflected for retiree group benefit plan purposes. This is because the liability weighting should be higher for low service employees under the typical retiree group benefit plan than under a pension plan.

Mortality

Mortality should also represent actual expectations. As in pensions, pre-retirement mortality, which is low, is generally not critical. Postretirement mortality becomes more critical because of the nature of health benefits. Mortality for an individual 30 years after retirement in a pension plan isn't as critical as it is in a retiree health plan. The reason is that pension benefits generally do not have a "cost-of-living" adjustment as do health benefits. Therefore, the value of the $1 benefit thirty years from now under the pension plan may only be worth $0.25 (or less) in today's dollar versus the full $1.00 in a retiree health valuation (assuming health costs increase at the same rate as inflation). If health costs are assumed to increase even just 1 percent more than general inflation, the $1.00 benefit today is worth $1.35 thirty years from now. For retiree group benefit plans that have implemented a "cap" on the employer obligation (e.g., the company will not pay more than the amount they paid in 2000 for any individual), the affect of mortality on the obligations will be similar to pension plans.

Disability

Disability may or may not be significant in a retiree group benefit valuation. Individuals who become disabled are usually covered under the active plans. Under some plans, they are considered to be disabled retirees and are covered under the retiree plan. If the disabled person is covered under the retiree plan, the actuary should consider the additional cost in the valuation because of impaired health. Since a disabled person could be very young, the coverage period under the retiree plan will be very long. They may also be covered under a government plan (e.g., Medicare covers disabled persons after 29 months in the U.S.). The primary point in selecting the disability assumptions is that they could be more significant in retiree group benefit valuations than in pension valuations. Because of differing disability requirements, the disability assumptions may also be different than under the pension plan.

Medical Claim costs for those under disability range from 8 to 12 times the average active cost rate in the first few years of disability and grade down rapidly to around two times active costs in about five years. Dependents may also be eligible for coverage at standard claim cost rates.

Retirement Incidence

A pension plan usually has reduction factors for employees who retire before age 65. These factors are intended to actuarially adjust the age 65 benefit at early retirement. Under most retiree group benefit plans, an employee retiring at age 55 receives a much greater total retiree benefit than an employee retiring at age 65 because the actuarial present value of benefits increases dramatically the younger a person is at retirement, especially under a retiree health valuation. This is in large part due to the availability of enhanced government benefits in the U.S. and Canada (Medicare starting at age 65 in the U.S. and post-65 drug benefits in Canada). Therefore, the retirement incidence rate becomes more important in retiree group benefit valuations because the level of benefit is not adjusted by retirement age. A pension plan valuation may be able to use an implicit assumption of actuarial equivalence by assuming everyone retires at age 65, but a retiree group benefit valuation definitely cannot.

In addition to the above assumptions that are used in pension plan valuations, a number of other assumptions must be established for a retiree group benefit valuation. Economic assumptions include:

- current retiree plan costs,
- current retiree contributions,
- Health care cost trend rate,
- Medicare Part B premium increase, and
- retiree contribution increase.

Additional demographic assumptions are:

- plan participation,
- spouse plan continuation after death of retiree,
- dependent children plan termination, and
- health plan options (if not considered in plan costs above).

The remainder of this section will discuss these additional assumptions in more detail.

Current Plan Costs and Contributions

A pension plan benefit is generally based on an employee's service and, sometimes, pay at retirement. Likewise, the retiree life insurance amount is generally based on salary at retirement. The life insurance amount may reduce after retirement to a minimum level. Typical retiree health plan benefits, however, are based on whatever the health plan costs are at the time of retirement. In order to determine what that amount might be, the actuary must develop a realistic estimate of both the current plan costs and the retiree contributions, and project them into the future.

Retiree and dependent contributions are generally a flat dollar amount depending upon whether or not the retiree is eligible for Medicare. The plan sponsor should have these amounts readily available. There should also be a policy for how these amounts are determined (e.g., 10 percent of expected plan costs). This policy may be written or unwritten. For purposes of FAS 106, if the policy is unwritten, there should be a clear history of setting the contribution level under the assumed approach.

The plan costs are usually more difficult to determine. Health plan costs for retirees are often "buried" in the total plan costs for all participants – active employees and retirees together. Since health care costs generally increase with age, retirees under age 65 will have much higher costs than the average active employee. Since retirees over age 65 have substantial coverage under the Medicare program, their costs are much less than the under age-65 retiree group. Health care costs by five-year age groups are sometimes used to value retiree health plans. As a general rule, health care costs for retirees under age 65 are 150 to 200 percent of the cost for active employees, and the costs for retirees over age 65 are generally 40 to 80 percent of active employee costs. These relationships will vary depending on the demographic profile of the group and plan design.

For plans that consider disabled employees as retirees, their average costs range from 150 percent to 400 percent of active employees' costs. The large range is due to many factors, including:

- maturity of disabled population (health care costs tend to be very high at the beginning of disability – 8 to 12 times active rates – a and level off in later years to around two times),

- incidence of Medicare eligibility (Medicare will be primary if the disabled employee is considered retired by meeting specific eligibility tests after 24 months of receiving Social Security benefits), and

- definition of disability (strict definitions will tend to have higher health care costs).

For some valuations, it may be necessary to value some benefits or services separately. For example, an employer subject to FAS 109, *Accounting for Income Taxes*, may need to separate out the value of the prescription drug benefits, in particular the retiree drug subsidy paid by the government. Since the subsidy is tax-free, under FAS 109, a deferred tax asset is established for the future tax benefit of the subsidy. Since it is specifically for prescription drug benefits, it may be easier to explicitly value this benefit separately from the other benefits rather than using a total cost and blended health care cost trend rate so that the results are consistently valued with and without the value of the subsidy.

Incurred versus Paid Claims

The claims data typically received for analysis covers claims paid during a given period of time. These claims must be projected to the appropriate valuation period based on what is expected to be incurred during the year.

The difference between paid and incurred is a timing issue. The difference in time is the period beginning when the services are provided and ending when the benefit payment is made. There are various techniques used to determine this difference from a simple factor approach (a multiplier of 1.02 or 1.04) to sophisticated claim lag analysis. The actual claim lag development process is beyond the scope of this text.

For a stable population, the factor approach may be derived in different ways. One is to assume that the population is stable with a relatively predictable health care cost trend rate. The adjustment would be based on an assumption that the incurred and unpaid claim liability at the end of a year is about equal to a fixed percentage of paid claims (e.g., 20 percent of annual paid claims). If the trend rate is equal to 15 percent, the adjustment factor would be equal to

$$1.026 = [1.00 + 1.00 \times 0.20 - (1.00 \times 0.20 \div 1.15)]$$

Incurred claims is the best measure to use in a retiree health plan valuation because they represent the employer's actual costs of providing the benefit for the current year. FAS 106 requires the use of incurred claims.

Health Care Cost Trend Rate

This is the rate used to project current plan costs into the future. Trends used by underwriters typically include the effect of inflation, utilization (both intensity and mix of services), advancements in technology, plan design effects, cost shifting, aging and population changes. Note that for a retiree health plan valuation, the last two components (aging and population changes) are generally handled directly in the valuation process and should not be included in the trend assumption. Health care inflation trends in the 1980s, early 1990s and early 2000s have ranged from 10 to 20 percent for plans with low initial deductibles. Trend rates in the mid-1990s were relatively low at zero to 5 percent. The actuary should keep in mind that this assumption should represent long-term trends.

The health care cost inflation trend rate selected for a particular plan should represent the underlying trends of the services provided by the plan. In some cases, it may be appropriate to use different health care trend rates for different categories of service (e.g., hospital, professional, lab/x-ray, drugs and other). This would automatically adjust the total plan trend to appropriate levels and would be useful in situations where an employer sponsors more than one plan with different benefits. Even if this approach is not used, it must be considered in setting the initial levels of trend. For example, if the plan only covers hospital charges, recent trends have been relatively low (5 to 8 percent). If the plan only covers prescription drugs, recent trends have been high (18 to 24 percent).

Consideration should also be given to the relationship of health care expenditures to the gross domestic product (GDP). In recent years, increases in health care expenditures have exceeded the increase in GDP. Figure 9.1 shows this historical growth.

Historical Health Care as Percent of GDP

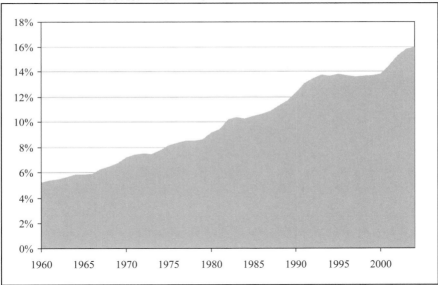

Figure 9.1

From 1960 to 2004, national health expenditures as a percent of GDP increased from 5.2 percent to 16.0 percent. The per capita GDP grew 6.2 percent per year on average during this time while the health care component grew 8.9 percent. This implies that the non-health care component grew 5.9 percent per year. Using an assumption that this relationship will continue in the future yields unlikely results. Keep in mind when doing an analysis of this type that the health care trends observed for insured plans are only a portion of the total increase in the health care services component of GDP. In addition to insured plans, this component of GDP includes services paid by the government (principally Medicare, Medicaid and Aid to Dependent Children), the providers (unpaid bills and indigent care) and out-of-pocket costs by the population in general.

With this understanding, assume that the non-health care components of GDP increase at 6 percent per year, and health care components increase at 9 percent per year. These assumptions will yield the results shown in Figure 9.2.

Projected Health Care as Percentage of GDP

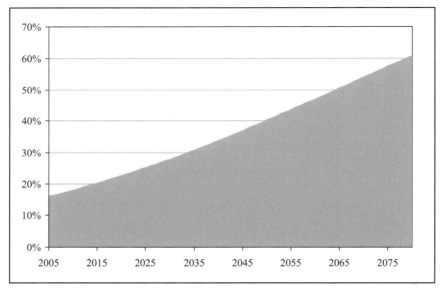

Figure 9.2

The illustration above shows that increases in health care expenditures cannot continue to severely outpace the rest of the components of GDP as it has historically. A more likely result is that health expenditures may increase to a more significant portion of GDP such as 20 or 30 percent, but will then be controlled and limited once that level is reached.

A key consideration of the 2000 Medicare Technical Review Panel[2] in selecting the long-term health care cost trend rate for the Medicare program was sustainability of the differential between national health care

---

[2] Technical Review Panel on the Medicare Trustees Reports, *Review of Assumptions and Methods of the Medicare Trustees' Financial Projections*, [1].

expenditure (NHE) growth and GDP growth. Assuming a one-percentage point differential between NHE and GDP resulted in a 27 percent share of health care in 2075 before demographic effects. After such changes – primarily the aging of the population – are accounted for, the NHE share of GDP would be about 38 percent of GDP. Figure 9.3 shows these results for other alternatives. Note that the % GDP line is the actual historical NHE as a percent of GDP; and GDP+0%, GDP+1%, and GDP+2% are three different projections assuming health care costs grow at 0%, 1%, and 2%, respectively, above total GDP growth rate.

NHE as Share of GDP Under Alternative Growth Scenarios

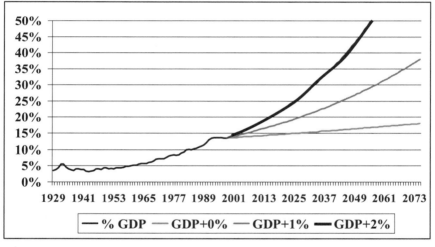

Figure 9.3

A key assumption in the above analysis is that the health plan cost trend under review increases at the same rate as national health care expenditures. For shorter periods of time, this assumption is generally not considered valid because of differences in the covered populations. In the long-term, however, most agree that the differences diminish. Any assumption regarding long-term health care trends should account for the sustainability of the trend in relation to the total economy.

The Technical Panel ultimately settled on recommending a long-term cost trend rate equal to one percentage point above per capita GDP increases for the Medicare trust funds. Besides sustainability, other considerations made included historical experience, the key drivers of the historical cost trends, how the key drivers may vary in the future compared to the past, the role of managed care in slowing recent historical experience, and other forecasts of long-term cost trends.

The use of health care trend assumptions that begin at current levels and grade down over a period of years to a lower level equal to some real rate plus inflation, seems appropriate. This is the preferred assumption for FAS 106 valuations by many actuaries and accountants.

Figure 9.4 illustrates this concept, showing the basic components of the assumed health care trend both today and the future year n.

Comparison of Health Care Cost Trend Rates Today and Year n

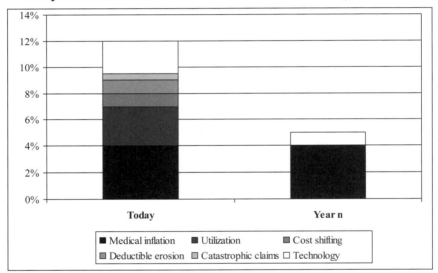

Figure 9.4

The above graph shows health care trend declining from an annual 12 percent per year increase to 5 percent per year. All of the principal components are expected to decline except the underlying medical inflation rate. Note that aging is not a factor in the trend rates shown. That assumption is usually taken into account explicitly in the health care cost assumptions by developing age-related costs.

A key assumption in developing a select and ultimate set of trend assumptions is the length of the select period. Experienced practitioners have used select periods ranging from as low as five years to as long as 35 years. Most valuations performed today are using five to ten year select periods.

Medicare Benefit Increase

Medicare benefits tend to increase at a lower rate than other health care costs because of the nature of the reimbursement procedures and plan design of the Medicare program. Employer programs are benefactors of these controls because providers generally cannot charge more than what they accept from Medicare. Physicians who accept assignment from Medicare (i.e., they accept Medicare payment in full because of the "assignment" contract they signed with Medicare) cannot charge more to their patients than what Medicare allows. These physicians are also classified as participating physicians. Physicians who have not agreed to accept assignment (non-participating physicians) cannot charge more than 115 percent of the Medicare allowable charge. In addition, hospitals cannot charge more than the Medicare allowable charge levels.

Service Mix

Different types of services (e.g., hospital, professional, lab & x-ray, prescription drugs) have historically increased at different rates. As alluded to above, different groups (e.g., Medicare-eligible retirees and others) may have different underlying cost increase trends. These differences need to be taken into account in determining appropriate trend rates, at least in the short-term. Many experts find that simply estimating long-term health care trends to be a very daunting task, let alone trying to distinguish different trend rates by types of service. Therefore, most assume that long-term cost increases are the same for all services.

Recent prescription drug cost trends have underlined the importance of developing trend rates by service. The key reason is that prescription drugs have become an increasing percentage of Medicare patient's health care expenditures. For the typical employer plan that coordinates with Medicare, prescription drugs are 60 to 70 percent of plan costs. For pre-65 retiree plans, drugs are about 20 percent of total costs. With other medical service costs increasing at trends of about 10 percent per year, this creates a significant difference in expected plan costs between pre- and post-65 retirees.

Prescription drug plan cost trends in the early 2000s have been between 15 and 25 percent compared to 8 to 12 percent for other medical services. The drug cost trend moderated somewhat by 2006 but was still higher than services. The following chart illustrates how the initial health care cost trend rates may be set for pre- and post-65 retirees.

	Pre-65 Retiree		Post-65 Retiree	
	Trend Rate	Percent of Total	Trend Rate	Percent of Total
Prescription drugs	13%	20%	13%	65%
Other medical services	9%	80%	9%	35%
Total	10%	100%	12%	100%

The above development suggests that post-65 retiree trend rates should be much higher than pre-65 retiree trend rates—at least initially. Over time, most experts would not try to estimate different trend rates by service category so would assume that they converge. This implies that the pre- and post-65 trend rates should also converge.

Gross versus Net Plan Cost Trend

A component of the plan cost trend discussed previously is the effect of plan design. If plan design features such as deductibles, out-of-pocket maximums, and per visit copays are defined as fixed dollar amounts and do not change from year to year, there will be an additional cost increase due to *leveraging*. The leveraging effect is due to more claims above the dollar limits. This is best illustrated by an example:

Deductible Leveraging Illustration #1

		Year 1	Change	Year 2
(1)	Covered expense	$ 2,000	10.0%	$ 2,200
(2)	Plan deductible	250	0.0%	250
(3)	Expense subject to coinsurance: (1) – (2)	1,750	11.4%	1,950
(4)	Coinsurance percentage	80%	0.0%	80%
(5)	Benefit payable: (3) – (4)	1,400	11.4%	1,560

The above example focuses on a single claim. When determining the total effect of the fixed dollar provisions on health care trend it is important to consider its effect on a distribution of claims. That is, its effect on the 5 percent of claims that average $200 as well as the 5 percent of claims averaging $50,000 needs to be determined. There are other sources to the plan design leveraging that occur at different claim levels. These include claims that were previously below the deductible and are now over, claims that move from being paid at 80 percent and are now paid at 100 percent because of the out-of-pocket maximum and claims affected by the per visit copays.

This plan leveraging, if any, may increase the pre-age 65 plan costs between 0.25 and 2.0 percent, depending on plan design. The plan leveraging component of trend may increase post-age 65 plan costs from none for plans that use the standard coordination of benefits (COB) method of Medicare integration to 2.0 to 4.0 percent for plans using a Medicare carveout form of integration.

The following illustrates the impact of leveraging on a sample claim for a Medicare-eligible retiree under both standard COB and carveout:

Deductible Leveraging Illustration #2

	Year 1	Change	Year 2
(1) Covered expense	$ 10,000	6.0%	$ 10,600
(2) Medicare payment:			
(a) Medicare allowable	9,700	6.0%	10,280
(b) Medicare deductible	124	6.0%	131
(c) Medicare coinsurance	80%	0.0%	80%
(d) Medicare payment	7,660	6.0%	8,120
(3) Regular plan benefit			
(a) Covered expense	10,000	6.0%	10,600
(b) Plan deductible	250	0.0%	250
(c) Coinsurance percentage	80%	0.0%	80%
($1,000 OOP max)			
(d) Regular plan benefit	8,750	6.9%	9,350
(4) Standard COB			
(a) Total not paid by Medicare: (1) – (2)	2,340	6.0%	2,480
(b) Regular plan benefit	8,750	6.9%	9,350
(c) Benefit payable: lesser of (a) or (b)	2,340	6.0%	2,480
(5) Carveout			
(a) Regular plan benefit	8,750	6.9%	9,350
(b) Medicare payment	7,660	6.0%	8,120
(c) Benefit payable: (a) – (b)	1,090	12.8%	1,230

For both pre- and post-age 65 plan costs, the effect of the plan leveraging slowly diminishes over time as the relative values of the fixed dollar amounts become less and less valuable relative to the total plan costs. For example, using the same plan as before except with a larger covered expense, shows how the leveraging is reduced.

Deductible Leveraging Illustration #3

		Year 1	Change	Year 2
(1)	Covered expense	$ 6,000	10.0%	$ 6,60
(2)	Plan deductible	250	0.0%	250
(3)	Expense subject to coinsurance: (1) – (2)	5,750	10.4%	6,350
(4)	Coinsurance percentage	80%	0.0%	80%
(5)	Benefit payable: (3) – (4)	4,600	10.4%	5,080

The leveraging impact has declined from 1.4 percent (shown in Illustration #1) to 0.4 percent with the increased covered expense.

The above illustrations point out another phenomenon that should be considered. If the actuary is assuming the health care trend on covered expenses will grade down over a 15 year period, the trend on net plan costs will have a much longer grading period due to the plan leveraging.

If the plan's provisions are indexed to actual plan cost increases, there will be no plan leveraging. If the provisions are indexed to something other than cost increases (e.g., general CPI) the effect of the leveraging will be somewhat reduced.

Under FAS 106, the health care trend that is required to be disclosed is the trend on gross plan costs (covered expenses). If the actuary is using a net plan cost trend in the valuation, it would generally need to be translated to a gross plan cost trend, at least for disclosure purposes. Some auditors may accept disclosure of the net plan trend as long as that fact is disclosed in the footnotes.

Medicare Part B Premium Increase

Some employers pay for their retirees' Medicare Part B premiums. If they do, an assumption is required to reflect future increases in the premium. Since these premiums are somewhat related to the benefits received, a rate close to the Medicare inflation assumption might be used. This increase rate may not be equal to the Medicare inflation assumption in the near future if the government continues to increase the retiree's share of the cost of the program.

Note that the Part B premiums could be constrained by law for some years as reflected in the 2006 Medicare Trustees report. The following table shows the rates set for those five years.

Part B Premiums

Year	Monthly Rate
2005	$ 78.20
2006	88.50
2007	98.20
2008	98.20
2009	98.30
2010	102.20

The Trustees report is generally a good source for setting Part B premium assumptions, but care should be made in its direct use. The report will generally comment on unusual aspects of any projected cost. For example, the 2006 report states that the "leveling out [of the 2007-09 premium rates] is a result of the current-law physician payment system combined with the large increase required for the 2006 financing in order to take a step toward restoring the Part B account assets. Note that the current-law physician payment updates and the resultant current-law Part B financing rates are very unlikely to occur before legislative changes intervene."[3]

Retiree Contribution Increase

For plans that require retiree contributions, an assumption must be made regarding how they increase. Generally, a plan sponsor policy of increasing these retiree contributions has been established. The assumption should consider whether this policy will continue in the future and, if not, how it might change.

---

[3] *2006 Annual Report of the Board of Trustees of the Federal Hospital Insurance and Federal Supplementary Medicare Insurance Trust Funds*, The Board of Trustees, [4].

Depending on the plan sponsor's contribution policy, this assumption may take on many forms. It may be:

- a flat percentage increase assumption (e.g., 5 percent),
- increased at the same rate as the retiree plan costs are assumed to increase, or
- increased based on increases in the active plan costs which may be different than retiree plan cost increases.

For an employer that has established a defined dollar approach of providing health benefits, the retiree contribution is the difference between the projected plan cost and the dollar limit. Briefly, a defined dollar benefit plan limits the employer's retiree health care costs in any one period to a specified dollar amount. Any costs above this dollar limit is paid by the retiree in the form of a retiree contribution.

It is critical that appropriate costs be used in this type of projection. For example, the pre-65 retiree contribution rate is often based on a blended active and pre-65 retiree rate. A statement that the employer costs are "fixed" at $2,000 per year does not always appropriately describe the real employer obligation. For example, if active only costs are $3,500 and pre-65 retiree costs are $7,000, and a blended rate with 80 percent active and 20 percent retirees is $4,200, using a blended rate develops a retiree contribution of $2,200 ($4,200 – $2,000). Using a pre-65 retiree rate would mean retirees should be charged $5,000 ($7,000 – $2,000). If retirees are charged $5,000, the employer obligation is the stated cap of $2,000. However, if the retiree is charged $2,200, the employer obligation is actually $4,800 ($7,000 – $2,200). If costs then increase 10 percent the next year, the blended rate will increase about 10 percent to $4,620 and the retirees would be charged $2,620. The actual employer subsidy will increase to $5,080 ($7,000 × 1.10 – $2,620) or six percent higher than last year. Costs are limited to less than health care cost trend but they are inflationary.

If the actuary assumes a retiree contribution increase rate that is greater than the plan cost increase rate, care should be taken that illogical results do not occur, such as negative employer costs.

Plan Participation

If a retiree group plan requires retiree contributions, not all retirees will elect coverage. An assumption of plan participation will, therefore, be required. A separate assumption of retiree versus dependent coverage may be appropriate, especially if there are different employer subsidy levels. This assumption is generally developed from the employer's own experience.

In general, the more retirees are required to contribute, the less likely they are to participate in the plan. Care should be given in selecting assumptions whenever a decision is made by the employer to change the level of retiree contributions, whether up or down.

Consideration should also be given to the level of claims for the retirees and their dependents who stay in the plan. Their health care claims per capita will, on average, be higher than if all eligible retirees elected coverage. For example, assume that because the company introduces retiree contributions for the first time equal to 50 percent of plan costs, 80 percent will continue plan coverage. Also assume that of those 80 percent remaining they have about 88 percent of the claims. Therefore, the actuary can explicitly assume that 80 percent will participate in the plan, but plan costs per capita will increase 10 percent ($88 \div 80$) because of the change from non-contributory status. Alternatively, an implicit assumption of 88 percent participation can be assumed. As time passes, this 88 percent assumption will have to be adjusted because the 10 percent "selection" effect will be inherent in the calculated claim cost amount.

For plans that allow retirees to drop out of coverage while they have other coverage available, the actuary should also consider including an assumption of returning retirees from the census of current opt outs.

Spouse Plan Continuation

Most health care plans allow spouses to continue coverage under the plan after the retiree dies. Continuation in the plans may be on the condition that the spouse pays the required premium. If the surviving spouse must make a contribution, an assumption needs to be included to indicate what percentage of these spouses elect coverage.

Dependent Children Plan Termination

Health care plans generally allow dependent children to be covered under the plan up to a certain age (i.e., the limiting age). Most employers do not maintain the age of a dependent child on their records so assumptions need to be made regarding when the dependent reaches the limiting age. Costs for dependent children may be indirectly included with the spouse costs. For example, assuming 25% percent of retirees covering spouses under age 65 have dependent children, the assumed spouse cost would be set equal to the under age 65 actual spouse cost plus 0.25 times the dependent children cost.

Plan Design Change

A valuation may also account for future plan design changes because of the nature of retiree group benefits (i.e., the benefits may be amended or terminated at the plan sponsor's discretion). Under FAS 106, this may be arguably considered as part of the substantive plan if there has been a history of changes in the past. This assumption may be handled explicitly in the valuation as a separate global plan change or termination assumption, or implicitly through lower health care cost trend rates.[4]

SELECTION OF ACTUARIAL ASSUMPTIONS

As was highlighted above, it is very important that all assumptions chosen for a retiree group benefit valuation accurately represent future expectations. Certain assumptions are more critical than their pension counterpart.

Economic assumptions should be selected to complement each other. Use of a discount rate of 7 percent and a level health care inflation assumption of 12 percent may be reasonable when viewed separately, however, they do not appear to be reasonable when used together. This is primarily because they would have to share a common underlying general inflation level, say 5 percent. A 2 percent spread between the discount rate and inflation seems reasonable but a long-term 7 percent spread for the trend rate does not. Used separately, the discount rate could have a 5 percent underlying inflation and the 12 percent trend could have a 9 percent underlying inflation.

---

[4] This concept was introduced by Jeffrey Petertil in his paper, *Measuring Terminable Postretirement Obligations* in the North American Actuarial Journal [32].

In order to be consistent with the pension valuation, the assumptions chosen for the retiree group benefit valuation should follow as closely as possible. If the population being valued is not the same or the pension assumptions are not reasonable for a retiree group benefit valuation, different assumptions may be warranted.

As mentioned in the actuarial assumption section above, certain assumptions must be chosen more carefully for retiree group benefit valuations than for pension valuations. Among these are turnover, mortality and retirement incidence.

Initial plan cost for a retiree health valuation is often the most difficult valuation assumption to develop. The premium rates/claim costs used by the plan sponsor often need to be adjusted for the valuation. The term "premium" will be used to represent either premium rates or claim costs. Common problems found with premiums are outlined below.

Under age 65 premiums

These often include active employees. Actual costs for retirees under 65 are generally 150 to 225 percent of the costs for active employees.

Composite premiums

Rates may be determined as costs per employee. The rate will therefore include the cost of all dependents, spouses and children. Using these rates implicitly assumes that the current distribution of retirees and dependents will not be different in the future. This may not be true if the underlying costs or retiree contribution levels will be changed.

Spouse/dependent premium

Spouse and dependent premiums and claims are often classified by the age of the retiree. Therefore, if the retiree is over age 65, even if the dependents are under age 65, they may be classified with the retiree, i.e. over 65.

Old premium structure

The premium structure between active and retiree rates are often developed initially and never adjusted for actual costs. If the premium structure (i.e. the cost differences for retirees versus active employees, retiree spouses versus active spouses, etc.) has not been updated in several years, the relationship may not be valid.

Missing data

Claims data for all benefits payable to retirees are sometimes missing data for a portion of the total plan costs. This may happen if there is more than one claims payer for the plan. Common omissions are claims for stand-alone programs such as prescription drug card plans, mail-order drug plans, behavioral health/chemical dependency programs, vision/hearing and dental plans.

Different plans

Often, the plan costs developed for current retirees are different for future retirees because of different plan provisions. This may be due to grandfathering provisions when plans are changed, acquisition and adoption of other plans, or retirees from closed divisions.

Costs by Age

In addition to the potential problems above, plan costs should, if possible, be developed by age. Based on available data, it is evident that costs vary by age, but few plan sponsors will have enough retirees to develop such costs. The actuary will thus have to develop these costs using relative value adjustments.

For example, if the actuary assumes that costs, on the average, increase 3.0 percent per year from age 65 to 75 and 0.5 percent per year from 75 to 85; and the plan has the following age distribution, costs can be developed by age.

Demographics

Age Group	Number
65 to 69	200
70 to 74	350
75 to 79	300
80 to 84	100
85 to 89	40
90+	10
Total	1,000

Assuming costs over age 65 for the above group are $2,000 per year, costs by age group may be developed as follows:

Age-Related Costs

Age Group	Number	Relative Value	Plan Cost
65 to 69	200	1.000	1,668
70 to 74	350	1.148	1,915
75 to 79	300	1.286	2,145
80 to 84	100	1.392	2,322
85 to 89	40	1.449	2,417
90 +	10	1.471	2,454
Total	1,000	1.199	2,000

The relative values were developed by setting the age 65 to 69 group at 1.000 and each group above was increased by the assumed aging factors by age. The total relative value (1.199) is the average, weighted by the number in each age group. The plan cost is the average cost ($2,000) divided by the average relative value (1.199) times the relative value in each age group. The above plan cost rates by age would then be used as the first year cost rates in the valuation. These rates are projected in the valuation using the health care trend rate assumption to establish future plan rates at the various ages.

Note that since health care costs by age tend to be exponential and varying by age, it is better to develop age-related costs using the above methodology than assuming that the average cost for the group is applicable to the average aged retiree. The average age methodology only works if costs by age were linear for all ages. This phenomenon was referred to as "warping" in a paper by Jeff Petertil on aging curves for health care benefits.[5] And, it becomes more pronounced for longer age periods being averaged. The paper illustrates the overstatement for varying durations of age periods and using a flat 3 percent and 5 percent per year aging assumption. The following table shows the results.

---

[5] Petertil, Jeffrey P., "Aging Curves for Health Care Costs in Retirement," *North American Actuarial Journal*, 2005 [33].

Average Age Overstatement

Age Period	Aging Curve Assumption 3%	5%
2 years	<0.1%	<1.0%
10 years	1.1%	3.0%
20 years	4.4%	12.1%

If ages are averaged over a ten year period, the error of assuming the average cost represents the rate at the average age may be one to three percent. Since the age curve does have annual changes between three and five percent per year between the ages of 40 and 65, the above errors may be more prevalent for pre-65 retiree analysis depending on the distribution of covered members.

ACTUARIAL METHODS FOR PENSION PLANS

This section provides a brief framework of actuarial methods used to value pension plans. Other material dealing specifically with pension plan valuations should be reviewed to gain a better understanding of the details.

Actuarial methods are generally divided into two major categories – immediate gain methods and spread gain methods. The primary difference between the two is how experience gains and losses are recognized.

Experience gains and losses occur when the actuarial assumptions used in the prior year's valuation do not exactly match what actually occurred during the year. Experience gains occur when the actual liability at the end of the year is less than the expected end-of-year liability. Losses occur when the actual liability is greater than the expected liability. Gains reduce future plan costs and losses increase future plan costs.

An immediate gain actuarial method is one that explicitly produces a gain or loss each year. A spread gain method does not produce an explicit gain or loss but, instead, automatically spreads it to future funding years along with the other liabilities of the plan.

Examples of immediate gain methods are:

- Unit credit
  - Traditional
  - Projected

- Entry age normal

- Attained age

Examples of spread gain methods are:

- Frozen initial liability
  - Entry age normal
  - Attained age

- Aggregate

Immediate Gain Methods

The use of all immediate gain actuarial methods results in two components – a normal cost and an actuarial accrued liability. The normal cost represents the costs assigned to the current year. The actuarial accrued liability represents costs assigned to all prior years. Another way to view it is that the actuarial accrued liability is the present value of past normal costs.

Traditional Unit Credit

The traditional unit credit method defines its normal cost as the present value of benefits expected to be earned in the current year. For example, if an employee earns a benefit equal to $10/month during the year, payable at age 65, the normal cost is equal to the present value of a deferred annuity of $10/month payable at age 65. The actuarial accrued liability is the present value of all benefits earned to date. For example, if the same employee has worked 20 years and, therefore, has earned a benefit of $200/month ($10 times 20 years), the actuarial liability is the present value of the $200/month benefit.

The following provides a simplified formula for the normal cost (NC) and actuarial accrued liability (AAL):

(1)
$$NC_x = (B_{x+1} - B_x) \times \frac{N_y}{D_x}$$

(2)
$$AAL_x = B_x \times \frac{N_y}{D_x}$$

where:

x	=	current age
y	=	retirement age
B_x	=	Accrued benefit at age x
D_x	=	Commutation function: $D_x = \ell_x v^x$
N_x	=	Commutation function: $N_x \equiv \sum\limits_{x}^{\infty} D_z$
NC_x	=	Normal cost at age x
AAL_x	=	Actuarial accrued liability at age x

Projected Unit Credit

This is a variation of the traditional unit credit method. Some plans cannot easily determine how much of a benefit is earned in a given year. For example, assume a pension plan benefit is equal to 1-percent times pay at retirement times years of service at retirement. The benefit earned in the current year is not easily determined. Using the appropriate assumptions, however, a benefit at retirement may be developed and then assigned to the current year.

Assume an individual has 20 years of service and earns $100,000 at retirement and has a benefit equal to $20,000 per year. You could then prorate this benefit to his working career by dividing by 20 and assuming that he earns the benefit in $1,000 increments per year. The normal cost is then equal to the present value of a $1,000 per year annuity payable at age 65. If he has ten years of service as of the valuation date, the actuarial liability is equal to the present value of a $10,000 per year annuity payable at age 65 ($1,000 times 10 years). Alternate ways to develop the prorated benefit are to weight the allocation by salary earned over the participant's career or by benefit accrual rates.

The following illustrates the projected unit credit NC and AAL values, assuming benefits are allocated prorata by service:

(3)
$$NC_x = \frac{B_y \times \frac{N_y}{D_x}}{y - e}$$

(4)
$$AAL_x = NC_x \times (x - e)$$

where:

e = age at entry into plan (when benefit credit begins)

Entry Age Normal

The entry age normal actuarial method derives the projected benefit at retirement and allocates the present value through the years from entry age to retirement age. These costs are allocated to specific years based on either pay or service, depending on whether or not the benefit is based on pay. Again, the actuarial accrued liability is the present value of past normal costs. This allocation, based on service, is developed as follows:

(5)
$$B_y \times \frac{N_y}{D_x} = \frac{NC_x \times (N_e - N_y)}{D_x}$$

which can be rearranged as follows:

(6)
$$NC_x = B_y \times \frac{N_y}{N_e - N_y}$$

If the costs are allocated by pay, the following equations would be used:

(7)
$$B_y \times \frac{N_y}{D_x} = NC_x \times \frac{{}^S N_e - {}^S N_y}{{}^S D_x}$$

which can be rearranged as follows:

$$(8) \qquad NC_x = \frac{B_y \times N_y \times {}^{S}D_x}{({}^{S}N_e - {}^{S}N_y) \times D_x}$$

where:

$$sN_x, sD_x = \text{Commutation functions with salary scale}$$

The actuarial accrued liability is equal to:

$$(9) \qquad AAL_x = NC_x \times \frac{N_e - N_x}{D_x}$$

or

$$(10) \qquad AAL_x = NC_x \times \frac{{}^{S}N_e - {}^{S}N_x}{{}^{S}D_x}, \text{with salary}$$

Attained Age

The attained age actuarial method is a blend of the unit credit method and a level premium allocation of future costs. One starts by developing the actuarial accrued liability using the same method as the unit credit method. Then the normal cost is determined by allocating the excess of the actuarial present value of benefits over the unit credit actuarial accrued liability on a level basis from the valuation date to the assumed retirement date based on either pay or service, depending on whether or not the benefit is based on pay. The actuarial accrued liability under the projected unit credit method can be expressed as follows:

$$(11) \qquad AAL_x = B_y \times \frac{N_y}{D_x} \times \frac{x-e}{y-e}$$

alternatively, the traditional unit credit method could be used:

$$(12) \qquad AAL_x = B_x \times \frac{N_y}{D_x}$$

If the normal costs are developed based on the projected unit credit actuarial accrued liability, the following equations would be used:

$$(13) \qquad NC_x = \frac{B_y \times \frac{N_y}{D_x} - AAL_x}{\frac{N_x - N_y}{D_x}} = \frac{B_y \times \frac{N_y}{D_x} - B_y \times \frac{N_y}{D_x} \times \frac{x-e}{y-e}}{\frac{N_x - N_y}{D_x}}$$

which can be rearranged as follows:

$$(14) \qquad NC_x = B_y \times \frac{N_y}{N_x - N_y} \times \frac{y-x}{y-e}$$

using the traditional unit credit method, the following formula could be derived:

$$(15) \qquad NC_x = B_x \times \frac{N_y}{N_x - N_y}$$

Spread Gain Methods

Unlike the immediate gain methods, the spread gain actuarial methods defines only a normal cost that includes provision for all benefits for which no assets or past service liabilities have been set aside.

Aggregate

The aggregate actuarial cost method is the basic spread gain method. As the name indicates, it develops the normal cost based on values in aggregate. That is, present values of various amounts are determined for each individual and summed together. In general, the total normal cost factor for the plan is equal to the sum of the present value of all future benefits minus plan assets, divided by the present value of future salaries. The normal cost factor is then multiplied by the current total salaries of the plan participants to determine the normal cost. This may be represented as follows:

$$(16) \qquad NCF_t = \frac{PVFB_t - AV_t}{PVFS_t}$$

(17)
$$NC_t = CE_t \times NCF_t$$

where:

NCF_t	=	normal cost factor at time t
$PVFB_t$	=	present value of future benefits
AV_t	=	asset value
$PVFX_t$	=	present value of future salaries
NC_t	=	normal cost
CE_t	=	total current earnings

Frozen Initial Liability

This is a variation of the aggregate method. The initial valuation performed for the plan results in an actuarial accrued liability amount by using some immediate gain method. This cost method often has its description expanded depending on the immediate gain method used to develop the frozen initial liability amount. For example, if the entry age normal method is used, the method would be called the "frozen entry age" cost method or if a unit credit method is used, it is called the "frozen attained age" cost method. The actuarial accrued liability amount that is determined the first time this method is adopted is called the initial liability. This liability amount is "frozen" and is amortized in the future assuming no gains or losses. The normal cost factor at any point in time is equal to the sum of the present value of future benefits minus the unamortized initial liability minus plan assets, divided by the present value of future salaries. This normal cost factor is multiplied by the current total salaries, just as in the aggregate cost method to derive the current year's normal cost.

The initial valuation is developed as follows:

(18)
$$NCF_0 = \frac{PVFB_0 - FIL_0 - AV_0}{PVFS_0}$$

(19)
$$NC_0 = CE_0 \times NCF_0$$

where:

FIL_0 = unamortized frozen initial liability at time 0

Subsequent valuations are determined as follows:

(20) $$FIL_t = (FIL_{t-1} + NC_{t-1}) \times (1+i) - C_{t-1}^i$$

(21) $$NCF_t = \frac{PVFB_t - FIL_t - FIL_t - AV_t}{PVFS_t}$$

(22) $$NC_t = CE_t \times NCF_t$$

where:

C_t^i = Contribution with interest paid during time t

Under either the Aggregate or the Frozen Initial Liability methods, the actuary could choose to allocate future costs as a level dollar amount rather than as a level percentage of pay, as was illustrated above. This may be accomplished by using non-salary-related commutation functions in the normal cost factor development and multiplying the resulting factor by the number of active participants.

General

One should keep in mind that the present values developed above have been greatly simplified. The commutation functions defined above will normally be developed using multiple decrements. Some of the commutation factors included salary increase assumptions. In practice, computers make these calculations using an iterative approach.

For example, the present value of a retirement benefit might be developed as follows:

(23) $$PVFB_x = \sum_{j}^{\infty} \frac{l_j \times {}^r q_j \times B_j \times \ddot{a}_j \times v^{j-x}}{l_x}$$

where:

$PVFB_x$	=	present value of future pension benefits
l_j	=	number alive at age j
${}^r q_j$	=	probability of retirement at age j

$$B_j \quad = \quad \text{benefit at age } j$$

$$\ddot{a}_j \quad = \quad \text{annuity at age } j$$

$$v^{j-x} \quad = \quad \text{interest discount}$$

$$j \quad = \quad \text{earliest retirement age}$$

Last-Year-of-Life Model[6]

Another way to develop the present values included in a valuation is via a last-year-of-life (LYOL) modeling of the future expected claim costs. In essence, the model will consider health care costs in two separate components—an ongoing maintenance (survivor) cost and a last year of life (decedent) cost. The survivor cost is the average cost for individuals who survive any given year of experience. And, the decedent cost is the average cost for individuals who die in a year.

There have been several studies demonstrating the large difference in costs. The following table shows results from a 1992 study. Prior studies show substantially the same result.

Payments by Survival Status and Age

Age	Average Cost per Decedent	Average Cost per Survivor	Ratio of Decedent Cost to Survivor Cost
55-59	$ 25,306	$ 2,314	10.9
60-64	27,378	3,243	8.4
65-69	3,704	734	5.0
70-74	3,834	777	4.9
75-79	3,515	840	4.2
80-84	2,889	766	3.8
85-89	2,297	758	3.0
90 +	2,196	595	3.7

Source: Actuarial Research Clearing House 1993.3, p. 298

Most plans will not have credible data to develop their own LOYL claim tables but they may be derived by assuming ratios such as the above. For example, if the age 70-74 costs are $2,000, on average, and q_{72} is 0.05

---

[6] Adam J. Reese, "Development of the Last-Year-of-Life Valuation Model for Retiree Medical Plans," *North American Actuarial Journal*, 2000 [35]. Copyright 2000 by the Society of Actuaries, Schaumburg, Illinois. Reprinted with permission.

and we use the above ratio of 4.9, the survivor and decedent costs may be derived as follows.

$$(24) \quad \text{Expected cost} = \$2,000 = (D \times q_{72}) + (S \times p_{72})$$

$$= \left(\frac{D}{S} \times S \times q_{72}\right) + (S \times p_{72})$$

$$= (4.9 \times S \times q_{72}) + (S \times p_{72})$$

$$= (4.9 \times S \times 0.05) + (S \times 0.95)$$

$$S = \$2,000 \div 1.1950 = \$1,674$$

$$D = 4.9 \times \$1,674 = \$8,201$$

The above arithmetic implies that survivors make up $1,590 of the $2,000 average expected cost and decedents make up the remaining $410. It also shows that 20 percent of the costs are for the five percent of individuals who die during the year.

A key aspect of this type of modeling is that it automatically adjusts the morbidity curve (the aging curve) for health care costs when changing mortality tables. Included in the paper is an illustration of the effect of changing the mortality table for a group on the accounting obligation.

Mortality Table	Average Claims Cost Model	LYOL Model
UP 84	$ 500 M	$ 500 M
GAM 83	599 M	565 M
GAM 94	617 M	578 M

The LOYL model does not completely moderate improvements in mortality but it does dampen its effect as show above.

ACTUARIAL METHODS FOR LIFE AND HEALTH PLANS

All of the actuarial cost methods that are used for pension plans can be adapted for use with retiree group benefit plans. The only thing that changes is the definition of the benefit. Instead of a benefit that may be based on salary, service and age at retirement, you will have a benefit based on health plan costs at the time of retirement plus, in most cases, the cost of health plan increases after retirement. Unlike most pension plans, retiree group benefit plans usually do not pay benefits to employees terminating before they are eligible for retirement. New and innovative plan designs that have been implemented in the last ten years may vary the benefit costs or the retiree contributions on service, age, and marital status at retirement.

Due to the differing nature of the health plan, the actuary may find it necessary to divide the plan into several components. A logical division would be to split the costs associated with total eligible health plan expenses and those reimbursed by Medicare. Therefore the net present value cost of the plan would be the present value of the total eligible expenses minus the present value of Medicare reimbursed expenses. Algebraically, this may be expressed as follows:

(25)
$$PVTH_x = \sum_{j}^{\infty} \frac{l_j \times {}^r q_j \times B_j \times {}^T \ddot{a}_j \times v^{j-x}}{l_x}$$

(26)
$$PVM_x = \sum_{j}^{64} \frac{l_{65} \times {}^r q_j \times M_{65} \times {}^M \ddot{a}_{65} \times v^{65-x}}{l_x}$$

$$+ \sum_{65}^{\infty} \frac{l_j \times {}^r q_j \times M_j \times {}^M \ddot{a}_j \times v^{j-x}}{l_x}$$

(27)
$$PVNH_x = PVTH_x - PVM_x$$

where:

$PVTH_x$	=	present value of total health plan benefit
l_j	=	number alive at age j
${}^r q_{jj}$	=	probability of retirement at age j
B_j	=	benefit at age j (increased at total health trend assumption from age x)
$T\ddot{a}_j$	=	increasing annuity at age j (increasing at total health trend assumption)
v^{j-x}	=	interest discount

$$
\begin{aligned}
PVM_x &= \text{present value of Medicare benefit} \\
M_j &= \text{Medicare benefit at age } j \text{ (increased at} \\
&\quad \text{Medicare increase assumption from age } x) \\
^M\ddot{a}_j &= \text{increasing annuity at age } j \text{ (increasing at} \\
&\quad \text{Medicare increase assumption)} \\
PVNH_x &= \text{present value of net health plan benefit}
\end{aligned}
$$

Note that both B_j and M_j above represent benefits payable at the attained age j and therefore include any health/Medicare inflation from age x. For example, assume an individual is currently age 50, gross medical cost at age 65 is currently equal to \$3,000 and medical inflation is 10 percent per year. The B_j variable in the above formula for an age 65 retirement is \$12,532 (\$3,000 times 1.10^{65-50}).

From a practical perspective, the above calculations would be done on a seriatim basis with each projected benefit checked so that the net amount is not negative.

As mentioned above, all of the actuarial methods used for pension plans may be used to value retiree group benefit plans. A specific method is required for complying with Financial Accounting Standard No. 106 (FAS 106). This and other modifications of the pension methods that have been used in practice to value retiree group benefit plans are briefly described below.

Modified Projected Unit Credit

This is basically the required "attribution" method under FAS 106. Retiree group benefits typically do not have a rate of benefit accrual. Any employee who retires from active employment will receive the benefit. The projected unit credit cost method may be modified to meet this definition.

For example, assume a plan provides full benefits after retirement under the pension plan and we have an employee hired at age 35, eligible to retire at age 55 and assumed to retire at age 60. The regular projected unit credit method would accrue the benefits in equal amounts over 25 years (60 – 35). The employee would have accrued one-fifth (5 ÷ 25) of his benefit at age 40, three-fifths (15 ÷ 25) at 50 and four-fifths (20 ÷ 25) at 55. He would not accrue the full benefit until actual assumed retirement at age 60.

FAS 106 requires different treatment. The standard requires that benefits be attributed to years prior to the date of full eligibility for benefits instead of expected retirement dates. Under this plan, the benefit should be fully accrued by the earliest retirement age of age 55. Therefore, in this example, the employee would be assumed to have accrued one-fourth [5 ÷ (55 − 35)] of his benefit at age 40, three-fourths at 50 (15 ÷ 20) and the full benefit at age 55.

Delayed Funding Eligibility

Any actuarial method described above may be used. The difference is that only participants who meet high age and service requirements will be included in the calculations. Sample requirements might be age 45 with 15 years of service or a rule of 60 requirement (age plus service greater than or equal to 60). The rationale for this type of approach is that only participants who will most likely receive a retiree group benefit in the future are included. The plan sponsor will not be valuing benefits for younger employees who may or may not make it to retirement. This type of method has been used to provide some degree of advance accrual for a plan sponsor.

Modified Entry Age

This method has been used for welfare benefit fund calculations. The standard entry age normal method is used with a service allocation and entry age defined as the later of age at date of hire or date the welfare benefit fund was adopted. This method will therefore satisfy the requirement that benefits be funded over the working lifetime of employees.

SELECTION OF ACTUARIAL METHODS

There may be reasons to select an actuarial method consistent with the method used to value the pension plan. There are, however, often different objectives in the two types of valuations. Modifications may be introduced in order to meet specific objectives of the retiree group benefit plan valuation.

FAS 106 requires the use of the projected unit credit method with an allocation of costs that generally goes from hire age to the full eligibility age. This is the age when the employee has rendered all of the service necessary to receive all of the benefits under the plan. For most plans, this is the earliest retirement age. Under certain circumstances the costs may be allocated over different periods of time depending on how benefits are earned.

In general, the entry age normal actuarial cost method will produce the most conservative (i.e., fastest) funding. The traditional unit credit will usually produce the most liberal (i.e., slowest) funding. The aggregate, frozen initial liability, and projected unit credit methods will often produce a funding level between entry age and unit credit. This will depend on the amortization period of any unfunded actuarial accrued liability included in the funding amount.

The GASB standards allow the use of six main methods: entry age, attained age, frozen entry age, frozen attained age, projected unit credit, and aggregate. It is imperative for the actuary to not only understand the impact the selection of the method has on current year costs but also to be able to communicate the longer term differences of the alternative methods.

Pension literature that addresses the selection of actuarial cost methods will be applicable for retiree group benefit valuations. Further commentary on this subject is beyond the scope of this textbook.[7]

EXPERIENCE GAINS AND LOSSES

The immediate gain methods described above (entry age and unit credit) produce gains and losses each year. The generalized formula for calculating the gain/loss is:

(28) $$Exp\ UAL_{t+1} = (UAL_t + NC_t) \times (1+i) - C_t^i$$

(29) $$Gain/(loss) = Exp\ UAL_{t+1} - UAL_{t+1}$$

where:

$Exp\ UAL_{t+1}$	=	Expected unfunded actuarial liability
UAL_{t+1}	=	Actual unfunded actuarial liability
NC_t	=	Normal cost
i	=	interest rate
C_t^i	=	Contribution (with interest)

---

[7] For further information, see [3].

Gains and losses may be identified by each source. That is, the actuary can determine the gain and loss for each separate actuarial assumption. This is done by isolating each assumption by itself and determining the difference between what actually happened and what was expected. For example, the gain or loss due to plan cost changes may be estimated as follows:

(30) $$Gain/(loss) = AL_{t+1} - \frac{PC_t \times (1+m)}{PC_{t+1}} \times AL_{t+1}$$

where:

$$PC_t = \text{plan cost at time } t$$
$$m = \text{expected health trend}$$

Again, pension literature may be reviewed to develop a more detailed understanding of gains and losses by source.[8]

"ROLL-FORWARD" VALUATIONS

ASOP 6 allows the use of a "roll-forward" valuation from year to future years as long as an actual calculation is performed every three years. The actuarial liability is generally rolled forward by first assuming that there are no gains or losses. That is, the expected actuarial liability is used – similar to the expected unfunded liability calculated in the prior section. The expected actuarial liability may be determined as follows:

(31) $$Exp\ AL_{t+1} = (AL_t + NC_t) \times (1+i) - B_t^i$$

This expected actuarial liability may be further adjusted if actual claim rates are known to be higher or lower than just using the prior year's claim rate increased by the valuation health care cost trend rate assumption. Generally, a linear adjustment is made for this estimate. That is, if the actual increase in the cost rate was $j\%$ and the expected increase was $i\%$, the adjustment would be as follows:

(32) $$Adj\ AL_{t+1} = Exp\ AL_{t+1} \times \frac{1+j}{1+i}$$

---

[8] For example, see [3].

A similar adjustment may be made for demographics – either the total number or a change in the make-up (i.e., age and gender). When making such an adjustment, consideration should be given to differences by group (i.e., actives versus pre- and post-65 retirees), plan type, and location.

The estimation of the normal cost in a roll-forward valuation is generally equal to the prior year's normal cost increased by the ultimate trend rate. This estimate is derived as follows:

$$(33) \quad PVB_x^z = \sum_{t=0}^{\infty} {}_t p_x \times r_{x+t} \times B_0^z \times \prod_{j=0}^{t-1}(1+h_{z+j})$$

where:

$$\begin{aligned} PVB &= & \text{present value of projected benefits} \\ {}_t p_x &= & \text{probability of survival to duration } t \\ r_{x+t} &= & \text{probability of being retired at } x+t \\ B_0^z &= & \text{initial benefit amount in year } z \\ h_{z+j} &= & \text{health care trend in year } z+j \end{aligned}$$

$$(34) \quad PVB_x^{z+1} = \sum_{t=0}^{\infty} {}_t p_x \times r_{x+t} \times B_0^{z+1} \times \prod_{j=0}^{t-1}(1+h_{z+1+j})$$

$$(35) \quad B_0^{z+1} = B_0^z \times (1+h_z)$$

$$(36) \quad PVB_x^{z+1} = \sum_{t=0}^{\infty} {}_t p_x \times r_{x+t} \times B_0^z \times (1+h_z) \times \prod_{j=0}^{t-1}(1+h_{z+1+j})$$

$$(37) \quad PVB_x^{z+1} = \sum_{t=0}^{\infty} {}_t p_x \times r_{x+t} \times B_0^z \times \prod_{j=0}^{t}(1+h_{z+j})$$

$$(38) \quad PVB_x^{z+1} = \sum_{t=0}^{\infty} {}_t p_x \times r_{x+t} \times B_0^z \times (1+h_{z+t}) \times \prod_{j=0}^{t-1}(1+h_{z+j})$$

If we assume that for most persons aged x benefits don't commence until after the select period (i.e., time t is beyond the select period), the term h_{z+t} is a constant equal to the ultimate trend rate h_{ult}.

(39)
$$PVB_x^{z+1} = (1+h_{ult}) \times \sum_{t=0}^{\infty} {}_t p_x \times r_{x+t} \times B_0^z \times \prod_{j=0}^{t-1} (1+h_{z+j})$$

(40)
$$PVB_x^{z+1} = (1+h_{ult}) \times PVB_x^z$$

(41)
$$NC_x^z = PVB_x^z \times \frac{1}{FEA - e}$$

(42)
$$NC_x^{z+1} = PVB_x^{z+1} \times \frac{1}{FEA - e}$$

therefore:

(43)
$$NC_x^{z+1} = NC_x^z \times (1+h_{ult})$$

Note that the above illustrates the formula for the projected unit credit method normal cost development. Similar proofs can be made for other actuarial cost methods.

Assuming a stable population from year to year implies that total normal cost also increases at the ultimate health care trend rate. The assumption that most active participants do not commence benefit payments until after the select period is usually not true for select periods longer than five years. Therefore, the actuary should use his judgment about how much greater the service cost should be increased over the ultimate trend rate assumption.

SUMMARY

This chapter has provided a brief discussion of the valuation of retiree group benefit plans. It is not intended to provide precise detail on the valuation process, but rather to provide some basic principles.

As noted throughout this textbook, these valuations are a blend of both pension and group actuarial techniques. As such, it is important that the actuary/actuaries be familiar with both disciplines to perform retiree group benefit valuations. This may be accomplished by having a team of pension and group actuaries, or by actuaries very familiar with both disciplines.

APPENDIX A
RETIREE GROUP BENEFIT DESIGN

The following tables provide a summary of the key plan design features of retiree group benefit programs offered in 2006. They are summarized from Hewitt Associates' SpecBook survey of large employers in the U.S.[1] They represent the provisions of retiree group benefit plans that current active employees are eligible to receive. Many employers have employees and retirees eligible for different provisions that are often more generous.

Prevalence of Medical Coverage

	Salaried		Hourly	
	Number	Percent	Number	Percent
Pre-65 and post-65 coverage				
Employer subsidized	339	35.7%	105	45.5%
Retiree pays all	129	13.6	25	10.8
Pre-65 retirees pay all; post-65 subsidized	11	1.2	1	0.4
Post-65 retirees pay all; pre-65 subsidized	14	1.5	3	1.3
Subtotal	493	51.9	134	58.0
Post-65 coverage only				
Employer subsidized	3	0.3	0	0.0
Retiree pays all	2	0.2	0	0.0
Subtotal	5	0.5	0	0.0
Pre-65 coverage only				
Employer subsidized	70	7.4	18	7.8
Retiree pays all	40	4.2	12	5.2
Subtotal	110	11.6	30	13.4
No Coverage	342	36.0	66	28.6
Total employers	950	100.0	231	100.0

---

[1] © Hewitt Associates, 2005 SpecBook summary (generally large, private-sector employers including 950 employers in salaried survey and 231 in hourly survey).

An important aspect of retiree group benefits is the age and service an employee has at retirement which determines whether or not they are eligible for the benefit. It is often stated as an age and service requirement but sometimes a function of age plus service (i.e., "points") and other variants. The most common is age 55 with at least 10 years of service.

Eligibility Requirements

		Salaried		Hourly	
		Number	Percent	Number	Percent
Age and service requirement					
Age	**Service**				
<55	<10	6	0.9%	3	1.8%
<55	10	21	3.5	5	3.0
55	<10	59	9.8	14	8.5
55	10	222	36.8	51	30.9
55	15	45	7.5	8	4.9
55	20	10	1.7	2	1.2
55	>20	3	0.5	0	0.0
56-59	7-20	5	0.8	0	0.0
60	10	13	2.2	5	3.0
60	15	3	0.5	0	0.0
60	20	1	0.2	0	0.0
>60	5-25	8	1.2	2	1.2
Age requirement only					
Age					
55		6	1.0%	2	1.2%
62		2	0.3	0	0.0
Service requirement only					
	Service				
	5	3	0.5%	3	1.8%
	7	1	0.2	1	0.6
	10	4	0.7	0	0.0
	20	1	0.2	2	1.2
Age and points requirement					
Age	**Points**				
55	65	1	0.2%	0	0.0%
55	70	7	1.2	2	1.2
55	75+	3	0.5	0	0.0
56-59	65-85	2	0.3	1	0.6
60	75	2	0.3	0	0.0
60	80	2	0.3	1	0.6

Eligibility Requirements (continued)

			Salaried		Hourly	
			Number	Percent	Number	Percent
Service and points requirement						
	Service	Points				
	10	65-75	3	0.5%	0	0.0%
Age, service and points requirement						
Age	Service	Points				
<55	5-15	55-75	4	0.7%	0	0.0%
55	5	65	2	0.3	0	0.0
55	10	70	1	0.2	0	0.0
55	10	75	4	0.7	1	0.6
Points only requirement						
		Points				
		65	4	0.7%	0	0.0%
		70	1	0.2	0	0.0
		75	1	0.2	2	1.2
Two or more alternatives						
35.2%				126	20.9%	58
Other			10	1.7%	2	1.2%
Total employees			603	100.0%	165	100.0%

Most pre-65 retiree health plans are a continuation of the active health plan.

Type of Pre-65 Medical Coverage

	Salaried		Hourly	
	Number	Percent	Number	Percent
Same as active plan	504	83.6%	136	82.4%
Special retiree plan	95	15.8	28	17.0
Other	4	0.7	1	0.6

There are a variety of ways that retiree contributions are determined. Generally, contributions are the same for all retirees and dependents but sometimes they may vary by age or service.

Type of Pre-65 Medical Contribution

	Salaried		Hourly	
	Number	**Percent**	**Number**	**Percent**
No retiree contributions required	12	2.0%	21	12.7%
Required for retiree and spouse: All retirees pay same amount	149	24.7	35	21.2
Retiree pays 100% of cost	180	29.9	42	25.5
Credits or allowance provided to offset retiree cost	15	2.5	4	2.4
Required for retiree and spouse: Amount paid is based on age	10	1.7	2	1.2
Required for retiree and spouse: Amount paid is based on service	101	16.7	29	17.6
Credits or allowance provided based on service	44	7.3	10	6.1
Required for retiree and spouse: Amount paid is based on age and service	20	3.3	5	3.0
Credits or allowance provided based on age and service	7	1.2	2	1.2
Required for retiree and spouse: Amount paid is based on other factors	34	5.6	3	1.8
Whether or not required depends on service and/or age	2	0.3	3	1.8
Whether or not required depends on option selected by retiree	1	0.2	0	0.0
Other	5	0.8	2	1.2
Employer contribution to purchase individual coverage	18	3.0	0	0.0
Paid from retiree medical spending account	5	0.8	7	4.2
Total employers	603	100.0%	165	100.0

After FAS 106 was passed, several employers placed limits on their contribution to retiree medical plans. These have commonly been called "capped" plans because the employer obligation is capped at a defined dollar amount.

Pre-65 Retirees:
Defined Dollar Approach for Employer Contributions

	Salaried		Hourly	
	Number	**Percent**	**Number**	**Percent**
Defined dollar approach limits current employer cost	171	28.4%	40	24.2%
Defined dollar approach with cap set at some future time	2	0.3	3	1.8
Defined dollar approach with indexed limit	15	2.5	2	1.2
Retiree pays 100% of cost	180	29.8	42	25.5
Other	9	1.5	8	4.9
No defined dollar cap to employer subsidy	226	37.5	70	42.4
Total employers	603	100.0	165	100.0

Most post-65 plans revert back to an indemnity-type plan that utilizes the Medicare fee schedule as the basis for determining benefits. Sometimes, providers may bill amounts greater than the fee schedule but that is limited by law. The following table provides the various methods used to integrate with the Medicare program.

Post-65 Retirees: Type of Medical Coverage

	Salaried		Hourly	
	Number	Percent	Number	Percent
Active plan with Medicare carve-out	224	45.0%	57	42.5%
Active plan with Medicare coordination of benefits	28	5.6	5	3.7
Special retiree plan with Medicare carve-out	82	16.5	21	15.7
Special retiree plan with Medicare coordination of benefits	4	0.8	1	0.8
Medicare supplement	125	25.1	43	32.1
Medicare risk HMO	5	1.0	0	0.0
Retiree medical spending account	18	3.6	2	1.5
Other	9	1.8	4	3.0
Data not provided	3	0.6	1	0.8
Total employers	498	100.0	134	100.0

Generally, the retiree contribution strategies are similar for pre- and post-65 retirees but they are not always the same. The following table provides the methods used for post-65 benefits.

Post-65 Retirees: Medical Contributions

	Salaried		Hourly	
	Number	**Percent**	**Number**	**Percent**
No retiree contributions required	15	3.0%	23	17.2%
Required for retiree and spouse: All retirees pay same amount	109	21.9	28	20.9
Retiree pays 100% of cost	146	29.3	30	22.4
Credits or allowance provided to offset retiree cost	13	2.6	2	1.5
Required for retiree and spouse: Amount paid is based on age	3	0.6	1	0.8
Required for retiree and spouse: Amount paid is based on service	84	16.9	21	15.7
Credits or allowance provided based on service	44	8.8	8	6.0
Required for retiree and spouse: Amount paid is based on age and service	19	3.8	4	3.0
Credits or allowance provided based on age and service	5	1.0	2	1.5
Required for retiree and spouse: Amount paid is based on other factors	22	4.4	2	1.5
Whether or not required depends on service and/or age	0	0.0	1	0.8
Other	2	0.4	2	1.5
Employer contribution to purchase individual coverage	1	0.2	0	0.0
Paid from retiree medical spending account	32	6.4	8	6.0
Data not provided	3	0.6	2	1.5
Total employers	498	100.0%	134	100.0

For employers placing limits on their contribution to pre-65 retiree medical plans, similar limits are placed on post-65 plans albeit at lower dollar limits because of the cost difference.

Post-65 Retirees:
Defined Dollar Approach for Employer Contributions

	Salaried		Hourly	
	Number	**Percent**	**Number**	**Percent**
Defined dollar approach limits current employer cost	154	30.9%	30	22.4%
Defined dollar approach with cap set at some future time	4	0.8	7	5.2
Defined dollar approach with indexed limit	13	2.6	2	1.5
Retiree pays 100% of cost	146	29.3	30	22.4
Other	1	0.2	4	3.0
Data not provided	3	0.6	2	1.5
No defined dollar cap to employer subsidy	177	35.5	59	44.0
Total employers	498	100.0	134	100.0

APPENDIX B
MEDICARE PART D

This appendix includes key references for the employer alternatives under the Medicare Modernization Act.

MEDICARE MODERNIZATION ACT
Title I, Section 101 of the legislative language under the MMA regarding the retiree drug subsidy alternative for employers and unions.

Special Rules for Employer-Sponsored Programs

Section 1860D–22

(a) *Subsidy Payment*
   (1) *In general.* The Secretary shall provide in accordance with this subsection for payment to the sponsor of a qualified retiree prescription drug plan (as defined in paragraph (2)) of a special subsidy payment equal to the amount specified in paragraph (3) for each qualified covered retiree under the plan (as defined in paragraph (4)). This subsection constitutes budget authority in advance of appropriations Acts and represents the obligation of the Secretary to provide for the payment of amounts provided under this section.
   (2) *Qualified retiree prescription drug plan defined.* For purposes of this subsection, the term 'qualified retiree prescription drug plan' means employment-based retiree health coverage (as defined in subsection (c)(1)) if, with respect to a part D eligible individual who is a participant or beneficiary under such coverage, the following requirements are met:
      (A) *Attestation of actuarial equivalence to standard coverage.* The sponsor of the plan provides the Secretary, annually or at such other time as the Secretary may require, with an attestation that the actuarial value of prescription drug cover-

age under the plan (as determined using the processes and methods described in section 1860D–11(c)) is at least equal to the actuarial value of standard prescription drug coverage.

(B) *Audits*. The sponsor of the plan, or an administrator of the plan designated by the sponsor, shall maintain (and afford the Secretary access to) such records as the Secretary may require for purposes of audits and other oversight activities necessary to ensure the adequacy of prescription drug coverage and the accuracy of payments made under this section. The provisions of section 1860D–2(d)(3) shall apply to such information under this section (including such actuarial value and attestation) in a manner similar to the manner in which they apply to financial records of PDP sponsors and MA organizations.

(C) P*rovision of disclosure regarding prescription drug coverage*. The sponsor of the plan shall provide for disclosure of information regarding prescription drug coverage in accordance with section 1860D–13(b)(6)(B).

(3) *Employer And Union Special Subsidy Amounts*.

(A) *In general*. For purposes of this subsection, the special subsidy payment amount under this paragraph for a qualifying covered retiree for a coverage year enrolled with the sponsor of a qualified retiree prescription drug plan is, for the portion of the retiree's gross covered retiree plan-related prescription drug costs (as defined in subparagraph (C)(ii)) for such year that exceeds the cost threshold amount specified in subparagraph (B) and does not exceed the cost limit under such subparagraph, an amount equal to 28 percent of the allowable retiree costs (as defined in subparagraph (C)(i)) attributable to such gross covered prescription drug costs.

(B) *Cost Threshold And Cost Limit Applicable*.

(i) *In general*. Subject to clause (ii)—

(I) the cost threshold under this subparagraph is equal to $250 for plan years that end in 2006; and

(II) the cost limit under this subparagraph is equal to $5,000 for plan years that end in 2006.

(ii) *Indexing*. The cost threshold and cost limit amounts specified in subclauses (I) and (II) of clause (i) for a plan year that ends after 2006 shall be adjusted in the same manner as the annual deductible and the annual out-of-pocket threshold, respectively, are annually adjusted under paragraphs (1) and (4)(B) of section 1860D–2(b).

(C) *Definitions.* For purposes of this paragraph:

  (i) *Allowable retiree costs.* The term 'allowable retiree costs' means, with respect to gross covered prescription drug costs under a qualified retiree prescription drug plan by a plan sponsor, the part of such costs that are actually paid (net of discounts, chargebacks, and average percentage rebates) by the sponsor or by or on behalf of a qualifying covered retiree under the plan.

  (ii) *Gross covered retiree plan-related prescription drug costs.* For purposes of this section, the term 'gross covered retiree plan-related prescription drug costs' means, with respect to a qualifying covered retiree enrolled in a qualified retiree prescription drug plan during a coverage year, the costs incurred under the plan, not including administrative costs, but including costs directly related to the dispensing of covered part D drugs during the year. Such costs shall be determined whether they are paid by the retiree or under the plan.

  (iii) *Coverage year.*—The term 'coverage year' has the meaning given such term in section 1860D–15(b)(4).

(4) *Qualifying covered retiree defined.* For purposes of this subsection, the term 'qualifying covered retiree' means a part D eligible individual who is not enrolled in a prescription drug plan or an MA–PD plan but is covered under a qualified retiree prescription drug plan.

(5) *Payment methods, including provision of necessary information.* The provisions of section 1860D–15(d) (including paragraph (2), relating to requirement for provision of information) shall apply to payments under this subsection in a manner similar to the manner in which they apply to payment under section 1860D–15(b).

(6) *Construction.* Nothing in this subsection shall be construed as—

  (A) precluding a part D eligible individual who is covered under employment-based retiree health coverage from enrolling in a prescription drug plan or in an MA–PD plan;

  (B) precluding such employment-based retiree health coverage or an employer or other person from paying all or any portion of any premium required for coverage under a prescription drug plan or MA–PD plan on behalf of such an individual;

(C) preventing such employment-based retiree health coverage from providing coverage—

   (i) that is better than standard prescription drug coverage to retirees who are covered under a qualified retiree prescription drug plan; or

   (ii) that is supplemental to the benefits provided under a prescription drug plan or an MA–PD plan, including benefits to retirees who are not covered under a qualified retiree prescription drug plan but who are enrolled in such a prescription drug plan or MA–PD plan; or

(D) preventing employers to provide for flexibility in benefit design and pharmacy access provisions, without regard to the requirements for basic prescription drug coverage, so long as the actuarial equivalence requirement of paragraph (2)(A) is met.

(b) *Application of MA Waiver Authority.* The provisions of section 1857(i) shall apply with respect to prescription drug plans in relation to employment-based retiree health coverage in a manner similar to the manner in which they apply to an MA plan in relation to employers, including authorizing the establishment of separate premium amounts for enrollees in a prescription drug plan by reason of such coverage and limitations on enrollment to part D eligible individuals enrolled under such coverage.

(c) *Definitions.* For purposes of this section:

   (1) *Employment-based retiree health coverage.* The term 'employment-based retiree health coverage' means health insurance or other coverage of health care costs (whether provided by voluntary insurance coverage or pursuant to statutory or contractual obligation) for part D eligible individuals (or for such individuals and their spouses and dependents) under a group health plan based on their status as retired participants in such plan.

   (2) *Sponsor.* The term 'sponsor' means a plan sponsor, as defined in section 3(16)(B) of the Employee Retirement Income Security Act of 1974, in relation to a group health plan, except that, in the case of a plan maintained jointly by one employer and an employee organization and with respect to which the employer is the primary source of financing, such term means such employer.

(3) *Group health plan*. The term 'group health plan' includes such a plan as defined in section 607(1) of the Employee Retirement Income Security Act of 1974 and also includes the following:

    (A) *Federal and state governmental plans*. Such a plan established or maintained for its employees by the Government of the United States, by the government of any State or political subdivision thereof, or by any agency or instrumentality of any of the foregoing, including a health benefits plan offered under chapter 89 of title 5, United States Code.

    (B) *Collectively bargained plans*. Such a plan established or maintained under or pursuant to one or more collective bargaining agreements.

    (C) *Church plans*. Such a plan established and maintained for its employees (or their beneficiaries) by a church or by a convention or association of churches which is exempt from tax under section 501 of the Internal Revenue Code of 1986.

Section 1202 Exclusion From Gross Income of Certain Federal Subsidies for Prescription Drug Plans

(a*) In general*. Part III of subchapter B of chapter 1 of the Internal Revenue Code of 1986 is amended by inserting after section 139 the following new section:

Section 139A Federal Subsidies For Prescription Drug Plans

Gross income shall not include any special subsidy payment received under section 1860D–22 of the Social Security Act. This section shall not be taken into account for purposes of determining whether any deduction is allowable with respect to any cost taken into account in determining such payment."

(b) *Alternative Minimum Tax Relief.* Section 56(g)(4)(B) of such Code is amended by inserting "or 139A" after ''section 114."

(c) *Conforming amendment*. The table of sections for part III of subchapter B of chapter 1 of such Code is amended by inserting after the item relating to section 139 the following new item:

Sec. 139A. Federal subsidies for prescription drug plans.

MMA Retiree Drug Subsidy Regulations

The following are the final regulations addressing the retiree drug subsidy.

Subpart R – Payments to Sponsors of Retiree Prescription Drug Plans

§423.880 Basis and Scope

(a) *Basis*. This subpart is based on section 1860D-22of the Act, as amended by section 101 of the Medicare Prescription Drug, Improvement, and Modernization Act of2003 (MMA).
(b) *Scope*. This section implements the statutory requirement that a subsidy payment be made to sponsors of qualified retiree prescription drug plans.

§423.882 Definitions

For the purposes of this subpart, the following definitions apply:

Allowable retiree costs, in accordance with section 1860D-22(a)(3)(C)(i) of the Act, means gross covered retiree plan-related prescription drug costs that are actually paid (net any manufacturer or pharmacy discounts, chargebacks, rebates, and similar price concessions) by either the qualified retiree prescription drug plan or the qualifying covered retiree (or on the qualifying covered retiree's behalf).

Benefit option means a particular benefit design, category of benefits, or cost-sharing arrangement offered within a group health plan.

Employment-based retiree health coverage means coverage of health care costs under a group health plan based on an individual's status as a retired participant in the plan, or as the spouse or dependent of a retired participant. The term includes coverage provided by voluntary insurance coverage, or coverage as a result of a statutory or contractual obligation.

Gross covered retiree plan-related prescription drug costs, or *gross retiree costs* means, for a qualifying covered retiree who is enrolled in a qualified retiree prescription drug plan during a plan year, non-administrative costs incurred under the plan for Part D drugs during the year, whether paid for by the plan or the retiree, including costs directly related to the dispensing of Part D drugs.

Group health plans include plans as defined in section 607(1) of ERISA, 29 U.S.C. §1167(1). They also include the following plans:

(1) A Federal or State governmental plan, which is a plan providing medical care that is established or maintained for its employees by the Government of the United States, by the government of any State or political subdivision of a State (including a county or local government), or by any agency or instrumentality or any of the foregoing, including a health benefits plan offered under chapter 89 of Title 5, United States Code (the Federal Employee Health Benefit Plan (FEHBP)).

(2) A collectively bargained plan, which is a plan providing medical care that is established or maintained under or by one or more collective bargaining agreements.

(3) A church plan, which is a plan providing medical care that is established and maintained for its employees or their beneficiaries by a church or by a convention or association of churches that is exempt from tax under section 501 of the Internal Revenue Code of 1986 (26 U.S.C.501).

(4) An account-based medical plan such as a Health Reimbursement Arrangement (HRA) as defined in Internal Revenue Service Notice 2002-45, 2002-28 I.R.B. 93, a health Flexible Spending Arrangement (FSA) as defined in Internal Revenue Code (Code) section 106(c)(2), a health savings account (HSA) as defined in Code section 223, or an Archer MSA as defined in Code section 220, to the extent they are subject to ERISA as employee welfare benefit plans providing medical care (or would be subject to ERISA but for the exclusion in ERISA section 4(b), 29 U.S.C.§ .§1003(b), for governmental plans or church plans).

> *Part D drug* is defined in §423.100 of this part.
> *Part D eligible individual* is defined in §423.4 of this part.

Qualified retiree prescription drug plan means employment-based retiree health coverage that meets the requirements set forth in §423.884 of this chapter for a Part D eligible individual who is a retired participant or the spouse or dependent of a retired participant under the coverage.

Qualifying covered retiree means a Part D eligible individual who is: a participant or the spouse or dependent of a participant; covered under employment-based retiree health coverage that qualifies as a qualified retiree prescription drug plan; and not enrolled in a Part D plan. For this purpose, the determination of whether an individual is covered under employment-based retiree health coverage is made by the sponsor in accordance with the rules of its plan. For purposes of this subpart, however, an individual is presumed not to be covered underemployment-based retiree health coverage if, under the Medicare Secondary Payer rules in §411.104 of this chapter and related CMS guidance, the person is considered to be receiving coverage by reason of current employment status. The presumption applies whether or not the Medicare Secondary Payer rules actually apply to the sponsor. For this purpose, a sponsor also may treat a person receiving coverage under its qualified retiree prescription drug plan as the dependent of a qualifying covered retiree in accordance with the rules of its plan, regardless of whether that person constitutes the qualifying covered retiree's dependent for Federal or State tax purposes.

Retiree drug subsidy amount, or *subsidy payment*, means the subsidy amount paid to sponsors of qualified retiree prescription drug coverage under §423.886(a).

Standard prescription drug coverage is defined in §423.100 of this part.

Sponsor is a plan sponsor as defined in section 3(16)(B) of the Employee Retirement Income Security Act of1974 (ERISA), 29 U.S.C. 1002(16)(B), except that, in the case of a plan maintained jointly by one employer and an employee organization and for which the employer is the primary source of financing, the term means the employer.

Sponsor agreement means an agreement by the sponsor to comply with the provisions of this subpart.

§423.884 Requirements for Qualified Retiree Prescription Drug Plans

(a) *General*. Employment-based retiree health coverage is considered to be a qualified retiree prescription drug plan if all of the following requirements are satisfied:
  (1) An actuarial attestation is submitted in accordance with paragraph (d) of this section. The rules for submitting attestations as part of subsidy applications are described in paragraph (c) of this section.
  (2) Part D eligible individuals covered under the plan are provided with creditable coverage notices in accordance with §423.56.

(3) Records are maintained and made available for audit in accordance with paragraph (f) of this section and §423.888(d).

(b) *Disclosure of information.* The sponsor must have a written agreement with its health insurance issuer (as defined in 45 CFR 160.103), or group health plan (as applicable) regarding disclosure of information to CMS, and the issuer or plan must disclose to CMS, on behalf of the sponsor, the information necessary for the sponsor to comply with this subpart.

(c) *Application*
  (1) *Submitting an application.* The sponsor (or its designee) must submit an application for the subsidy to CMS that is signed by an authorized representative of the sponsor. The application must be provided in a form and manner specified by CMS.
  (2) *Required information.* In connection with each application the sponsor (either directly or through its designee) must submit the following:
    (i) Employer Tax ID Number (if applicable).
    (ii) Sponsor name and address.
    (iii) Contact name and email address.
    (iv) Actuarial attestation that satisfies the standards specified in paragraph (d) of this section and any other supporting documentation required by CMS for each qualified retiree prescription drug plan for which the sponsor seeks subsidy payments.
    (v) A list of all individuals the sponsor believes (using information reasonably available to the sponsor when it submits the application) are qualifying covered retirees enrolled in each prescription drug plan (including spouses and dependents, if Medicare-eligible), along with the information about each person listed below in this paragraph:
      (A) Full name.
      (B) Health Insurance Claim (HIC) number or Social Security number.
      (C) Date of birth.
      (D) Gender.
      (E) Relationship to the retired employee.
    (vi) A sponsor may satisfy paragraph (c)(2)(v) of this section by entering into a voluntary data sharing agreement (VDSA) with CMS (or any other arrangement CMS may make available).
    (vii) A signed sponsor agreement.
    (viii) Any other information specified by CMS.

(3) *Terms and conditions.* To receive a subsidy payment, the sponsor (through the signed sponsor agreement or as otherwise specified by CMS) must specifically accept and agree to:
  (i) Comply with the terms and conditions of eligibility for a subsidy payment set forth in this regulation and in any related CMS guidance;
  (ii) Acknowledge that the information in the application is being provided to obtain Federal funds; and
  (iii) Require that all subcontractors, including plan administrators, acknowledge that information provided in connection with the subcontract is used for purposes of obtaining Federal funds.

(4) *Signature by sponsor.* An authorized representative of the requesting sponsor must sign the completed application and certify that the information contained in the application is true and accurate to the best of the sponsor's knowledge and belief.

(5) *Timing.*
  (i) *General rule.* An application for a given plan year must be submitted by no later than 90 days prior to the beginning of the plan year, unless a request for an extension has been filed and approved under procedures established by CMS.
  (ii) *Transition rule.* For plan years that end in2006, an application must be submitted by September 30, 2005 unless a request for an extension has been filed and approved under procedures established by CMS.

(6) *Updates.* The sponsor (or the designee) must provide updates to CMS in a manner specified by CMS of the information required in paragraph (c)(2) of this section on a monthly basis or at a frequency specified by CMS.

(7) *Data match.* Once the full application for the subsidy payment is submitted, CMS —
  (i) Matches the names and identifying information of the individuals submitted as qualifying covered retirees with the Medicare Beneficiary Database (MBD) to determine which retirees are Part D eligible individuals who are not enrolled in a Part D plan.
  (ii) Provides information concerning the results of the search in paragraph (c)(7)(i) of this paragraph (such as names and other identifying information, if necessary) to the sponsor (or to a designee).

(d) *Actuarial attestation-general.* The sponsor of the plan must provide to CMS an attestation in a form and manner specified by CMS that the actuarial value of the retiree prescription drug coverage under the plan is at least equal to the actuarial value of the defined standard prescription drug coverage (as defined at §423.100). The attestation must meet all of the following standards.

(1) Contents of the attestation include the following assurances:
   (i) The actuarial gross value of the retiree prescription drug coverage under the plan for the plan year is at least equal to the actuarial gross value of the defined standard prescription drug coverage under Part D for the plan year in question.
   (ii) The actuarial net value of the retiree prescription drug coverage under the plan for that plan year is at least equal to the actuarial net value of the defined standard prescription drug coverage under Part D for the plan year in question.
   (iii) The actuarial values must be determined using the methodology in paragraph (d)(5) of this section.

(2) The attestation must be made by a qualified actuary who is a member of the American Academy of Actuaries. Applicants may use qualified outside actuaries, including (but not limited to) actuaries employed by the plan administrator or an insurer providing benefits under the plan. If an applicant uses an outside actuary, the attestation can be submitted directly by the outside actuary or by the plan sponsor.

(3) The attestation must be signed by a qualified actuary and must state that the attestation is true and accurate to the best of the attester's knowledge and belief.

(4) The attestation must contain an acknowledgement that the information being provided in the attestation is being used to obtain Federal funds.

(5) *Methodology.*
   (i) Basis of the attestation. The attestation must be based on generally accepted actuarial principles and any actuarial guidelines established by CMS in this section or in future guidance. To the extent CMS has not provided guidance on a specific aspect of the actuarial equivalence standard under this section, an actuary providing the attestation may rely on any reasonable interpretation of this section and section 1860D-22(a) of the Act consistent with generally accepted actuarial principles in determining actuarial values.
   (ii) *Specific rules for determining the actuarial value of the sponsor's retiree prescription drug coverage.*

(A) The gross value of coverage under the sponsor's retiree prescription drug plan must be determined using the actual claims experience and demographic data for Part D eligible individuals who are participants and beneficiaries in the sponsor's plan, provided that sponsors without creditable data due to their size or other factors, may use normative databases as specified by CMS. Sponsors may use other actuarial approaches specified by CMS as an alternative to the actuarial valuation specified by this paragraph (d)(5)(ii)(A).

(B) The net value of coverage provided under the sponsor's retiree prescription drug plan must be determined by reducing the gross value of such coverage as determined under paragraph (d)(5)(ii)(A) of this section by the expected premiums paid by Part D eligible individuals who are plan participants or their spouses and dependents. For sponsors of plans that charge a single, integrated premium or contribution to their retirees for both prescription drug coverage and other types of medical coverage, the attestation must allocate a portion of the premium/contribution to prescription drug coverage under the sponsor's plan, under any method determined by the sponsor or its actuary.

(iii) *Specific rules for calculating the actuarial value of defined standard prescription drug coverage under Part D.*

(A) The gross value of defined standard prescription drug coverage under Part D must be determined using the actual claims experience and demographic data for Part D eligible individuals in the sponsor's plan, provided that sponsors without credible data due to their size or other factors may use normative databases as specified by CMS. Sponsors may use other actuarial approaches specified by CMS as an alternative to the actuarial valuation specified by this paragraph (d)(5)(iii)(A).

(B) To calculate the net value of defined standard prescription drug coverage under Part D, the gross value of defined standard prescription drug coverage under Part D as determined by paragraph (d)(5)(iii)(A) of this section is reduced by the following amounts:

(1) The monthly beneficiary premiums (as defined in §423.286) expected to be paid for standard prescription drug coverage; and

(2) An amount calculated to reflect the impact on the value of defined standard prescription drug coverage of supplemental coverage provided by the sponsor. Sponsors may use other actuarial approaches specified by CMS as an alternative to the actuarial valuation specified in this paragraph (d)(5)(iii)(B)(2).

(C) The valuation of defined standard prescription drug coverage for a given plan year is based on the initial coverage limit cost-sharing and out-of-pocket threshold for defined standard prescription drug coverage under Part D in effect at the start of such plan year. The attestation, however, must be submitted to CMS no later than 60 days after the publication of the Part D coverage limits for the upcoming calendar year otherwise, such valuation is based on the initial coverage limit, cost-sharing amounts, and out-of-pocket threshold for defined standard prescription drug coverage under Part D for the upcoming calendar year.

(D) Example. If a sponsor's retiree prescription drug plan operates under a plan year that ends March 30, the attestation for the year April 1, 2007-March 30, 2008 is based on the coverage limit, cost-sharing and out-of-pocket threshold that apply to defined standard prescription drug coverage under Part D in 2007 provided the attestation is submitted within 60 days after the publication of the Part D coverage limits for 2008. If the attestation is submitted more than 60 days after the 2008 coverage limits have been published, the 2008 coverage limits would apply.

(iv) Employment-based retiree health coverage with two or more benefit options. For the assurance required under paragraph (d)(1)(i) of this section, the assurance must be provided separately for each benefit option for which the sponsor requests a subsidy under this subpart. For the assurance required under paragraph (d)(1)(ii) of this section, the assurance may be provided either separately for each benefit option for which the sponsor provided assurances under paragraph (d)(1)(i) of this section, or in the aggregate for all benefit options for which the sponsor provided assurances under paragraph (d)(1)(i) of this section.

(6) *Timing*.
  (i) *Annual submission*. The attestation must be provided annually at the time the sponsor's subsidy application is submitted, or at such other times as specified by CMS in further guidance.
  (ii)Submission following material change. The attestation must be provided no later than 90 days before the implementation of a material change to the drug coverage of the sponsor's plan that impacts the actuarial value of the coverage.

(e) Disclosure of creditable prescription drug coverage status. The sponsor must disclose to all of its retirees and their spouses and dependents eligible to participate in its plan who are Part D eligible individuals whether the coverage is creditable prescription drug coverage under §423.56 in accordance with the notification requirements under that section.

(f) Access to records for audit. The sponsor (and where applicable, its designee) must meet the requirements of §423.888(d). Failure to comply with §423.888(d) may result in nonpayment or recoupment of all or part of a subsidy payment.

§423.886 Retiree Drug Subsidy Amounts.

(a) *Amount of subsidy payment*.
  (1) For each qualifying covered retiree enrolled with the sponsor of a qualified retiree prescription drug plan in a plan year, the sponsor receives a subsidy payment in the amount of 28percent of the allowable retiree costs (as defined in §423.882) in the plan year for such retiree attributable to gross retiree costs between the cost threshold and the cost limit as defined in paragraph (b) of this section. The subsidy payment is calculated by first determining gross retiree costs between the cost threshold and cost limit, and then determining allowable retiree costs attributable to the gross retiree costs. For this purpose and where otherwise relevant in this subpart, plan year is the calendar, policy, or fiscal year on which the records of a plan are kept.
  (2) *Transition provision*. For a qualified retiree prescription drug plan that has a plan year which begins in calendar year 2005 and ends in calendar year 2006, the subsidy for the plan year must be determined in the following manner. Claims incurred in all months of the plan year (including claims incurred in 2005) are taken into account in determining which claims fall within the

cost threshold and cost limit for the plan year. The subsidy amount is determined based only on costs incurred on and after January 1, 2006.

(b) *Cost threshold and cost limit.* The following cost threshold and cost limits apply—

    (1) Subject to paragraph (b)(3) of this section, the cost threshold under this section is equal to $250 for plan years that end in 2006.

    (2) Subject to paragraph (b)(3) of this section, the cost limit under this section is equal to $5,000 for plan years that end in 2006.

    (3) The cost threshold and cost limit specified in paragraphs (b)(1) and (b)(2) of this section, for plan years that end in years after 2006, are adjusted in the same manner as the annual Part D deductible and the annual Part D out-of-pocket threshold are adjusted annually under §423.104(d)(1)(ii) and (d)(5)(iii)(B), respectively.

§423.888 Payment methods, including provision of necessary information.

(a) *Basis.* The provisions of §423.301 through§423.343, including requirements to provide information necessary to ensure accurate subsidy payments, govern payment under §423.886 except to the extent the provisions in this section specify otherwise.

(b) *General payment rules.* Payment under §423.886 is conditioned on provision of accurate information. The information must be submitted, in a form and manner and at the times provided in this paragraph and under other guidance specified by CMS, by the sponsor or its designee.

    (1) *Timing.* Payment can be made on a monthly, quarterly or annual basis, as elected by the plan sponsor under guidance specified by CMS, unless CMS determines that the options must be restricted because of operational limitations.

        (i) *Monthly or quarterly payments.* If the plan sponsor elects for payment on a monthly or quarterly basis, it must provide information described in paragraph (b)(2)(i) of this section on the same monthly or quarterly basis, or at such time as CMS specifies.

        (ii) *Annual payments.* If the sponsor elects an annual payment, it must submit to CMS actual rebate and other price concession data within 15 months after the end of the plan year.

(2) *Submission of cost data*
    (i) *Monthly or quarterly payments.* If the plan sponsor elects to receive payment on a monthly or quarterly basis, it must submit to CMS, in a manner specified by CMS, the gross covered retiree plan-related prescription drug costs (as defined in§423.882) incurred for its qualifying covered retirees during the payment period for which it is claiming a subsidy payment and any other data CMS may require. Except as otherwise provided by CMS in future guidance, the sponsor must also submit, using historical data and generally accepted actuarial principles, an estimate of the extent to which its expected allowable retiree costs differs from the gross covered retiree plan-related prescription drug costs, based on expected rebates and other price concessions for the upcoming plan year. The estimate must be used to reduce the periodic payments for the plan year. Final allocation of price concession data must occur after the end of the year under the reconciliation provisions of paragraph (b)(4) of this section.

    (ii) *Annual payments.* If the plan sponsor elects a one-time final annual payment, it must submit, in a manner specified by CMS, within 15 months, or within any other longer time limit specified by CMS, after the end of the plan year, the total gross covered retiree plan-related prescription drug costs (as defined in §423.882) for the plan year for which it is claiming a subsidy payment, actual rebate and other price concession data described in paragraph (b)(1)(ii) of this section, and any other data CMS may require. The alternative is that the sponsor can elect an interim annual payment, in which case it must submit the following to CMS, at a time and in a manner specified by CMS: the gross covered retiree plan-related prescription drug costs (as defined in §423.882) incurred for all of its qualifying covered retirees during the payment period for which it is claiming a subsidy payment; an estimate (using historical data and generally accepted actuarial principles) of the difference between such gross costs and allowable costs (based on expected rebates and other price concessions for the upcoming plan year); and any other data CMS may require.

(3) *Payment by CMS.* CMS makes payment after the sponsor's submission of the cost data at a time and in a manner to be specified by CMS.

(4) *Reconciliation*

    (i) Sponsors who elect either monthly, quarterly or an interim annual payment must submit to CMS, within 15 months, or within any other longer time limit specified by CMS, after the end of its plan year, the total gross covered retiree plan-related prescription drug costs (as defined in §423.882), in a manner specified by CMS; actual rebate and other price concession data for the plan year in question; and any other data CMS may require.

    (ii) Upon receiving this data, CMS adjusts the payments made for the plan year in question in a manner to be specified by CMS.

(5) *Special rule for insured plans*

    (i) *Interim payments.* Sponsors of group health plans that provide benefits through health insurance coverage (as defined in 45 CFR 144.103) and that choose either monthly payments, quarterly payments or an interim annual payment in paragraphs (b)(1) and (b)(2) of this section , may elect to determine gross covered plan-related retiree prescription drug costs for purposes of the monthly, quarterly or interim annual payments based on a portion of the premium costs paid by the sponsor (or by the qualifying covered retirees) for coverage of the covered retirees under the group health plan. Premium costs that are determined, using generally accepted actuarial principles, may be attributable to the gross prescription drug costs incurred by the health insurance issuer (as defined in 45 CFR§144.103) for the sponsor's qualifying covered retirees, except that administrative costs and risk charges must be subtracted from the premium.

    (ii) *Final payments.* At the end of the plan year, actual gross retiree plan-related prescription drug costs incurred by the insurer (or the retiree), and the allowable costs attributable to the gross costs, are determined for each of the sponsor's qualifying covered retirees and submitted for reconciliation after the end of the plan year as specified in paragraph (b)(4)of this section. The data for the reconciliation can be submitted directly to CMS by the insurer in a manner to be specified by CMS. Upon receiving this data, CMS adjusts the payments made for the relevant plan year in a manner to be specified by CMS.

(c) *Use of information provided.* Officers, employees and contractors of the Department of Health and Human Services, including the Office of Inspector General (OIG), may use information collected under this section only for the purposes of, and to the extent necessary in, carrying out this subpart including, but not limited to, determination of payments and payment-related oversight and program integrity activities, or as otherwise required bylaw. This restriction does not limit OIG authority to conduct audits and evaluations necessary for carrying out these regulations.

(d) *Maintenance of records.*
    (1) The sponsor of the qualified retiree prescription drug plan (or a designee), as applicable, must maintain, and furnish to CMS or the OIG upon request, the records enumerated in paragraph (d)(3) of this section. The records must be maintained for 6 years after the expiration of the plan year in which the costs were incurred for the purposes of audits and other oversight activities conducted by CMS to assure the accuracy of the actuarial attestation and the accuracy of payments.

    (2) CMS or the OIG may extend the 6-year retention requirement for the records enumerated in paragraph (d)(3) of this section in the event of an ongoing investigation, litigation, or negotiation involving civil, administrative or criminal liability. In addition, the sponsor of the qualified retiree prescription drug plan (or a designee),as applicable, must maintain the records enumerated in paragraph (d)(3) of this section longer than 6 years if it knows or should know that the records are the subject of an ongoing investigation, litigation or negotiation involving civil, administrative or criminal liability.

    (3) The records that must be retained are:
        (i) Reports and working documents of the actuaries who wrote the attestation submitted in accordance with §423.884(a).
        (ii) All documentation of costs incurred and other relevant information utilized for calculating the amount of the subsidy payment made in accordance with §423.886,including the underlying claims data.
        (iii) Any other records specified by CMS.

    (4) CMS may issue additional guidance addressing recordkeeping requirements, including (but not limited to) the use of electronic

§423.890 Appeals

(a) *Informal Written Reconsideration.*
    (1) *Initial Determinations.* A sponsor is entitled to an informal written reconsideration of an adverse initial determination. An initial determination is a determination regarding the following:
        (i) The amount of the subsidy payment.
        (ii) The actuarial equivalence of the sponsor's retiree prescription drug plan.
        (iii) If an enrollee in a retiree prescription drug plan is a qualifying covered retiree; or
        (iv) Any other similar determination (as determined by CMS) that affects eligibility for, or the amount of, a subsidy payment.
    (2) *Effect of an Initial Determination Regarding the Retiree Drug Subsidy.* An initial determination is final and binding unless reconsidered in accordance with this paragraph (a) of this section.
    (3) *Manner and Timing for Request.* A request for reconsideration must be made in writing and filed with CMS within 15 days of the date on the notice of adverse determination.
    (4) *Content of Request.* The request for reconsideration must specify the findings or issues with which the sponsor disagrees and the reasons for the disagreements. The request for reconsideration may include additional documentary evidence the sponsor wishes CMS to consider.
    (5) *Conduct of Informal Written Reconsideration.* In conducting the reconsideration, CMS reviews the subsidy determination, the evidence and findings upon which it was based, and any other written evidence submitted by the sponsor or by CMS before notice of the reconsidered determination is made.
    (6) *Decision of the Informal Written Reconsideration.* CMS informs the sponsor of the decision orally or through electronic mail. CMS sends a written decision to the sponsor on the sponsor's request.
    (7) *Effect of CMS Informal Written Reconsideration.* A reconsideration decision, whether delivered orally or in writing, is final and binding unless a request for hearing is filed in accordance with paragraph (b) of this section, or it is revised in accordance paragraph (d) of this section.

(b) *Right to Informal Hearing.* A sponsor dissatisfied with the CMS reconsideration decision is entitled to an informal hearing as provided in this section.

(1) *Manner and Timing for Request.* A request for a hearing must be made in writing and filed with CMS within 15 days of the date the sponsor receives the CMS reconsideration decision.

(2) *Content of Request.* The request for informal hearing must include a copy of the CMS reconsideration decision (if any) and must specify the findings or issues in the decision with which the sponsor disagrees and the reasons for the disagreements.

(3) *Informal Hearing Procedures.*

    (i) CMS provides written notice of the time and place of the informal hearing at least 10 days before the scheduled date.

    (ii) The hearing is conducted by a CMS hearing officer who neither receives testimony nor accepts any new evidence that was not presented with the reconsideration request. The CMS hearing officer is limited to the review of the record that was before CMS when CMS made both its initial and reconsideration determinations.

    (iii) If CMS did not issue a written reconsideration decision, the hearing officer may request, but not require, a written statement from CMS or its contractors explaining CMS' determination, or CMS or its contractors may, on their own, submit the written statement to the hearing officer. Failure of CMS to submit a written statement does not result in any adverse findings against CMS and may not in any way be taken into account by the hearing officer in reaching a decision.

(4) *Decision of the CMS Hearing Officer.* The CMS hearing officer decides the case and sends a written decision to the sponsor, explaining the basis for the decision.

(5) *Effect of hearing Officer Decision.* The hearing officer decision is final and binding, unless the decision is reversed or modified by the Administrator in accordance with paragraph (c) of this section.

(c) *Review by the Administrator*

(1) A sponsor that has received a hearing officer decision upholding a CMS initial or reconsidered determination may request review by the Administrator within 15 days of receipt of the hearing officer's decision.

(2) The Administrator may review the hearing officer's decision, any written documents submitted to CMS or to the hearing officer, as well as any other information included in the record of the hearing officer's decision and determine whether to uphold, reverse or modify the hearing officer's decision.

(3) The Administrator's determination is final and binding.

(d) *Reopening*

(1) *Ability to Reopen.* CMS may reopen and revise an initial or reconsidered determination upon its own motion or upon the request of a sponsor:

(i) Within 1 year of the date of the notice of determination for any reason.

(ii) Within 4 years for good cause.

(iii) At any time when the underlying decision was obtained through fraud or similar fault.

(2) *Notice of Reopening*

(i) Notice of reopening and any revisions following the reopening are mailed to the sponsor.

(ii) Notice of reopening specifies the reasons for revision.

(3) *Effect of Reopening.* The revision of an initial or reconsidered determination is final and binding unless—

(i) The sponsor requests reconsideration in accordance with paragraph (a) of this section;

(ii) A timely request for a hearing is filed under paragraph (b) of this section;

(iii) The determination is reviewed by the Administrator in accordance with paragraph (c) of this section; or

(iv) The determination is reopened and revised in accordance with paragraph (d) of this section.

(4) *Good Cause.* For purposes of this section, CMS finds good cause if —

(i) New and material evidence exists that was not readily available at the time the initial determination was made;

(ii) A clerical error in the computation of payments was made; or

(iii) The evidence that was considered in making the determination clearly shows on its face that an error was made.

(5) For purposes of this section, CMS does not find good cause if the only reason for reopening is a change of legal interpretation or administrative ruling upon which the initial determination was made.

(6) A decision by CMS not to reopen an initial or reconsidered determination is final and binding and cannot be appealed.

§423.892 Change of Ownership

(a) *Change of ownership.* Any of the following constitutes a change of ownership:

    (1) *Partnership.* The removal, addition, or substitution of a partner, unless the partners expressly agree otherwise as permitted by applicable State law.

    (2) *Asset sale.* Transfer of all or substantially all of the assets of the sponsor to another party.

    (3) *Corporation.* The merger of the sponsor's corporation into another corporation or the consolidation of the sponsor's organization with one or more other corporations, resulting in a new corporate body.

(b) *Change of ownership, exception.* Transfer of corporate stock or the merger of another corporation into the sponsor's corporation, with the sponsor surviving, does not ordinarily constitute change of ownership.

(c) *Advance notice requirement.* A sponsor that has a sponsor agreement in effect under this part and is considering or negotiating a change in ownership must notify CMS at least 60 days before the anticipated effective date of the change.

(d) *Assignment of agreement.* When there is a change of ownership as specified in paragraph (a) of this section, and this results in a transfer of the liability for prescription drug costs, the existing sponsor agreement is automatically assigned to the new owner.

(e) *Conditions that apply to assigned agreements.* The new owner to whom a sponsor agreement is assigned is subject to all applicable statutes and regulations and to the terms and conditions of the sponsor agreement.

§423.894 Construction

Nothing in this part must be interpreted as prohibiting or restricting:

(a) A Part D eligible individual who is covered underemployment-based retiree health coverage, including a qualified retiree prescription drug plan, from enrolling in a Part D plan;

(b) A sponsor or other person from paying all or any part of the monthly beneficiary premium (as defined in §423.286) for a Part D plan on behalf of a retiree (or his or her spouse or dependents);

(c) A sponsor from providing coverage to Part D eligible individuals under employment-based retiree health coverage that is —

(1) Supplemental to the benefits provided under a Part D plan; or

(2) Of higher actuarial value than the actuarial value of standard prescription drug coverage (as defined in §423.104(d)); or

(d) Sponsors from providing for flexibility in the benefit design and pharmacy network for their qualified retiree prescription drug coverage, without regard to the requirements applicable to Part D plans under §423.104, as long as the requirements under §423.884 are met.

CMS GUIDANCE ON ACTUARIAL EQUIVALENCE FOR RETIREE DRUG SUBSIDY

The following guidance was released by CMS to assist actuaries in determining the actuarial equivalence of employer/union sponsored plans to the Medicare program for the purposes of the retiree drug subsidy.

CMS GUIDANCE ON THE ACTUARIAL EQUIVALENCE STANDARD FOR THE RETIREE DRUG SUBSIDY
April 7, 2005

Introduction

Subpart R of the Title I Medicare Modernization Act (MMA) Final Rule, published in the January 28, 2005 *Federal Register*, implements §1860D-22 of the Social Security Act, which authorizes subsidy payments to the sponsor of a qualified retiree prescription drug plan. Among the qualification requirements is that a qualified actuary submit an attestation to CMS that the plan's actuarial value is at least equal to the actuarial value of defined standard prescription drug coverage under Part D of Medicare. The final rule defines the actuarial equivalence standard, requires that an attestation be based on generally accepted actuarial principles, and states some specific rules on how to apply the attestation in various situations. This guidance is intended to further clarify several issues relating to the methodology for actuarial equivalence attestations and to make it less burdensome for actuaries to complete the actuarial attestation.

Of all the options available for employers and unions under the MMA, the retiree drug subsidy provides the most continuity for existing retiree prescription drug plans. It is the least burdensome option to administer and provides the most design flexibility as long as the sponsor's plan is at least actuarially equivalent to the defined standard prescription drug benefit under Part D. See the Retiree Drug Subsidy: Why Employers and Union Plan Sponsors Should Consider It, April 6, 2005, paper outlining the 5 easy steps to apply for the retiree drug subsidy.

Background

The standard for actuarial equivalence in Subpart R is a two-prong test in which the sponsor's retiree prescription drug program must provide coverage to its Medicare beneficiaries the value of which is at least equal to the value of the coverage the same beneficiaries would receive under the defined standard prescription drug coverage. The first prong is the "gross value" test in which the expected amount of paid claims for Medicare beneficiaries under the sponsor's plan must be at least equal to the expected amount of paid claims for the same beneficiaries under the defined standard prescription drug coverage, including catastrophic coverage available when an individual's out-of-pocket expenses exceed a specified threshold ($3,600 in 2006). See 42 CFR §423.884(d)(1)(i).

The second prong is the "net value" test in which the net value of the sponsor's plan must be at least equal to the net value of the defined standard prescription drug coverage. See §423.884(d)(1)(ii). The net value of the sponsor's plan is calculated by subtracting the retiree premium/contribution from the gross value of the sponsor's plan. See §423.884(d)(5)(ii)(B)(1). The net value of defined standard prescription drug coverage under Part D is calculated by subtracting the prescribed national beneficiary premium from the gross value of the defined standard prescription drug coverage.

For those sponsors that plan to supplement the coverage provided under Part D for their retirees that choose Part D, an additional adjustment to the net value of Part D is permitted that accounts for the impact that the sponsor's supplemental coverage will have on the value of defined standard prescription drug coverage under Part D. See §423.884(d)(5)(ii)(B)(2). By delaying the point at which the individual receives catastrophic coverage under Part D, the supplemental coverage will lower the value of defined standard prescription drug coverage to their plan participants. This anticipated reduction in the value of the defined standard prescription drug coverage under Medicare Part D plan to the plan's retirees resulting from supplemental plan will be referred to in this guidance as the "Medicare Supplemental Adjustment" value.

Clarifications to the Regulation

Premiums

Pursuant to §423.884(d)(5)(iii)(B)(1), in calculating the net value of the defined standard prescription drug coverage under Part D for purposes of the second prong of the actuarial equivalence test, the beneficiary premium is subtracted from the gross value of Part D. This guidance clarifies that the national average beneficiary premium can be used to determine the beneficiary premium for this purpose. One should use the national average beneficiary premium for the same year from which the Part D coverage limits are being utilized for the test. Alternatively, the beneficiary premium can be determined by multiplying the gross value of Part D by 25.5%. In either case, there is no requirement to account for beneficiaries in the plan who may be eligible for reduced premiums (or enhanced benefits) through the low-income subsidy provisions of Subpart P of the final rule (§423.771 et. seq.).

Calculating the Value of Drug Coverage under the Sponsor's Plan

In calculating the gross value of the sponsor's plan under §423.884(d)(1)(i), this guidance clarifies that only prescription drugs that are Part D drugs as defined in §423.882 can be considered; however, the drugs do not necessarily have to be in any Part D plan's formulary to be included in the calculation. Generally, Part D drugs are prescription drugs that are not covered by Part A or Part B of Medicare and may not be excluded from coverage under §1860D-2(e)(2)(A) of the Social Security Act. See the discussion of the definition of "Gross covered retiree plan-related prescription drug costs" in the Subpart R preamble to the final rule at 70 FR 4403 and a discussion paper titled "Medicare Part B Versus Part D Coverage Issues" which can be found at www.cms.hhs.gov/pdps/PARTB-Ddocument.pdf. Conversely, in calculating the value of defined standard prescription drug coverage under Part D, all Part D drugs are considered, including those that the sponsor's plan does not cover.

Eligibility for Medicare Supplemental Adjustment

In §423.884(d)(5)(iii)(B)(2), for purposes of the net value prong of the actuarial equivalence test, the value of the defined standard prescription drug coverage under Part D can be adjusted to reflect the impact of a sponsor's plan supplementing Part D for those beneficiaries in the sponsor's plan who enroll in Part D. This guidance clarifies that the adjustment can only be made by those sponsors who actually supplement the Part D coverage of the Medicare-eligible beneficiaries in their plan who enroll in Part D. A sponsor has flexibility in providing such supplemental coverage. For example, it can design its retiree drug plan to be secondary to any Part D plan selected by a retiree, or it can designate specific Part D arrangements under which the supplemental coverage is provided (including through customized Part D arrangements providing enhanced coverage pursuant to a waiver for the sponsor's retiree coverage). The attestation must take into account any restrictions in beneficiary accessibility to the supplemental coverage by prorating for the share of retirees who have access to the supplemental coverage in determining the impact on the Medicare Supplemental Adjustment value.

The final rule does not require that sponsors supplement Part D coverage for their retirees who enroll in a Part D plan. However, they cannot take into account the Medicare Supplemental Adjustment value pursuant to §423.884(d)(5)(iii)(B)(2) if they do not supplement Part D for a retiree who enrolls in Part D.

Sponsors interested in the Medicare Supplemental Adjustment but concerned about the ability to coordinate their benefits with Part D coverage should be aware that CMS is facilitating the establishment of a coordination of benefits system that will provide, by January 1, 2006, real time, point-of-sale coordination between Medicare Part D and supplemental plans such as employer and union-sponsored plans. Such a system should provide for cost-effective coordination between Medicare and retiree health plans, including those in which a sponsor is providing the coverage to qualify for the Medicare Supplemental Adjustment.

Benefit Options within a Plan

A benefit option is defined in §423.882 of the final rule as a particular benefit design, category of benefits, or cost-sharing arrangement offered within a group health plan.

The final rule in §423.884(d)(5)(iv) provides sponsors with plans with multiple benefit options the flexibility to submit the actuarial equivalence attestation either for each benefit option separately or in the aggregate for options that meet the "gross value" test. That is, each benefit option must separately pass the gross test, but the plan can pass the net test by testing benefit options on an aggregated or separate basis.

This guidance clarifies that the sponsor's attestation can combine either all of the benefit options that meet the gross value test or one or more subsets of those options for purposes of applying the "net value" test and submitting the actuarial attestation. The sponsor (working with its actuary) determines the number of options to be combined for this purpose. If the sponsor combines two or more benefit options, the sponsor may not claim the subsidy for those benefit options excluded from the net value calculation, even if those options meet the gross test.

In applying the gross value and net value test to each benefit option separately (or in the aggregate to a subset of the options), it will be within the discretion of the attesting actuary, in accordance with actuarial standards, to determine the applicability of plan experience across benefit options. For example, an actuary may determine that aggregate plan experience is not applicable to each benefit option even if these benefit options are being aggregated for testing purposes and instead may apply the plan experience unique to each benefit option. Conversely, an actuary may decide to apply the aggregate plan experience to each individual benefit option if the experience segregated by individual benefit option is non-existent or is an unreliable indication of costs.

Integrated Health and Drug Situations

In the final rule it is indicated that sponsors of plans that charge a single, integrated premium or contribution to their retirees for both medical and drug coverage have the complete discretion and flexibility to allocate any portion of the premium to the drug coverage for the purpose of the net value test of actuarial attestation. See §423.884(d)(5)(ii)(B).

This guidance addresses plans that have integrated cost sharing for medical and prescription benefits. Integrated cost-sharing is based on plan experience (unlike premiums, which is a factor of plan design). Accordingly, for benefit plans where the plan design covers both prescription drugs and other medical costs (for example, integrated out-of-pocket limits, integrated deductibles, integrated plan maximums, etc.), an actuary must be able to reasonably estimate and allocate the cost-sharing provisions and cost of benefits for prescription drugs. This allocation can be based upon either actual plan cost experience or on future cost projections. Once this allocation is made, then the value allocated to the drug coverage must pass the gross value test of the actuarial attestation.

Sample Calculation and Simplified Computations for the Actuarial Equivalence Test

Sample Calculation

To assist actuaries in determining the Medicare Supplemental Adjustment, the appendix to this guidance includes a sample calculation showing the steps for the actuarial equivalence test using the "Medicare Supplemental Adjustment." The sample calculation for actuarial equivalence testing utilizes standard actuarial techniques for calculating values of deductibles and coinsurance on a probability distribution, which was previously released by CMS. For plans with co-pay cost-sharing structures, similar techniques would need to be utilized. Further explanation on the techniques and parameters is provided in the appendix.

Simplified Calculations

For those plans that pass the two-prong actuarial equivalence test without the Medicare Supplemental Adjustment, there is no requirement to calculate the adjustment for the "net value" test. Furthermore, if the attesting actuary, in his/her professional judgment, is certain that the sponsor's plan is at least actuarially equivalent to Part D without performing the calculation of either the "gross value" test or the "net value" test, then it is within the actuary's professional discretion as to whether the calculations need to be made to support the attestation. For example, if a retiree drug plan that covers both brand and generic drugs, has a $100 deductible, pays 80% of the cost of drugs with the beneficiary paying the remaining 20% as coinsurance, and the sponsor pays 90% of the premium, this plan would clearly be actuarially equivalent to the defined standard prescription drug benefit under Part D and there would be no need to do the specific calculations.

Normative Data Sets

Certain retiree prescription drug plans may not have sufficiently reliable plan data to use to determine whether the plan's coverage is at least actuarially equivalent to the defined standard prescription drug coverage under Part D. It will be within the discretion of the attesting actuary, in accordance with actuarial standards, whether a plan has sufficiently reliable data for the computation. The attesting actuary may find that utilizing an appropriate normative data set is appropriate as indicated in §423.884(d)(5)(ii)(A) and (d)(5)(iii)(A) of the final rule. Possible normative data sets are:

1. The accepted normative data set tools of the industry provided that the data reflect the demographics and other risk characteristics of the group and are appropriately segregated; or

2   The vendor "block of business" data set.

The calculation of actuarial equivalence should rely on plan experience to the extent that the experience is reasonable and credible. If reasonable and credible experience is not available, the calculations should reflect reasonable actuarial methods that take into account the demographics and other risk characteristics of the group.

Appendix

Sample Calculation

The sample calculation, enclosed in an excel spreadsheet, assumes the employer plan has a $50 deductible and 20% retiree cost sharing. While actuaries will have the ability to review this plan and determine without further calculation that this plan is actuarially equivalent in the first prong, the sample calculation provides the mechanics to demonstrate this. Additionally, the employer plan is assumed to have a retiree premium share arrangement of 40%. However, with the excel spreadsheet, the user can vary the premium share arrangement to create some variations of the sample. In fact, most important plan parameters can be varied. This sample calculation mechanism is not automatically approved for creating actuarial attestations. The actuary must be able to create an opinion that the attestation meets all applicable actuarial standards, including the appropriateness of data and tools used in the calculation, and as set forth in the guidance.

The spreadsheet contains 3 tabs in addition to the Medicare pricing data previously released on October 8, 2004 (Tables 1-4). The Summary Sheet contains all of the parameters utilized in the actuarial equivalence and subsidy calculations. The Working Sheet contains the actuarial calculations on the probability distribution (Table 4) described above. These calculations include: the value of the Medicare Standard Plan (in component pieces, the first layer and the second, catastrophic layer), the value of the subsidy payment, and a detailed calculation demonstrating the calculation of the "Medicare Supplemental Adjustment Value." The detailed calculation assumes that the employer plan would pursue a "carve-out" approach to integrating with Medicare Part D, whereby the retiree cost-sharing would be calculated as if there were no primary plan, and then the employer plan calculates their cost as the difference between (1) the sum of the retiree cost and the Medicare benefit and (2) the eligible expense.

All claim cost calculations are performed in the Summary Sheet and posted to the "AE Test" tab to demonstrate the mathematics involved in calculating the two prongs described above.

Notice that all of the formulas are intact in the excel spreadsheet, which will allow for maximum clarity in understanding the mathematics involved in the calculations, specifically the "Medicare Supplemental Adjustment Value."

Summary Sheet

Summary of Parameters and Calculations
(see AE Test tab for actual test mechanics)

Parameters (2006 values)

Medicare Part D Standard Plan Premium	**$440**
Medicare Part D Standard Plan Deductible	**$250**
End of First Layer of Benefit	**$2,250**
Out-of-Pocket Maximum	**$3,600**
Employer subsidy lower threshold	**$250**
Employer subsidy upper threshold	**$5,000**
Employer subsidy payment amount	**28%**

Employer Plan Specifics

Annual Deductible	**$50**
Coinsurance of Plan	**80%**
Plan Out-of-Pocket Maximum	**None**
Estimated Eligible Charge Level (*)	**$17,800**

(*) If secondary, the eligible charge level when the Medicare Catastrophic coverage would be primary due to fulfillment of the Medicare _Out-of-Pocket Maximum. Please note that the formula in the cell only works for deductible/coinsurance plans which have lower deductibles and greater coinsurance than the Medicare first layer of benefits.

Calculations (see working sheet tab for detail)

		Column
Eligible Charges for Population, on average	$2,963.37	D
Medicar3e value, first layer (75% benefit)	$1,046.67	H
Medicare value, catastrophic layer	$447.15	J
Medicare value, Standard Plan no Supplement	$2,493.82	K
Employer Subsidy	$632.94	L
Employer Plan value, Employer Primary	$2,335.15	R
Employer Plan value, Employer Secondary	$1,233.15	AA

Medicare Value if Employer Supplemental

Medicare value, first layer (75% benefit)	$1,046.67	S
Medicare value, catastrophic layer	$64.83	W
Medicare value, Standard Plan with Supplement	$1,111.50	Z
Supplemental Adjustment (+)	− $382.32	

(+) If an Employer Plan is secondary, the Medicare Catastrophic Coverage will begin at $17,800 in eligible charges, reducing the value of the Catastrophic Layer. The value reduction is the difference between the value of Medicare with no Supplemental coverage, and the value with Supplemental coverage.

AE Test Sheet

Sample Actuarial Equivalence Calculation

	Employer Plan	Medicare D Standard Plan
(1) Eligible Expenses	$2,963	$2,963
(2) Plan Expenses (*)	$2,335	$1,494
(2) (a) Supplemental Adjustment (+)		− $382
(3) Adjusted Plan Expenses	$2,335	$1,112
(4) Retiree Contributions	$934	$381
(40% Employer Plan, 25.5% Medicare D Standard Plan)		
(5) Net Value	$1,401	$731

AE Test Result (Review (5))	Pass
(If Employer Plan Net Value < Medicare Net Value Plan Fails)	
Creditable Coverage test (Review (2))	Pass
(If Employer Plan Gross Value	

< Medicare Gross Value Plan Fails)

(*), (+) See descriptions in Summary Sheet

Extract of Working Sheet

Working Sheet: Distribution of Prescription drug expenses for Medicare beneficiaries:

1998 MCBS updated to 1006 and adjusted for under-reporting of drug expenses, estimated price discounts and other cost-management savings under the MMA, and induced utilization due to insurance effect.

Lowest Bound	Upper Bound	Fraction of Beneficiaries $\{f(x)\}$	Mean R_x Expense $\{x\}$
$0.00	$0.00	0.1106	$0.00
$0.01	$100.00	0.0159	$47.20
$100.01	$200.00	0.0138	$147.96
$200.01	$300.00	0.0154	$246.27
$300.01	$400.00	0.0137	$354.63
$400.01	$500.00	0.0142	$453.18
$500.01	$600.00	0.0128	$549.49
$600.01	$700.00	0.0148	$650.40
$700.01	$800.00	0.0157	$741.69
$800.01	$900.00	0.0133	$847.10
$900.01	$1,000.00	0.0147	$948.14
$1,000.01	$1,100.00	0.0196	$1,050.55

Claim Cost $\{x\} \cdot \{f(s)\}$	Medicare Benefit (first layer)	Retiree Spending (for TrOOP)	Medicare Benefit (second layer)	Total Medicare Benefit	Plan Sponsor Subsidy Payment
$0.00	0.00	$0.00	$0.00	0.00	0.00
$0.75	0.00	$47.20	$0.00	0.00	0.00
$2.04	0.00	$147.96	$0.00	0.00	0.00
$3.79	0.00	$246.27	$0.00	0.00	0.00
$4.86	78.47	$276.16	$0.00	78.47	29.30
$6.44	152.39	$300.80	$0.00	152.39	56.89
$7.03	224.62	$324.87	$0.00	244.62	83.86
$9.63	300.30	$350.10	$0.00	300.30	112.11
$11.64	368.77	$372.92	$0.00	368.77	137.67
$11.27	447.83	$399.28	$0.00	447.83	167.19
$13.94	523.61	$424.54	$0.00	523.61	195.48
$20.59	600.41	$450.14	$0.00	600.41	224.15

Total plan (ded + coinsurance)	Plan in Medicare (ded layer)	Plan in Medicare (first layer)	Plan in Coverage Gap	Subtotal Plan Spend	Medicare Benefit (first layer)	Plan pays secondary (first layer)
$0	$0	$0	$0	$0	0.00	$0
$0	$0	$0	$0	$0	0.00	$0
$78	$78	$0	$0	$78	0.00	$78
$157	$157	$0	$0	$157	0.00	$157
$244	$160	$84	$0	$244	78.47	$165
$323	$160	$163	$0	$323	152.39	$170
$400	$160	$240	$0	$400	224.62	$175
$480	$160	$320	$0	$480	300.30	$180
$553	$160	$393	$0	$553	368.77	$185
$638	$160	$478	$0	$638	447.83	$190
$719	$160	$559	$0	$719	523.61	$195
$800	$160	$640	$0	$800	600.41	$200

Retiree Spending (for Plan OOP) (first pass)	Retiree Spending (for Plan TrOOP)	Medicare Benefit (second layer)	Retiree cost share in second layer (before Plan OOP)	Total Retiree Cost (with Plan OOP)	Total Medicare Cost	Total Plan / Employer Cost
$0.00	$0	$0	$0	$0	$0	$0
$47.20	$47	$0	$0	$47	$0	$0
$69.59	$70	$0	$0	$70	$0	$78
$89.25	$89	$0	$0	$89	$0	$157
$110.93	$111	$0	$0	$111	$78	$165
$130.64	$131	$0	$0	$131	$152	$170
$149.90	$150	$0	$0	$150	$225	$175
$170.08	$170	$0	$0	$170	$300	$180
$188.34	$188	$0	$0	$188	$369	$185
$209.42	$209	$0	$0	$209	$448	$190
$229.63	$230	$0	$0	$230	$524	$195
$250.11	$250	$0	$0	$250	$600	$200

Employer Waivers

CMS issued three guidance documents on employer waivers. These documents clarify the rules regarding employer waivers for direct contracting with PDPs.

First CMS Guidance Document

Part D Waiver Guidance for Employer/Union Retiree Coverage
February 11, 2005

Introduction

Employer Options

The MMA provides employers and unions with a number of options for providing prescription drug coverage to their retirees.

- An employer or union sponsor with coverage that is at least as good as Medicare's Part D defined standard prescription drug benefit can receive a tax-free retiree drug subsidy that pays 28 percent of a retiree's drug costs (as defined by the regulation) between $250 and $5,000 in 2006. The subsidy only applies to retirees eligible for but not enrolled in a Medicare Prescription Drug Plan or a Medicare Advantage Plan (such as an HMO or PPO), cost plan, or PACE plan with prescription drug coverage (collectively, a "Part D plan").

- Another available option is for an employer or union to encourage its retirees to enroll in a Part D plan and then provide them with additional benefits. There are several ways that sponsors could supplement the standard Medicare drug benefit, such as:

  o Setting up their own separate supplemental plans and coordinating benefits with the coverage provided by the Part D plans their retirees enroll in, in much the same way they currently supplement the standard Medicare Part A and B benefits;

  o Paying for enhanced coverage offered under a Part D plan that subsidizes more of their retirees' cost-sharing and provide additional benefits;

  o Making special arrangements with Part D plans to provide an employer-only plan with customized drug benefits for their retirees pursuant to CMS waivers (discussed in more detail below); and

  o Providing the customized drug benefits for their retirees by becoming Part D plans pursuant to CMS waivers.

Overview of Standard Part D Benefit Design

In 2006, standard Part D coverage features a $250 deductible. After that, the plan pays on average approximately 75 percent of the beneficiary's drug costs up to $2,250. Once a beneficiary spends $3,600 out-of-pocket, Medicare will cover about 95 percent of all remaining costs, with 80 percent coming in the form of federal reinsurance. Part D plans can bid based on different benefit designs that reduce the deductible or modify other cost-sharing elements of the standard Part D benefit in a package, provided it has the same actuarial value or better than the defined standard benefit. The equivalent actuarial value applies with respect to various aspects of the benefit, including the value of the benefit at the initial coverage limit ($2,250 in 2006).

Employer Group Waivers

Part D plans are subject to specific standards concerning enrollment, beneficiary protections, plan design, and a variety of other issues. However, section 1860D-22(b) of the Social Security Act (Act) says that the provisions of section 1857(i) of the Act shall apply with respect to prescription drug plans in relation to employment-based retiree health coverage in a manner similar to the manner in which they apply to an MA plan in relation to employers or unions, including authorizing the establishment of separate premium amounts for enrollees of the employer/union-sponsored group prescription drug plan and limitations on enrollment in such plan to Part D eligible individuals participating in the sponsor's employment-based retiree health coverage. Section 1857(i)(1) of the Act provides that to facilitate the offering of MA plans under contracts between MA organizations and employers, labor organizations, and employer/union funds, the Secretary may waive or modify requirements that hinder the design of, the offering of, or the enrollment in such MA plans. Section 1857(i)(2) of the Act provides the Secretary with similar waiver authority to facilitate the offering of MA plans by employers, labor organizations, or employer/union funds to their retirees.

Policy Goals

In considering the extent to which it will exercise its waiver authority, CMS will consider a number of important goals, including:

- Providing group plan sponsors with maximum flexibility and minimum administrative burden with regard to requirements that would hinder the design of, the offering of, or the enrollment in, Part D plans offered to their retirees so they will keep offering – and retirees can retain – high quality retiree prescription drug coverage;

- Adhering to budgetary constraints; and

- Considering the appropriate protections that Medicare enrollees may expect when enrolling in a Part D plan.

Scope of Guidance

This initial guidance solely addresses employer group waivers that CMS will provide for retiree prescription drug coverage provided under the last two types of arrangements described above – an employer or union making a customized arrangement with a Medicare Prescription Drug Plan or Medicare Advantage Plan with prescription drug coverage, or becoming such a plan itself. It is not intended to address standards that apply under any other employer or union option (the waiver provisions referenced above are not applicable for such other options).

Discussed below are several Part D requirements dealing with timing and entry for which employer group waivers will be approved by CMS. These waivers will automatically apply and will not need to be granted on an individual basis.

In the near future, CMS will release additional waiver guidance detailing other employer group waivers CMS will approve. Examples of additional waiver areas may include, but are not limited to marketing materials requirements, drug formulary requirements, and pharmacy access requirements, among others. In the meantime, the waivers that CMS will currently approve are listed below.

CMS will also consider additional waiver requests relating to specific requirements not addressed in this document or in future guidance on a case-by-case basis.

Approved Part D Employer Group Waivers

Part D Timeline for Retiree Group Plans

Part D plans must submit various types of materials to CMS for review by certain specified deadlines. For example, a notice of intent to apply must be filed with CMS by February 18th. For plan year 2006, CMS will permit flexibility in these timeframes by allowing employer/union-sponsored prescription drug plan or MA-PD plan materials to be submitted by the following deadlines:

March 23, 2005 Notice of intent to apply must be submitted to CMS
April 18, 2005   PDP or MA-PD applications must be submitted to CMS
June 6, 2005   PDP or MA-PD formularies must be submitted to CMS
Further guidance will be issued regarding any possible changes in the deadlines for submitting bids for employer-sponsored prescription drug coverage (individual market Part D plan bids must be submitted by June 6, 2005).

State Licensure and Solvency Requirements

In general, a Part D sponsor must be organized and licensed under State law as a risk-bearing entity eligible to offer health insurance or health benefits coverage in each State in which it offers coverage (42 C.F.R. 423.504 (b) (2)). However, an employer/union applying to become a PDP or MA-PD solely for purposes of providing prescription drug coverage to its retirees will not have to meet state licensing requirements as a condition of being a Medicare prescription drug sponsor. However, CMS will require such entities to certify that they meet solvency standards and/or have other safeguards that CMS will identify in additional guidance.

Governmental Entity Requirements

In general, governmental entities are not permitted to be PDP or MA-PD sponsors (section 1860D-41 (a)(13) of the Act). However, CMS will waive that requirement for governmental entities applying to sponsor a PDP or MA-PD plan for their retirees, such as for state retirement funds and municipal or local government plans.

Enrollment Requirements

In general, Part D plans have to accept all Medicare-eligible beneficiaries who reside in their service area. Through our waiver authority, CMS will allow employer or union-sponsored group plans approved as PDPs or MA-PD plans to restrict enrollment solely to their retirees.

Service Area Requirements

In general, Part D plans can only cover beneficiaries in the service areas in which they operate. However under our waiver authority, for employers/unions which directly contract with CMS to sponsor their own PDP or MA-PD plans, coverage can extend to all of their retirees, regardless of whether they reside in one or more other PDP or MA regions in the nation.

Minimum Enrollment Requirements

In general, Part D plans must meet minimum enrollment standards (42 C.F.R. 423.512 (a)). CMS will waive this requirement for employer/union-sponsored retiree group plans approved as PDPs or MA-PD plans.

For More Information

A significant amount of information regarding Part D plans (including applications, formulary information, a place to register for user group calls, and other implementation materials) can be found at:
www.cms.hhs.gov/pdps/.

Questions about employer group waivers can be submitted to:
epog@cms.hhs.gov.

Second CMS Guidance Document

**Additional Part D Waiver Guidance for
Employer/Union Retiree Coverage
March 9, 2005**

Introduction

Employer Options

The MMA provides employers and unions with a number of options for providing prescription drug coverage to their retirees.

- An employer or union sponsor with coverage that is at least as good as Medicare's Part D defined standard prescription drug benefit can receive a tax-free retiree drug subsidy that pays 28 percent of a retiree's drug costs (as defined by the regulation) between $250 and $5,000 in 2006. The subsidy only applies to retirees eligible for but not enrolled in a Medicare Prescription Drug Plan or a Medicare Advantage (MA) Plan (such as an HMO or PPO), cost plan, or PACE plan with prescription drug coverage (collectively, a "Part D plan"). Under the subsidy rules described in 42 CFR 423.880 et. seq., sponsors have substantial flexibility to qualify for subsidy payments under the existing health plans.

- Another available option is for an employer or union to encourage its retirees to enroll in a plan providing Part D benefits and then provide them with additional coverage. There are several ways that sponsors could supplement the standard Medicare drug benefit, such as:

  o Retaining substantial flexibility to design and offer their own separate supplemental coverage that coordinates benefits with the coverage provided by the Part D plans their retirees enroll in, in much the same way they currently lower non-prescription drug costs by supplementing the standard Medicare Part A and B benefits;

  o Paying for enhanced coverage offered under a Part D plan that subsidizes more of their retirees' cost-sharing and provides additional benefits;

  o Making special arrangements with MA plans to purchase customized benefits, including drug benefits, for their retirees pursuant to CMS waivers (discussed in more detail below), or to rely on such waivers to purchase customized benefits from other Part D sponsors (defined in 42 CFR 423.4) that provide prescription drug-only plans; and

o Providing the customized Part D plan benefits for their retirees by contracting with CMS to become Part D plan sponsors themselves and obtaining CMS waivers.

Waiver Authority

CMS has the authority under sections 1860D-22(b) and 1857(i) of the Social Security Act (Act) to waive or modify Part D requirements that hinder the design of, the offering of, or the enrollment in an employer or union Part D retiree plan. In considering the extent to which it will exercise its waiver authority, CMS will consider a number of important goals, including:

- Providing group plan sponsors with maximum flexibility and minimum administrative burden with regard to requirements that would hinder the design of, the offering of, or the enrollment in, Part D plans offered to their retirees so they will keep offering — and retirees can retain — high quality retiree prescription drug coverage;

- Recognizing and supporting the goal of employers to offer coordinated care plans to their Medicare-eligible retirees like they do for other retired (and active) health plan participants;

- Adhering to budgetary constraints; and

- Considering the appropriate protections that Medicare enrollees may expect when enrolling in a Part D plan.

Scope of Guidance

This guidance waives or modifies Part D requirements and elements of the Part D application process that CMS believes hinder the design, offering of or enrollment in employer or union retiree Part D coverage. Given the erosion of retiree coverage over time, the different ways in which employer and union retiree coverage have historically been regulated and designed as compared to standards for Part D benefits, and the limited time available for employers, unions and Part D sponsors to consider available options under the MMA, CMS believes the guidance is needed to ensure that the customized Part D benefit is a viable option for employers and unions seeking to retain high quality retiree coverage. At the same time, the guidance has been designed to take into account important policy goals and beneficiary protections built into the Part D rules, and budgetary considerations.

The waivers listed below are in addition to those described in the waiver guidance for employer/union retiree coverage issued on February 11, 2005 at www.cms.hhs.gov/medicarereform/pdbma/employer.asp. The waivers will automatically apply and will not need to be granted to each employer or union Part D plan on an individual basis. Waivers are not applicable to the other MMA options described above for employers and unions, and this guidance is not intended to address standards that apply under any of those other options.

CMS will release further guidance relating to Medicare Part D waivers that will be granted automatically to employer or union retiree group plans. CMS will also consider additional waiver requests relating to specific requirements not addressed in this document or in future guidance on a case-by-case basis.

For the waivers described below, references are provided to relevant sections of the PDP application at www.cms.hhs.gov/pdps/PDPApplication.pdf and Part D regulation. The guidance also indicates which waivers apply only to arrangements involving employer or union direct contracts with CMS, and which waivers apply both to the direct contract arrangements and to employer or union plans offered by other Part D sponsors.

Part D Employer Group Waivers in Addition to Those in CMS February 11, 2005 Guidance

Management and Operations Requirements

Application Sections 3.1 and 3.16

Available for Employer/Union Direct Contracts Only
In general, an entity seeking to contract with CMS as a Part D sponsor must have policy-making bodies exercising oversight and control to ensure actions are in the best interest of the organization and its enrollees, appropriate personnel and systems relating to prescription drug services, administration and management, and an executive manager whose appointment and removal are under the control of the policy-making body,

pursuant to 42 CFR 423.504 (b) (4)(i)-(iii). An employer or union directly contracting with CMS as a Part D sponsor may be subject to other, potentially different standards governing its management and operations, such as ERISA fiduciary requirements, state law standards, and certain oversight standards created under the Sarbanes-Oxley Act. In most cases they will also contract with business associates to provide the prescription drug benefit services. To reflect these issues and avoid imposing additional (and potentially conflicting) government oversight that may hinder employers and unions from considering direct Part D contracts with CMS, the requirements of 423.504(b)(4) noted above are waived if the employer or union (or to the extent applicable, the business associate with which it contracts for prescription drug benefit services) is subject to ERISA fiduciary requirements or similar state or federal law standards. However, such entities (or their business associates) are not relieved from the record retention standards applicable to other Part D sponsors in 42 CFR 423.505(d) (section 3.16 of the PDP application).

In addition, Part D sponsors must meet bonding and insurance standards described in 42 CFR 423.504(b)(4)(iv)-(v). CMS may, on a case-by-case basis, provide flexibility to an employer or union directly contracting with CMS as a Part D sponsor upon a demonstration that different federal or state legal standards (such as ERISA bonding requirements) are satisfied.

Cost Sharing Requirements

Regulation Sections 423.104(d) and (e)

*Available for Employer/Union Direct Contracting Plans
and MA-PD and PDP Retiree-only Plans*
In general, a Part D plan can offer alternative or enhanced prescription drug coverage (i.e., coverage that differs from defined standard prescription drug coverage) if certain actuarial equivalence standards are met. For example, section 423.104(e)(5) requires that the coverage be designed to provide for the payment of costs incurred for covered part D drugs equal to the initial coverage limit defined in 42 CFR 423.104(d)(3) ($2,250 in 2006) that is equal to or greater than what a part D plan offering defined standard prescription drug coverage would pay between such limit and the deductible at section 423.104(d)(1) ($250 in 2006). (Throughout that range, defined standard prescription drug coverage covers on average 75 percent of the costs and beneficiaries pay on average 25 percent.)

Retiree coverage offered by employers and unions has often differed from the defined standard benefit design in Part D. For example, many arrangements offer lower deductibles or provide coverage for claims incurred in the Part D coverage gap. By contrast, within the range between the deductible and the initial coverage limit, these designs may provide somewhat less coverage than defined standard prescription drug coverage under Part D. To provide beneficiaries with more choices and enable employers and unions to continue offering retirees their familiar coverage, CMS will waive the section 423.104(e)(5) actuarial equivalence test for Part D plans offered exclusively to employer or union retirees. (This waiver applies to employer/unions directly contracting with CMS as Part D sponsors, and Part D plans offered by other Part D sponsors).

However, this guidance is not intended to waive other actuarial equivalence standards in section 423.104(e), including (but not limited to) the requirement in section 423.104(e)(3) that the total or gross value of the coverage be at least equal to the total or gross value of defined standard coverage and the requirement in 423.104(e)(2) regarding catastrophic coverage. Thus, for example, a retiree Part D plan that requires beneficiary coinsurance that on average is greater than 25 percent may still satisfy actuarial equivalence by instead offering a lower deductible, or by providing coverage above the initial coverage limit, if the gross value coverage standard, the catastrophic coverage, and other requirements are satisfied.

Solvency Requirements

Application Section 3.1.3 and Appendix X

Available for Employer/Union Direct Contracts Only
Under certain circumstances, Part D sponsors are permitted to operate without state licensure for certain periods. If they do, they are subject to specified solvency standards and other requirements described in appendix X of the PDP application. (See www.cms.hhs.gov/pdps/SolvencyStandardsforWaiveredEntities.pdf.) In the February 11, 2005 guidance, CMS noted that in regards to an employer/union applying to become a Part D sponsor for purposes of providing prescription drug coverage to its retirees, certain solvency and other standards will be required if state licensure is waived for that entity.

This guidance clarifies that if the employer or union does not meet the standards described in appendix X of the PDP application, CMS may in its discretion approve, on a case-by-case basis, waivers of such requirements upon a demonstration from the entity that its fiscal soundness is commensurate with its financial risk and that through other means the entity can assure that claims for benefits paid for by CMS and beneficiaries will be covered. In all cases, CMS will require that the employer or union's contracts and sub-contracts provide beneficiary hold harmless provisions described in appendix X and other CMS guidance.

Pharmacy Access Requirements

Application Section 3.4

*Available for Employer/Union Direct Contracting Plans
and MA-PD and PDP Retiree-only Plans*

Part D plans cannot limit coverage to only mail order prescription drugs. In addition, Part D plans must meet specific standards in section 423.120(a)(1) regarding the assembling of broad networks of retail pharmacies to provide convenient access to beneficiaries. While waivers of the mail order only-prohibition will not be granted, CMS also recognizes different circumstances surrounding retiree coverage as compared to other Part D plans. For example, an employer or union arrangement may have only a small numbers of retirees concentrated in a local area within a large region. Employers and unions also have an interest in ensuring their retirees have adequate pharmacy access.

To facilitate the offering of such plans and maximize flexibility, CMS will waive other specific Part D retail pharmacy access standards in 423.120(a) for Part D plans for employer or union retirees upon receipt of an attestation that the plan's networks are sufficient to meet the needs of its retiree population, including situations involving emergency access. For example, this might be the case if a sponsor provides similar or identical provider networks to pre-Medicare eligible health plan participants. However, CMS may review the adequacy of the pharmacy networks and potentially require expanded access in the event of beneficiary complaints or for other reasons it determines in order to ensure that the plan's network is sufficient to meet the needs of its retiree population.

Marketing/Beneficiary Communications Requirements

Application Section 3.10

*Available for Employer/Union Direct Contracting Plans
and MA-PD and PDP Retiree-only Plans*

In general, CMS establishes guidelines on the content and format of beneficiary plan documents, including marketing materials, and requires CMS prior approval (423.50 (a)). Additional standards governing the disclosure of Part D plan information are described or cross-referenced in section 423.128. Many Part D plans offered only to employer/union re-tirees are subject to alternative disclosure standards under other laws (e.g., under ERISA). To avoid subjecting such plans to unneces-sary/conflicting standards of review, CMS will waive such specific Part D marketing/beneficiary communications requirements upon receipt of an attestation that the plans comply with the alternative disclosure stan-dards. However, such materials must be provided to CMS at the time of use and to beneficiaries on a timely basis, and CMS may review these materials in the event of beneficiary complaints or for other reasons it determines to ensure the information adequately informs Medicare bene-ficiaries about their rights and obligations under the plan.

Reporting Requirements

Application Section 3.13

Available for Employer/Union Direct Contracts Only

In general, Part D plan Sponsors must report certain information to CMS, to their enrollees, and to the general public, such as the cost of their op-erations and financial statements, under 42 CFR 423.514 (a). To avoid imposing additional and possibly conflicting public disclosure obliga-tions that would hinder the offering of employer or union direct contract arrangements, CMS will modify these reporting requirements to require information regarding such arrangements be reported to enrollees and to the general public to the extent required by other law (including ERISA or securities laws) or by contract.

Timetable for Employer Plans

The February 11 guidance provided extended timetables for submission of notice of intent to apply, applications, and formularies with respect to employer/union Part D plans.

This guidance clarifies that MA-PDs and PDPs serving the non-employer or union group market already file notices of intent to apply (for new plans), and thus it will not be necessary for these plans that wish to offer customized employer/union-only plans to file additional notices of intent to apply. Also, they will not need to file separate applications for the employer or union group coverage but will file by April 18, 2005 an addendum (to be supplied by CMS) identifying certain provisions of the Part D application expected to differ for their employer customers, and/or provisions for which they are requesting additional waivers. Further, separate formulary submissions will be required to the extent a formulary differs for a given product. Information relating to bids for employer or union retiree plans will be addressed separately in other guidance.

Process to File a Notice of Intent for Direct Contract Plans: As stated in the February 11 guidance, the deadline for submission for of a Notice of Intent to Apply for employer/union direct contracts has been extended to March 23, 2005. The process involves submission of three documents that can be located on the employer page of the CMS Website www.cms. hhs.gov/medicarereform/pdbma/employer.asp. These documents include: 1) Notice of Intent Form for an Employer/Union PDP Direct Contract; 2) CMS Connectivity Request Form; and 3) Application for Access to CMS Computer Systems. This information was posted on March 4, 2005.

For More Information

A significant amount of information regarding Part D plans (including applications, formulary information, a place to register for user group calls, and other implementation materials) can be found at: www.cms.hhs.gov/pdps.

Questions about employer group waivers can be submitted to www.mmaissuesform.cms.hhs.gov/.

Third CMS Waiver Guidance Document

ADDITIONAL PART D WAIVER GUIDANCE FOR EMPLOYER/UNION RETIREE COVERAGE
April 6, 2005

Introduction

CMS has the authority under sections 1860D-22(b) and 1857(i) of the Social Security Act (Act) to waive or modify Part D requirements added by the Medicare Modernization Act (MMA) that hinder the design of, the offering of, or the enrollment in an employer or union-sponsored Part D retiree plan (including a Medicare Prescription Drug Plan (PDP) or a Medicare Advantage (MA) Plan with prescription drug coverage). Although an employer or union-sponsored MA-PD may be offered to both retirees and active employees (and their dependents) who are Medicare beneficiaries, in accordance with section 1860D-22(b) of the Act, an employer or union-sponsored PDP may only be offered to retirees. In considering the extent to which it will exercise its waiver authority, CMS will consider a number of important goals, including:

● Providing group Part D plan sponsors (defined as Part D Organizations offering group plans and employers or unions who directly contract with CMS) with maximum flexibility and minimum administrative burden with regard to requirements that would hinder the design of, the offering of, or the enrollment in, Part D plans offered to their retirees (and active employees in the case of a MA-PD) so they will keep offering – and retirees can retain – high quality retiree prescription drug coverage;

● Adhering to budgetary constraints; and

● Considering the appropriate protections that Medicare enrollees may expect when enrolling in a Part D plan.

This guidance waives or modifies Part D requirements and elements of the Part D application process that CMS believes hinder the design, offering of or enrollment in employer or union-sponsored Part D coverage. Given the erosion of retiree coverage over time, the different ways in which employer and union retiree coverage have historically been regulated and designed as compared to standards for Part D benefits, and the limited time available for employers, unions and Part D Organizations to consider available options under the MMA, CMS believes the guidance is needed to ensure that the customized Part D benefit is a viable option for employers and unions seeking to retain high quality retiree coverage. At the same time, the guidance has been designed to take into account important policy goals and beneficiary protections built into the Part D rules, and budgetary considerations.

The waivers listed below supplement and modify those described in the waiver guidance for employer/union retiree coverage issued on February 11, 2005 and the additional waiver guidance issued on March 9, 2005 at www.cms.hhs.gov/medicarereform/pdbma/employer.asp. The waivers will automatically apply and will not need to be granted to each employer or union Part D plan on an individual basis. Except as noted, the waivers in this guidance apply both to Part D plans in which employers and unions directly contract with CMS to be Part D sponsors, and to other entities contracting with employer or unions to offer employer or union-sponsored Part D plans.

Waivers are not applicable to other MMA options for employers and unions providing prescription drug coverage to their retirees. For example, waivers do not apply to employers or unions electing to receive a tax-free 28% retiree drug subsidy with respect to retirees receiving coverage that is at least as good as Medicare's Part D defined standard prescription drug benefit. This guidance is not intended to address standards that apply under any of those other options.

CMS will consider additional waiver requests relating to specific requirements not addressed in this document or in our prior guidance on a case-by-case basis.

Service Area for Employer/Union Group Plans
Offered by MA-PDs and PDPs that Serve the Non-Group Market

Background

Under most MMA options available to employers and unions sponsoring drug coverage – including the 28% retiree drug subsidy program – sponsors can select the entities providing or administering such coverage without Medicare regulation of the regions of the country served by those entities. However, service area conditions apply to drug coverage for Medicare beneficiaries through Medicare Advantage (MA) plans, and through MA plans offering prescription drug coverage (MA-PDs) and prescription drug plans (PDPs), as follows:

- Prior to the passage of the MMA, CMS permitted the service area identified for an employer or union-sponsored MA plan to be larger or smaller than the service area offered by the same MA organization provided the MA organization offered at least one MA plan to individuals somewhere in the same state as it offered the employer or union-sponsored plan. The area offered within the state to individuals could be an area smaller than the state (e.g. at least one county).

- Under the MMA, PDPs and Regional MA-PDs must offer coverage to all individuals who reside in one or more specified regions. The MMA did not change the service area for local MA plans. On February 11, 2005, CMS released guidance that allows employer and union direct contracting PDPs and MA-PDs plans to restrict enrollment to retirees only. Further, the guidance waived service area requirements for an employer/union retiree plan if the employer/union directly contracts with CMS as a PDP sponsor or MA organization. Thus, for these direct contracting employer-union plans, coverage can be extended to all retirees, regardless of where they reside in the nation.

This guidance addresses service area-related issues for employer/union-sponsored Part D arrangements not discussed in the February 11 guidance – i.e., those MA-PDs and PDPs that do not involve direct contracts between CMS and the employer or union.

MA-PDs

Service Area Rules
CMS service area rules for MA plans prior to passage of the MMA will continue to apply to local MA-PD plans (and MA-only plans). Thus, if an MA organization provides coverage to individuals in any part of a State, it can offer an employer/union-sponsored MA-PD plan in any area within that State or throughout the entire State.

An MA Organization offering a MA-PD regional plan to individuals residing in a particular MA region may offer an employer/union sponsored MA-PD plan in any area within the MA region or throughout the entire MA region. CMS may, on a case-by-case basis, grant a waiver to permit a regional MA or MA-PD providing coverage under an employer or union-sponsored retiree plan to extend coverage to the employer or union retirees living outside such region.

Out of Service Area Coverage Options
Employers and unions sponsoring retiree coverage through an MA-PD have several options for providing coverage outside that MA-PD's service area. They include:

- receiving payments under the 28% retiree drug subsidy program for qualifying prescription drug coverage, and providing hospitalization and other health benefits that supplement benefits provided to the retirees under Medicare Parts A and B;

- providing prescription drug coverage for out-of-region retirees through a separate, stand-alone PDP (under rules described below) and providing hospitalization and other health benefits that supplement Medicare Parts A and B; or

- using an MA-PD that partners with or enters into reciprocal arrangements with other MA-PDs that can provide the coverage in those other service areas.

Retiree-Only Group PDPs

Service Area Rules. A PDP sponsor is permitted to offer a retiree–only PDP plan to employers or unions in a given PDP region of the country if the sponsor - either itself or through subcontractors or other partners - provides PDP coverage to Part D eligible individuals (non-retirees) in that region. Moreover, through the waiver authority permitted in section 1860D-22(b) of the Social Security Act, CMS will permit such PDP sponsors to expand coverage under such plans to retirees residing in other regions through contracts and other arrangements it chooses to use in providing such expanded coverage.

For these purposes, an employer is treated as being in the PDP region where the most substantial portion of its employees reside. A multiemployer union fund is treated as being in the PDP region where the most substantial portion of its participants reside.

Example 1 An employer has 600,000 employees, of whom 400,000 live in California and 200,000 live in Florida. A PDP sponsor that serves the non-group market in California (or that contracts or partners with an entity serving the non-group market in California) can offer a PDP sponsored by the employer that not only serves the employer's California retirees, but also those retirees in Florida or any other state in the nation.

Example 2 An employer has 100,000 employees, of whom 45,000 live in New York, with the remainder spread out in smaller numbers among 20 other states. A PDP sponsor that serves the non-group market in New York (or that contracts or partners with an entity serving the non-group market in New York) can offer a PDP sponsored by the employer that not only serves the employer's New York retirees, but also the retirees residing in the other 20 states where they reside.

A PDP sponsor that does not meet the substantial portion test described above for a given employer or union may provide retiree-only PDP coverage for the retirees in any region where the PDP provides PDP coverage to individuals (non-retirees).

The foregoing service area rules are summarized in this table:

Region for Non-Retiree Coverage	Largest Region for Employer/Union Retiree Group Coverage
No coverage in non-retiree market	Employer/union-sponsored PDP coverage prohibited. However, other MMA options are available for nationwide coverage, including the 28% retiree drug subsidy for qualifying retiree prescription drug plans. (Entities can offer prescription drug coverage that qualifies for the 28% subsidy without being a PDP sponsor.)
Region where most substantial portion of employees (or for union funds, participants) reside	Nationwide
Region other than where most substantial portion of employees (or for union funds, participants) reside	Limited to that same region

Out of Service Area Coverage Options

An employer or union that currently provides retiree prescription drug coverage through an entity that does not meet the above standards has options for continuing to use such entity and receive prescription drug-related assistance under the MMA. For example, the employer or union can:

- receive payments under the 28% retiree drug subsidy program for qualifying prescription drug coverage (as noted above, such rules do not require entities to be PDP sponsors or offer coverage to non-retirees); or

- provide separate prescription drug coverage that supplements PDP coverage obtained by its retirees.

In addition, the prescription drug vendor can use subcontractors or partners that qualify as PDPs as a means of providing PDP coverage under the rules described above.

Submission of Part D Bids

For the non-group market, Part D bids must be submitted to CMS by June 6, 2005 for the 2006 year. In the initial Employer/Union Part D waiver guidance issued by CMS on February 11, CMS extended the dates for submission of notices of intent, applications and formularies for Part D plans offered by an employer or union directly contracting with CMS and employer or union-sponsored Part D plans offered by MA Organizations and PDP sponsors also offering Part D plans to the non-group market. These extended timeframes will give employers and unions more time to consider the various options available to them under the Medicare Modernization Act. With this waiver guidance, CMS will provide flexibility on the timing of submission of employer or union-sponsored Part D plan bids (both direct contract and MA-PD and PDP group plan), with a modified payment method described below.

Timing

Because of the flexibility to retain current drug benefit designs and vendors, CMS expects and encourages most employers to avail themselves of the tax free 28% subsidy for retiree drug coverage in 2006. However CMS recognizes that some employers, such as state and local governments, do not receive the full tax benefits of the subsidy and may prefer to enroll their retirees in a Part D plan. Thus, for 2006, CMS will use the employer/union waiver authority to extend the deadline for submission of Part D bids for employer or union-sponsored retiree plans to July 1, 2005, provided that bids for regional MA-PD employer/union plans will be required by June 6, 2006 to calculate the regional MA benchmark. CMS will not include employer or union Part D bids in the calculation of the Part D national average monthly bid amount or the low income premium benchmark amounts in 2006.

Design

Part D plan sponsors (both Part D plans and employer/union direct contractors) will submit Part D bids for employer or union retiree coverage in a manner similar to the flexible method offered to MA Organizations in the past. Under this approach, CMS will require group Part D plan sponsors to submit bids for employer or union-sponsored plans only for the standardized Part D coverage. They will not submit separate bids in 2006 for each employer/union benefit design variation. Any supplemental prescription drug coverage will be provided separately pursuant to a private agreement between the Part D plan sponsor and the employer/union, or in the case of a direct contract will be provided separately by the employer or union.

These private supplemental coverage arrangements cannot reduce the value of the basic standardized Part D benefit design. For example, supplemental coverage cannot impose a cap that would preclude group members from realizing the full value of coverage under the standard Part D benefit. To assure that the actuarial equivalence of the standard Part D benefit design is maintained, CMS will require that the Part D plan sponsor that is submitting the Part D bid for the standard benefit design also provide an attestation that the total employer or union sponsored plan (including adjusting for any supplemental coverage) is providing at least the standard Part D coverage, including (for 2006) a deductible no higher than $250, full coverage between the deductible and the $2250 initial coverage limit (for which the standard Part D benefit pays 75% and the beneficiary pays 25%), and catastrophic coverage after the $3600 true out-of-pocket limit is met. (If the group plan sponsor avails itself of the waiver offered in the March 9, 2005 employer waiver guidance that permitted flexibility to offset increased cost sharing between the $250 deductible and initial coverage limit by other design changes that ensure the plan is at least actuarially equivalent to Part D, the attestation must reflect that modified design.)

Payment

CMS believes the above waivers are necessary to remove administrative burdens that would hinder the offering of employer and union-sponsored Part D plans, including the approval of such plans. As a condition of providing such waivers, however, risk corridor payments (which assist Part D plan sponsors entering a new market without any experience to mitigate any losses or gains by sharing these losses or gains with Medicare) will not apply to group Part D employer or union-sponsored plans.

In addition, CMS will modify the way catastrophic reinsurance is paid. CMS will not make a prospective payment for reinsurance but will include the group plans in the normal Part D reinsurance reconciliation at year end. Since no prospective payments will have been made during the year, the result of the year end process will be the full reinsurance payment due to the plan. We expect that most employers will be providing enhanced drug coverage through supplemental arrangements and these reinsurance payments will be small as a result of the application of True Out of Pocket Costs (TrOOP) rule. Low Income Subsidies (discussed below) will be paid through the normal Part D process, which involves an estimate as part of the bid with a reconciliation at year end. Thus, this payment method should provide administrative flexibility to both retiree plan sponsors and CMS.

Finally, the federal Part D direct subsidy risk adjusted payment will be based on the national benchmark rather than on the bid submitted by the employer or union plan sponsor.

Uniform Premium Requirements

In general, each Part D plan that provides coverage in the non-employer market must charge a uniform premium for each beneficiary enrolled in that plan. Further, the premium for each beneficiary in a defined standard Part D plan is determined by the difference between the plan's bid and the national benchmark. That amount (referred to here as the "standard Part D beneficiary premium") is established through the bidding process. The plan can also charge up to 100% of the value of any supplemental prescription drug coverage provided in conjunction with the Part D plan.

Under its waiver authority, CMS will allow the employer or union sponsoring a Part D plan to have flexibility to determine how much of a plan enrollee's Part D monthly beneficiary premium they will subsidize, subject to the following conditions. First, an employer or union sponsor can subsidize different amounts for different classes of enrollees in a plan provided such classes are reasonable and based on objective business criteria, such as years of service, business location, job category, and nature of compensation (e.g. salaried v. hourly). Different classes cannot be based on eligibility for the Low Income Subsidy described below. Second, the premium cannot vary for individuals within a given class of enrollees. Third, an enrollee cannot be charged more than the sum of his or her standard part D beneficiary premium and 100% of the premium for his or her supplemental prescription drug coverage (if any). Thus, direct subsidy payments from CMS to the Part D plan must be passed through to reduce the amount that the beneficiary pays. Part D sponsors that offer MA-PD or PDP plans to employers or unions will be required to obtain in writing from such employers or unions their agreement that they will satisfy the requirements of this waiver with respect to the premiums charged to their participants.

Low Income Subsidy

In general, the Low Income Subsidy (LIS) provisions of Subpart P of the final rule for the Medicare prescription drug benefit (423.771 et. seq.) apply to employer and union-sponsored Part D plans in the same manner as they apply to other Part D plans. For each beneficiary entitled to the LIS, CMS pays the beneficiary's premium (up to the low income premium subsidy amount) and cost sharing obligations minus the beneficiary's cost-sharing responsibilities under the LIS rules.

Premium

CMS will require that the LIS premium subsidy that CMS is paying on behalf of the LIS eligible retiree be passed through to that retiree under rules similar to those described above with respect to the uniform premium requirements. In other words, the monthly premium subsidy amount for a beneficiary eligible for the low-income subsidy must first be used to reduce the portion of the monthly beneficiary premium paid for by the beneficiary, with any remainder then used to reduce the employer's premium contribution. For example, if under the terms of the retiree plan, the beneficiary is responsible for paying $20 of a $40 monthly premium with the employer paying the remaining $20, a monthly low income premium subsidy amount of $35 would be used first to reduce the beneficiary's liability to $0, and then to reduce the employer's liability from $20 to $5. In the case of Part D sponsors that provide MA-PD or PDP plans to employer/union retiree plans, the Part D sponsors must obtain written agreements from such employers or unions indicating that they will satisfy these requirements with respect to the premium contributions collected from their retirees. Such Part D sponsors will also identify the LIS-eligible retirees for the employers/unions or their prescription drug providers, as necessary.

If the low income premium subsidy amount is less than the beneficiary premium contribution under the employer or union-sponsored part D plan (including any beneficiary premium contribution for supplemental benefits), employer and union plan sponsors should communicate with their LIS retirees the premium impact of remaining in the employer plan versus enrolling as an individual in another Part D plan.

Cost Sharing

Benefits provided in an employer or union-sponsored retiree-only Part D plan cannot be determined based on the retiree's LIS eligibility. In addition, for an LIS retiree in a retiree-only plan receiving a waiver, CMS will pay only the cost-sharing obligations imposed on the retiree under the plan. For this purpose, the employer/union plan must be designed to include supplemental coverage offered by the Part D sponsor to the employer or union, with the supplemental coverage primary to the LIS program.

For example, a Part D plan that provides benefits exclusively to employer X's retirees has a $100 deductible. For expenses incurred by a full subsidy eligible individual, CMS's payments to the plan will be determined based on that $100 deductible (minus any minimal co-pays an individual is responsible for under 42 CFR 423.782(a)). CMS payments will not be based on the assumption the plan has a $250 deductible (as reflected in Part D standard prescription drug coverage).

Finally, the Part D sponsor of a retiree plan will be required (like other Part D plan sponsors) to submit as part of its bid an estimate of its LIS cost sharing, and submit at the end of the year information needed for a final reconciliation. The estimate must take into account the aggregate effect on LIS payments of any supplemental coverage(s) not submitted as part of the bid to CMS.

Premium Withholding for Employer/Union Sponsored Group Plans

Under the MMA, Part D plans must permit their enrollees, at their option, to pay their Part D premium through deductions from their Social Security checks, Railroad Retirement checks, or Federal annuity. When employers also contribute to the beneficiary's Part D premium, in whole or in part, operationally for 2006 it will be extremely difficult for both plans and CMS to factor in the employer contribution and adjust the amount of the premium that should be deducted from the beneficiary's Social Security or other check. Thus, CMS will waive the requirement that the employer/union-sponsored Part D plan provide beneficiaries the option to pay their premium through Social Security withholding. Thus, the premium withhold option will not be available for enrollees in employer-union sponsored group plans. These plans will be required to bill the beneficiary and/or the employer directly (as Part C plans do today).

Non Calendar Year for Employer Only Part D Plans

Many employers, particularly public employers, determine benefits and enroll individuals on plan years that differ from the calendar year. Many of these plan years are mandated by state laws or federal law, or union contracts.

CMS will use its waiver authority to permit employer or union-sponsored Part D plans to determine benefits (including deductibles, out-of-pocket limits, etc.) on a non-calendar year basis. However, bids and other submissions to CMS, along with CMS payments, will be determined on a calendar year basis, in a process similar to the process currently used for employer and union-sponsored MA plans. Under that process:

- Applications, formularies and bids for such plans must be submitted at the same time as calendar-year employer and union-sponsored Part D plans for the calendar year that follows the calendar year of submission.

- In a given month the standard Part D beneficiary premium (as discussed in the section above regarding uniform premiums) will be based on the difference between the plan's bid and the national average monthly bid amount benchmark for the calendar year in which that month falls.

- The plan must be actuarially equivalent to defined standard coverage for the portion of its plan year that falls in a given calendar year. A plan will meet this standard if it is actuarially equivalent for the calendar year in which the plan year starts and no design change is made for the remainder of the plan year. In no event can a plan increase during the plan year the out-of-pocket limit at which catastrophic coverage begins.

- Medicare direct subsidy payments will be based on the national average monthly bid amount benchmark for the calendar year for which the direct subsidy is being paid.

- LIS payments and reconciliations will be determined based on the calendar year for which the payments are made.

Catastrophic reinsurance payments and (to the same extent as other employer or union-sponsored Part D plans) risk corridor payments will not be made available to such employer or union-sponsored Part D plans. However, the waiver of catastrophic reinsurance payments does not change the requirement for such plans to provide catastrophic coverage comparable to the standard benefit, though eligibility for such catastrophic coverage under the plan can be determined on a plan year basis.

For plan years that begin in 2005, the following special transition rules apply. CMS payments (direct subsidy and LIS) will apply for the period beginning January 1, 2006, based on applications, formularies and bids submitted in 2005 at the times described above and in other waiver guidance. Plans will be required to track deductibles and other beneficiary expenditures from the start of the plan year. Plan design and beneficiary premiums must meet the other standards applicable to Part D employer group plans starting January 1, 2006. Of course, another option for non-calendar year plans is to take the 28% subsidy for the partial year.

CMS will allow members of an employer or union Part D retiree plan that operates on a non-calendar year basis to leave such plan and enroll in another Part D plan through a special enrollment period (SEP) at the beginning of the month following the end of the employer/union plan year.

Group Enrollment

To the extent the employer or union is a beneficiary's authorized representation under applicable law, with the authority to act on behalf of the beneficiary for purposes of enrollment in a Part D plan, an employer or union may enroll the beneficiary into its Part D plan. If the employer or union is not a beneficiary's authorized representation, CMS will waive individual enrollment provisions under 423.32 to allow employer group plans to enroll their retirees under a special group enrollment process. In addition, the employer will also be required to provide CMS with any information it has on other insurance coverage for purposes of coordination of benefits.

As part of the group enrollment process, all beneficiaries must be advised that the employer intends to enroll them into the Part D plan that the employer or union is offering unless the beneficiary affirmatively opts out of such enrollment. This information must be provided at least 30 days prior to the effective date of a beneficiary's enrollment in the employer or union-sponsored Part D plan. The information must also include a summary of benefits offered under the employer or union-sponsored plan, an explanation of how to get more information on such plan, and an explanation of how to contact Medicare for information on other Part D plans that might be available to the beneficiaries. In addition, all information necessary to effectuate enrollment must be submitted electronically consistent with instructions that CMS will provide at a future date.

For More Information

A significant amount of information regarding Part D plans (including applications, formulary information, a place to register for user group calls, and other implementation materials) can be found at: www.cms.hhs.gov/pdps. Questions about employer group waivers can be submitted to www.mmaissuesform.cms.hhs.gov.

APPENDIX C
KEY IRS CODE AND REGULATIONS

This appendix includes key references for the Internal Revenue Code and regulations as of March 2006 regarding welfare benefit funds and medical accounts in a pension plan (IRC §401(h)).

WELFARE BENEFIT FUND RULES

TITLE 26 – INTERNAL REVENUE CODE
Subtitle A – Income Taxes
CHAPTER 1 – NORMAL TAXES AND SURTAXES
Subchapter D – Deferred Compensation, Etc.
PART I – PENSION, PROFIT-SHARING, STOCK BONUS PLANS, ETC.
Subpart D – Treatment of Welfare Benefit Funds

IRC Section 419
Treatment of Funded Welfare Benefit Plans

(a) *General rule*

Contributions paid or accrued by an employer to a welfare benefit fund—

(1) shall not be deductible under this chapter, but

(2) if they would otherwise be deductible, shall (subject to the limitation of subsection (b)) be deductible under this section for the taxable year in which paid.

(b) *Limitation*

The amount of the deduction allowable under subsection (a)(2) for any taxable year shall not exceed the welfare benefit fund's qualified cost for the taxable year.

(c) *Qualified cost*

For purposes of this section—

(1) In general

Except as otherwise provided in this subsection, the term "qualified cost" means, with respect to any taxable year, the sum of—

(A) the qualified direct cost for such taxable year, and

(B) subject to the limitation of section 419A(b), any addition to a qualified asset account for the taxable year.

(2) *Reduction for funds after-tax income*

In the case of any welfare benefit fund, the qualified cost for any taxable year shall be reduced by such fund's after-tax income for such taxable year.

(3) *Qualified direct cost*

(A) In general

The term "qualified direct cost" means, with respect to any taxable year, the aggregate amount (including administrative expenses) which would have been allowable as a deduction to the employer with respect to the benefits provided during the taxable year, if—

(i) such benefits were provided directly by the employer, and

(ii) the employer used the cash receipts and disbursements method of accounting.

(B) *Time when benefits provided*

For purposes of subparagraph (A), a benefit shall be treated as provided when such benefit would be includible in the gross income of the employee if provided directly by the employer (or would be so includible but for any provision of this chapter excluding such benefit from gross income).

(C) *60-month amortization of child care facilities*

(i) *In general*

In determining qualified direct costs with respect to any child care facility for purposes of subparagraph (A), in lieu of depreciation the adjusted basis of such facility shall be allowable as a deduction ratably over a period of 60 months beginning with the month in which the facility is placed in service.

(ii) *Child care facility*

The term "child care facility" means any tangible property which qualifies under regulations prescribed by the Secretary as a child care center primarily for children of employees of the employer; except that such term shall not include any property—

(I) not of a character subject to depreciation; or

(II) located outside the United States.

(4) *After-tax income*
  (A) *In general*
    The term "after-tax income" means, with respect to any taxable year, the gross income of the welfare benefit fund reduced by the sum of—
    (i) the deductions allowed by this chapter which are directly connected with the production of such gross income, and
    (ii) the tax imposed by this chapter on the fund for the taxable year.
  (B) *Treatment of certain amounts*
    In determining the gross income of any welfare benefit fund—
    (i) contributions and other amounts received from employees shall be taken into account, but
    (ii) contributions from the employer shall not be taken into account.
(5) *Item only taken into account once*
  No item may be taken into account more than once in determining the qualified cost of any welfare benefit fund.

(d) *Carryover of excess contributions*
  If—
  (1) the amount of the contributions paid (or deemed paid under this subsection) by the employer during any taxable year to a welfare benefit fund, exceeds
  (2) the limitation of subsection (b),
    such excess shall be treated as an amount paid by the employer to such fund during the succeeding taxable year.

(e) *Welfare benefit fund*
  For purposes of this section—
  (1) *In general*
    The term "welfare benefit fund'" means any fund—
    (A) which is part of a plan of an employer, and
    (B) through which the employer provides welfare benefits to employees or their beneficiaries.
  (2) *Welfare benefit*
    The term "welfare benefit" means any benefit other than a benefit with respect to which—
    (A) section 83(h) applies,
    (B) section 404 applies (determined without regard to section 404(b)(2)), or
    (C) section 404A applies.

(3) *Fund*

The term "fund" means—

(A) any organization described in paragraph (7), (9), (17), or (20) of section 501(c),

(B) any trust, corporation, or other organization not exempt from the tax imposed by this chapter, and

(C) to the extent provided in regulations, any account held for an employer by any person.

(4) *Treatment of amounts held pursuant to certain insurance contracts*

(A) In general

Notwithstanding paragraph (3)(C), the term "fund" shall not include amounts held by an insurance company pursuant to an insurance contract if —

(i) such contract is a life insurance contract described in section 264(a)(1), or

(ii) such contract is a qualified nonguaranteed contract.

(B) *Qualified nonguaranteed contract*

(i) In general

For purposes of this paragraph, the term "qualified nonguaranteed contract" means any insurance contract (including a reasonable premium stabilization reserve held thereunder) if—

(I) there is no guarantee of a renewal of such contract, and

(II) other than insurance protection, the only payments to which the employer or employees are entitled are experience rated refunds or policy dividends which are not guaranteed and which are determined by factors other than the amount of welfare benefits paid to (or on behalf of) the employees of the employer or their beneficiaries.

(ii) *Limitation*

In the case of any qualified nonguaranteed contract, subparagraph (A) shall not apply unless the amount of any experience rated refund or policy dividend payable to an employer with respect to a policy year is treated by the employer as received or accrued in the taxable year in which the policy year ends.

(f) *Method of contributions, etc., having the effect of a plan*
If—
(1) there is no plan, but
(2) there is a method or arrangement of employer contributions or benefits which has the effect of a plan,
this section shall apply as if there were a plan.

(g) *Extension to plans for independent contractors*
If any fund would be a welfare benefit fund (as modified by subsection (f)) but for the fact that there is no employee-employer relationship—
(1) this section shall apply as if there were such a relationship, and
(2) any reference in this section to the employer shall be treated as a reference to the person for whom services are provided, and any reference in this section to an employee shall be treated as a reference to the person providing the services.

Section 419A
Qualified Asset Account; Limitation on Additions to Account

(a) *General rule*
For purposes of this subpart and section 512, the term "qualified asset account" means any account consisting of assets set aside to provide for the payment of -
(1) disability benefits,
(2) medical benefits,
(3) SUB or severance pay benefits, or
(4) life insurance benefits.

(b) *Limitation on additions to account*
No addition to any qualified asset account may be taken into account under section 419(c)(1)(B) to the extent such addition results in the amount in such account exceeding the account limit.

(c) *Account limit*
For purposes of this section —
(1) *In general*
Except as otherwise provided in this subsection, the account limit for any qualified asset account for any taxable year is the amount reasonably and actuarially necessary to fund —
(A) claims incurred but unpaid (as of the close of such taxable year) for benefits referred to in subsection (a), and
(B) administrative costs with respect to such claims.

(2) *Additional reserve for post-retirement medical and life insurance benefits*

The account limit for any taxable year may include a reserve funded over the working lives of the covered employees and actuarially determined on a level basis (using assumptions that are reasonable in the aggregate) as necessary for—

(A) post-retirement medical benefits to be provided to covered employees (determined on the basis of current medical costs), or

(B) post-retirement life insurance benefits to be provided to covered employees.

(3) *Amount taken into account for SUB or severance pay benefits*

(A) In general

The account limit for any taxable year with respect to SUB or severance pay benefits is 75 percent of the average annual qualified direct costs for SUB or severance pay benefits for any 2 of the immediately preceding 7 taxable years (as selected by the fund).

(B) Special rule for certain new plans

In the case of any new plan for which SUB or severance pay benefits are not available to any key employee, the Secretary shall, by regulations, provide for an interim amount to be taken into account under paragraph (1).

(4) Limitation on amounts to be taken into account

(A) *Disability benefits*

For purposes of paragraph (1), disability benefits payable to any individual shall not be taken into account to the extent such benefits are payable at an annual rate in excess of the lower of—

(i) 75 percent of such individual's average compensation for his high 3 years (within the meaning of section 415(b)(3)), or

(ii) the limitation in effect under section 415(b)(1)(A).

(B) *Limitation on SUB or severance pay benefits*

For purposes of paragraph (3), any SUB or severance pay benefit payable to any individual shall not be taken into account to the extent such benefit is payable at an annual rate in excess of 150 percent of the limitation in effect under section 415(c)(1)(A).

(5) Special limitation where no actuarial certification

    (A) *In general*

        Unless there is an actuarial certification of the account limit determined under this subsection for any taxable year, the account limit for such taxable year shall not exceed the sum of the safe harbor limits for such taxable year.

    (B) *Safe harbor limits*

      (i) *Short-term disability benefits*

          In the case of short-term disability benefits, the safe harbor limit for any taxable year is 17.5 percent of the qualified direct costs (other than insurance premiums) for the immediately preceding taxable year with respect to such benefits.

      (ii) *Medical benefits*

          In the case of medical benefits, the safe harbor limit for any taxable year is 35 percent of the qualified direct costs (other than insurance premiums) for the immediately preceding taxable year with respect to medical benefits.

      (iii) *SUB or severance pay benefits*

          In the case of SUB or severance pay benefits, the safe harbor limit for any taxable year is the amount determined under paragraph (3).

      (iv) *Long-term disability or life insurance benefits*

          In the case of any long-term disability benefit or life insurance benefit, the safe harbor limit for any taxable year shall be the amount prescribed by regulations.

(d) Requirement of separate accounts for post-retirement medical or life insurance benefits provided to key employees

    (1) *In general*

      In the case of any employee who is a key employee -

      (A) a separate account shall be established for any medical benefits or life insurance benefits provided with respect to such employee after retirement, and

      (B) medical benefits and life insurance benefits provided with respect to such employee after retirement may only be paid from such separate account.

      The requirements of this paragraph shall apply to the first taxable year for which a reserve is taken into account under subsection (c)(2) and to all subsequent taxable years.

(2) *Coordination with section 415*
For purposes of section 415, any amount attributable to medical benefits allocated to an account established under paragraph (1) shall be treated as an annual addition to a defined contribution plan for purposes of section 415(c). Subparagraph (B) of section 415(c)(1) shall not apply to any amount treated as an annual addition under the preceding sentence.

(3) *Key employee*
For purposes of this section, the term "key employee" means any employee who, at any time during the plan year or any preceding plan year, is or was a key employee as defined in section 416(i).

(e) Special limitations on reserves for medical benefits or life insurance benefits provided to retired employees

(1) *Reserve must be nondiscriminatory*
No reserve may be taken into account under subsection (c)(2) for post-retirement medical benefits or life insurance benefits to be provided to covered employees unless the plan meets the requirements of section 505(b) with respect to such benefits (whether or not such requirements apply to such plan). The preceding sentence shall not apply to any plan maintained pursuant to an agreement between employee representatives and 1 or more employers if the Secretary finds that such agreement is a collective bargaining agreement and that post-retirement medical benefits or life insurance benefits were the subject of good faith bargaining between such employee representatives and such employer or employers.

(2) *Limitation on amount of life insurance benefits*
Life insurance benefits shall not be taken into account under subsection (c)(2) to the extent the aggregate amount of such benefits to be provided with respect to the employee exceeds $50,000.

(f) *Definitions and other special rules*
For purposes of this section —

(1) *SUB or severance pay benefit*
The term "SUB or severance pay benefit" means –
(A) any supplemental unemployment compensation benefit (as defined in section 501(c)(17)(D)), and
(B) any severance pay benefit.

(2) *Medical benefit*
The term "medical benefit" means a benefit which consists of the providing (directly or through insurance) of medical care (as defined in section 213(d)).

(3) *Life insurance benefit*
The term "life insurance benefit" includes any other death benefit.

(4) *Valuation*
For purposes of this section, the amount of the qualified asset account shall be the value of the assets in such account (as determined under regulations).

(5) *Special rule for collective bargained and employee pay-all plans*
No account limits shall apply in the case of any qualified asset account under a separate welfare benefit fund —
(A) under a collective bargaining agreement, or
(B) an employee pay-all plan under section 501(c)(9) if —
(i) such plan has at least 50 employees (determined without regard to subsection (h)(1)), and
(ii) no employee is entitled to a refund with respect to amounts in the fund, other than a refund based on the experience of the entire fund.

(6) *Exception for 10-or-more employer plans*
(A) In general
This subpart shall not apply in the case of any welfare benefit fund which is part of a 10 or more employer plan. The preceding sentence shall not apply to any plan which maintains experience-rating arrangements with respect to individual employers.
(B) 10 or more employer plan

For purposes of subparagraph (A), the term "10 or more employer plan" means a plan —
(i) to which more than 1 employer contributes, and
(ii) to which no employer normally contributes more than 10 percent of the total contributions contributed under the plan by all employers.

(7) *Adjustments for existing excess reserves*
(A) Increase in account limit
The account limit for any of the first 4 taxable years to which this section applies shall be increased by the applicable percentage of any existing excess reserves.
(B) *Applicable percentage*
For purposes of subparagraph (A) —

	The applicable
In the case of:	percentage is:

The first taxable year to which this section applies 80
The second taxable year to which this section applies.............. 60
The third taxable year to which this section applies 40
The fourth taxable year to which this section applies................ 20

(C) *Existing excess reserve*

For purposes of computing the increase under subparagraph (A) for any taxable year, the term "existing excess reserve" means the excess (if any) of —

    (i) the amount of assets set aside at the close of the first taxable year ending after July 18, 1984, for purposes described in subsection (a), over

    (ii) the account limit determined under this section (without regard to this paragraph) for the taxable year for which such increase is being computed.

(D) *Funds to which paragraph applies*

This paragraph shall apply only to a welfare benefit fund which, as of July 18, 1984, had assets set aside for purposes described in subsection (a).

(g) *Employer taxed on income of welfare benefit fund in certain cases*

    (1) *In general*

In the case of any welfare benefit fund which is not an organization described in paragraph (7), (9), (17), or (20) of section 501(c), the employer shall include in gross income for any taxable year an amount equal to such fund's deemed unrelated income for the fund's taxable year ending within the employer's taxable year.

    (2) *Deemed unrelated income*

For purposes of paragraph (1), the deemed unrelated income of any welfare benefit fund shall be the amount which would have been its unrelated business taxable income under section 512(a)(3) if such fund were an organization described in paragraph (7), (9), (17), or (20) of section 501(c).

    (3) *Coordination with section 419*

If any amount is included in the gross income of an employer for any taxable year under paragraph (1) with respect to any welfare benefit fund —

    (A) the amount of the tax imposed by this chapter which is attributable to the amount so included shall be treated as a contribution paid to such welfare benefit fund on the last day of such taxable year, and

(B) the tax so attributable shall be treated as imposed on the fund for purposes of section 419(c)(4)(A).

(h) *Aggregation rules*

For purposes of this subpart —

(1) *Aggregation of funds*

(A) Mandatory aggregation

For purposes of subsections (c)(4), (d)(2), and (e)(2), all welfare benefit funds of an employer shall be treated as 1 fund.

(B) Permissive aggregation for purposes not specified in subparagraph (A)

For purposes of this section (other than the provisions specified in subparagraph (A)), at the election of the employer, 2 or more welfare benefit funds of such employer may (to the extent not inconsistent with the purposes of this subpart and section 512) be treated as 1 fund.

(2) *Treatment of related employers*

Rules similar to the rules of subsections (b), (c), (m), and (n) of section 414 shall apply.

(i) *Regulations*

The Secretary shall prescribe such regulations as may be appropriate to carry out the purposes of this subpart. Such regulations may provide that the plan administrator of any welfare benefit fund which is part of a plan to which more than 1 employer contributes shall submit such information to the employers contributing to the fund as may be necessary to enable the employers to comply with the provisions of this section.

§1.419–1T Treatment of welfare benefit funds. (Temporary)

Q–1: What does section 419 of the Internal Revenue Code provide?

A–1: Section 419 prescribes limitations upon deductions for contributions paid or accrued with respect to a welfare benefit fund. Under section 419 (a) and (b), an employer's contributions to a welfare benefit fund are not deductible under section 162 (relating to trade or business expenses) or section 212 (relating to expenses for production of income) but, if the requirements of section 162 or 212 are otherwise met, are deductible under section 419 for the taxable year of the employer in which paid to the extent of the welfare benefit fund's qualified cost (within the meaning of section 419(c)(1)) for the taxable year of the fund that relates to such taxable year of the employer. Under section 419(g), section 419 and this section shall also apply to the deduction by a taxpayer of contributions with respect to a fund that would be a welfare benefit fund but for the fact that there is no employer-employee relationship between the person providing the services and the person for whom the services are provided. Contributions paid to a welfare benefit fund after section 419 becomes effective with respect to such contributions are deemed to relate, first, to amounts accrued and deducted (but not paid) by the employer with respect to such fund before section 419 becomes effective with respect to such contributions and thus shall not be treated as satisfying the payment requirement of section 419. See paragraph (b) of Q&A–5 for special deduction limits applicable to employer contributions to welfare benefit funds with excess reserves.

Q–2: When do the deduction rules of section 419, as enacted by the Tax Reform Act of 1984, become effective?

A–2: (a) Section 419 generally applies to contributions paid or accrued with respect to a welfare benefit fund after December 31, 1985, in taxable years of employers ending after that date. See Q&A–9 of this regulation for special rules relating to the deduction limit for the first taxable year of a fiscal year employer ending after December 31, 1985. (b) In the case of a welfare benefit fund which is part of a plan maintained pursuant to one or more collective bargaining agreements (1) between employee representatives and one or more employers, and (2) that are in effect on July 1, 1985 (or ratified on or before such date), sections 419 shall not apply to contributions paid or accrued in taxable years beginning before the termination of the last of the collective bargaining agreements pursuant to which the plan is maintained (determined without regard to any extension thereof agreed to after July 1, 1985). For purposes of the preceding sentence, any plan amendment made pursuant to a collective bargaining agreement relating to the plan which amends the plan solely to conform to any requirement added under section 511 of the Tax Reform Act of 1984 (i.e., requirements under sections 419, 419A, 512(a)(3)(E), and 4976) shall not be treated as a termination of such collective bargaining agreement. See §1.419A–2T for special rules relating to the application of section 419 to collectively bargained welfare benefit funds. (c) Notwithstanding paragraphs (a) and (b), section 419 applies to any contribution of a facility to a welfare benefit fund (or other contribution, such as cash, which is used to acquire, construct, or improve such a facility) after June 22, 1984, unless such facility is placed in service by the fund before January 1, 1987, and either (1) is acquired or improved by the fund (or contributed to the fund) pursuant to a binding contract in effect on June 22, 1984, and at all times thereafter, or (2) the construction of which was begun by or for the welfare benefit fund before June 22, 1984. See Q&A–11 of this regulation for special rules relating to the application of section 419 to the contribution of a facility to a welfare benefit fund (and to the contribution of other amounts, such as cash, used to acquire, construct, or improve such a facility) before section 419 generally becomes effective with respect to contributions to the fund.

Q–3. What is a "welfare benefit fund" under section 419?

A–3. (a) A "welfare benefit fund" is any fund which is part of a plan, or method or arrangement, of an employer and through which the employer provides welfare benefits to employees or their beneficiaries. For purposes of this section, the term "welfare benefit" includes any benefit other than a benefit with respect to which the employer's deduction is governed by section 83(h), section 404 (determined without regard to section 404(b)(2)), section 404A, or section 463. (b) Under section 419(e)(3) (A) and (B), the term "fund" includes any organization described in section 501(c) (7), (9), (17) or (20), and any trust, corporation, or other organization not exempt from tax imposed by chapter 1, subtitle A, of the Internal Revenue Code. Thus, a taxable trust or taxable corporation that is maintained for the purpose of providing welfare benefits to an employer's employees is a "welfare benefit fund." (c) Section 419(e)(3)(C) also provides that the term "fund" includes, to the extent provided in regulations, any account held for an employer by any person. Pending the issuance of further guidance, only the following accounts, and arrangements that effectively constitute accounts, as described below, are "funds" within section 419(e)(3)(C). A retired lives reserve or a premium stabilization reserve maintained by an insurance company is a "fund," or part of a "fund," if it is maintained for a particular employer and the employer has the right to have any amount in the reserve applied against its future years' benefit costs or insurance premiums. Also, if an employer makes a payment to an insurance company under an "administrative services only" arrangement with respect to which the life insurance company maintains a separate account to provide benefits, then the arrangement would be considered to be a "fund." Finally, an insurance or premium arrangement between an employer and an insurance company is a "fund" if, under the arrangement, the employer has a right to a refund, credit, or additional benefits (including upon termination of the arrangement) based on the benefit or claims experience, administrative cost experience, or investment experience attributable to such employer. However, an arrangement with an insurance company is not a "fund" under the previous sentence merely because the employer's premium for a renewal year reflects the employer's own experience for an earlier year if the arrangement is both cancellable by the insurance company and cancellable by the employer as of the end of any policy year and, upon cancellation by either of the parties, neither of the parties can receive a refund or additional amounts or benefits and neither of the parties can incur a residual liability beyond the end of the policy year (other than, in the case of the insurer, to provide benefits with respect to claims incurred before cancellation). The determination whether either of the parties can receive a refund or additional amounts or benefits or can incur a residual liability upon cancellation of an arrangement will be made by examining both the contractual rights and obligations of the parties under the arrangement and the actual practice of the insurance company (and other insurance companies) with respect to other employers upon cancellation of similar arrangements. Similarly, a disability income policy does not constitute a "fund" under the preceding provisions merely because, under the policy, an employer pays an annual premium so that employees who became disabled in such year may receive benefit payments for the duration of the disability.

Q–4: For purposes of determining the section 419 limit on the employer's deduction for contributions to the fund for a taxable year of the employer, which taxable year of the welfare benefit fund is related to the taxable year of the employer?

A–4: The amount of an employer's deduction for contributions to a welfare benefit fund for a taxable year of the employer is limited to the "qualified cost" of the welfare benefit fund for the taxable year of the fund that is related to such taxable year of the employer. The taxable year of the welfare benefit fund that ends with or within the taxable year of the employer is the taxable year of the fund that is related to the taxable year of the employer. Thus, for example, if an employer has a calendar taxable year and it makes contributions to a fund having a taxable year ending June 30, the "qualified Cost" of the fund for the taxable year of the fund ending on June 30, 1986, applies to limit the employer's deduction for contributions to the fund in the employer's 1986 taxable year. In the case of employer contributions paid directly to an account or arrangement with an insurance company that is treated as a welfare benefit fund for the purposes of section 419, the policy year will be treated as the taxable year of the fund. See Q&A–7 of this regulation for special section 419 rules relating to the coordination of taxable years for the taxable year of the employer in which a welfare benefit fund is established and for the next following taxable year of the employer.

Q–5: What is the "qualified cost" of a welfare benefit fund for a taxable year under section 419?

A–5: (a) Under section 419(c), the "qualified cost" of a welfare benefit fund for a taxable year of the fund is the sum of: (1) The "qualified direct cost" of such fund for such taxable year of the fund, and (2) the amount that may be added to the qualified asset account for such taxable year of the fund to the extent that such addition does not result in a total amount of such account as of the end of such taxable year of the fund that exceeds the applicable account limit under section 419A(c). However, in calculating the qualified cost of a welfare benefit fund for a taxable year of the fund, this sum is reduced by the fund's "after-tax income" (as defined in section 419(c)(4)) for such taxable year of the fund. Also, the qualified cost of a welfare benefit fund is reduced further under the provisions of paragraph (b) of this Q&A. (b)(1) Pursuant to section 419A(i), notwithstanding section 419 and §1.419– 1T, contributions to a welfare benefit fund during any taxable year of the employer beginning after December 31, 1985, shall not be deductible for such taxable year to the extent that such contributions result in the total amount in the fund as of the end of the last taxable year of the fund ending with or within such taxable year of the employer exceeding the account limit applicable to such taxable year of the fund (as adjusted under section 419A(f)(7)). Solely for purposes of this subparagraph, (i) contributions paid to a welfare benefit fund during the taxable year of the employer but after the end of the last taxable year of the fund that relates to such taxable year of the employer, and (ii) contributions accrued with respect to a welfare benefit fund during the taxable year of the employer or during any prior taxable year of the employer (but not actually paid to such fund on or before the end of a taxable year of the employer) and deducted by the employer for such or any prior taxable year of the employer, shall be treated as an amount in the fund as of the end of the last taxable year of the fund that relates to the taxable year of the employer. Contributions that are not deductible under this subparagraph are in excess of the qualified cost of the welfare benefit fund for the taxable year of the fund that relates to the taxable year of the employer and thus are treated as contributed to the fund on the first day of the employer's next taxable year. (2) Paragraph (b)(1) of this section shall not apply to contributions with respect to a collectively bargained welfare benefit fund within the meaning of §1.419A–2T. In addition, paragraph (b)(1) of this section shall not apply to any taxable year of an employer beginning after the end of the earlier of the following taxable years: (i) the first taxable year of the employer beginning after December 31, 1985, for which the employer's deduction limit under section 419 (after the application of paragraph (b)(1) of this section) is at least equal to the qualified direct cost of the fund for the taxable year (or years) of the fund that relates to such first taxable year of the employer, or (ii) the first taxable year of the employer beginning after December 31, 1985, with or within which ends the first taxable year of the fund with respect to which the total amount in the fund as of the end of such taxable year of the fund does not exceed the account limit for such taxable year of the fund (as adjusted under section 419A(f)(7)). (3) For example, assume an employer with a taxable year ending June 30 and a welfare benefit fund with a taxable year ending January 31. During its taxable year ending June 30, 1987, and on or before January 31, 1987, the employer contributes $250,000 to the fund, and during the remaining portion of its taxable year ending June 30, 1987, the employer contributes $200,000. The qualified direct cost of the fund for its taxable year ending January 31, 1987, is $500,000, the account limit applicable to such taxable year (after the adjustment under section 419A(f)(7)) is $750,000, and the total amount in the fund as of January 31, 1987, is $800,000. Before the application of this paragraph, the employer may deduct the entire $450,000 contribution for its taxable year ending June 30, 1987. However, under this paragraph, the excess of (i) the sum of the total amount in the fund as of January 31, 1987 ($800,000), and employer contributions to the fund after January 31, 1987, and on or before June 30, 1987 ($200,000), over (ii) the account limit applicable to the fund for its taxable year ending January 31, 1987 ($750,000), is $250,000. Thus, under this paragraph, only $200,000 of the $450,000 contribution the employer made during its taxable year ending June 30, 1987, is deductible for such taxable year. If the excess were $450,000 or greater, no portion of the $450,000 contribution would be deductible by the employer for its taxable year ending June 30, 1987. Such nondeductible contributions are in excess of the fund's qualified cost for the taxable year related to the employer's taxable year and thus are deemed to be contributed on the first day of the employer's next taxable year. (c) See Q&A–7 of this regulation for special rules relating to the calculation of the qualified cost of a welfare benefit fund for an Initial Fund Year and an Overlap Fund Year (as defined in Q&A–7). See Q&A–11 of this regulation for special rules relating to the application of section 419 to the contribution to a welfare benefit fund of a facility (and to the contribution of other amounts, such as cash, used to acquire, construct, or improve a facility) before section 419 generally becomes effective with respect to contributions to the fund. See §1.419A–2T for special rules relating to certain collectively bargained welfare benefit funds.

Q–6: What is the "qualified direct cost" of a welfare benefit fund under section 419(c)(3)?

A–6: (a) Under section 419(c)(3), the "qualified direct cost" of a welfare benefit fund for any taxable year of the fund is the aggregate amount which would have been allowable as a deduction to the employer for benefits provided by such fund during such year (including insurance coverage for such year) if (1) such benefits were provided directly by the employer and (2) the employer used the cash receipts and disbursements method of accounting and had the same taxable year as the fund. In this regard, a benefit is treated as provided when such benefit would be includible in the gross income of the employee if provided directly by the employer (or would be so includible but for a provision of chapter 1, subtitle A, of the Internal Revenue Code excluding it from gross income). Thus, for example, if a calendar year welfare benefit fund pays an insurance company in July 1986 the full premium for coverage of its current employees under a term health insurance policy for the twelve month period ending June 30, 1987, the insurance coverage will be treated as provided by the fund over such twelve month period. Accordingly, only the portion of the premium for coverage during 1986 will be treated as a "qualified direct cost" of the fund for 1986; the remaining portion of the premium will be treated as a "qualified direct cost" of the fund for 1987. The "qualified direct cost" for a taxable year of the fund includes the administrative expenses incurred by the welfare benefit fund in delivering the benefits for such year. (b) If, in a taxable year of a welfare benefit fund, the fund holds an asset with a useful life extending substantially beyond the end of the taxable year (e.g., buildings, vehicles, tangible assets, and licenses) and, for such taxable year of the fund, the asset is used in the provision of welfare benefits to employees, the "qualified direct cost" of the fund for such taxable year of the fund includes the amount that would have been allowable to the employer as a deduction under the applicable Code provisions (e.g., sections 168 and 179) with respect to the portion of the asset used in the provision of welfare benefits for such year if the employer had acquired and placed in service the asset at the same time the fund received and placed in service the asset, and the employer had the same taxable year as the fund. This rule applies regardless of whether the fund received the asset through a contribution of the asset by the employer or through an acquisition or the construction by the fund of the asset. For example, assume that in 1986 a calendar year employer contributes recovery property under section 168(c) to a welfare benefit fund with a calendar taxable year to be used in the provision of welfare benefits. The employer will be treated as having sold the property in such year and thus will recognize gain to the extent that the fair market value of the property exceeds the employer's adjusted basis in the property. In this regard, see section 1239(d). Also, the employer will be treated as having made a contribution to the fund in such year equal to the fair market value of the property. Finally, the qualified direct cost of the welfare benefit fund for 1986 will include the amount that the employer could have deducted in 1986 with respect to the portion of the property used in the provision of welfare benefits if the employer had acquired the property in 1986 and had placed the property in service when the fund actually placed the property in service. Similarly, for example, assume that in 1986 a welfare benefit fund purchases and places in service a facility to be used in the provision of welfare benefits. The qualified direct cost of the fund for 1986 will include the amount that the employer could have deducted with respect to such facility if the employer had purchased and placed in service the facility at the same time that the fund purchased and placed in service the facility. (c) The qualified direct cost of a welfare benefit fund does not include expenditures by the fund that would not have been deductible if they had been made directly by the employer. For example, a fund's purchase of land in a year for an employee recreational facility will not be treated as a qualified direct cost because, if made directly by the employer, the purchase would not have been deductible under section 263. See also sections 264 and 274. (d) Notwithstanding the preceding paragraphs, the qualified direct cost of a welfare benefit fund with respect to that portion of a child care facility used in the provision of welfare benefits for a year will include the amount that would have been allowable to the employer as a deduction for the year under a straight-line depreciation schedule for a period of 60 months beginning with the month in which the facility is placed in service under rules similar to those provided for section 188 property under §1.188–1(a). For purposes of this section, a "child care facility" is tangible property of a charactersubject to depreciation that is located in the United States and specifically used as an integral part of a "qualified child care center facility" within the meaning of §1.188–1(d)(4). (e) See Q&A–7 of this regulation for special section 419 rules relating to the calculation of the qualified direct cost of a welfare benefit fund for an Initial Fund Year and an Overlap Fund Year (as defined in Q&A–7). See Q&A–11 of this regulation for special rules relating to the contribution to a welfare benefit fund of a facility (and to the contribution of other amounts, such as cash, used to acquire, construct, or improve a facility) before section 419 generally becomes effective with respect to contributions to the fund.

Q–7: What special rules apply for purposes of determining the section 419 limit on the employer's deduction for contributions to a welfare benefit fund for the taxable year of the employer in which the fund is established and for the next following taxable year of the employer?

A–7: (a) If the taxable year of a welfare benefit fund is the same as the taxable year of the employer, there are no special rules that apply for purposes of determining the section 419 limit on an employer's deduction for contributions to the fund for either the taxable year of the employer in which the fund is established or the next following taxable year of the employer. However, if the taxable year of a welfare benefit fund is different from the taxable year of the employer, the general section 419 rules are modified by the special rules set forth below for purposes of determining the section 419 deduction limit for the taxable year of the employer in which a fund is established and for the next following taxable year of the employer. (b) If a welfare benefit fund is established after December 31, 1985, during a taxable year of an employer and either (i) the first taxable year of the fund ends after the close of such taxable year of the employer, or (ii) the first taxable year of the fund is six months or less and ends before the close of such taxable year of the employer and the second taxable year of the fund begins before and ends after the close of such taxable year of the employer, the taxable year of the fund that contains the closing day of such taxable year of the employer will be treated as an "Overlap Fund Year." For purposes of determining the limit on the employer's deduction for contributions to a welfare benefit fund for the taxable year of the employer in which the fund was established, the period between the beginning of the fund's Overlap Fund Year and the end of the employer's taxable year in which the Overlap Fund Year began will be treated as a taxable year of the fund ("Initial Fund Year"). (c) The qualified cost of a welfare benefit fund for its Initial Fund Year will be equal to the qualified direct cost of the fund for such Initial Fund Year. The qualified cost of a fund for its Overlap Fund Year will be determined under the general rules of Q&A–5 of this regulation and section 419(c), with the exception that such qualified cost will be reduced by the employer contributions made during the Initial Fund Year and deductible by the employer for the taxable year of the employer in which the Overlap Fund Year of the fund begins. (d) Assume that an employer with a calendar taxable year establishes on July 1, 1986, a welfare benefit fund with a taxable year ending on June 30. The fund's first taxable year from July 1, 1986, to June 30, 1987, is an Overlap Fund Year. The employer contributes $1,000 to the fund during its taxable year ending December 31, 1986 (i.e., during the period between July 1, 1986, and December 31, 1986, which is also the Initial Fund Year) and another $1,500 to the fund during its taxable year ending December 31, 1987. Assume further that the qualified direct cost of the fund for the Initial Fund Year is $900 and that the qualified cost for the Overlap Fund Year is $2,500 (prior to the reduction required by paragraph (c) of this Q&A). Under the special rules of paragraphs (b) and (c), the employer may deduct $900 for its taxable year ending on December 31, 1986, and $1,600 for its taxable year ending on December 31, 1987. If the qualified direct cost of the fund for the Initial

Fund Year had been $1,050 and the qualified cost for the Overlap Fund Year had been $2,500 (prior to the reduction required by paragraph (c) of this Q&A), the employer's deduction for its taxable year ending December 31, 1986, would have been $1,000 and its deduction for its taxable year ending December 31, 1987, would have been $1,500. (e) Assume that an employer with a calendar taxable year establishes on March 1, 1986, a welfare benefit fund with a taxable year ending June 30. Thus, the fund has a short first taxable year ending June 30, 1986, an Overlap Fund Year from July 1, 1986, until June 30, 1987, and an ongoing June 30 taxable year. The employer contributes $1,750 to the fund during the employer's taxable year ending December 31, 1986— $750 during the short first taxable year of the fund and $1,000 during the Initial Fund Year (i.e., the period between July 1, 1986, and December 31, 1986)—and $1,500 to the fund during its taxable year ending December 31, 1987. Assume that the qualified cost of the fund for the short first taxable year of the fund is $800, the qualified direct cost for the Initial Fund Year is $900, and the qualified cost for the Overlap Fund Year is $2,500 (prior to the reduction required by paragraph (c) of this Q&A). Under the special rules of paragraphs (b) and (c), the employer may deduct $1,700 for its taxable year ending December 31, 1986, and $1,550 for its taxable year ending December 31, 1987.

Q–8: How does section 419 treat an employer's contribution with respect to a welfare benefit fund in excess of the applicable deduction limit for a taxable year of the employer?

A–8: (a) If an employer makes contributions to a welfare benefit fund in a taxable year of the employer and such contributions (when combined with prior contributions that are deemed under the rule of this Q&A and section 419(d) to have been made in such taxable year) exceed the section 419 deduction limit for such taxable year of the employer, the excess amounts are deemed to be contributed to the fund on the first day of the next taxable year of the employer. Such deemed contributions are combined with amounts actually contributed by the employer to the fund during the next taxable year and may be deductible for such year, subject to the otherwise applicable section 419 deduction limit for such year. (b) Contributions to a welfare benefit fund on or before December 31, 1985, that were not deductible by the employer for any taxable year of the employer ending on or before December 31, 1985, or for the first taxable year of the employer ending after December 31, 1985, as pre-1986 contributions (see Q&A–9 of this regulation) are deemed to be contributed to the fund on January 1, 1986, However, see Q&A–11 of this regulation for special rules relating to the contribution to a welfare benefit fund of amounts (such as cash) used to acquire, construct, or improve a facility before section 419 generally becomes effective with respect to contributions to the fund. Generally, such contributions (to the extent that they were made after June 22, 1984 and on or before December 31, 1985) are treated as nondeductible pre-1986 contributions and are deemed to be contributed in the form of a facility at the same time as when the facility is placed in service by the fund.

Q–9: How does an employer with a fiscal taxable year calculate its deduction limit for contributions with respect to a welfare benefit fund for the first taxable year of the employer ending after December 31, 1985?

A–9: (a) If the first taxable year of an employer ending after December 31, 1985 (or, if applicable under paragraph (b) of Q&A–2 of this section, the first taxable year of an employer beginning after termination of the last of the collective bargaining agreements pursuant to which the fund is maintained) is a fiscal year, the employer's deduction for such taxable year for contributions to a welfare benefit fund that is not a collectively bargained welfare benefit fund under §1.419A–2T is limited to the greater of the following two amounts: (1) The contributions paid to the fund during such first taxable year up to the qualified cost of the welfare benefit fund for the taxable year of the fund that relates to such taxable year of the employer, and (2) the contributions paid to the fund during the 1985 portion of such first taxable year of the employer ("the pre-1986 contributions") to the extent that such pre-1986 contributions are deductible under the rules governing the deduction of such contributions before section 419 generally becomes effective (including the rules set forth in Q&A–10 of this regulation, modified for purposes of this Q&A–9 by substituting "December 31, 1986" for "December 31, 1985" in paragraph (c)). See Q&A–11 of this regulation for special rules relating to the contribution to a welfare benefit fund of a facility (and to the contribution of other amounts, such as cash, used to acquire, construct, or improve such a facility) before section 419 generally becomes effective with respect to contributions to such fund. (b) For example, assume that an employer with a taxable year ending June 30, contributes to a welfare benefit fund with a taxable year ending

January 31. This employer contributes $1,000 to the fund between July 1, 1985, and December 31, 1985, and an additional $500 to the fund between January 1, 1986, and June 30, 1986. Assume further that the qualified direct cost of the fund for the taxable year of the fund ending January 31, 1986, is $500 and that the qualified cost for such taxable year is $800. Under the deduction rule set forth above, the employer's deduction for its taxable year ending June 30, 1986, is the greater of two amounts: (1) The contributions made during such full taxable year ($1,500) up to the qualified cost of the fund with respect to such taxable year ($800), and (2) the pre-1986 contributions ($1,000) to the extent that such pre-1986 contributions are deductible under the pre-section 419 rules. In determining the extent to which the pre-1986 contributions are deductible under the pre-section 419 rules, the rules contained in Q&A–10 apply as though December 31, 1985, in paragraph (c) were December 31, 1986. Assuming that only $875 is deductible under the pre-section 419 rules, because $875 is greater than $800, this employer may deduct $875 for its first taxable year ending after December 31, 1985. This full $875 deduction for 1985 is deemed to consist entirely of pre-1986 contributions.

Q–10: How do the rules of sections 263, 446(b), 461(a), and 461(h) apply in determining whether contributions with respect to a welfare benefit fund are deductible for a taxable year?

A–10: (a) Both before and after the effective date of section 419 (see Q&A–2 of this regulation), an employer is allowed a deduction for taxable year for contributions paid or accrued with respect to a "welfare benefit fund" (as defined in Q&A–3 of this regulation and section 419(e)) only to the extent that such contributions satisfy the requirements of section 162 or 212. These requirements must be satisfied after the effective date of section 419 because 419 requires that (among other requirements) contributions to a welfare benefit fund satisfy the requirements of section 162 or 212. (b) Except as provided in paragraphs (c) and (d), in determining the extent to which contributions paid or accrued with respect to welfare benefit fund satisfy the requirements of section 162 or 212 for a taxable year (both before and after section 419 generally becomes effective with respect to such contributions), the rules of sections 263, 446(b), 461(a) (including the rules that relate to the creation of an asset with a useful life extending substantially beyond the close of the taxable year), and 461(h) (to the extent that such section is effective with respect to such contributions) are generally applicable. (c) Notwithstanding paragraph (b), under the authority of section 7805(b), the rules of sections 263, 446(b), and 461(a) shall not be applied in determining the extent to which an employer's contribution with respect to a welfare benefit fund is deductible under section 162 or 212 with respect to any taxable year of the employer ending on or before December 31, 1985, to the extent that, for such taxable year, (1) the contribution was made pursuant to a bona fide collective bargaining agreement requiring fixed and determinable contributions to a collectively bargained welfare benefit fund (as defined in §1.419A–2T), or (2) the contribution was not in excess of the amount deductible under the principles of Revenue Rulings 69–382, 1969–2 C.B. 28; 69–478, 1969–2 C.B. 29; and 73–599, 1973–2 C.B. 40, modified as appropriate for benefits for active employees. (d) Notwithstanding paragraph (b), in determining the extent to which contributions paid or accrued with respect to a welfare benefit fund are deductible under section 419, the rules of sections 263, 446(b), and 461(a) will be treated as having been satisfied to the extent that such contributions satisfy the otherwise applicable rules of section 419. Thus, for example, contributions to a welfare benefit fund will not fail to be deductible under section 419 merely because they create an asset with a useful life extending substantially beyond the close of the taxable year if such contributions satisfy the otherwise applicable requirements of section 419. (e) In determining the extent to which contributions with respect to a welfare benefit fund satisfy the requirements of section 461(h) for any taxable year for which section 461(h) is effective, pursuant to the authority under section 461(h)(2), economic performance occurs as contributions to the welfare benefit fund are made. Solely for purposes of section 461(h), in the case of an employer's taxable year ending on or after July 18, 1984, and on or before March 21, 1986, contributions made to the welfare benefit fund after the end of such taxable year and on or before March 21, 1986 shall be deemed to have been made on the last day of such taxable year.

Q–11: What special section 419 rules apply to the payment or accrual with respect to a welfare benefit fund of a facility (and the payment or accrual of other amounts, such as cash, used to acquire, construct, or improve such a facility)?

A–11: (a)(1) In the case of an employer's payment or accrual with respect to a welfare benefit fund after June 22, 1984, and on or before December 31, 1985 (or, if applicable under paragraph (b) of Q&A–2 of this regulation, before section 419 generally becomes effective with respect to contributions to such fund), of a facility, the rules of section 419, §1.419–1T, and §1.419A–2T generally apply to determine the extent to which such contribution is deductible by the employer for its taxable year of contribution. For this purpose, however, the facility is to be treated as the only contribution made to the fund and the qualified cost of the fund for the taxable year of the fund in which the facility was contributed is to be equal to the qualified direct cost directly attributable to the facility (as determined under Q&A–6 of this regulation). Also, for this purpose, the welfare benefit fund to which the facility was contributed may not be aggregated with any other fund. For purposes of this Q&A, "facility" means any tangible asset with a useful life extending substantially beyond the end of the taxable year (e.g., vehicles, buildings) and any intangible asset (e.g., licenses) related to a tangible asset, whether or not such asset is used in the provision of welfare benefits. See, however, paragraph (c) of Q&A–2 of this regulation for a binding contract exception. (2) For example, assume that an employer and a welfare benefit fund each has a calendar taxable year and that, during 1985, the employer contributes to the fund $200,000 in cash and a facility with a fair market value of $100,000. Such facility is used in the provision of welfare benefits under the fund. The employer is treated as having sold the facility in such year and thus will recognize gain to the extent that the fair market value of the facility exceeds the employer's adjusted basis in the facility. In this regard, see section 1239(d). The extent to which the facility contribution is deductible by the employer for its 1985 taxable year is determined as though it were the only contribution made by the employer to the fund during such year and the qualified cost of the fund for the taxable year of the fund in which the contribution was made (i.e., the 1985 taxable year) were equal to the amount that would have been allowable to the employer as a deduction for such year under the applicable Code provisions with respect to the portion of the facility used in the provision of welfare benefits for such year if the employer had placed in service the facility at the time the fund placed in service the facility and if the employer had the same taxable year as the fund. If, under these assumptions, the employer would have been allowed a $10,000 deduction with respect to the facility for the 1985 taxable year, the fund's qualified cost for its 1985 taxable year would be only

$10,000. Thus, only $10,000 of the $100,000 facility contribution would be deductible by the employer for its 1985 taxable year (i.e., the taxable year of the employer with or within which the applicable taxable year of the fund ends). However, in determining the extent to which the $200,000 in cash is deductible by the employer for its 1985 taxable year, the $100,000 facility is not to be disregarded. Thus, if under the applicable pre-section 419 rules the employer is allowed for 1985 a total deduction of only $175,000, the employer would be permitted a deduction for 1985 of $175,000 ($10,000 with respect to the facility and $165,000 of the cash contribution). The nondeductible portion of the cash contribution is to be treated as contributed to the fund on the first day of the next taxable year of the employer. If under the applicable pre-section 419 rules the employer were allowed a total deduction of $300,000 for 1985, the employer would be permitted a deduction for 1985 of only $210,000 ($10,000 with respect to the facility and the full $200,000 cash contribution). (3) For example, assume that an employer has a June 30 taxable year and maintains a welfare benefit fund with a taxable year ending January 31. During the 1985 portion of its taxable year ending June 30, 1986, the employer contributes $50,000 in cash and a facility with a fair market value of $100,000; and during the 1986 portion of such taxable year, the employer contributes another $75,000 in cash to the fund. The facility is used in the provision of welfare benefits under the fund. Under the rules of Q&A–9 of this regulation, the employer's deduction for its June 30, 1986, taxable year is limited to the greater of the following two amounts: (i) The contributions paid to the fund during such taxable year ($225,000) up to the qualified cost of the fund for the taxable year of the fund ending January 31, 1986, and (ii) the contributions paid to the fund during the 1985 portion of the employer's taxable year ending June 30, 1986 ("the pre-1986 contributions") ($150,000) to the extent that such pre-1986 contributions are deductible under the rules governing the deduction of such contributions before section 419 is generally effective with respect to the fund. For purposes of this rule, the contribution of the facility on or before December 31, 1985, is to be treated as a pre-1986 contribution and the rules of section 419 and this Q&A are to be treated as rules governing the deduction of such contribution before section 419 generally becomes effective with respect to the fund. Thus, in determining the extent to which the facility is deductible as a pre-1986 contribution under the rules before section 419 generally becomes effective, the facility is treated as the only contribution to the welfare benefit fund and the qualified cost of such fund for the taxable year of the fund in which the facility was contributed is the amount that would have been allowable to the employer as a deduction with respect to the portion of the facility used in the provision of welfare benefits if the employer had placed in service the facility at the same time that the fund placed in service the facility and the employer's taxable year ended on January 31, 1986. (b)(1) The preceding rules shall also apply for purposes of determining when and the extent to which an employer may deduct contributions or other items and amounts after June 22, 1984 and on or before December 31, 1985 (or, if applicable under paragraph (b) of Q&A–2 of this regulation, before section 419 generally becomes effective with respect to contributions to the fund) that are not facilities (e.g., cash contributions) to a welfare benefit fund that are used by the fund to acquire, construct, or improve a facility. The most recent non-facility contributions made to a welfare benefit fund before the facility in question is placed in service by the fund (up to the fair market value of the facility at such time) are to be treated as used by the fund for the acquisition, construction, or improvement (as the case may be) of such facility. To the extent that contributions before such a facility is placed in service are not at least equal to the value of the facility at such time, contributions after such date (up to the value of the facility at the time it is placed in service) are treated as used for acquisition, construction, or improvement of the facility. Such nonfacility contributions, to the extent that they were made after June 22, 1984, and on or before December 31, 1985 (or, if applicable under paragraph (b) of Q&A–2 of this regulation, before section 419 generally becomes effective with respect to contributions to the fund), are not deductible by the employer as non-facility contributions for any year. Instead, the employer is permitted a deduction with respect to such contributions only under the rules of this Q&A as though the employer had contributed a facility to the fund at the same time that the fund placed in service the facility in question and, at such time, the facility had a fair market value equal to the total of such non-facility contributions. (2) For example, assume that an employer and a welfare benefit fund each has a calendar taxable year and during 1985 the fund acquired and placed in service a facility with a fair market value of $100,000 to be used in the provision of welfare benefits. Further, during July 1984 the employer contributed $150,000 in cash to the fund and, during the portion of 1985, before the facility was placed in service by the fund, the employer contributed another $75,000 in cash to the fund; during the remaining portion of 1985, the employer contributed $125,000 in cash. The facility is used in the provision of welfare benefits under the fund. Because $25,000 of the employer's 1984 contribution is treated under this rule as used for the acquisition of a facility, such $25,000 is not deductible by the employer for 1984. For purposes of determining the employer's deduction for 1985, the employer will be treated as having contributed $125,000 in cash and a facility with a fair market value of $100,000. The employer's deduction for its 1985 taxable year will be determined under the rules relating to the contribution of a facility after June 22, 1984, and on or before December 31, 1985. (3) For example, assume that an employer and a welfare benefit fund each has a calendar taxable year and during 1986 the fund placed in service a facility with a fair market value of $100,000 to be used in the provision of welfare benefits. During 1985, the employer contributed $125,000 in cash to the fund. During the portion of 1986 before the facility was placed in service, the employer contributed $60,000 in cash, and during the remaining portion of 1986, the employer contributed another $75,000 in cash. The facility is used in the provision of welfare benefits under the fund. Because $40,000 of its 1985 cash contribution is treated under this rule as used for the acquisition of the facility, such $40,000 is not deductible by the employer for 1985. For purposes of determining the employer's deduction for 1986, the employer will be treated as though it had contributed a $40,000 facility to the fund at the time the fund placed the facility in service. (c) For purposes of calculating the "existing excess reserve amount" under Q&A–1 of §1.419A–1T and the "existing reserves for post-retirement medical or life insurance benefits" under Q&A–4 of §1.512(a)–5T (but not the exempt function income under Q&A–3 of §1.512(a)–5T), the amount set aside as of any applicable date is to be reduced to the extent that contributions originally included in such amount are subsequently treated under this Q&A as used for the acquisition, construction, or improvement of an asset excluded from the calculation of the total amount set aside under paragraph (b) of §1.512(a)–5T (or would be so treated under this Q&A if it applied to such asset). The reduction required under this paragraph applies for purposes of calculating the "existing excess reserve amount" and the "existing reserves for post-retirement medical or life insurance benefits" for all taxable years of the welfare benefit fund.

[T.D. 8073, 51 FR 4323, Feb. 4, 1986; 51 FR 7262, Mar. 3, 1986; 51 FR 11303, Apr. 2, 1986]

§1.419A–1T Qualified Asset Account Limitation of Additions to Account. (Temporary)

Q–1: What does the transition rule under section 419A(f)(7) provide?

A–1: Section 419A(f)(7) provides that, in the case of a welfare benefit fund that was in existence on July 18, 1984, the account limit (as determined under section 419A(c)) for each of the first four taxable years of the fund that relate to taxable years of the employer ending after December 31, 1985 (or, if applicable under paragraph (b) of Q&A–2 of §1.419–1T, taxable years of the employer beginning after the termination of the last of the collective bargaining agreements pursuant to which the plan is maintained) shall be increased by the following percentages of the "existing excess reserve amount":

	Percent
First taxable year	80
Second taxable year	60
Third taxable year	40
Fourth taxable year	20

For purposes of this section, the "existing excess reserve amount" for any taxable year of a fund is the excess of (a) the assets actually set aside for purposes described in section 419A(a) at the close of the first taxable year of the fund ending after July 18, 1984 (calculated in the manner set forth in Q&A–3 of §1.512(a)–3T, and adjusted under paragraph (c) of Q&A–11 of §1.419–1T), reduced by employer contributions to the fund before the close of such first taxable year to the extent that such contributions are not deductible for the taxable year of the employer with or within which such taxable year of the fund ends and for any prior taxable year of the employer, over (b) the account limit which would have applied to the taxable year of the fund for which the excess is being computed (without regard to this transition rule). A welfare benefit fund is treated as in existence on July 18, 1984, for purposes of this transition rule only if amounts were actually set aside in such fund on such date to provide welfare benefits enumerated under section 419A.

[T.D. 8073, 51 FR 4329, Feb. 4, 1986, as amended at 51 FR 11303, Apr. 2, 1986]

§1.419A–2T Qualified asset account limitation for collectively bargained funds. (Temporary)

Q–1: What account limits apply to welfare benefit funds that are maintained pursuant to a collective bargaining agreement?

A–1: Contributions to a welfare benefit fund maintained pursuant to one or more collective bargaining agreements and the reserves of such a fund generally are subject to the rules of sections 419, 419A, and 512. However, neither contributions to nor reserves of such a collectively bargained welfare benefit fund shall be treated as exceeding the otherwise applicable limits of section 419(b), 419A(b), or 512(a)(3)(E) until the earlier of: (i) The date on which the last of the collective bargaining agreements relating to the fund in effect on, or ratified on or before, the date of issuance of final regulations concerning such limits for collectively bargained welfare benefit funds terminates (determined without regard to any extension thereof agreed to after the date of issuance of such final regulations), or (ii) the date 3 years after the issuance of such final regulations.

Q–2: What is a welfare benefit fund maintained pursuant to a collective bargaining agreement for purposes of Q&A–1?

A–2: (1) For purposes of Q&A–1, a collectively bargained welfare benefit fund is a welfare benefit fund that is maintained pursuant to an agreement which the Secretary of Labor determines to be a collective bargaining agreement and which meets the requirements of the Secretary of the Treasury as set forth in paragraph 2 below. (2) Notwithstanding a determination by the Secretary of Labor that an agreement is a collective bargaining agreement, a welfare benefit fund is considered to be maintained pursuant to a collective bargaining agreement only if the benefits provided through the fund were the subject of arms-length negotiations between employee representatives and one or more employers, and if such agreement between employee representatives and one or more employers satisfies section 7701(a)(46) of the Code. Moreover, the circumstances surrounding a collective bargaining agreement must evidence good faith bargaining between adverse parties over the welfare benefits to be provided through the fund. Finally, a welfare benefit fund is not considered to be maintained pursuant to a collective bargaining agreement unless at least 50 percent of the employees eligible to receive benefits under the fund are covered by the collective bargaining agreement. (3) In the case of a collectively bargained welfare benefit fund, only the portion of the fund (as determined under allocation rules to be provided by the Commissioner) attributable to employees covered by a collective bargaining agreement, and from which benefits for such employees are provided, is considered to be maintained pursuant to a collective bargaining agreement. (4) Notwithstanding the preceding paragraphs and pending the issuance of regulations setting account limits for collectively bargained welfare benefit funds, a welfare benefit fund will not be treated as a collectively bargained welfare benefit fund for purposes of Q&A–1 if and when, after July 1, 1985, the number of employees who are not covered by a collective bargaining agreement and are eligible to receive benefits under the fund increases by reason of an amendment, merger, or other action of the employer or the fund. In addition, pending the issuance of such regulations, for purposes of applying the 50 percent test of paragraph (2) to a welfare benefit fund that is not in existence on July 1, 1985, "90 percent" shall be substituted for "50 percent".

[T.D. 8034, 50 FR 27428, July 3, 1985]

IRC Section 401(h)
Medical Account Rules

TITLE 26 — INTERNAL REVENUE CODE
Subtitle A — Income Taxes
CHAPTER 1 — NORMAL TAXES AND SURTAXES
Subchapter D — Deferred Compensation, Etc.
PART I — PENSION, PROFIT-SHARING, STOCK BONUS PLANS, ETC.
Subpart A — General Rule

Section 401
Qualified Pension, Profit-sharing, and Stock Bonus Plans

(h) *Medical, etc., benefits for retired employees and their spouses and dependent*
Under regulations prescribed by the Secretary, and subject to the provisions of section 420, a pension or annuity plan may provide for the payment of benefits for sickness, accident, hospitalization, and medical expenses of retired employees, their spouses and their dependents, but only if -

    (1) such benefits are subordinate to the retirement benefits provided by the plan,

        (2) a separate account is established and maintained for such benefits,

        (3) the employer's contributions to such separate account are reasonable and ascertainable,

    (4) it is impossible, at any time prior to the satisfaction of all liabilities under the plan to provide such benefits, for any part of the corpus or income of such separate account to be (within the taxable year or thereafter) used for, or diverted to, any purpose other than the providing of such benefits,

    (5) notwithstanding the provisions of subsection (a)(2), upon the satisfaction of all liabilities under the plan to provide such benefits, any amount remaining in such separate account must, under the terms of the plan, be returned to the employer, and

    (6) in the case of an employee who is a key employee, a separate account is established and maintained for such benefits payable to such employee (and his spouse and dependents) and such benefits (to the extent attributable to plan years beginning after March 31, 1984, for which the employee is a key employee) are only payable to such employee (and his spouse and dependents) from such separate account.

For purposes of paragraph (6), the term "key employee" means any employee, who at any time during the plan year or any preceding plan year during which contributions were made on behalf of such employee, is or was a key employee as defined in section 416(i). In no event shall the requirements of paragraph (1) be treated as met if the aggregate actual contributions for medical benefits, when added to actual contributions for life insurance protection under the plan, exceed 25 percent of the total actual contributions to the plan (other than contributions to fund past service credits) after the date on which the account is established.

§1.401–14 Inclusion of Medical Benefits for Retired Employees in Qualified Pension or Annuity Plans

(a) *Introduction.* Under section 401(h) a qualified pension or annuity plan may make provision for the payment of sickness, accident, hospitalization, and medical expenses for retired employees, their spouses, and their dependents. The term "medical benefits described in section 401(h)" is used in this section to describe such payments.

(b) *In general*—(1) *Coverage.* Under section 401(h), a qualified pension or annuity plan may provide for the payment of medical benefits described in section 401(h) only for retired employees, their spouses, or their dependents. To be "retired" for purposes of eligibility to receive medical benefits described in section 401(h), an employee must be eligible to receive retirement benefits provided under the pension plan, or else be retired by an employer providing such medical benefits by reason of permanent disability. For purposes of the preceding sentence, an employee is not considered to be eligible to receive retirement benefits provided under the plan if he is still employed by the employer and a separation from employment is a condition to receiving the retirement benefits.

(2) *Discrimination.* A plan which provides medical benefits described in section 401(h) must not discriminate in favor of officers, shareholders, supervisory employees, or highly compensated employees with respect to coverage and with respect to the contributions or benefits under the plan. The determination of whether such a plan so discriminates is made with reference to the retirement portion of the plan as well as the portion providing the medical benefits described in section 401(h). Thus, for example, a plan will not be qualified under section 401 if it discriminates in favor of employees who are officers or shareholders with respect to either portion of the plan.

(3) *Funding medical benefits.* Contributions to provide the medical benefits described in section 401(h) may be made either on a contributory or noncontributory basis, without regard to whether the contributions to fund the retirement benefits are made on a similar basis. Thus, for example, the contributions to fund the medical benefits described in section 401(h) may be provided for entirely out of employer contributions even though the retirement benefits under the plan are determined on the basis of both employer and employee contributions.

(4) *Definitions.* For purposes of section 401(h) and this section:
   (i) The term dependent shall have the same meaning as that assigned to it by section 152, and
   (ii) The term medical expense means expenses for medical care as defined in section 213(e)(1).

(c) *Requirements*. The requirements which must be met for a qualified pension or annuity plan to provide medical benefits described in section 401(h) are set forth in subparagraphs (1) through (5) of this paragraph.

(1) *Benefits*.

(i) The plan must specify the medical benefits described in section 401(h) which will be available and must contain provisions for determining the amount which will be paid. Such benefits, when added to any life insurance protection provided for under the plan, must be subordinate to the retirement benefits provided by such plan. For purposes of this section, life insurance protection includes any benefit paid under the plan on behalf of an employee-participant as a result of the employee-participant's death to the extent such payment exceeds the amount of the reserve to provide the retirement benefits for the employee-participant existing at his death. The medical benefits described in section 401(h) are considered subordinate to the retirement benefits if at all times the aggregate of contributions (made after the date on which the plan first includes such medical benefits) to provide such medical benefits and any life insurance protection does not exceed 25 percent of the aggregate contributions (made after such date) other than contributions to fund past service credits.

(ii) The meaning of the term *subordinate* may be illustrated by the following example:

Example. The X Corporation amends its qualified pension plan to provide medical benefits described in section 401(h) effective for the taxable year 1964. The total contributions under the plan (excluding those for past service credits) for the taxable year 1964 are $125,000, allocated as follows: $100,000 for retirement benefits, $10,000 for life insurance protection, and $15,000 for medical benefits described in section 401(h). The medical benefits described in section 401(h) are considered subordinate to the retirement benefits since the portion of the contributions allocated to the medical benefits described in section 401(h) ($15,000) and to life insurance protection after such medical benefits were included in the plan ($10,000), or $25,000, does not exceed 25 percent of $125,000. For the taxable year 1965, the X Corporation contributes $140,000 (exclusive of contributions for past service credits) allocated as follows: $100,000 for retirement benefits, $10,000 for life insurance protection, and $30,000 for medical benefits described in section 401(h). The medical benefits described in section 401(h) are considered subordinate to the retirement benefits since the aggregate contributions allocated to the medical benefits described in section 401(h) ($45,000) and to life insurance protection after such medical benefits were included in the plan ($20,000) or $65,000 does not exceed 25 percent of $265,000, the aggregate of the contributions made in 1964 and 1965.

(2) *Separate accounts.* Where medical benefits described in section 401(h) are provided for under a qualified pension or annuity plan, a separate account must be maintained with respect to contributions to fund such benefits. The separation required by this section is for recordkeeping purposes only. Consequently, the funds in the medical benefits account need not be separately invested. They may be invested with funds set aside for retirement purposes without identification of which investment properties are allocable to each account. However, where the investment properties are not allocated to each account, the earnings on such properties must be allocated to each account in a reasonable manner.

(3) *Reasonable and ascertainable.* Section 401(h) further requires that amounts contributed to fund medical benefits therein described must be reasonable and ascertainable. For the rules relating to the deduction of such contributions, see paragraph (f) of §1.404(a)–3. The employer must, at the time he makes a contribution, designate that portion of such contribution allocable to the funding of medical benefits.

(4) *Impossibility of diversion prior to satisfaction of all liabilities.* Section 401(h) further requires that it must be impossible, at any time prior to the satisfaction of all liabilities under the plan to provide for the payment of medical benefits described in section 401(h), for any part of the corpus or income of the medical benefits account to be (within the taxable year or thereafter) used for, or diverted to, any purpose other than the providing of such benefits. Consequently, a plan which, for example, under its terms, permits funds in the medical benefits account to be used for any retirement benefit provided under the plan does not satisfy the requirements of section 401(h) and will not qualify under section 401(a). However, the payment of any necessary or appropriate expenses attributable to the administration of the medical benefits account does not affect the qualification of the plan.

(5) *Reversion upon satisfaction of all liabilities.* The plan must provide that any amounts which are contributed to fund medical benefits described in section 401(h) and which remain in the medical benefits account upon the satisfaction of all liabilities arising out of the operation of the medical benefits portion of the plan are to be returned to the employer.

(6) *Forfeitures.* The plan must expressly provide that in the event an individual's interest in the medical benefits account is forfeited prior to termination of the plan an amount equal to the amount of the forfeiture must be applied as soon as possible to reduce employer contributions to fund the medical benefits described in section 401(h).

(d) *Effective date.* This section applies to taxable years of a qualified pension or annuity plan beginning after October 23, 1962.

[T.D. 6722, 29 FR 5072, Apr. 14, 1964]

§1.404(a)–3 Contributions of an employer to or under an employees' pension trust or annuity plan that meets the requirements of section 401(a); application of section 404(a)(1).

(f)(1) Amounts contributed by an employer under the plan for the funding of medical benefits described in section 401(h) as defined in paragraph (a) of §1.401–14 must satisfy the general requirements which are applicable to deductions allowable under section 404 and which are set forth in §1.404(a)–1 including, for example, the requirements described in paragraph (b) of such section. Accordingly, such amounts must constitute an ordinary and necessary expense relating to either the trade or business or the production of income and must not, when added to all other compensation paid by the employer to the employee on whose behalf such a contribution is made, constitute more than reasonable compensation. However, in determining the amount which is deductible with respect to contributions to provide retirement benefits under the plan, amounts contributed for the funding of medical benefits described in section 401(h) shall not be taken into consideration.

(2) The amounts deductible with respect to employer contributions to fund medical benefits described in section 401(h) shall not exceed the total cost of providing such benefits. The total cost of providing such benefits shall be determined in accordance with any generally accepted actuarial method which is reasonable in view of the provisions and cov-

erage of the plan, the funding medium, and other applicable considerations. The amount deductible for any taxable year with respect to such cost shall not exceed the greater of—

(i) An amount determined by distributing the remaining unfunded costs of past and current service credits as a level amount, or as a level percentage of compensation, over the remaining future service of each employee, or

(ii) 10 percent of the cost which would be required to completely fund or purchase such medical benefits.

In determining the amount deductible, an employer must apply either subdivision (i) of this subparagraph for all employees or subdivision (ii) of this subparagraph for all employees. If contributions paid by an employer in a taxable year to fund such medical benefits under a pension or annuity plan exceed the limitations of this subparagraph but otherwise satisfy the conditions for deduction under section 404, then the excess contributions are carried over and are deductible in succeeding taxable years of the employer which end with or within taxable years of the trust for which it is exempt under section 501(a) in order of time to the extent of the difference between the amount paid and deductible in each succeeding year and the limitation applicable to such year under this subparagraph. For purposes of subdivision (i) of this subparagraph, if the remaining future service of an employee is one year or less, it shall be treated as one year.

[T.D. 6500, 25 FR 11685, Nov. 26, 1960, as amended by T.D. 6722, 29 FR 5073, Apr. 14, 1964; T.D. 7165, 37 FR 5025, Mar. 9, 1972]

TITLE 26 — INTERNAL REVENUE CODE
Subtitle A — Income Taxes
CHAPTER 1 — NORMAL TAXES AND SURTAXES
Subchapter D — Deferred Compensation, Etc.
PART I — PENSION, PROFIT-SHARING, STOCK BONUS PLANS, ETC.
Subpart E — Treatment of Transfers to Retiree Health Accounts

Sec. 420. Transfers of excess pension assets to retiree health accounts

(a) *General rule*
If there is a qualified transfer of any excess pension assets of a defined benefit plan (other than a multiemployer plan) to a health benefits account which is part of such plan –
  (1) a trust which is part of such plan shall not be treated as failing to meet the requirements of subsection (a) or (h) of section 401 solely by reason of such transfer (or any other action authorized under this section),
  (2) no amount shall be includible in the gross income of the employer maintaining the plan solely by reason of such transfer,
  (3) such transfer shall not be treated –
    (A) as an employer reversion for purposes of section 4980, or
    (B) as a prohibited transaction for purposes of section 4975, and
  (4) the limitations of subsection (d) shall apply to such employer.

(b) *Qualified transfer*
For purposes of this section –
  (1) In general
    The term "qualified transfer" means a transfer –
    (A) of excess pension assets of a defined benefit plan to a health benefits account which is part of such plan in a taxable year beginning after December 31, 1990,
    (B) which does not contravene any other provision of law, and
    (C) with respect to which the following requirements are met in connection with the plan –
      (i) the use requirements of subsection (c)(1),
      (ii) the vesting requirements of subsection (c)(2), and
      (iii) the minimum cost requirements of subsection (c)(3).
  (2) Only 1 transfer per year
    (A) In general
      No more than 1 transfer with respect to any plan during a taxable year may be treated as a qualified transfer for purposes of this section.

(B) Exception

A transfer described in paragraph (4) shall not be taken into account for purposes of subparagraph (A).

(3) Limitation on amount transferred

The amount of excess pension assets which may be transferred in a qualified transfer shall not exceed the amount which is reasonably estimated to be the amount the employer maintaining the plan will pay (whether directly or through reimbursement) out of such account during the taxable year of the transfer for qualified current retiree health liabilities.

(4) Special rule for 1990

(A) In general

Subject to the provisions of subsection (c), a transfer shall be treated as a qualified transfer if such transfer –

(i) is made after the close of the taxable year preceding the employer's first taxable year beginning after December 31, 1990, and before the earlier of –

(I) the due date (including extensions) for the filing of the return of tax for such preceding taxable year, or

(II) the date such return is filed, and

(ii) does not exceed the expenditures of the employer for qualified current retiree health liabilities for such preceding taxable year.

(B) Deduction reduced

The amount of the deductions otherwise allowable under this chapter to an employer for the taxable year preceding the employer's first taxable year beginning after December 31, 1990, shall be reduced by the amount of any qualified transfer to which this paragraph applies.

(C) Coordination with reduction rule

Subsection (e)(1)(B) shall not apply to a transfer described in subparagraph (A).

(5) Expiration

No transfer made after December 31, 2013, shall be treated as a qualified transfer.

(c) Requirements of plans transferring assets

(1) Use of transferred assets

(A) In general

Any assets transferred to a health benefits account in a qualified transfer (and any income allocable thereto) shall be used only to pay qualified current retiree health liabilities (other than liabilities of key employees not taken into account under subsection (e)(1)(D)) for the taxable year of the transfer (whether directly or through reimbursement).

(B) Amounts not used to pay for health benefits

    (i) In general

        Any assets transferred to a health benefits account in a qualified transfer (and any income allocable thereto) which are not used as provided in subparagraph (A) shall be transferred out of the account to the transferor plan.

    (ii) Tax treatment of amounts

        Any amount transferred out of an account under clause (i) —

        (I) shall not be includible in the gross income of the employer for such taxable year, but

        (II) shall be treated as an employer reversion for purposes of section 4980 (without regard to subsection (d) thereof).

(C) Ordering rule

For purposes of this section, any amount paid out of a health benefits account shall be treated as paid first out of the assets and income described in subparagraph (A).

(2) Requirements relating to pension benefits accruing before transfer

(A) In general

The requirements of this paragraph are met if the plan provides that the accrued pension benefits of any participant or beneficiary under the plan become nonforfeitable in the same manner which would be required if the plan had terminated immediately before the qualified transfer (or in the case of a participant who separated during the 1-year period ending on the date of the transfer, immediately before such separation).

(B) Special rule for 1990

In the case of a qualified transfer described in subsection (b)(4), the requirements of this paragraph are met with respect to any participant who separated from service during the taxable year to which such transfer relates by recomputing such participant's benefits as if subparagraph (A) had applied immediately before such separation.

(3) Minimum cost requirements

(A) In general

The requirements of this paragraph are met if each group health plan or arrangement under which applicable health benefits are provided provides that the applicable employer cost for each taxable year during the cost maintenance period shall not be less than the higher of the applicable employer costs for each of the 2 taxable years immediately preceding the taxable year of the qualified transfer.

(B) Applicable employer cost

For purposes of this paragraph, the term "applicable employer cost" means, with respect to any taxable year, the amount determined by dividing –

    (i) the qualified current retiree health liabilities of the employer for such taxable year determined –

        (I) without regard to any reduction under subsection (e)(1)(B), and

        (II) in the case of a taxable year in which there was no qualified transfer, in the same manner as if there had been such a transfer at the end of the taxable year, by

    (ii) the number of individuals to whom coverage for applicable health benefits was provided during such taxable year.

(C) Election to compute cost separately

An employer may elect to have this paragraph applied separately with respect to individuals eligible for benefits under title XVIII of the Social Security Act at any time during the taxable year and with respect to individuals not so eligible.

(D) Cost maintenance period

For purposes of this paragraph, the term "cost maintenance period" means the period of 5 taxable years beginning with the taxable year in which the qualified transfer occurs. If a taxable year is in two or more overlapping cost maintenance periods, this paragraph shall be applied by taking into account the highest applicable employer cost required to be provided under subparagraph (A) for such taxable year.

(E) Regulations

    (i) In general –

The Secretary shall prescribe such regulations as may be necessary to prevent an employer who significantly reduces retiree health coverage during the cost maintenance period from being treated as satisfying the minimum cost requirement of this subsection.

    (ii) Insignificant cost reductions permitted –

        (I) In general –

An eligible employer shall not be treated as failing to

meet the requirements of this paragraph for any taxable year if, in lieu of any reduction of retiree health coverage permitted under the regulations prescribed under clause (i), the employer reduces applicable employer cost by an amount not in excess of the reduction in costs which would have occurred if the employer had made the maximum permissible reduction in retiree health coverage under such regulations. In applying such regulations to any subsequent taxable year, any reduction in applicable employer cost under this clause shall be treated as if it were an equivalent reduction in retiree health coverage.

(II) Eligible employer –

For purposes of subclause (I), an employer shall be treated as an eligible employer for any taxable year if, for the preceding taxable year, the qualified current retiree health liabilities of the employer were at least 5 percent of the gross receipts of the employer. For purposes of this subclause, the rules of paragraphs (2), (3)(B), and (3)(C) of section 448(c) shall apply in determining the amount of an employer's gross receipts.

(d) *Limitations on employer*

For purposes of this title –

(1) Deduction limitations

No deduction shall be allowed –

(A) for the transfer of any amount to a health benefits account in a qualified transfer (or any retransfer to the plan under subsection (c)(1)(B)),

(B) for qualified current retiree health liabilities paid out of the assets (and income) described in subsection (c)(1), or

(C) for any amounts to which subparagraph (B) does not apply and which are paid for qualified current retiree health liabilities for the taxable year to the extent such amounts are not greater than the excess (if any) of –

(i) the amount determined under subparagraph (A) (and income allocable thereto), over

(ii) the amount determined under subparagraph (B).

(2) No contributions allowed

An employer may not contribute after December 31, 1990, any amount to a health benefits account or welfare benefit fund (as defined in section 419(e)(1)) with respect to qualified current retiree health liabilities for which transferred assets are required to be used under subsection (c)(1).

(e) *Definition and special rules*
For purposes of this section –
(1) Qualified current retiree health liabilities
For purposes of this section –
(A) In general
The term "qualified current retiree health liabilities" means, with respect to any taxable year, the aggregate amounts (including administrative expenses) which would have been allowable as a deduction to the employer for such taxable year with respect to applicable health benefits provided during such taxable year if –
(i) such benefits were provided directly by the employer, and
(ii) the employer used the cash receipts and disbursements method of accounting.

For purposes of the preceding sentence, the rule of section 419(c)(3)(B) shall apply.
(B) Reductions for amounts previously set aside
The amount determined under subparagraph (A) shall be reduced by the amount which bears the same ratio to such amount as –
(i) the value (as of the close of the plan year preceding the year of the qualified transfer) of the assets in all health benefits accounts or welfare benefit funds (as defined in section 419(e)(1)) set aside to pay for the qualified current retiree health liability, bears to
(ii) the present value of the qualified current retiree health liabilities for all plan years (determined without regard to this subparagraph).
(C) Applicable health benefits
The term "applicable health benefits" means health benefits or coverage which are provided to –
(i) retired employees who, immediately before the qualified transfer, are entitled to receive such benefits upon retirement and who are entitled to pension benefits under the plan, and
(ii) their spouses and dependents.

(D) Key employees excluded

If an employee is a key employee (within the meaning of section 416(i)(1)) with respect to any plan year ending in a taxable year, such employee shall not be taken into account in computing qualified current retiree health liabilities for such taxable year or in calculating applicable employer cost under subsection (c)(3)(B).

(2) Excess pension assets

The term "excess pension assets" means the excess (if any) of –

(A) the amount determined under section 412(c)(7)(A)(ii), over

(B) the greater of –

   (i) the amount determined under section 412(c)(7)(A)(i), or

   (ii) 125 percent of current liability (as defined in section 412(c)(7)(B)).

The determination under this paragraph shall be made as of the most recent valuation date of the plan preceding the qualified transfer.

(3) Health benefits account

The term "health benefits account" means an account established and maintained under section 401(h).

(4) Coordination with section 412

In the case of a qualified transfer to a health benefits account –

(A) any assets transferred in a plan year on or before the valuation date for such year (and any income allocable thereto) shall, for purposes of section 412, be treated as assets in the plan as of the valuation date for such year, and

(B) the plan shall be treated as having a net experience loss under section 412(b)(2)(B)(iv) in an amount equal to the amount of such transfer (reduced by any amounts transferred back to the pension plan under subsection (c)(1)(B)) and for which amortization charges begin for the first plan year after the plan year in which such transfer occurs, except that such section shall be applied to such amount by substituting "10 plan years" for "5 plan years."

(f) *Qualified transfers to cover future retiree health costs and collectively bargained retiree health benefits.* –

(1) In general.—An employer maintaining a defined benefit plan (other than a multiemployer plan) may, in lieu of a qualified transfer, elect for any taxable year to have the plan make –

(A) a qualified future transfer, or

(B) a collectively bargained transfer.

Except as provided in this subsection, a qualified future transfer and a collectively bargained transfer shall be treated for purposes of this title and the Employee Retirement Income Security Act of 1974 as if it were a qualified transfer.

(2) Qualified future and collectively bargained transfers. – For purposes of this subsection –

(A) In general. – The terms 'qualified future transfer' and 'collectively bargained transfer' mean a transfer which meets all of the requirements for a qualified transfer, except that –

(i) the determination of excess pension assets shall be made under subparagraph (B),

(ii) the limitation on the amount transferred shall be determined under subparagraph (C),

(iii) the minimum cost requirements of subsection (c)(3) shall be modified as provided under subparagraph (D), and

(iv) in the case of a collectively bargained transfer, the requirements of subparagraph (E) shall be met with respect to the transfer.

(B) Excess pension assets. –

(i) In general. – In determining excess pension assets for purposes of this subsection, subsection (e)(2) shall be applied by substituting '120 percent' for '125 percent'.

(ii) Requirement to maintain funded status. – If, as of any valuation date of any plan year in the transfer period, the amount determined under subsection (e)(2)(B) (after application of clause (i)) exceeds the amount determined under subsection (e)(2)(A), either –

(I) the employer maintaining the plan shall make contributions to the plan in an amount not less than the amount required to reduce such excess to zero as of such date, or

(II) there is transferred from the health benefits account to the plan an amount not less than the amount required to reduce such excess to zero as of such date.

(C) Limitation on amount transferred. – Notwithstanding subsection (b)(3), the amount of the excess pension assets which may be transferred –

  (i) In the case of a qualified future transfer shall be equal to the sum of –

    (I) If the transfer period includes the taxable year of the transfer, the amount determined under subsection (b)(3) for such taxable year, plus

    (II) In the case of all other taxable years in the transfer period, the sum of the qualified current retiree health liabilities which the plan reasonably estimates, in accordance with guidance issued by the Secretary, will be incurred for each of such years, and

  (ii) In the case of a collectively bargained transfer, shall not exceed the amount which is reasonably estimated, in accordance with the provisions of the collective bargaining agreement and generally accepted accounting principles, to be the amount the employer maintaining the plan will pay (whether directly or through reimbursement) out of such account during the collectively bargained cost maintenance period for collectively bargained retiree health liabilities.

(D) Minimum cost requirements. –

  (i) In general. – The requirements of subsection (c)(3) shall be treated as met if –

    (I) In the case of a qualified future transfer, each group health plan or arrangement under which applicable health benefits are provided provides applicable health benefits during the period beginning with the first year of the transfer period and ending with the last day of the 4th year following the transfer period such that the annual average amount of such the applicable employer cost during such period is not less than the applicable employer cost determined under subsection (c)(3)(A) with respect to the transfer, and

    (II) In the case of a collectively bargained transfer, each collectively bargained group health plan under which collectively bargained health benefits are provided provides that the collectively bargained employer cost for each taxable year during the collectively bargained cost maintenance period shall not be less than the amount specified by the collective bargaining agreement.

(ii) Election to maintain benefits for future transfers. – An employer may elect, in lieu of the requirements of clause (i)(I), to meet the requirements of subsection (c)(3) by meeting the requirements of such subsection (as in effect before the amendments made by section 535 of the Tax Relief Extension Act of 1999) for each of the years described in the period under clause (i)(I).

(iii) Collectively bargained employer cost. – For purposes of this subparagraph, the term 'collectively bargained employer cost' means the average cost per covered individual of providing collectively bargained retiree health benefits as determined in accordance with the applicable collective bargaining agreement. Such agreement may provide for an appropriate reduction in the collectively bargained employer cost to take into account any portion of the collectively bargained retiree health benefits that is provided or financed by a government program or other source.

(E) Special rules for collectively bargained transfers. –

  (i) In general. – A collectively bargained transfer shall only include a transfer which –

    (I) is made in accordance with a collective bargaining agreement,

    (II) before the transfer, the employer designates, in a written notice delivered to each employee organization that is a party to the collective bargaining agreement, as a collectively bargained transfer in accordance with this section, and

    (III) involves a plan maintained by an employer which, in its taxable year ending in 2005, provided health benefits or coverage to retirees and their spouses and dependents under all of the benefit plans maintained by the employer, but only if the aggregate cost (including administrative expenses) of such benefits or coverage which would have been allowable as a deduction to the employer (if such benefits or coverage had been provided directly by the employer and the employer used the cash receipts and disbursements method of accounting) is at least 5 percent of the gross receipts of the employer (determined in accordance with the last sentence of subsection (c)(2)(E)(ii)(II)) for such taxable year, or a plan maintained by a successor to such employer.

        (ii) Use of assets. – Any assets transferred to a health benefits account in a collectively bargained transfer (and any income allocable thereto) shall be used only to pay collectively bargained retiree health liabilities (other than liabilities of key employees not taken into account under paragraph (6)(B)(iii)) for the taxable year of the transfer or for any subsequent taxable year during the collectively bargained cost maintenance period (whether directly or through reimbursement).

(3) Coordination with other transfers. – In applying subsection (b)(3) to any subsequent transfer during a taxable year in a transfer period or collectively bargained cost maintenance period, qualified current retiree health liabilities shall be reduced by any such liabilities taken into account with respect to the qualified future transfer or collectively bargained transfer to which such period relates.

(4) Special deduction rules for collectively bargained transfers. – In the case of a collectively bargained transfer –

    (A) the limitation under subsection (d)(1)(C) shall not apply, and

    (B) notwithstanding subsection (d)(2), an employer may contribute an amount to a health benefits account or welfare benefit fund (as defined in section 419(e)(1)) with respect to collectively bargained retiree health liabilities for which transferred assets are required to be used under subsection (c)(1)(B), and the deductibility of any such contribution shall be governed by the limits applicable to the deductibility of contributions to a welfare benefit fund under a collective bargaining agreement (as determined under section 419A(f)(5)(A)) without regard to whether such contributions are made to a health benefits account or welfare benefit fund and without regard to the provisions of section 404 or the other provisions of this section. The Secretary shall provide rules to ensure that the application of this paragraph does not result in a deduction being allowed more than once for the same contribution or for 2 or more contributions or expenditures relating to the same collectively bargained retiree health liabilities.

(5) Transfer period. – For purposes of this subsection, the term 'transfer period' means, with respect to any transfer, a period of consecutive taxable years (not less than 2) specified in the election under paragraph (1) which begins and ends during the 10-taxable-year period beginning with the taxable year of the transfer.

(6) Terms relating to collectively bargained transfers.—For purposes of this subsection –

(A) Collectively bargained cost maintenance period.—The term 'collectively bargained cost maintenance period' means, with respect to each covered retiree and his covered spouse and dependents, the shorter of –

    (i) the remaining lifetime of such covered retiree and his covered spouse and dependents, or

    (ii) the period of coverage provided10 by the collectively bargained health plan (determined as of the date of the collectively bargained transfer) with respect to such covered retiree and his covered spouse and dependents.

(B) Collectively bargained retiree health liabilities. –

    (i) In general. – The term 'collectively bargained retiree health liabilities' means the present value, as of the beginning of a taxable year and determined in accordance with the applicable collective bargaining agreement, of all collectively bargained health benefits (including administrative expenses) for such taxable year and all subsequent taxable years during the collectively bargained cost maintenance period.

    (ii) Reduction for amounts previously set aside. – The amount determined under clause (i) shall be reduced by the value (as of the close of the plan year preceding the year of the collectively bargained transfer) of the assets in all health benefits accounts or welfare benefit funds (as defined in section 419(e)(1)) set aside to pay for the collectively bargained retiree health liabilities.

    (iii) Key employees excluded. – If an employee is a key employee (within the meaning of section 416(I)(1)) with respect to any plan year ending in a taxable year, such employee shall not be taken into account in computing collectively bargained retiree health liabilities for such taxable year or in calculating collectively bargained employer cost under subsection (c)(3)(C).

(C) Collectively bargained health benefits. – The term 'collectively bargained health benefits' means health benefits or coverage which are provided to –

    (i) Retired employees who, immediately before the collectively bargained transfer, are entitled to receive such benefits upon retirement and who are entitled to pension benefits under the plan, and their spouses and dependents, and

(ii) If specified by the provisions of the collective bargaining agreement governing the collectively bargained transfer, active employees who, following their retirement, are entitled to receive such benefits and who are entitled to pension benefits under the plan, and their spouses and dependents.

(D) Collectively bargained health plan. – The term 'collectively bargained health plan' means a group health plan or arrangement for retired employees and their spouses and dependents that is maintained pursuant to 1 or more collective bargaining agreements.

§1.420-1 Significant reduction in retiree health coverage during the cost maintenance period.

(a) *In general*. Notwithstanding section 420(c)(3)(A), the minimum cost requirements of section 420(c)(3) are not met if the employer significantly reduces retiree health coverage during the cost maintenance period.

(b) *Significant reduction* — (1) In general. An employer significantly reduces retiree health coverage during the cost maintenance period if, for any taxable year beginning on or after January 1, 2002, that is included in the cost maintenance period, either —

(i) The employer-initiated reduction percentage for that taxable year exceeds 10 percent; or

(ii) The sum of the employer-initiated reduction percentages for that taxable year and all prior taxable years during the cost maintenance period exceeds 20 percent.

(2) Employer-initiated reduction percentage. The employer-initiated reduction percentage for any taxable year is the fraction B/A, expressed as a percentage, where:

A = The total number of individuals (retired employees plus their spouses plus their dependents) receiving coverage for applicable health benefits as of the day before the first day of the taxable year.

$B =$ The total number of individuals included in A whose coverage for applicable health benefits ended during the taxable year by reason of employer action.

(3) *Special rules for taxable years beginning before January 1, 2002.* The following rules apply for purposes of computing the amount in paragraph (b)(1)(ii) of this section if any portion of the cost maintenance period precedes the first day of the first taxable year beginning on or after January 1, 2002 –

    (i) *Aggregation of taxable years.* The portion of the cost maintenance period that precedes the first day of the first taxable year beginning on or after January 1, 2002 (the initial period) is treated as a single taxable year and the employer-initiated reduction percentage for the initial period is computed as set forth in paragraph (b)(2) of this section, except that the words "initial period" apply instead of "taxable year."

    (ii) *Loss of coverage.* If coverage for applicable health benefits for an individual ends by reason of employer action at any time during the initial period, an employer may treat that coverage as not having ended if the employer restores coverage for applicable health benefits to that individual by the end of the initial period.

(4) *Employer action* –

    (i) *General rule.* For purposes of paragraph (b)(2) of this section, an individual's coverage for applicable health benefits ends during a taxable year by reason of employer action, if on any day within the taxable year, the individual's eligibility for applicable health benefits ends as a result of a plan amendment or any other action of the employer (e.g., the sale of all or part of the employer's business) that, in conjunction with the plan terms, has the effect of ending the individual's eligibility. An employer action is taken into account for this purpose regardless of when the employer action actually occurs (e.g., the date the plan amendment is executed), except that employer actions occurring before the later of December 18, 1999, and the date that is 5 years before the start of the cost maintenance period are disregarded.

    (ii) *Special rule.* Notwithstanding paragraph (b)(4)(i) of this section, coverage for an individual will not be treated as having ended by reason of employer action merely because such coverage ends under the terms of the plan if those terms were adopted contemporaneously with the provision under which the individual became eligible for retiree health coverage. This paragraph (b)(4)(ii) does not apply with respect to plan terms adopted contemporaneously with a plan amendment that restores coverage for applicable health benefits before the end of the initial period in accordance with paragraph (b)(3)(ii) of this section.

(iii) *Sale transactions*. If a purchaser provides coverage for retiree health benefits to one or more individuals whose coverage ends by reason of a sale of all or part of the employer's business, the employer may treat the coverage of those individuals as not having ended by reason of employer action. In such a case, for the remainder of the year of the sale and future taxable years of the cost maintenance period –

(A) For purposes of computing the applicable employer cost under section 420(c)(3), those individuals are treated as individuals to whom coverage for applicable health benefits was provided (for as long as the purchaser provides retiree health coverage to them), and any amounts expended by the purchaser of the business to provide for health benefits for those individuals are treated as paid by the employer;

(B) For purposes of determining whether a subsequent termination of coverage is by reason of employer action under this paragraph (b)(4), the purchaser is treated as the employer. However, the special rule in paragraph (b)(4)(ii) of this section applies only to the extent that any terms of the plan maintained by the purchaser that have the effect of ending retiree health coverage for an individual are the same as terms of the plan maintained by the employer that were adopted contemporaneously with the provision under which the individual became eligible for retiree health coverage under the plan maintained by the employer.

(c) *Definitions*. The following definitions apply for purposes of this section:

(1) *Applicable health benefits*. Applicable health benefits means applicable health benefits as defined in section 420(e)(1)(C).

(2) *Cost maintenance period*. Cost maintenance period means the cost maintenance period as defined in section 420(c)(3)(D).

(3) *Sale.* A sale of all or part of an employer's business means a sale or other transfer in connection with which the employees of a trade or business of the employer become employees of another person. In the case of such a transfer, the term purchaser means a transferee of the trade or business.

(d) *Examples.* The following examples illustrate the application of this section:

Example 1.

(i) Employer W maintains a defined benefit pension plan that includes a 401(h) account and permits qualified transfers that satisfy section 420. The number of individuals receiving coverage for applicable health benefits as of the day before the first day of Year 1 is 100. In Year 1, Employer W makes a qualified transfer under section 420. There is no change in the number of individuals receiving health benefits during Year 1. As of the last day of Year 2, applicable health benefits are provided to 99 individuals, because 2 individuals became eligible for coverage due to retirement and 3 individuals died in Year 2. During Year 3, Employer W amends its health plan to eliminate coverage for 5 individuals, 1 new retiree becomes eligible for coverage and an additional 3 individuals are no longer covered due to their own decision to drop coverage. Thus, as of the last day of Year 3, applicable health benefits are provided to 92 individuals. During Year 4, Employer W amends its health plan to eliminate coverage under its health plan for 8 more individuals, so that as of the last day of Year 4, applicable health benefits are provided to 84 individuals. During Year 5, Employer W amends its health plan to eliminate coverage for 8 more individuals.

(ii) There is no significant reduction in retiree health coverage in either Year 1 or Year 2, because there is no reduction in health coverage as a result of employer action in those years.

(iii) There is no significant reduction in Year 3. The number of individuals whose health coverage ended during Year 3 by reason of employer action (amendment of the plan) is 5. Since the number of individuals receiving coverage for applicable health benefits as of the last day of Year 2 is 99, the employer-initiated reduction percentage for Year 3 is 5.05 percent (5/99), which is less than the 10 percent annual limit.

(iv) There is no significant reduction in Year 4. The number of individuals whose health coverage ended during Year 4 by reason of employer action is 8. Since the number of individuals receiving coverage for applicable health benefits as of the last day of Year 3 is 92, the employer-initiated reduction percentage for Year 4 is 8.70 percent (8/92), which is less than the 10 percent annual limit. The sum of the employer-initiated reduction percentages for Year 3 and Year 4 is 13.75 percent, which is less than the 20 percent cumulative limit.

(v) In Year 5, there is a significant reduction under paragraph (b)(1)(ii) of this section. The number of individuals whose health coverage ended during Year 5 by reason of employer action (amendment of the plan) is 8. Since the number of individuals receiving coverage for applicable health benefits as of the last day of Year 4 is 84, the employer-initiated reduction percentage for Year 5 is 9.52 percent (8/84), which is less than the 10 percent annual limit. However, the sum of the employer-initiated reduction percentages for Year 3, Year 4, and Year 5 is 5.05 percent + 8.70 percent + 9.52 percent = 23.27 percent, which exceeds the 20 percent cumulative limit.

Example 2.

(i) Employer X, a calendar year taxpayer, maintains a defined benefit pension plan that includes a 401(h) account and permits qualified transfers that satisfy section 420. X also provides lifetime health benefits to employees who retire from Division A as a result of a plant shutdown, no health benefits to employees who retire from Division B, and lifetime health benefits to all employees who retire from Division C. In 2000, X amends its health plan to provide coverage for employees who retire from Division B as a result of a plant shutdown, but only for the 2-year period coinciding with their severance pay. Also in 2000, X amends the health plan to provide that employees who retire from Division A as a result of a plant shutdown receive health coverage only for the 2-year period coinciding with their severance pay. A plant shutdown that affects Division A and Division B employees occurs in 2000. The number of individuals receiving coverage for applicable health benefits as of the last day of 2001 is 200. In 2002, Employer X makes a qualified transfer under section 420. As of the last day of 2002, applicable health benefits are provided to 170 individuals, because the 2-year period of benefits ends for 10 employees who retired from Division

A and 20 employees who retired from Division B as a result of the plant shutdown that occurred in 2000.

(ii) There is no significant reduction in retiree health coverage in 2002. Coverage for the 10 retirees from Division A who lose coverage as a result of the end of the 2-year period is treated as having ended by reason of employer action, because coverage for those Division A retirees ended by reason of a plan amendment made after December 17, 1999. However, the terms of the health plan that limit coverage for employees who retired from Division B as a result of the 2000 plant shutdown (to the 2-year period) were adopted contemporaneously with the provision under which those employees became eligible for retiree coverage under the health plan. Accordingly, under the rule provided in paragraph (b)(4)(ii) of this section, coverage for those 20 retirees from Division B is not treated as having ended by reason of employer action. Thus, the number of individuals whose health benefits ended by reason of employer action in 2002 is 10. Since the number of individuals receiving coverage for applicable health benefits as of the last day of 2001 is 200, the employer-initiated reduction percentage for 2002 is 5 percent (10/200), which is less than the 10 percent annual limit.

(e) *Regulatory effective date.* This section is applicable to transfers of excess pension assets occurring on or after December 18, 1999.

[66 Fed. Reg. 32897-32901 (June 20, 2001)]

APPENDIX D
CASES REGARDING
RETIREE HEALTH CARE

Due to the nature of collectively bargained versus nonunion court decisions, the following summary of key court cases separate these two groups of cases.

COLLECTIVELY BARGAINED CASES

The following summarize the key court cases involving collectively bargained plans and retiree group benefit plans.

UAW v. Yard Man, Inc.
716 F.2d. 1476 (6th Cir. 1983)

Employer closed a plant in 1975 and active employees lost benefits immediately. Two years later, retiree benefits were terminated when CBA expired. The court held that the parties intended to provide lifetime retiree welfare benefits because the CBA had ambiguous provisions regarding the nature and duration of retiree life and health benefits, the CBA placed specific durational limits on other benefits (e.g., the savings and pension plans), the fact that the employer continued benefits to retirees after the plan closing and terminated active employee coverages, and retiree benefits were deemed to be "status" benefits.

➢ Judgment for the retirees.

Bower v. Bunker Hill Co.
725 F.2d. 1221 (9th Cir. 1984)

The company terminated medical coverage for active and retired employees when operations closed down. The court held that the CBA did not explicitly state whether retiree medical benefits were vested or not because there was no explicit expiration date. The SPD included a disclaimer of lifetime coverage but the court found it to be inadequate because it was printed in substantially smaller type than the rest of the document. Other statements from management may have led employees to believe that they were entitled to lifetime benefits. During a recent strike, the company continued retiree health benefits which indicated that the benefits were tied to the CBA.

➢Judgment for the retirees.

UAW v. Cadillac Malleable Iron
728 F.2d. 807 (6th Cir. 1984)

The employer terminated retiree life and health benefits at the expiration of the CBA. The court stated that there is no legal presumption that retiree benefits vest on retirement unless it is explicitly stated by all parties. However, in this case, the bargaining history and statements made at exit interviews with retirees provided demonstration that the employer's intent was to provide lifetime benefits.

➢Judgment for the retirees.

Dubuque Packing Co. v. United Food & Commercial Workers Local 150-A
756 F.2d. 66 (8th Cir. 1985)

The company notified the union that it was going to close a plant and agreed with the union to extend the CBA for about one year. The company issued a statement that all retiree benefits would terminate at the end of that extension. The court found that the CBA language and the actions of the parties in the course of the dealings indicated an intent that the right to benefits vested on retirement. The court stated that the right to receive retiree benefits came from the retirees' status as a past employee and is not dependent on any continued relationship with the company.

➢Judgment for the retirees.

District 29, UMWA v. Royal Coal Co.
768 F.2d. 588 (4th Cir. 1985)

The company closed down a mining operation and terminated life and health benefits at the termination of the CBA. The court found that both parties intended to limit the retiree benefits to the term of the CBA.

➢Judgment for the employer.

Policy v. Powell Pressed Steel Co.
770 F.2d 609 (6th Cir. 1985)

Plaintiffs, retired employees of defendant company, brought a class action to compel defendant to resume providing health insurance benefits for a certain group of retirees. The CBA between the company and plaintiffs' union had an expiration time and defendant contended the health insurance benefits could not survive the agreement. The court held that although the collective bargaining agreement had an expiration period, it unambiguously provided for survival of health insurance benefits for certain retirees. The court held that failure to provide a mechanism for funding pensioners' health insurance benefits did not necessarily imply that retiree benefits were not intended to survive the collective bargaining agreement.

➢ Judgment in favor of the retirees.

In re White Farm Equipment Co.
788 F.2d. 1186 (6th Cir. 1986)
After sale to another company, the buyer discontinued retiree health coverage. The bankruptcy court initially ruled in favor of the employer relying on the view that SPDs indicated that the employer had an unqualified right to terminate or amend the plans. The district court disagreed and attempted to fashion a federal common law principle stating that retiree benefits are in exchange for required service while employed and therefore vest on retirement. The 6th Circuit rejected the notion of vesting and reversed the district court's opinion.

➢Judgment for the employer.

District 29, UMWA v. UMWA 1974 Benefit Plan and Trust
826 F.2d. 280 (4th Cir. 1987)
In a prior related case, the court found that the union and the employer intended to limit the retiree benefits to the term of the CBA. In this later case, the court found that the union and the trust fund did intend that the benefits were for life and that the benefit trust was intended to be a safety net in the event the former employer was neither able to nor required to provide benefits.

➢Judgment for the retirees.

United Steelworkers v. Textron, Inc.
836 F.2d. 6 (1st Cir. 1987)
The company sold a division to another company who agreed to assume liability for the retiree life and health benefits. The union asked Textron to guarantee the benefits and after discussions, the company finally agreed to pay the premiums. After a short time, the company stopped paying the premiums due to its financial situation and the union sought injunction to

prohibit Textron from ceasing payments. The court found that the CBA indicated an intent to provide retirees benefits after the expiration of the contract. In addition, retirement exit interviews did not suggest that benefits may terminate and there was documentation showing that Textron management wanted the buyer to pay the retiree benefit for life and that there were estimates of the cost for providing the benefits.

➢ Judgment in favor of the retirees.

Anderson v. Alpha Portland Industries, Inc.
836 F.2d 1512 (8th Cir. 1988)

Plaintiffs, a group of former employees of defendants, brought an action under ERISA and the NLRA after defendants decided to terminate all retiree health and life insurance benefits when the existing CBA expired. Plaintiffs claimed that the welfare benefits were vested lifetime benefits that could not be terminated. The court ruled that welfare plans did not vest as a matter of law, and plaintiffs had the burden of proving the parties intended that the duration of benefits was not tied to the agreement that created them. Plaintiffs relied upon a faulty summary plan description given them by defendants; however, the court held that plaintiffs did not show significant reliance on the summary sufficient to secure relief.

➢ Judgment in favor of the employer.

United Paperworkers International Union v. Champion International Corp.
908 F.2d 1252 (5th Cir. 1990)

Plaintiffs filed a class action alleging breach of a CBA and ERISA for increasing retirees' medical insurance premiums. The CBA provided medical insurance under an early retirement plan through age 65. The monthly premium, taken by pension reduction, was $15.50, which was derived from the Medicare Part B premium at the time the plan was implemented. The premium amount was subsequently increased to correspond with increases in the Medicare Part B premium. Retirees argue that "equal to" the Medicare Part B premium means equal to the premium at the time of the contract's drafting. The employer argues that "equal to" the Medicare Part B premium implies that the premium at any given time must match the Part B premium. The court found the contract language to be ambiguous, requiring an examination of extrinsic evidence to determine the objective intent of the parties.

➢ Case remanded to district court.

Senn V. United Dominion Industries, Inc.
951 F.2d 806 (7th Cir. 1992)
Defendant acquired the assets of the plaintiffs' former employer. Under the purchase agreement the defendant agreed to provide retiree health and life benefits. A new CBA was then struck by the defendant and the union. The agreement provided that the defendant was no longer responsible for providing retirees any medical or life insurance coverage. Plaintiff sued the defendant for declaratory and injunctive relief as well as damages under the LMRA and sought clarification of their benefits under ERISA. The court reversed the granting of a permanent injunction, ordering the defendant to provide benefits to the plaintiffs because ERISA does not provide for the vesting of benefits, which is covered by the most recent CBA.

➢ Judgment for the employer.

Bidlack v. Wheelabrator Corp.,
993 F.2d 603 (7th Cir. 1993)
Plaintiffs, retired employees, filed a class action claiming that collective bargaining agreements between defendant company and the union representing them conferred lifetime rights to certain health benefits. The court held that the parol evidence rule, which enforces integration clauses by barring evidence of side agreements, did not bar the use of extrinsic evidence to clarify the meaning of an ambiguous text. Because the contract was ambiguous, both sides should be allowed to introduce extrinsic evidence for clarification.

➢ Judgment for the retirees.

John Morrell & Co. v. United Food & Commercial Workers International Union
37 F.3d 1302 (8th Cir. 1994)
Employer sought a declaratory judgment that it could unilaterally modify or terminate retiree health benefits. Court held that health benefits were non-vested benefits, which the employer could modify or terminate.

➢ Judgment for employer.

United Rubber v. Pirelli Armstrong Tire Corporation
873 F.Supp. 1093 (M.D. Tenn. 1994)
The Court found all of the requirements for equitable estoppel and denied the employer the right to terminate retiree medical. Particularly, the Court found that the employer consistently told the retirees that their benefits were

for life and that it used the benefits as an inducement to employment and as a substitute for present wages. Further, the retirees had no knowledge that the employer could terminate their benefits until they received a letter after the fact, and the retirees relied upon the representations by working for the employer, by foregoing present wages for future benefits, and by retiring and not making any other arrangements for health benefits.

➤ Judgment in favor of the retirees.

American Federation of Grain Millers v. International Multifoods Corp. 116 F.3d 976 (2nd Cir. 1997)

Retirees brought suit alleging that the employer promised vested medical benefits to its retirees in CBAs and in ERISA plan documents. The court held that: (1) the CBA did not obligate the employer to provide medical benefits after the agreement expired; (2) ERISA plan did not promise vested retiree benefits; and (3) SPD sufficiently alerted participants that the employer has a right to amend the plan.

➤ Judgment for employer.

Pabst Brewing Co. v. Corrao 161 F.3d 434 (7th Cir. 1998)

Employer amended its welfare plan and life insurance plan to terminate eligibility of retirees and their dependents for coverage under the welfare plan and to terminate death benefits for certain union retirees. Employer then initiated litigation in a "class action complaint" for declaratory judgment that the elimination of benefits did not violate ERISA or other law, but no class was ever certified. Retirees counterclaimed that the CBAs gave retirees lifetime rights to health and life insurance benefits because benefits clauses in the CBA did not specify that benefits would last only for the term of the agreement. The court found that the CBA defendant was under at the time of retirement included a statement that promised health and life benefits for the term of the agreement and referred to the benefit provisions of the appendix.

➤ Judgment for employer.

International Union, United Auto., Aero. & Agric. Implement Workers of America v. BVR Liquidating, Inc. 190 F.3d 768 (6th Cir. 1999)

Plaintiff unions and employees sued defendant companies to enforce provisions of their CBAs following defendants' closure of a Michigan production plant. Plaintiffs contended retirees' rights to health care benefits provided for in the insurance agreements had vested and defendants had violated the agreements by terminating these benefits. Defendants argued the benefits were limited in duration to the term of the CBA. The court affirmed summary judgment for plaintiffs, holding the CBA contained ambiguous provisions making consideration of extrinsic evidence proper, and the extrinsic evidence proffered by plaintiffs supported plaintiffs' interpretation of the CBA and demonstrated there was no genuine issue of material fact as to the parties' intent and that lifetime retiree health care benefits had vested under the CBA.

➤ Judgment for the retirees.

International Union, United Auto., Aero. & Agric. Implement Workers of America v. Skinner Engine Co.
188 F.3d 130 (3rd Cir. 1999)

The court found that the primary question on appeal was whether life and medical insurance benefits provided to retired employees under various CBAs vested at the time of each employee's retirement or were terminable by the employer at the expiration of the collective bargaining agreement under which the right to the benefits was provided. Appellants were representatives of a class of former, retired, hourly employees of appellee. The court found that the language of the CBAs did not unambiguously vest lifetime medical and life insurance benefits for retirees and that certain testimony was extrinsic evidence and did not create an ambiguity precluding summary judgment. The court found that the breach of fiduciary duty claim was properly dismissed because appellants failed to persuade that appellee was obligated under ERISA to inform its employees that retiree benefits may at some point in the future be modified or changed. The court affirmed dismissal of the equitable estoppel claim because there was no evidence that showed that any of appellants considered the promise of lifetime health and life insurance benefits in timing their retirements.

➤ Judgment for the employer.

Joyce v. Curtiss-Wright Corp.
171 F.3d 130 (2nd Cir. 1999)

Plaintiff retirees sued defendant employer under ERISA and the LMRA protesting the termination of their health insurance. Under the framework established in Multifoods, the language contained in the collective bargaining agreement and the insurance plan (1) was unambiguous, and

(2) did not operate to vest the retirees' benefits. Under Multifoods, plaintiffs did not have to point to unambiguous language to support a claim. Rather, it was enough to point to written language capable of reasonably being interpreted as creating a promise on the part of defendant to vest plaintiff's benefits. Here, however, plaintiffs failed to identify language that affirmatively operated to imply vesting.

➢ Judgment for the employer.

Maurer v. Joy Techs., Inc
212 F.3d 907 (6th Cir. 2000)
After employer changed appellees' retirement health benefit plans, appellees filed suit alleging violations of the LMRA, ERISA, and claimed promissory estoppel. Plaintiffs asserted that their benefits, acquired pursuant to a CBA, could not unilaterally be altered. The court held first that the retirement benefits for those retiring before August 19, 1991, vested as lifetime benefits and survived the termination of the CBA. However, those plaintiffs retiring after August 19, 1991, did not hold vested retirement benefits. The reservation of rights clearly included retirees, was distributed to them, and was not disputed until the instant suit was filed.

➢Judgment in part for employer and in part for retirees.

UAW v. Rockford Powertrain, Inc.
350 F.3d. 698 (7th Cir. 2003)
The company reduced its subsidy to the retiree medical plan and terminated the retiree life insurance plan. The union filed suit against the company for changing the plans in the middle of contract agreement period. The court found that the CBA and the SPDs clearly reserved the right of the employer to make such changes.

➢Judgment in favor of the employer.

Hourly Retirees of Debtor v. Erie Forge & Steel Inc.
418 F.3d. 270 (3rd Cir. 2005)
The company sent a notice to retirees during a bankruptcy proceeding that it will terminate its retiree medical benefits. The union agreed to allow the company to modify its plan. A group of retirees opposed the settlement however the court ruled that the union did not act under a conflict of interest and that the union can continue to represent the retirees.

➢Judgment in favor of the employer and union.

Cherry v. Auburn Gear, Inc.
441 F.3d. 476 (7th Cir. 2006)
The employer terminated retiree benefits and retirees argued that their CBA provided for lifetime benefits. The court ruled that the CBA limited benefits to the term of the agreement and past history of changing benefits under various agreements further supported the parties understanding of the benefit limitation. In addition, the court found the CBA to be unambiguous.

➤Judgment in favor of the employer.

NONUNION CASES

The following summarize the key court cases involving nonunion plans and retiree group benefit plans.

Eardman v. Bethlehem Steel Corp.
607 F.Supp. 196 (WD NY 1984)
The company notified retirees that it was amending the retiree medical plan to introduce retiree contributions, deductibles, hospital precertification, a lifetime benefit limit. The retirees claimed that the company could not change their plan. The court found for the retirees because there was not adequate reservation of rights by the employer to amend or terminate the plan. The plan documents were ambiguous; exit interviews implied lifetime benefits and the latest SPD did not contain a reservation of rights to change the plan. The court also implied that retiree benefits are status benefits and continue as long as their retirement status continues.

➤Judgment for the retirees.

Hansen v. White Motor Corp.
788 F.2d. 1186 (6th Cir. 1986)
After White Farm filed for bankruptcy and was sold to White Farm USA, the company notified nonunion retirees that it would no longer subsidize the retiree benefits but would continue to offer its plans on a fully contributory basis. The court found that ERISA exempts welfare plans from its vesting rules and employers have the right to terminate welfare plans. However, the termination clause in the company's SPD was ambiguous and therefore ruled in favor of the retirees.

➤Judgment for the retirees.

Moore v. Metropolitan Life
856 F.2d. 488 (2nd Cir. 1988)

The company amended its retiree medical plan by increasing the plan's deductibles. Retirees argued that the company did not have the right to change the cost sharing provisions of the plan. The court reviewed plan documents that clearly gave the employer the right to amend or terminate the plan at any time. Any other written or oral communication was irrelevant because of the unambiguous plan document language. The court ruled that ERISA does not require automatic vesting of welfare benefits.

➤Judgment for the employer.

Musto v. American General Corp.
861 F.2d. 879 (6th Cir. 1988)

The company introduced retiree contributions for some retirees and increased contributions for others. A retiree class action suit claimed that they had the vested contractual right to veto any proposed changes to the retiree medical plan. The court reviewed all plan documentation including the group insurance policy and SPDs and found that the documents were not ambiguous and gave the employer a clear right to amend or terminate coverage at any time and to change premium contributions. In addition, the employer did not make any promises – orally or in writing – that the retiree medical benefits were vested.

➤Judgment in favor of employer.

Alday V. Container Corporation of America
906 F.2d 660 (11th Cir. 1990)

Employer modified the benefits, substantially raised the employee contributions of its retiree health insurance plan, and reduced the maximum lifetime benefits available under the plan. Appellant brought action on behalf of himself and all similarly situated employees against the employer, its parent company, and its pension consultant, alleging that the modification of the plan violated ERISA, and breached the appellees' fiduciary duties. Appellant also alleged that appellees were estopped from altering the terms of the plan because they had induced him into believing that the plan's terms would not change, and he relied upon that representation. The court concluded that there were no material facts in dispute.

➤ Judgment for the employer.

Jensen v. Sipco, Inc.
38 F.3d 945, 952 (8ᵗʰ Cir. 1994)

Retirees sued employer alleging entitlement to vested medical benefits. Court held that the employer intended to provide retirees with vested medical benefits.

➢ Judgment for retirees.

Gable v. Sweetheart Cup Co, Inc.
35 F.3d 851 (4ᵗʰ Cir. 1994)

Retirees brought an action alleging that a reduction in medical payments violated ERISA. Court held that the employer did not vest retiree's health benefits and did not waive the right to modify the plan.

➢ Judgment for employer.

Jensen v. Sipco, Inc.
38 F.3d 945 (8ᵗʰ Cir. 1994)

Successor employer was denied the right to charge premiums on retiree medical because the original SPD did not reserve the right to amend or modify the retiree medical plan. The burden is on the employee to show that the benefits were vested – any promise by the company must be incorporated, in some fashion, into the formal written ERISA plan. The Court ruled favorably for the employees based on the overwhelming extrinsic evidence that the original employer intended for the rights to vest upon retirement.

➢ Judgment in favor of the retirees.

Curtiss-Wright Corporation v. Schoonejongen
514 U.S. 73, 115 (S. Ct. 1995)

Retirees sued employer under ERISA for wrongful termination of post-retirement health care benefits. Supreme Court Held that: (1) clause in plan constitution stating that "the Company" reserved the right at any time to amend the plan adequately set forth procedure for identifying persons with amendment authority, and procedure for amending plan, as required by ERISA; and (2) on remand, question was whether plan's amendment procedure was followed, or, if not, whether any subsequent actions served to ratify amended provision ex post.

➢ Judgment in part for employer and remanded.

Helwig v. Kelsey-Hayes Company
93 F.3d 243 (6th Cir. 1996)

Retirees sued employer claiming that employer reduced their health care benefits in violation of ERISA. Court held that: (1) retirees demonstrated reasonable likelihood of success on the merits of the case; (2) the SPDs made clear promises of lifetime coverage and contained no valid provisions reserving the right to modify or terminate benefits; and (3) benefits vested upon retirement.

➤ Judgment for retirees.

Diehl v. Twin Disc, Inc.
102 F.3d 301 (7th Cir. 1996)

Retirees brought action against employer arising out of employer's modification of their insurance coverage. Court held that: (1) employees has vested right to life and medical insurance for lifetime of the employee; and (2) remand was required to determine whether employer's modifications of retiree's insurance benefits coverage brought benefits below the level of coverage they had under welfare insurance agreement prior to modification.

➤ Judgment in part for retirees and remanded.

Varity Corporation v. Howe
516 U.S. 489, 116 (S. Ct. 1996)

[NOTE: This case does not specifically address retiree medical benefits. It is included here for its decision regarding an employer's fiduciary responsibility with regard to employee benefits.]

Employer persuaded employees to transfer to a new entity established by the employer and represented that the employees' benefits would remain secure. Those employees later lost their non-pension benefits. Supreme Court held that employer breached its fiduciary duty under ERISA by misrepresenting to employees that their benefits would be secure if they transferred, since employer acted in its role as plan administrator and not employer in making such representation and, therefore, was a plan fiduciary. Employer did not act solely in interest of plan participants when it knowingly deceived plan participants for purpose of saving employer's money at participants' expense.

➤ Judgment for retirees.

Pisciotta v. Teledyne Industries, Inc.
91 F.3d 1326 (9th Cir. 1996)

Retirees brought suit alleging that modification in retiree health benefits violated ERISA. Court held, among other things, that: (1) insurance booklet issued to employees did not constitute an SPD under ERISA; (2) employer's reservation of right to modify or terminate employee welfare benefits was effective; and (3) retirees would not be allowed to amend complaint to include a cause of action for promissory estoppel.

➢ Judgment for employer.

Sengpiel v. B. F. Goodrich Co.
156 F.3d 660 (6th Cir. 1998)

The plaintiffs, salaried retirees of the B.F. Goodrich Company ("BFG") challenged the 1985 transfer of their retirement benefits to a newly formed company, the Uniroyal Goodrich Tire Company ("UGTC") and subsequent reductions in those benefits by UGTC and its successor in interest, Michelin North America, Inc. ("Michelin"). The court found that actions taken by BFG to implement its decision to spin off its tire division did not trigger ERISA's fiduciary duties and retirees were in the same or better position after the transfer. The court also held that retirees' welfare benefits were not vested at the time of their retirement because no language in the SPDs clearly expressed an intent to vest the benefits.

➢ Judgment for the employer.

Bierman v. Pirelli Armstrong Tire Corp.
162 F.3d 1163 (8th Cir. 1998)

Former employees of Pirelli Armstrong Tire Corporation's Des Moines, Iowa, tire plant claimed that Pirelli violated ERISA and state law when it terminated retiree health insurance benefits in 1994. At the time of the retiree benefits termination, plaintiffs were active Pirelli salaried employees and participants in Pirelli's Salaried Health Benefits Plan. Though the benefits termination had no immediate effect on plaintiffs, they contend that it wrongfully deprived them of vested rights to future retirement health benefits. Pirelli expressly "reserved the right to terminate or amend the Health Plan at any time and from time to time by action of the Committee." Plaintiffs argue that references in earlier Plan documents and oral assurances over the years that salaried employees would be eligible for retirement health benefits are sufficient evidence of vested rights. The court concluded that plaintiffs could not recover under ERISA because there was no promise to provide vested benefits incorporated into the Plan. The court rejected plaintiffs' state law estoppel claims as preempted by and inconsistent with ERISA.

➤ Judgment for the employer.

Salamouni v. Daiwa Bank
139 F.3d 902 (7th Cir. 1998)

Retiree claimed employer illegally denied him medical insurance benefits following his retirement. The employer had explicitly reserved the right to amend its plan.

➤ Judgment for employer.

Sprague v. General Motors Corp.
133 F.3d 388 (6th Cir. 1998)

Retirees brought suit to require employer to furnish them with basic health care coverage at no cost for life. The SPD reserved the right to amend its plans. Accordingly, the employer was not estopped from amending the plan.

➤ Judgment for employer.

Algren v. Pirelli Armstrong Tire Corp.
197 F.3d 915 (8th Cir. 1999)

Plaintiffs, former employees, brought action against defendant employer claiming pension and benefits plan committee violated ERISA when they terminated retiree health care benefits in 1994. The plan unambiguously conditioned retiree health benefits upon qualified retirement, and plaintiffs had no evidence of documents indicating otherwise. Plaintiffs had no vested right to retiree health benefits in advance of retirement, and none of the plaintiffs retired before defendant terminated the benefits. Plaintiffs' employment was terminated at a time when they were still active employees. State-law promissory estoppel claims were preempted by ERISA. Any federal-law claim of estoppel, whether under federal common law or ERISA itself, failed because the representations relied upon were contrary to the language of the plan.

➤ Judgment for the employer.

Erie County Retirees Ass'n v. County of Erie
220 F.3d 193 (3rd Cir. 2000)

Medicare-eligible retirees claimed that the County violated the Age Discrimination in Employment Act (ADEA) by treating them less favorably than retirees under age 65 with respect to health coverage. The trial court found that the ADEA did not apply and dismissed the claim. The court concluded that appellants had established a claim of age discrimination because they were individuals within the meaning of the ADEA and the County had treated them differently when they offered them different health coverage than was offered to non-Medicare-eligible retirees. The coverage would not violate the ADEA only if the County met the equal benefit or equal cost standard.

➢ Judgment for the retirees. Erie County has filed a petition to be heard in the US Supreme Court.

In re Unisys Corp. Retiree Med. Benefits Litig.
2000 U.S. Dist. LEXIS 22347 (E.D. Pa. 2000)

Successor employer terminated all medical coverage and instituted new plans with increased premiums. Summary judgment was granted to the employer for employees who involuntarily retired and retirees who had knowledge of the reservation of rights clause. However, summary judgment was not awarded to the employer for retirees who presented a colorable claim that they mistakenly relied on the representation that they would have retiree medical for life if they retired because of certain ambiguities in information disclosed to them.

➢ Judgment in favor of employer.

Deboard v. Sunshine Mining
24 EBC 1289 (10th Cir. 2000)

Plaintiffs sought to enforce promise of lifetime insurance benefits as inducement for early retirement. Court relied on informational letter sent to participants outlining the benefits they would receive upon early retirement. Court determined a new ERISA Plan was created based on information letters sent to all eligible participants – the letter specified a funding mechanism and gave the employer ongoing operational and administrative responsibility. The Court failed to decide whether the new plan incorporated the right to amend clause from the original plan because the clause itself was ambiguous.

➢ Judgment in favor of the retirees.

Hughes v. 3M Retiree Medical Plan
281 F.3d 786 (8ᵗʰ Cir. 2001)

Employer able to increase retiree medical premiums even though participants received a booklet stating that post-retirement medical benefits would be for retirees' lifetime. However, the SPD explicitly reserved the employer's right to amend, modify, or terminate retiree medical benefit plan and did not contain any vesting language, therefore the court ignored the booklet as extrinsic evidence.

➤ Judgment in favor of employer.

Danis v. Cutler Food
2001 U.S. Dist. LEXIS 14355 (D. Conn. 2001)

Successor employer not responsible for retiree medical. The most recent plan did not contain retiree medical and clearly revoked all prior plans – since welfare benefits are normally not vested the employee only has a claim if his benefit was vested. The court rejected a letter stating he would receive substantially similar benefits as before as creating a vested life-time benefit stating that the support for a promise must come within the text of the plan documents themselves. Where an ERISA plan is silent as to vesting or reserves the right to amend and terminate at any time, extrinsic evidence such as informal communications between an employer and plan beneficiaries cannot amend the plan to create a promise of vested benefits absent a showing tantamount to proof of fraud.

➤ Judgment in favor of employer.

Richmond v. NCR Corp.,
227 F.Supp.2d 802 (S.D. Ohio 2002).

Informational documents, describing special pension enhancement program that employer offered to encourage early retirement, did not contain representation that any welfare benefit, including health insurance, would vest upon employees' early retirement, and thus promissory estoppel did not require reinstatement of such benefits to early retirees after employer terminated or changed benefits.

➤ Judgment in favor of employer.

Stearns v. NCR Corp.
297 F.3d 706 (8ᵗʰ Cir. 2002).

For purposes of resolving dispute over applicability of provision reserving employer's right to modify or terminate retirement health care benefits that were part of early retirement program, intent to vest those benefits in program participants could not be implied from fact that releases signed by participants and employer's documents explaining program did not address vesting or cross-reference reservation-of-rights provision. Additionally, summary plan description need not disclose that welfare plan benefits are not vested.

➢ Judgment in favor of employer.

In re Bridge Info. Sys. of Am. Inc.
288 B.R. 565 (Bankr. E.D. Mo. 2002)
Employer could unilaterally terminate its welfare benefit plan at any time without notice to employees; plan, in specifying that employer had right to amend or terminate, sufficiently described procedure for terminating plan, and it did not purport to confer vested right to benefits on employees, but explicitly provided that employees would have no vested rights.

➢ Judgment in favor of employer.

Leuthner v. Blue Cross and Blue Shield of N.E. Pa.
270 F.Supp.2d 584 (M.D. Pa. 2003)
Existence of unequivocal reservation of rights clauses in summary plan descriptions of plan, providing that employer/sponsor might discontinue retiree health insurance coverage at any time, precluded any reasonable reliance on employer's provision of lifetime health benefits, and thus retirees did not have equitable estoppel claim based on employer's decision to eliminate certain retiree health care benefits.

➢ Judgment in favor of employer.

Grappone v. Combined Services, LLC
2004 WL 1724998 (D. N.H. 2004)
No provision in the plan or the summary plan description that purported to waive the right to terminate. Therefore, the termination of the welfare benefit was valid as to people in whom it had not yet vested.

➢ Judgment in favor of employer.

Vallone v. CNA Fin. Corp.
375 F.3d 623 (7th Cir. 2004)
Employer not estopped from denying "lifetime" health care benefits granted by early retirement package; early retirees were not told explicitly that the "lifetime" benefits were irrevocable, and early retirees

could not show reasonable reliance because plan documents contained numerous, unambiguous provisions reserving employer's right to amend, suspend or terminate the health care benefits.

➢ Judgment in favor of employer.

McCarthy v. Bowe Bell
2004 U.S. Dist. LEXIS 18547 (D. Md. 2004)
Court denied employer's motion to dismiss regarding the denial of payment of retiree medical. The employee and the employer entered into a settlement agreement when retiree terminated – the agreement promised prescription coverage for life. The representation resulted in a one-person ERISA Plan and allowed to go forward as an ERISA claim.

➢ Judgment in favor of the retirees.

Adams v. Tetley USA, Inc.,
363 F.Supp. 2d 94 (D. Conn. 2005)
Employer did not make promise, enforceable under ERISA, of employee lifetime medical benefits in negotiating individual early retirement plan, even though letters outlining employee's benefits did not reserve employer's right to terminate retiree medical program, where employer's regular retirees were subject to employer's reservation of right to terminate benefits, and neither letter promised any separate or different health benefits than those to which regular retirees were entitled. Additionally, employer made no promise of lifetime medical benefits upon which ERISA promissory estoppel claim could be based, inasmuch as employees' "understanding" that promise occurred did not meet objective test for promise, summary plan descriptions (SPD) could not reasonably be interpreted as promise of lifetime benefits, employer was not required to reiterate its reservation of right to terminate benefits in informal letters and communications, and, although executives mentioned to one employee possibility of "lifetime" health coverage, employee subsequently signed written agreement indicating otherwise.

➢ Judgment in favor of employer.

FEDERAL COURT OF APPEALS CIRCUITS

Most of the court cases cited above are federal appeals court decisions. They set precedent in their districts that must be followed in subsequent cases and may provide guidance in the decisions within other districts.

The following lists the districts and the states and territories included in its jurisdiction.

1ˢᵗ Circuit	Maine, Massachusetts, New Hampshire, Puerto Rico, Rhode Island
2ⁿᵈ Circuit	Connecticut, New York, Vermont
3ʳᵈ Circuit	Delaware, New Jersey, Pennsylvania, Virgin Islands
4ᵗʰ Circuit	Maryland, North Carolina, South Carolina, Virginia, West Virginia
5ᵗʰ Circuit	Louisiana, Mississippi, Texas
6ᵗʰ Circuit	Kentucky, Michigan, Ohio, Tennessee
7ᵗʰ Circuit	Illinois, Indiana, Wisconsin
8ᵗʰ Circuit	Arkansas, Iowa, Minnesota, Missouri, Nebraska, North Dakota, South Dakota
9ᵗʰ Circuit	Alaska, Arizona, California, Guam, Hawaii, Idaho, Montana, Nevada, Northern Mariana Islands, Oregon, Washington
10ᵗʰ Circuit	Colorado, Kansas, New Mexico, Oklahoma, Utah, Wyoming
11ᵗʰ Circuit	Alabama, Florida, Georgia
D.C.	District of Columbia

APPENDIX E

HEALTH PRACTICE NOTE 2006-3

Attestations of Actuarial Equivalence for Plan Sponsors Accepting a Retiree Drug Subsidy Under the Medicare Drug Program, by the American Academy of Actuaries Actuarial Equivalence Retiree Practice Note Work Group, dated March 2006, is reproduced with the permission of the American Academy of Actuaries. Copyright © 2006 American Academy of Actuaries. As the Academy updates and/or supplements its publications from time to time, the reader should refer to the Academy's website (www.actuary.org) to confirm whether any additions, changes, deletions, or modifications have been made to the foregoing practice note since March 2006, or whether the practice note has been superseded or supplemented since that time.

HEALTH PRACTICE NOTE 2006-3

MARCH 2006

Attestation of Actuarial Equivalence for
Plan Sponsors Accepting a Retiree Drug Subsidy
under the Medicare Drug Program

Developed by the
Actuarial Equivalence Retiree Practice Note Work Group
of the American Academy of Actuaries[1]

This practice note was prepared by a work group organized by the Health Practice Council of the American Academy of Actuaries. The work group was asked to:

> Review the new Centers for Medicare & Medicaid Services (CMS) regulations that require an Academy member to attest that an employer or union's prescription drug plan, in order to receive a retiree drug subsidy (RDS), meets the actuarial equivalence standard; and
> Publish a practice note addressing the procedural and professional aspects of the attestation.

The purpose of this practice note is to provide advisory guidance to the actuary attesting to the actuarial equivalence of a plan sponsor's[2] retiree health plans under the requirements of 42 CFR 423.884 for payments to sponsors of retiree prescription drug plans. The actuarial comparison of plan values required by the regulation will involve methods common to health actuaries but in an entirely new circumstance. This note provides examples of possible responses to certain situations and issues, but no representation of completeness is intended. Other approaches may also be reasonable and may be used. The draft of the practice note was exposed for public comment a few weeks before the first deadline for such attestations (August 2005). Appropriate alternatives to methods mentioned herein may develop over time and come into generally accepted use.

This practice note is based on interpretations of 42 CFR 423.884 and current CMS guidelines and requirements. The information in this practice note is not binding on any actuary and is not a definitive statement about what constitutes generally accepted practice in this area. This practice note has not been promulgated by the Actuarial Standards Board or by any other authoritative body. Regulations or other clarifying guidance promulgated subsequent to the date of publication of this practice note may make the practices described herein irrelevant or inappropriate.

E-1

The members of the work group responsible for this practice note are: Dale Yamamoto, chairperson; Al Bingham; Derek Guyton; Mark Olson; John Schubert; and Mark White. This group consists of actuaries experienced in working with employer and union groups that sponsor retiree health care plans. All members have the necessary expertise to provide technical guidance on this new actuarial certification process.

This final practice note takes into consideration the comments received during the comment period (August 2005 to Nov. 15, 2005). Additional comments are welcome as to the appropriateness of the practice note, frequency of updates, substantive disagreements, etc. Comments should be sent to the Academy's Federal Health Policy Analyst at the following address: American Academy of Actuaries, 1100 17th St. NW, 7th floor, Washington, DC 20036.

Health Practice Council

Practice Note — March 2006

**Attestation of Actuarial Equivalence for
Plan Sponsors Accepting a Retiree Drug Subsidy
under the Medicare Drug Program**

Table of Contents

I. Introduction

The Medicare program was established under Title XVIII of the Social Security Act of 1965. The program established hospital and medical care coverage for U.S. seniors over 65 and certain disabled individuals. The program is administered and regulated by the Centers for Medicare and Medicaid Services (CMS), an agency of the U.S. Department of Health and Human Services. Medicare is administered federally and financed with dedicated payroll taxes, premiums paid by (or on behalf of) beneficiaries, and general tax revenue.

The Medicare Prescription Drug, Improvement, and Modernization Act (MMA) of 2003 established a new voluntary outpatient prescription drug benefit effective as of Jan. 1, 2006. This new benefit is a substantial change to the Medicare program. The prescription drug benefit (also referred to as Medicare Part D) is provided by private plans authorized by CMS. The plans are either stand-alone prescription drug plans (PDPs) or Medicare Advantage Prescription Drug plans (MA-PDs) offering both medical and prescription drug coverage. These plans are required to offer a standard drug benefit described by the MMA but have the flexibility to vary the drug benefit as long as it is at least actuarially equivalent to the standard design. The MMA also provides for subsidized premiums and lower cost-sharing for eligible low-income beneficiaries.

In order to encourage employers and unions to maintain their retiree health care plans, the MMA provided a tax-exempt retiree drug subsidy for qualified retiree health plans that offer coverage on and after Jan. 1, 2006. Under the MMA regulations, a primary requirement for qualification to receive the subsidy is that the retiree health plan must provide a benefit design and subsidy level that is at least actuarially equivalent to the standard Medicare design and government subsidy level. The actuarial equivalence tests for subsidy qualification, which are the subject of this practice note, are different from those imposed on private PDPs.

To be eligible for the subsidy, the regulations require a plan sponsor to apply for the retiree drug subsidy each year. Included in the application is an attestation by a qualified actuary that the plan is at least actuarially equivalent to the Medicare Part D standard benefit. The MMA requires that the qualified actuary be a member of the American Academy of Actuaries, and Section VII of this practice note discusses appropriate qualifications. The actuarial attestation is required to specify that the plan meets the Gross and Net Value Tests required by the MMA under CMS rules and to acknowledge that the information is being used to obtain federal funds. The actual attestations of the Gross and Net Value Tests may be performed by one actuary for both tests or different actuaries for each test.

For Medicare beneficiaries delaying enrollment in the Part D program from their first eligibility, a late-enrollment penalty is assessed. If the beneficiary was enrolled in a prescription drug plan with benefits as good as the standard Medicare offering, however, the penalty will not apply. The regulations require plan sponsors providing such coverage to provide their retirees with a notice that their prescription drug plan is "creditable" coverage, thereby relieving the retiree from the late-enrollment penalty. Passing the "Gross Test" discussed in section III will satisfy the requirement that the benefits be at least equal to standard Medicare benefit.

This practice note offers guidance on the actuarial equivalence requirements for actuaries providing services to plan sponsors that receive the retiree drug subsidy, and does not apply to practice involving entities offering PDPs and MA-PDs.

II. Generally Accepted Actuarial Principles

In the hierarchy of generally accepted actuarial principles and practices, the Code of Professional Conduct and, by reference, the Actuarial Standards of Practice (ASOP) have the highest standing. Other items – such as practice notes, textbooks, examination study notes, and articles in professional journals – do not have the same binding authority. Since the actuarial attestation required for actuarial equivalence under the MMA is new, no ASOP has been adopted specifically and exclusively to apply to actuarial work performed to comply with CMS requirements.

The actuary may consider several existing ASOPs as valuable sources of guidance when performing the actuarial attestation, including:

No. 5: Incurred Health and Disability Claims
No. 6: Measuring Retiree Group Benefit Obligations
No. 8: Regulatory Filings for Rates and Financial Projections for Health Plans
No. 16: Actuarial Practice Concerning Health Maintenance Organizations and Other Managed-Care Health Plans
No. 23: Data Quality
No. 25: Credibility Procedures Applicable to Accident and Health, Group Term Life, and Property/Casualty Coverages
No. 31: Documentation in Health Benefit Plan Ratemaking
No. 41: Actuarial Communications
No. 42: Determining Health and Disability Liabilities Other Than Liabilities for Incurred Claims

In addition, generally accepted actuarial practices have been established in the health care field that are not published in the form of ASOPs. The actuarial equivalence testing is generally expected to rely heavily on the use of prescription drug price and utilization experience. The concepts of continuation tables and claim distributions will normally be used in this type of analysis. Appropriate adjustments will usually be made to project historical medical and prescription drug claim data to the plan year of the actuarial equivalence attestation and to possibly adjust for any benefit changes. It is usually preferable for an actuary to have experience in this or comparable work before performing actuarial attestations. Guidance in such work is beyond the scope of this practice note.

III. Actuarial Equivalence Concepts

"Actuarial equivalence" has a specific meaning in the context of the MMA and the subsequent regulatory guidance, but this meaning is not explicitly defined. This meaning under MMA may be different from an actuary's preconception of the term and warrants careful attention. The MMA concept of actuarial equivalence is applied in the determination of a Gross Test and a Net Test that affect the creditable coverage determination and qualification for the direct retiree drug subsidy of an eligible prescription drug plan.

4

◆ The Gross Test is tied to the determination of creditable coverage. If the Gross Test for a plan fails, then the plan will not provide creditable coverage. When a Medicare beneficiary eventually enrolls in a Medicare Part D plan, the plan will charge a penalty premium that is based on the number of months the beneficiary was not enrolled in a plan providing creditable coverage. The primary purpose of the penalty premium is to minimize enrollment timing by late enrolling Medicare beneficiaries. If the late enrollee transfers to a Medicare Part D plan from a plan providing creditable coverage, then there would not usually be a large adverse selection effect from those late enrollees, so no penalty is warranted. Therefore, from the Medicare perspective, the determination of creditable coverage is based on the level of the plan design relative to Medicare Part D.

◆ The Net Test is tied to the determination of a financial subsidy for plan sponsors. The plan sponsor is providing the financial support for the benefit and will receive any financial benefits of the subsidy payment itself. As a strictly financial measure, the portion of the benefit value paid for by the plan sponsor is compared with the portion of the Medicare Part D benefit value paid for by Medicare. In addition, an alternative form of the Net Test is allowed that recognizes the lost value of the catastrophic benefit due to the "True Out of Pocket" (TrOOP) adjustment. This alternative is used only where the plan sponsor's plan includes a continued supplemental benefit for those beneficiaries who enroll in Part D. In either case, the Net Test is a relative comparison of the plan sponsor's net financial support to the retiree with Medicare's net financial support to the retiree.

For each of these tests, the actuary will make a "pass/fail" determination for the plan. There is no gradation of partial creditability under the Gross Test or partial subsidy under the Net Test. The "all or nothing" result may lead some actuaries to feel uncomfortable that the law requires them to make a definitive statement regarding "equivalence." Actuarial analysis and projection is inherently an estimation exercise and hence is somewhat imprecise. In valuing health plans and prescription drug benefits, the actuary will make choices and assumptions about data sources used, projection methodologies, and other elements. The projected plan values will be an estimate rather than a precise number. To add complexity, pharmacy costs are influenced by the introduction of new technology (e.g., new medicines) and rapid changes in prices (e.g., when brand named drugs go off patent). The resulting uncertainty affects both elements in the Gross Test and Net Test—the value calculated for the Medicare Part D standard plan, and the value of the plan sponsor's retiree prescription drug plan.

This lack of precision may become a difficulty if the plan sponsor's Gross Test or Net Test result indicates that the plan sponsor's value just slightly exceeds the Medicare value. The actuary's attestation of actuarial equivalence may imply to the non-actuary a correct and solid finding, but that finding may instead be based on underlying statistical variation or on the actuary's choice of the data set used, the methodology applied, or the specific actuarial assumptions that were applied. If slight changes in the data set, the methodology, or the assumptions would cause the test result to fail, then the actuary would usually find it prudent to be prepared to explain the choice of a particular data set, methodology, or set of assumptions against other alternatives.

This variability takes on particular importance for actuarial equivalence testing, because the test results are used by the plan sponsor to qualify for the payment of federal funds subject to the False Claims Act. Since the audit review of the test will usually be performed well after the fact, there is some risk that more than one year of testing could be affected, compounding the impact of any changes resulting from the audit process. Thus, the actuary is advised to be aware of the defensibility of the data sources, methodology, and assumptions in concluding that the results of either the Gross Test or the Net Test are favorable. Sensitivity testing is not a requirement of CMS, but the actuary would normally be better prepared to address any challenges that might occur in the audit process if those issues were addressed with analysis at the time of the initial determination. The intent of the law is clearly to encourage the maintenance of private retiree health plan coverage of prescription drugs as an alternative to Part D. The actuary and the plan sponsor have considerable flexibility in defining coverage to meet actuarial equivalence, particularly under the Net Test, and sensitivity testing may aid that process.

IV. Summary of Regulations

Subpart R of the CMS regulations contains the rules pertinent to the retiree drug subsidy and the required actuarial attestation. The regulations require this attestation to be certified by a qualified actuary who is a member of the American Academy of Actuaries, and to be based on generally accepted actuarial principles and any actuarial guidelines established by CMS in the regulations or in future guidance. To the extent CMS has not provided guidance on a specific aspect of the actuarial equivalence standard, it seems likely that the attesting actuary may rely on any reasonable interpretation that is consistent with accepted actuarial principles in determining actuarial values.

The CMS regulations prescribe a "two prong test" to satisfy the actuarial equivalence testing. The first prong is a Gross Value Test and the second prong is a Net Value Test, taking into account the sponsor's contribution toward the financing of the coverage. CMS felt that this approach best supported the goal of maximizing the number of retirees that retain their employer or union-sponsored retiree prescription drug coverage and not creating windfalls to the sponsors. CMS also felt that this test best reflected Congressional intent.

To satisfy the Gross Test, the regulations require that the expected amount of paid claims for Part D drugs for Medicare beneficiaries under the sponsor's plan be at least equal to the expected amount of paid claims for the same beneficiaries under the defined standard prescription drug coverage, including catastrophic coverage available when an individual's out-of-pocket expenses exceed a specified threshold. Satisfying this Gross Test also satisfies the actuarial equivalence test for creditable coverage purposes.

In the final regulations, "employment-based retiree drug coverage satisfies the actuarial equivalence standard if its actuarial value (as determined after reducing the Gross Value of the benefit by expected retiree premiums) is at least equal to the Net Value of defined standard prescription drug coverage under Part D (as determined after reducing the Gross Value of the benefit by the expected monthly beneficiary premiums), with the Net Value of the defined standard prescription drug coverage reflecting the impact of employer or union-sponsored prescription drug coverage that would supplement the beneficiary's defined standard prescription drug coverage."

The Net Value of the sponsor's plan is calculated by subtracting the retiree premium/ contribution from the Gross Value of the sponsor's plan. The Net Value of the defined standard prescription drug coverage is calculated by subtracting the national beneficiary premium from the Gross Value of the defined standard prescription drug coverage. The national beneficiary premium may be the national average beneficiary premium for the applicable year, or may be determined by multiplying the Gross Value of the Part D benefit by 25.5 percent.

If the sponsor provides coverage that supplements Part D for those retirees who enroll in Part D, the Net Value of the defined standard prescription drug coverage may also be adjusted to recognize the lower catastrophic coverage because of the effect of TrOOP. This "Medicare Supplemental Adjustment" (as defined in the CMS guidance issued April 7, 2005) is based on the plan design of the supplemental coverage, which is important to recognize in cases where the supplemental benefit is different from the normal benefit available to retirees that do not enroll in a Part D plan.

The regulations require that each benefit option within a group health plan (defined as a particular benefit design, category of benefits, or cost-sharing arrangement) for which attestation is made must pass the Gross Test. The plan can pass the Net Test, however, by testing each option separately or by aggregating benefit options within a group health plan.

For plans in which the sponsor charges a single, integrated retiree premium/contribution for medical and drug coverage, the sponsor may allocate any portion of the premium to the drug coverage for the purpose of the Net Test of the actuarial attestation. For practical purposes of passing the Net Test, the obvious approach is to allocate all of the retiree contribution to the other, non-drug, medical coverage and administrative expenses, which requires ascertaining the actuarial cost of the other medical coverage. If the contribution is greater than the actuarial cost of the other medical coverage and expenses, then the excess must be allocated to the drug coverage. It will usually be important for any allocation, however, to be consistent with other documentation. For example, a plan sponsor offering separate medical and prescription drug plans, each with its own contribution structure would not be able to reallocate the retiree contributions across the two plans.

V. Claim Cost Sources

The purpose of this section is to provide guidance with respect to claim cost sources that the actuary may choose to consider in developing the support for the attestation of actuarial equivalence.

CMS has indicated that the calculations for the Gross and Net Tests should be based on the sponsor's own claims experience for participants who are Part D eligible individuals, when such data is available and credible enough to ensure that it provides a meaningful representation at all levels of claims for a given distribution. If there is not sufficient claims data at all levels to support a reasonable calculation of the actuarial values based on a sponsor's own claims data, CMS allows the use of alternative normative databases. CMS regulations state a preference, however, that normative data should only be used if the sponsor's specific data is either unavailable or is not credible. If the plan sponsor has many plans or benefit options, those with less credible data may be supplemented with the claims experience of those with more credible data to enhance the overall claims distribution.

If the actuary believes that the plan sponsor's data is insufficient for the evaluation, then the actuary may consider supplementing the plan sponsor's data with other sources that would provide additional credibility to the overall data set. Other data sources can be used, provided these additional data sources can reasonably be expected to reflect the characteristics of the plan design, demographics, and other factors. The other sources may be published claims distributions that can be adjusted to closely reflect the expected plan sponsor's retiree claim distribution. This might include claim distributions generally available for purchase in the marketplace. Other acceptable sources might include: (a) broad claim distribution data from pharmacy benefit managers or health plan administrators that may be made available to a plan sponsor, or (b) claims distribution data from a similar plan sponsor that is adjusted for differences between the two plan sponsors.

Actuaries are usually well advised to be careful when using data sources not from the plan sponsor, since these sources may require adjustments to more closely reflect the plan design, demographic, as well as utilization characteristics of the plan sponsor's retirees. Specifically, the actuary should become familiar with the data underlying any sources to determine whether they appropriately represent the plan sponsor's specific experience.

The actuary normally would disclose the data sources that have been used as well as any adjustments that may have been made.

VI. Methodology

This section provides an outline of the major steps that would usually be taken or considered in preparing the actuarial equivalence tests. The underlying data that will be used would normally be consistent with the guidance in the previous section.

There are four key steps in the testing process:

      A. Preparation for Testing
      B. Claim Cost Selection and Adjustment
      C. Gross Value Test
      D. Net Value Test

The attesting actuary is responsible for completing these four steps. These guidelines are not intended to be exhaustive or to cover every situation.

A.   **Preparation for Testing.** Before testing is done, the actuary usually reviews relevant plan descriptions. The requested information might include: the plan document, SPDs, enrollment materials, and other retiree communications materials. The actuary may rely on the plan sponsor's representations of changes to be made to the prescription drug benefits for the period covered by the attestation. Consideration would normally also be given to the substantive plan (as defined under Financial Accounting Statement No. 106) and any administrative procedures that significantly affect the benefits actually paid to retirees.

Other key preparation steps typically are:

1. Identify separate plans and the benefit options within each plan.[3]

   a. The definition of a plan can be difficult to determine. The preamble to the proposed Part D regulations states that CMS proposed to apply the ERISA plan definition, modeling the approach adopted by the Treasury Department at 26 CFR section 54.4980B-2, in the context of a group health plan. Specifically, CMS referred sponsors to Q&A-6 of that COBRA regulation, noting that all health benefits provided by a sponsor are presumed to be under a single plan unless it is clear from the plan instruments and operation that the plans are separate arrangements. Plan sponsors must determine what is a "plan" for purposes of combining benefit options in the actuarial equivalence test. The plan sponsors must also determine the benefit options within each plan, and the actuary should take into account the defined options. If questions exist, the plan sponsor's benefits counsel usually would be consulted.

   b. A variation in plan design cost-sharing provisions for the prescription drug benefit (expected for testing year) will normally create a separate benefit option, at the discretion of the plan sponsor.

   c. Variations in retiree contributions may create separate benefit options.

      i. Many plan sponsors have situations with differences in contributions between the former employee and dependents. The plan sponsor will determine whether to treat each such contribution schedule as one benefit option or as multiple benefit options.

      ii. Many plan sponsors have situations with differences in contributions among retirees with different lengths of service. The plan sponsor will determine whether to treat each such contribution schedule as one benefit option or as multiple benefit options.

   d. The plan sponsor will determine whether it is appropriate to include disability retirees under the age of 65 in testing and whether they create another benefit option.

   e. The actuary normally confirms the plan year for each plan (and therefore for each benefit option), the benefit in force for that plan year, and the impact (if any) of the plan year on testing. Non-calendar-year plans in particular should be identified due to the special treatment specified by the MMA and regulations.

2. Based on a preliminary review of the design and contributions for each plan, determine whether the plan can be certified as passing both the Gross and Net Tests without detailed calculations (as exemplified by the CMS guidance for simplified

9

calculations for creditable coverage) or whether the actuary believes that data-based testing is required for each plan. In the event a simplified testing approach is used, the actuary is usually well-advised to be prepared to provide documentation supporting his determination process. Such data might include aggregate historical claims experience, aggregate historical retiree contribution data, and similar elements. Refer to ASOP 41 "Actuarial Communications" for additional Guidance

B.   **Claim Cost Selection and Adjustment.** Historical claim experience for the plan and benefit option being tested is used if available and appropriately credible. Other normative data may be appropriate for the option being tested and would usually be adjusted for differences in demographics, design, and any other factors that may affect cost levels.

A claims continuation table of allowed charges would often be employed for Gross Value testing (unless data-based testing is not indicated), whether historical claims data or normative databases are being used. Other methods may also be used, including seriatim calculations based on historical data projected to the testing year, which will have similar data requirements and issues. The data selected for testing would normally be reviewed and adjusted as follows:

1.   Based on the data available, establish the credibility level of each benefit option being tested. ASOP No. 25 will likely offer useful guidance.

   a.   The levels of credibility achievable include:

      i.   The volume of claim data available is sufficient to produce a claim distribution that is fully credible (except perhaps in the 'tail').

      ii.   The volume of claim data available is sufficient to produce a cost per member per year that is fully credible.

      iii. The volume of claim data available is sufficient to produce a cost per member per year that is only partially credible and the use of normative data would usually be considered.

      iv.   The volume of claim data available is not sufficient to produce a cost per member per year that is even partially credible and normative data would, therefore, be used for actuarial equivalence testing.

   b.   The actuary may choose to consider combining the experience of multiple benefit options with the same or similar plan provisions to increase credibility.

2.   Where the analysis would be affected materially, adjust data used for each benefit option to:

   a.   An incurred basis (if appropriate);

10

b.　Exclude drugs not covered under Part D, even if payable under Part B, and include drugs covered under Part D but not covered by the plan sponsor's coverage;

c.　Reflect the (estimated) savings from any rebates not reflected in point-of-sale prices.

3.　Project costs to the testing year.

a.　Historical option-specific claims experience, preferably using allowed charges, will be trended appropriately. Use of separate trend rates for price and utilization would usually be considered.

b.　In most cases, the actual participant contribution rates for the testing year will be used. If not available, expected participant contributions may be used, applying the contribution policy.

c.　Costs for the sponsor's plan would be adjusted for any plan design changes.

C.　**Gross Value Test.** The Gross Value Test compares the benefit value of the plan sponsor's program to the benefit value of the standard Medicare benefit using generally accepted actuarial practices. The actuary usually considers each of the following steps in preparation of this test:

1.　Determine whether one of the simplified testing approaches applies or whether the full calculation will be performed. If a simplified method is used, document the basis for the simplified testing.

2.　For each benefit option, identify the prescription drug plan provisions that determine each participant's level of cost sharing. The actuary will usually decide whether any plan management features might affect the Gross Value of the option.

3.　For benefit options with plan provisions that apply to any covered plan expenses and are not solely applicable to prescription drug expenses, organize the combined plan provisions into separate plan provisions for prescription drugs and all other covered expenses. The organization would generally be based on historical medical and prescription drug claims experience for the plan.

a.　Special consideration would typically be given to plans with lifetime or annual benefit maximums that potentially can be reached in the testing year or that are demonstrably affecting the benefits paid from the plan.

b.　If data is available, the actuary would usually consider the amounts remaining under the plan for each member, restoration of benefits provisions, and similar items that are likely to significantly affect the amount of benefits paid in the testing year.

11

4. Establish the total allowed cost per member for the testing year to be used for each benefit option. This would be adjusted for factors such as non-covered drugs, expected discounts, utilization levels, or rebates, if the effects of these factors are material relative to the standard Medicare Part D coverage.

    a. If the plan design has a feature such as a low lifetime maximum benefit or pay-related deductibles that will affect individual participants uniquely, it may be necessary to perform a weighted average calculation to determine the average value of the plan design across all participants in a benefit option.

5. Apply the drug plan provisions to the selected claims continuance table or seriatim claims data to estimate the Gross Value of the sponsor's plan on a cost-per-member basis.

6. Apply the plan provisions for the standard Medicare Part D coverage to the selected claims continuance table or seriatim claims data to estimate the Gross Value of Part D for the group covered by the benefit option being tested on a cost-per-member basis.

    a. If the standard Medicare Part D plan provisions are notably different from the sponsor's plan, an assumption regarding behavioral changes to utilization would normally be considered.

7. If the Gross Value of the sponsor's plan meets or exceeds the Gross Value of Part D coverage for this group, the sponsor's plan passes the Gross Value Test. Note that the results of this test also document that the option provides creditable coverage. (CMS has also specified safe harbor conditions for the purpose of determining creditable coverage, but not for this Gross Value Test.)

8. If the Gross Value of the sponsor's plan is not significantly different from the Gross Value of Part D, the actuary would usually determine the sensitivity of the results to changes in the assumptions made, to the data projection methodology, or to the normative databases used (if any). The actuary and the plan sponsor have considerable flexibility in defining coverage to meet actuarial equivalence; sensitivity testing may aid in that process.

D. **Net Value Test.** The Net Value Test uses generally accepted actuarial practices to compare the Net Value provided under the sponsor's program to the Net Value provided under the standard Medicare Part D benefit. The actuary would normally consider each of the following steps (and perhaps reconsider after seeing preliminary results) in preparing this test:

1. Decide which benefit options will be combined for Net Value testing as allowed by the regulations and guidance.

2. Determine whether one of the simplified testing methods applies or, if not, perform the full calculation. If no testing is done, document the reasons for not performing the tests. All benefit options should be able to pass the simplified Gross Test individually in order to be aggregated.

12

3. Determine the dollar-weighted value for those options being combined to determine the:

   a. Weighted average Gross Value of the sponsor's plans;

   b. Weighted average Gross Value of Part D for this group;

   c. Weighted average of the contributions required from plan participants.

4. Calculate the Part D contribution value by one of the following methods:

   a. National average Part D premiums; or

   b. 25.5 percent of the (weighted) Gross Value of Part D for this group.

5. Determine the Net Value as the Gross Value of the sponsor's option(s) less the projected average contributions. The Gross Value of Part D, less the Part D contribution value, equals the preliminary Net Value for Part D.

   a. If the Net Value of the sponsor's options meets or exceeds the preliminary Net Value of Part D coverage for this group, the benefit options pass the Net Value Test.

   b. If not, the plan sponsor has the option of determining whether to provide a supplemental plan to retirees electing Part D coverage and directing the actuary to apply the Medicare Supplemental Adjustment to reduce the Net Value of Part D.

      i. The Medicare Supplemental Adjustment may only be applied if the plan sponsor has agreed to provide benefits exceeding the standard Part D coverage for participants electing to enroll in Part D.

      ii. The Medicare Supplemental Adjustment for each benefit option is determined using the same claim continuance table or seriatim claim data (adjusted as appropriate) selected to establish the Gross Value of Part D, using the process described in the regulatory guidance.

      iii. The design applied to the continuance table is required to be the design offered to those participants electing to enroll in Part D, even if this design is different from that provided to other participants.

6. The final Net Value for Part D equals the Gross Value of Part D, less the Part D contribution value, less the Medicare supplemental adjustment, if applicable.

   a. If the Net Value of the sponsor's options meets or exceeds the final Net Value of Part D coverage for this group, the benefit options pass the Net Value Test.

   b. If the Net Value of the sponsor's options is less than the final Net Value of Part D, the group does not pass the actuarial equivalence Net Value Test and the plan sponsor does not qualify for the related subsidy.

7. If the Net Value of the sponsor's plan is not significantly different from the Net Value of Part D (either before or after the supplemental benefit adjustment), the actuary would usually determine the sensitivity of the results to changes in the assumptions made, the data projection methodology, or the normative databases used (if any). The actuary and the plan sponsor have considerable flexibility in defining coverage to meet actuarial equivalence and sensitivity testing may aid that process. The results of the sensitivity tests should be discussed with the plan sponsor, highlighting circumstances under which the plan would fail testing and possible implications for future years.

CMS Guidelines

CMS has issued guidelines for some unique situations. One is on the determination of creditable coverage. The guidelines provide plan sponsors with the general concept of creditable coverage and provide some simplified test parameters. This topic is outside the scope of this practice note.

Account-based plans were addressed in another CMS guidance notification. The described accounts are more comparable to designs used for active employees but represent the only guidance available at the time of drafting this note. In brief, the guidance states:

1. Health reimbursement account (HRA) – If an HRA is offered with a high-deductible health plan (HDHP), then for creditable coverage determination, amounts contributed to an HRA in a given year should be treated as increasing the expected prescription drug claims payable from the non-account benefit for that year. Existing funds in the HRA that have been rolled over from prior years will not be factored into the value of the arrangements.

2. Flexible spending account (FSA) – An employer sponsoring an FSA shall disregard such a plan for purposes of determining whether an individual has creditable coverage.

3. Health savings accounts (HSA)/medical savings accounts (MSA) – These types of accounts cannot be taken into account in determining whether an HDHP qualifies as creditable coverage. Also, they cannot be taken into account to determine whether the HDHP can qualify for the retiree drug subsidy.

VII. Qualification

Certification of actuarial equivalence is considered a statement of actuarial opinion. Therefore, the signing actuary is subject to the Qualification Standards (Including Continuing Education Requirements) for Actuaries Issuing Statements of Actuarial Opinion in the United States. Under the Qualification Standards, the actuary should satisfy requirements for basic education, experience, and continuing education in the practice area before issuing a statement of actuarial opinion.

All actuaries, including those who work with retiree medical benefits in a valuation context, are usually prudent to recognize the importance of being careful in this area. Actuarial equivalence analysis as referenced in the law and regulations is, by its nature, a health bene-fit pricing analysis. While valuation experience alone may be helpful, it is, by itself, not sufficient qualification to perform this analysis or to attest to actuarial equivalence. The actuary may wish to refer to Section II for additional guidance and applicable Actuarial Standards of Practice. It is usually preferable for the actuary's work experience and continuing education to include health benefit system pricing and analysis.

VIII. Reports

This section provides an overview of suggested report documentation for the actuarial at-testation of actuarial equivalence for plan sponsors receiving a retiree drug subsidy. The term "report" in this practice note refers collectively to the "reports and working docu-ments" the plan sponsor (or their designee) is required to maintain. The actuary develops the reports in support of the actuarial work product. The plan sponsor (or their designee) is required to maintain for six years the actuarial attestation as well as the actuary's reports supporting the attestation. The actuary may choose to retain copies of the attestation and reports as well.

The reports will typically describe the relevant data, sources of data, material assumptions, methods, and process used in the actuarial equivalence comparison with enough clarity that another qualified actuary practicing in the same field could objectively evaluate the reason-ableness of the work product. The actuary normally explains the reason(s) for and describes the effect of any material changes in sources of data, assumptions, or methods from the last analysis. Generally speaking, there are five key areas to be documented:

A. Documentation of actuarial equivalence
B. Participant data
C. Summary of plan provisions
D. Total rates and retiree contributions
E. Actuarial assumptions and methods

The actuary develops appropriate documentation in support of the actuarial work product. The extent of the documentation typically includes the standard information outlined in ASOP No. 41. The documentation also usually includes the source(s) of data, material as-sumptions, methods, and the process by which actuarial equivalence was determined. The actuary generally also explains the reason(s) for and describes the effect of any material changes in the source(s) of data, assumptions, or methods from the last attestation.

A. Documentation of actuarial equivalence. The actuary normally documents how the plan sponsor's plans and options meet the test of actuarial equivalence to the Medicare program. The following key items are usually documented:

   ❖ The Gross Value Test.

   ❖ The process for determining the average retiree contribution under the sponsor plan(s).

   ❖ The Net Value Test.

15

The above three elements are the key for testing actuarial equivalence. The Gross Value Test and the Net Value Test are the actuarial equivalence tests spelled out in the Act and the regulations. The average retiree contribution under the plan is a key element that will drive results and usually deserves separate analysis.

1. Document the Gross Value of the plan sponsor's program to the total value of the standard Medicare benefit:

    a. Disclose any use of the actual claims experience of the plan sponsor;

    b. Disclose use of normative databases and describe in the assumptions and methods section.

2. Document the retiree contribution rate used under each plan and benefit option. If a rate is an average or a composite of contribution rates, document the development of that average in the assumptions and methods section, along with any commentary on projected enrollment.

3. Document the Net Value of the plan sponsor's benefit to the Net Value of the standard Medicare benefit:

    a. Disclose the assumed Medicare beneficiary contribution rate used;

    b. Disclose whether a supplemental benefit adjustment (i.e., adjustment for higher catastrophic benefit limit due to TrOOP) is used. If so, describe its derivation in the assumptions and methods section.

B. Participant data. A summary of the participant data would typically be provided in enough detail to determine key plans and benefit options. At a minimum, the total number of lives used for testing purposes would normally be provided. Documentation of the number of retirees, surviving spouses, dependent spouses, and other eligible dependents may be desirable if different total cost or contribution rates apply for these members.

C. Summary of plan provisions. Key plan provisions are normally documented for each benefit option within the group health plan. Specifically:

    1. Provisions of the group health plan, which will generally be the same for all benefit options. These provisions will usually include eligibility requirements (for retirees and dependents), a description of copays, coinsurance, benefit maximums, and retiree contributions; and

    2. Provisions of the benefit options within the group health plan. These provisions will normally describe differences among options within a group health plan.

D. Total rates and retiree contributions. Document detailed total costs and retiree contributions by plan and benefit option. The report will usually document both prescription

16

drug costs as well as other medical costs. This documentation will generally provide the source of cost rates (e.g., historical claims experience, exposure data, and the use of any normative data).

E. Actuarial assumptions and methods. This section typically details the methods used to value the plan sponsor's and Medicare's benefit and any assumptions used. The following documentation would usually be considered:

1. Demographic assumptions. Disclose the date of census data and any significant adjustments made.

2. Prescription drug claims cost. Disclose the experience period used to develop claim rates including: discussions of credibility and the use of normative data; the source of the claims and exposure data; and the trend rates used to project the claims to the evaluated plan year. Any plan changes made during the experience period or future changes anticipated for the projection year would also be documented. If the plan sponsor's plan design could be subject to leveraging due to fixed plan provisions, commentary would usually be included as to implicit or explicit assumptions used in the projection.

3. Medicare value. The Medicare value would normally be determined based on the underlying prescription drug costs from No. 2 (above). A description of the development of the value would normally be disclosed, including the method used. Describe any use of continuation tables, normative databases used, and use of seriatim modeling. Key assumptions used in projecting costs to the evaluated year would usually be disclosed. Note that since Medicare's plan design values are all indexed to cost trends, there is generally little or no leveraging due to plan provisions.

4. Allocation of Retiree Contributions. A description of how retiree contributions are allocated between the prescription drug and medical coverages would normally be disclosed.

The actuary's documentation would usually address the reasonableness or appropriateness of the assumptions and methodology used in the actuarial equivalence testing process. The chosen data, assumptions used, and adjustments made would usually be provided. The size and effect of any adjustments would usually be included, as well as a statement to the effect that the adjustments are mutually exclusive and are not being applied more than once. Examples of adjustments are those made because of demographics, plan design changes from historical data, and any other adjustments to actual data.

The actuarial attestation also requires affirmation that the actuary is a member of the American Academy of Actuaries and is qualified to render actuarial opinions that are contained in the report. The attestation report would usually also acknowledge that the information contained in the report is being used to obtain federal funds.

17

IX. Attestation Language

Sample Attestation Language[4]

XYZ, Inc.
Actuarial Equivalence Attestation of Prescription Drug Plan

This analysis has been prepared to demonstrate the actuarial equivalence of the *XYZ, Inc.* prescription drug program with the benefits provided by Medicare Part D. Such demonstration is required by the Medicare program to qualify *XYZ*'s programs for the retiree drug subsidy (RDS) provided under the Medicare Modernization Act of 2003 for plan years beginning Jan. 1, 2006. The certified, electronic attestation has been made on the CMS's Retiree Drug Subsidy Program website.

In conducting our analysis, we have relied on participant data, plan design, and prescription drug claim cost information supplied by *XYZ* and its pharmacy benefit manager. We have accepted the data without audit and have relied upon the sources for the accuracy of the data.

We have not reviewed the other information and data the plan sponsor submitted to CMS in order to qualify for the RDS. Except for the findings described in this report that certain plans are actuarially equivalent to the benefits provided by the Medicare Part D standard benefit, this report does not otherwise substantiate the basis of *XYZ*'s claim for the RDS.

The analysis was developed using generally accepted actuarial principles and practices and is considered to reflect reasonable expectations of anticipated plan experience. This analysis demonstrates actuarial equivalence in compliance with the CMS requirements under 42 CFR 423.884 and is in accordance with applicable laws and regulations. This analysis is not appropriate for any other purpose. The documentation of the methods and assumptions used in the development of the actuarial equivalence has been provided in this report. The actuarial equivalence certification that is associated with this attestation is for the plan year beginning Jan. 1, 2006.

The undersigned is a qualified actuary of *ABC*, a Member of the American Academy of Actuaries {mandatory} and an Associate / Fellow of the Society of Actuaries {if applicable}. I certify that I meet the qualification standards established by the American Academy of Actuaries and have followed the practice standards established periodically by the Actuarial Standards Board. I acknowledge that the information contained in this document is being used to obtain federal funds. All of the sections of the report are considered an integral part of the actuarial opinion.

John Q. Smith
Member, American Academy of Actuaries
Membership Number: xxxxx
Date

1. The American Academy of Actuaries is a national organization formed in 1965 to bring together, in a single entity, actuaries of all specializations within the United States. A major purpose of the Academy is to act as a public information organization for the profession. Academy committees, task forces and work groups regularly prepare testimony and provide information to Congress and senior federal policy-makers, comment on proposed federal and state regulations, and work closely with the National Association of Insurance Commissioners and state officials on issues related to insurance, pensions and other forms of risk financing. The Academy establishes qualification standards for the actuarial profession in the United States and supports two independent boards. The Actuarial Standards Board promulgates standards of practice for the profession, and the Actuarial Board for Counseling and Discipline helps to ensure high standards of professional conduct are met. The Academy also supports the Joint Committee for the Code of Professional Conduct, which develops standards of conduct for the U.S. actuarial profession.

2. *Plan sponsor* is used in this practice note to indicate both employer and union sponsors of prescription drug plans.

3. Note that this section states throughout that the plan sponsor will determine how to define both the plan and benefit options being offered to their retirees for purposes of the retiree drug subsidy application. This is to emphasize that the plan sponsor has the final responsibility for the definition of these two important definitions. The actuary, however, may play an important advisory role in the process because of the actuarial nature of the RDS program. The actuary should be well-versed in the rules to assist in this determination.

4. This sample attestation language is offered solely for educational purposes and is not intended to limit the content of individual actuaries' certifications. The actuary is encouraged to develop appropriate language for each attestation. The application process for requesting the retiree drug subsidy will include an attestation certification that the actuary will be required to sign electronically.

Appendix F
MEASURING RETIREE GROUP BENEFIT OBLIGATIONS

Actuarial Standard of Practice 6, *Measuring Retiree Group Benefit Obligations*, dated December 2001, is reproduced with the permission of the Actuarial Standards Board. Copyright © 2001 Actuarial Standards Board. As the Actuarial Standards Board (ASB) updates and/or supplements actuarial standards of practice (ASOPs) from time to time, the reader should refer to the ASB website (www.actuarialstandardsboard.org) to confirm whether any additions, changes, deletions, or modifications have been made to ASOP No. 6 since December 2001, or whether it has been superseded or supplemented since that time.

ACTUARIAL STANDARDS BOARD

Actuarial Standard
of Practice
No. 6

Measuring Retiree Group Benefit Obligations

Revised Edition

Developed by the
Task Force on Retiree Group Benefits of the
Actuarial Standards Board

Adopted by the
Actuarial Standards Board
December 2001

(Doc. No. 084)

T A B L E   O F   C O N T E N T S

APPENDIXES

March 2001

TO: Members of Actuarial Organizations Governed by the Standards
of Practice of the Actuarial Standards Board and Other Persons
Interested in Measuring Retiree Group Benefit Obligations

FROM: Actuarial Standards Board (ASB)

SUBJ: Actuarial Standard of Practice (ASOP) No. 6

This booklet contains the final version of the revision of ASOP No. 6. The original
title, *Measuring and Allocating Present Values of Retiree Health Care and Death
Benefits*, has been changed to *Measuring Retiree Group Benefit Obligations*. This
standard supersedes Actuarial Compliance Guideline (ACG) No. 3, *For Statement of
Financial Accounting Standards No. 106, Employers' Accounting for Postretirement
Benefits Other Than Pensions*, which has been repealed.

Background

The original ASOP No. 6 was effective October 17, 1988. ACG No. 3 was originally
effective December 1, 1992. During the time these documents were being developed,
the Financial Accounting Standards Board was raising the visibility of financial issues related to retiree group benefits with its development of Statement of Financial
Accounting Standard (SFAS) No. 106, *Employers' Accounting for Postretirement
Benefits Other Than Pensions*. Prior to the issuance of SFAS No. 106, most plan
sponsors provided and accounted for retiree group benefits on a pay-as-you-go basis.
The move to accrual accounting necessitated greater actuarial involvement. ASOP
No. 6 and ACG No. 3 were written with a high level of educational content because
the measurement of retiree group benefit obligations was an emerging practice area
that would be new to many actuaries.

In the 1990s, the ASB adopted standards related to data quality (ASOP No. 23),
credibility procedures (ASOP No. 25), documentation in health benefit plan ratemaking (ASOP No. 31), and the selection of pension assumptions (ASOP Nos. 27
and 35). As provided in this ASOP, these other ASOPs have application to actuaries
measuring retiree group benefit obligations.

Although the measurement of retiree group benefit obligations continues to develop
as an actuarial field within the profession, the ASB believes that practice in this field
has developed sufficiently to permit codification of acceptable current practices in a
revised ASOP No. 6. Thus, in 1999, the ASB convened a special task force of
knowledgeable practitioners in the retiree group benefits field to draft the revision of
this standard. The Task Force on Retiree Group Benefits was charged with (1) updating ASOP No. 6 to provide guidance to actuaries regarding acceptable practices and
to reduce the amount of educational material; (2) determining whether there was a

continuing need for ACG No. 3; and (3) evaluating the applicability to retiree group benefits of ASOPs written since the original adoption of ASOP No. 6.

Key Issues

As discussed in the exposure draft, this standard not only replaces the previous ASOP No. 6, but also supersedes ACG No. 3. In addition, this revised standard represents the following changes from the original ASOP No. 6:

1. This standard uses a model-building approach to the measurement of retiree group benefit obligations, as representative of contemporary practice.

2. The measurement model described in this standard includes the following three key components:

    a. the modeled plan provisions;

    b. the modeled population expected to receive retiree group benefits; and

    c. the model of current and projected benefit costs.

3. The standard requires that each of these three components be appropriately developed so as to sustain the integrity of the measurement. This generally requires the following:

    a. expertise in both the development of health care claims rates and the long-term projection of the covered population; and

    b. exclusion of very simplified methods or assumptions used in modeling complex plans and processes.

4. The standard emphasizes the use of the plan's experience for health care measurements, but allows for the use of appropriately adjusted premium rates or normative claim databases when the plan's experience is not fully credible.

5. The standard requires the actuary(s) issuing the actuarial opinion to take professional responsibility for overall appropriateness of the analysis, assumptions, and results.

6. The standard requires the actuary to use appropriate age bands if the claim rates are expected to vary significantly by age.

7. The standard allows the use of roll-forward measurement techniques to measurement dates that are less than three years after the original measurement date.

8. The standard places increased emphasis on the modeling of participant contributions in retiree group benefit measurements.

9. The standard calls for the application of ASOP Nos. 25, 27, 31, and 35 to the measurement of retiree group benefits.

10. The standard requires the actuary to compare projected claims to recent actual claims.

11. The standard includes guidance on the handling of differences between actual administrative practices and stated plan provisions.

12. The standard places increased emphasis on considering expected changes in plan design and covered population.

13. The standard requires the actuary to consider using different trend assumptions by line of coverage.

Exposure Draft

The exposure draft of this standard was issued in October 2000 with a comment deadline of March 31, 2001. The Task Force on Retiree Group Benefits carefully considered the twenty-two comment letters received. For a summary of the substantive issues contained in these comment letters, please see appendix 3.

The changes since the exposure draft that were incorporated into this standard include the following significant items:

1. The language regarding the appropriateness of the use of premium rates in setting the initial per capita claim rates was changed to allow more flexibility in using this approach, and the material on premium rates in appendix 2 was revised.

2. The requirement to use five-year age bands in the initial per capita health care rate was replaced by a more flexible requirement.

3. The language regarding the actuary's responsibility when actual administrative practices are not consistent with stated plan procedures was clarified to remove any apparent burden on the actuary to audit administrative practices.

4. The effective date of the standard was clarified, especially with respect to roll-forward measurements.

5. Several subsections of section 3 regarding the use of roll-forward techniques and the use of prescribed assumptions, methods, and other model components were moved to different areas of section 3.

The task force thanks all those who commented on the exposure draft. The task force also thanks John Stenson for his assistance during the drafting of this standard.

The ASB voted in December 2001 to adopt this standard.

ACTUARIAL STANDARD OF PRACTICE NO. 6

MEASURING RETIREE GROUP BENEFIT OBLIGATIONS

STANDARD OF PRACTICE

Section 1. Purpose, Scope, Cross References, and Effective Date

1.1 <u>Purpose</u>—This actuarial standard of practice (ASOP) provides guidance to actuaries when measuring obligations under a retiree group benefits plan.

1.2 <u>Scope</u>—This standard applies to actuaries when measuring any type of retiree group benefit obligation. Included in the scope of this standard are measurements made for the following purposes:

a. financial reporting, such as measurements made for purposes of compliance with SFAS No. 106;

b. cash-flow analyses;

c. plan funding, including the determination of participant contributions when such contributions are based on expected retiree group benefit costs;

d. cost projections, including those made in conjunction with establishing or modifying the plan's design; and

e. determinations of actuarial present values.

This standard highlights health and death benefits because they are the most common forms of retiree group benefits. This standard can provide guidance in situations involving other types of benefits, but does not apply to measurements of pension obligations or social insurance programs.

Throughout this standard, any reference to selecting assumptions, selecting a cost allocation policy, or to modeling also includes giving advice on selecting assumptions, selecting a cost allocation policy, or modeling. For instance, the actuary may advise the plan sponsor on selecting assumptions for Statement of Financial Accounting Standards (SFAS) No. 106, but the plan sponsor is ultimately responsible for selecting these assumptions. This standard applies to the actuarial advice given in such situations, within the constraints imposed by the relevant accounting standards.

If applicable law, regulation, or accounting standards contain requirements for a measurement of retiree group benefit obligations that conflict with this standard, the actuary should comply with the requirements of such applicable law, regulation, or accounting standards. Compliance with such applicable law, regulation, or accounting standards is not considered to be a deviation from this standard, provided the actuary discloses that the measurement was performed in compliance with applicable law, regulation, or accounting standards. Most of the current applicable laws, regulations, or accounting standards that may apply to specific measurements of retiree group benefit obligations are listed in appendix 2 under "Compliance with Other Requirements."

1.3 Cross References—When this standard refers to the provisions of other documents, the reference includes the referenced documents as they may be amended or restated in the future, and any successor to them, by whatever name called. If any amended or restated document differs materially from the originally referenced document, the actuary should consider the guidance in this standard to the extent it is applicable and appropriate.

1.4 Effective Date—This standard will be effective for measurements of retiree group benefit obligations with measurement dates on or after January 1, 2003 or, if roll-forward techniques are used, three years after the last full measurement before January 1, 2003.

Section 2. Definitions

The definitions below are defined for use in this actuarial standard of practice.

2.1 Actuarial Cost Method—A procedure for allocating the actuarial present value of future plan costs over time periods.

2.2 Adverse Selection—The actions of plan participants who are motivated directly or indirectly to take financial advantage of plan provisions, such as the choice of plan.

2.3 Contingent Participant—An individual who is not currently a participant but who may reasonably be expected to become a participant through his or her future action.

2.4 Contributions—A payment made by a participant to support a retiree group benefit plan. While plan sponsors and employers will contribute funds to subsidize retiree group benefits, in this standard *contributions* refer to periodic payments required from participants for their plan coverage.

2.5 Cost Allocation Policy—An actuarial cost method combined with defined procedures to account for plan assets (if any) and amortization of changes in plan obligations (such as those arising from plan changes, experience gains and losses, assumption changes, or changes in actuarial cost methods).

2.6 Covered Population—Active and retired participants, participating spouses and surviving spouses of participants who are eligible for benefit coverage under a retiree group benefit plan. The covered population may also include dependents and contingent participants.

2.7 Dedicated Assets—Assets designated by the plan sponsor for the exclusive purpose of satisfying the retiree group benefit obligations.

2.8 Dependents—Individuals, other than spouses, who are covered under a retiree group benefits plan by virtue of their relationship to a participating employee or retiree.

2.9 Measurement Date—The date as of which the retiree group benefit obligation is determined (sometimes referred to as the *valuation date*).

2.10 Measurement Period—The period subsequent to the measurement date during which the chosen assumptions or other model components apply.

2.11 Medicare-Eligible Participant—A participating individual who is entitled to Medicare benefits.

2.12 Medicare Integration—The approach to determining the portion of a Medicare-eligible claim that is paid by the plan, after adjustment for Medicare reimbursements for the same claim. Types of Medicare integration include the following:

    a.   Full Coordination of Benefits (Full COB)—The plan pays the difference between total eligible charges and the Medicare reimbursement amount, or the amount it would have paid in the absence of Medicare, if less.

    b.   Exclusion—The plan applies its normal reimbursement formula to the amount remaining after Medicare reimbursements have been deducted from total eligible charges.

    c.   Carve-Out—The plan applies its normal reimbursement formula to the total eligible charges, then subtracts the amount of Medicare reimbursement.

2.13 Normative Database—Data compiled from sources that are expected to be typical of the retiree group benefit plan, rather than from plan-specific experience. Examples of normative databases include published mortality and disability tables, proprietary premium rate manuals, and experience on similar retiree group benefit plans.

2.14 Participant—An individual who (a) is currently receiving benefit coverage under a retiree group benefit plan, or (b) is reasonably expected to receive benefit coverage under a retiree group benefit plan upon satisfying the plan's eligibility and participation requirements.

2.15 <u>Retiree Group Benefits</u>—Health, death, and other benefits (excluding retirement income benefits) that are provided during retirement to a group of individuals, on account of an employment relationship.

2.16 <u>Spouse</u>—A husband, wife, or domestic partner eligible for retiree group benefits.

2.17 <u>Stop-Loss Coverage</u>—Insurance protection providing reimbursement of all or a portion of claims in excess of a stated amount. Stop-loss coverage may be either individual or aggregate (sometimes referred to as *excess loss coverage*).

2.18 <u>Survivor</u>—A spouse or dependent who continues as a participant under the retiree group benefit plan following the death of a participating employee or retiree.

2.19 <u>Trend</u>—A measure of a rate of change, over time, of the per capita health care rates.

<u>Section 3. Analysis of Issues and Recommended Practices</u>

3.1 <u>General Overview</u>—When measuring retiree group benefit obligations, the actuary should do the following:

   a. develop a model that represents the following:

   1. known plan provisions as they currently exist and as they are anticipated in the measurement period (see section 3.2);

   2. the population covered by the benefits in question, which should reflect the current population and the anticipated population in the measurement period (see section 3.3); and

   3. current and projected benefit costs (see sections 3.4 and 3.5).

   b. evaluate the quality and consistency of data used in construction of the model, and make appropriate adjustments (see section 3.6);

   c. identify any significant administrative inconsistencies and make appropriate adjustments in the model or disclose the unresolved inconsistency (see section 3.7);

   d. select projection assumptions in addition to the assumptions developed as part of step (a) above (see section 3.8);

   e. measure the obligations and, when allocating costs to time periods, use an appropriate cost allocation policy (see section 3.9); and

4

    f.   review and test the results of the calculations (see sections 3.12 and 3.13).

Additionally, the standard contains guidance on using roll-forward techniques (see section 3.10), using prescribed assumptions, methods, or other model components (see section 3.11), and reliance on a collaborating actuary (see section 3.14).

Retiree health cost projections generally can be expected to vary within a large range of reasonableness. Notwithstanding the variability of reasonable results, the actuary should select each element of the model to sustain the integrity of the measurement.

3.2 Modeling Plan Provisions—In modeling the known provisions of the plan, the actuary should give appropriate consideration to the written plan documents, historical practices, administrative practices of the plan sponsor, governmental programs, communications to participants, and, depending on the purpose of the measurement, plan sponsor decisions and expected future benefit plan designs, as described in sections 3.2.1 and 3.2.2 below.

    3.2.1 Components of the Modeled Plan—The actuary should incorporate the significant elements of the known plan provisions into the model. The major components of the modeled plan include, but are not limited to, covered benefits; benefit limitations, exclusions, and cost-sharing provisions; participant contributions; health care delivery system attributes; and optional benefits. In some cases, it may also be appropriate to consider future changes and limits on plan sponsor costs. These considerations are discussed in more detail below.

        a.   Covered Benefits—Covered benefits may include reimbursements for covered services, fixed-dollar payments for covered events (such as death benefits), and other monetary benefits (such as Medicare premiums or defined dollar benefits).

        b.   Benefit Limitations, Exclusions, and Cost-Sharing Provisions—Benefit limitations and exclusions (such as a lifetime maximum benefit in a medical plan) may affect plan payments, and such effects will change over time. The actuary should also consider participant cost-sharing provisions (such as deductibles, copayments, coinsurance, and out-of-pocket limits).

        c.   Participant Contributions—Many plans require contributions from participants as a condition for their continued eligibility for plan coverage. The actuary should reflect the participant contributions in the model, as discussed below. In addition, participant contributions may affect both participation rates and adverse selection, thus affecting per capita claim rates.

5

1. Contribution Formula—In modeling the plan, the actuary should reflect actual contribution levels. There is a wide variation in how plan sponsors determine participant contributions (examples include flat amounts, amounts based on credited service at retirement, amounts based on retiree claims costs, and amounts based on combined active and retiree costs).

2. Contribution Reasonableness—The actuary should compare for reasonableness the stated basis for participant contributions to what has been implemented. See section 3.7, Administrative Inconsistencies, for further guidance.

3. Preretirement Active Employee Contributions—A plan may require preretirement contributions from active employees for them to earn eligibility for retiree group benefits. The actuary should consider how this may affect future benefit eligibility and plan sponsor costs.

4. Contributions as Defined by Limits on Plan Sponsor Costs—Some plans place an upper limit on the plan sponsor cost by designating a maximum average per capita amount to be paid in a year (these limits are commonly known as "caps"). Other plans limit total plan sponsor cost in any current or future period. The actuary should consider whether the limits will have a significant impact on the obligation. The actuary should consider how the plan sponsor is expected to implement these limits, when these limits are expected to be reached, their impact on participant contributions, and, thus, future participation, and, if appropriate, incorporate these limits into the modeled plan.

d. Health Care Delivery System Attributes—The actuary should consider that various health care delivery system attributes can affect costs differently. For example, certain delivery systems may "lock in" costs for an extended period of time because of their provider contracts.

e. Optional Benefits—The actuary should consider the effect of optional benefits. Optional benefits include coverage options (for example, choice of medical plans) and additional coverages (for example, contributory dental coverage). Optional benefits may require participant contributions, but also incur plan sponsor costs.

f. Anticipated Future Changes—After discussion with the plan sponsor, and depending upon the purpose of the measurement, the actuary may take into account future changes that the plan sponsor has represented an intention to implement or that are required by law to be implemented within a specified period. However, for some purposes, such as for compliance with SFAS No. 106, the actuary may consider only changes that have been communicated to plan participants or that result from the continuation of a historical pattern.

3.2.2 <u>Historical Practices</u>—When appropriate, the actuary should consider historical practices of the plan in developing the model. Historical practices include the following:

    a.   Claims Payment Practices—The actuary should consider whether there is significant inconsistency between the benefits provided and the plan sponsor's representation to the actuary of the terms of the plan. See section 3.7 for further guidance.

    b.   Cost-Sharing and Contribution Levels—The actuary should consider the plan sponsor's past pattern of cost-sharing and participant contributions.

    c.   Pattern of Plan Changes—The actuary should consider the plan sponsor's past practice or a pattern of regular changes in the retiree group benefit plan (such as benefits, cost-sharing, and participant contribution levels). Depending on the purpose of the measurement, the continuation of such past practices or patterns may warrant inclusion in the model.

    d.   Governmental Programs—For some purposes, to the extent that the plan integrates with Medicare and other governmental programs, the actuary should consider the historically enacted legislative and administrative policy changes in these programs.

3.2.3 <u>Reviewing the Modeled Plan</u>—For each measurement, the actuary should consider whether the model continues to reflect actual known plan provisions and practices. If the administration of the plan has significantly deviated from the plan as modeled, the actuary should consider whether this deviation is temporary or should be treated as a permanent plan change.

3.2.4 <u>Measurement Results by Category</u>—The actuary should consider whether the measurement results may need to be examined by category (for example, medical vs. dental, union vs. nonunion, retiree vs. spouse; plan paid vs. participant paid; payments before Medicare eligibility age vs. payments after Medicare eligibility age). This need may arise from either the nature of the assignment or from assessing the integrity of the measurement model.

3.3 Modeling the Covered Population—The projected size and demographic composition of the covered population has a significant impact on the measurement. The actuary should consider the need to model variations in the covered population (for example, when benefit eligibility varies by type of coverage). This standard does not require the use of open group measurements, although such measurements may be used when appropriate. These issues are discussed below.

    3.3.1 Census Data—The actuary should collect sufficient census data in order to make a reasonable estimate of the obligation. In certain circumstances, grouped data may be appropriate; in others, individual census data are required. For example, to ascertain the optional benefits elected by the retiree, the actuary may need to collect individual census data, including retiree contribution amounts.

    3.3.2 Employees Currently Not Accruing Benefits—Depending on the purpose of the measurement, the actuary should consider whether some or all of the employees currently not accruing service toward retiree group benefit eligibility may accrue service in the future and whether some or all of the employees currently not making required preretirement contributions may contribute in the future, and make appropriate allowance for them in the modeled population.

    3.3.3 Contingent Participants—The actuary should examine the census data and take appropriate measures to reflect individuals who are not current participants, but may reasonably be expected to become participants through their future actions. For example, the actuary may need to make a reentry assumption in situations where retirees have opted out of coverage at the time of retirement, but may later reenter the plan.

    3.3.4 Spouses and Survivors of Participants—The actuary should include in the modeled population participating spouses and survivors who are eligible for coverage. In doing so, the actuary should take into account that the plan's eligibility conditions and benefit levels for spouses and survivors may differ from the plan's eligibility conditions and benefit levels for retirees. Benefit coverage for the spouse of a retiree may continue subject to a contribution, continue for a limited period (for example, until Medicare eligibility or one year after the death of the retiree), or cease when the retiree dies. The actuary should generally model spouses separately from retirees because of differences in the timing of Medicare eligibility and in mortality between the retiree and spouse.

    3.3.5 Dependents—The actuary should consider whether the dependent obligation is significant and, if so, model dependents appropriately. For example, for plans that have liberal early retirement eligibility conditions, dependent coverage can significantly increase the overall number of

8

covered individuals and, therefore, have a significant effect on the size of the covered population.

3.3.6 <u>Appropriateness of Pension Plan Data</u>—Plan sponsors who do not maintain separate retiree group benefit plan databases may furnish pension plan data to represent the retiree group benefit plan covered population. In such cases, the actuary should make appropriate edits and adjustments. Examples of the types of edits and adjustments that may be required are discussed below.

a. Retirees Covered for Retiree Group Benefits but Not Receiving Pension Benefits—Employees may be participants in the retiree group benefits plan, but may no longer be participants in the pension plan (such as employees who received lump-sum pension payments). Spouses, dependents, and survivors of retirees may be eligible for retiree group benefits, but may not be in the pension plan census data.

b. Retirees Receiving Pension Benefits but Not Covered for Retiree Group Benefits—Employees may be participants in the pension plan, but may not be covered for retiree group benefits (such as employees who terminated with vested pension benefits now in payment status). Employees may be eligible for pension benefits upon retirement or disability, but may not satisfy the eligibility conditions or may have waived coverage for retiree group benefits.

c. Provisions Affecting Certain Employees—The pension plan may be frozen for a certain group of employees or may exclude employees due to age or service eligibility requirements, which might not affect their eligibility for other retiree group benefits.

3.3.7 <u>Use of Grouping</u>—The actuary may use grouping techniques when, in the actuary's judgment, grouping is not expected to unreasonably affect the measurement results. One such technique is to group participants based on common demographic characteristics (for example, age and service), where the obligation for each participant in the group is expected to be similar for commonly grouped individuals.

Another technique is to group plans with similar expected costs and features. A plan sponsor with multiple plan designs (for example, through various collective bargaining agreements) may not require separate measurement for each individual plan. Under such circumstances, the actuary, after evaluating the eligibility conditions and range of benefits provided, may decide it is appropriate to combine plans that have similar expected costs and group the covered populations of those plans. The actuary should disclose such combining of plans and grouping of populations.

9

3.4 <u>Modeling Initial Per Capita Health Care Rates</u>—The actuary should develop assumed per capita health care rates to be the basis of the initial annual benefit costs for estimating the future health care obligations. The accuracy of the measurement model depends in large part on its ability to forecast annual claims costs for the plan. In the actuarial development of health care rates, plan experience is generally considered the best predictor of future claims experience, preferable to sole reliance on normative claims databases or other measures. Therefore, preferred methods involve development of annual per capita health care rates from the claim experience of the retiree group benefit plan. In the absence of credible retiree group benefit plan experience data, the actuary may use other methods (such as methods that use premium rates and normative claims databases) to develop the per capita rates.

The ratemaking process generally involves (a) quantifying aggregate claims costs; (b) quantifying a measure of exposure to risk, usually the count of participants who were eligible for the plan during the period the claims were incurred; and (c) applying other information such as normative databases and premium rates as appropriate.

Multiple initial per capita health care rates may be appropriate due to the modeling of known plan provisions (section 3.2) and covered population (section 3.3) as well as claims experience (for example, different rates by gender, healthy vs. disabled, retirees vs. spouses or dependents).

The actuary should document the methods and procedures followed in developing the initial per capita health care rates, such that another actuary qualified in this practice area could assess the reasonableness of the initial per capita health care rates. The actuary should also document any significant actuarial judgments applied during the modeling process. ASOP No. 31, *Documentation in Health Benefit Plan Ratemaking*, provides relevant guidance to the actuary.

The sections that follow address aspects of ratemaking that are particularly important when projecting benefit costs for a long period. The actuary should consider the following elements, but is not required to include all these elements in the model.

3.4.1 <u>Net Aggregate Claims Data</u>—In most cases, the actuary's objective is the development of a net incurred claims rate. The actuary should, however, recognize the factors involved in distinguishing net claims from gross claims and incurred claims from paid claims, as discussed below.

a. Paid Claims—Aggregate claims data received by the actuary will usually be grouped by the dates of payment, not by the dates on which claims were incurred. The actuary should analyze the data for the likely difference between the level of paid claims for a period and the level of incurred claims for the same period. When the differences are significant, the actuary should make an adjustment, either to the historical paid claims or to the initial claims assumption, to account for the likely future level of claims activity. To the extent the difference may be due to the trend or the time value of money, the significance of the difference to the measurement of retiree group benefit obligations may be reduced, because the plan sponsor will usually have the use of the money between the time a claim is incurred and when it is paid.

b. Gross Claim Components—Aggregate claims data received by the actuary may show only net payments or may include cost-sharing components (such as deductibles and copayments), reimbursements, costs not covered, or other elements of gross claims. The actuary may determine the initial claims rate assumption from the net payments or the gross amounts.

3.4.2 Exposure Data—In developing an initial per capita health care rate, the actuary should obtain exposure data for the same time periods as the claims experience data that will be used. Since exposure data are historical in nature, the exposure data typically will be different from the census data used in modeling the future covered population. If the differences are significant, the actuary should review the data sets for consistency (see section 3.6).

It may be appropriate to segment the exposure data by age and gender or by retiree, spouse, or dependent. The actuary should obtain information to properly segment the population or employ reasonable assumptions as appropriate.

3.4.3 Use of Multiple Claims Experience Periods—The actuary should consider the use of multiple claims experience periods and adjust the experience of the various periods to comparable bases as described in sections 3.4.8, 3.4.10, and 3.4.11. When combining multiple experience periods, the actuary should consider the applicability of each period based upon elapsed time and changes required to adjust to comparable bases.

The actuary may consider smoothing the results to account for historical irregularities. The actuary may weight the experience periods as appropriate.

3.4.4 Credibility—There will be times when plan data are not available or wholly credible. In those instances, the actuary should make use of relevant normative databases or active plan experience on the same group, adjusted for age and expected differences in such items as utilization and plan design. The actuary may use these supplementary data and professional judgment to validate, adjust, or replace the plan experience data.

11

ASOP No. 25, *Credibility Procedures Applicable to Accident and Health, Group Term Life, and Property/Casualty Coverages*, provides guidance to the actuary when assigning credibility to sets of experience data.

3.4.5 Use of Premium Rates—Although an analysis of the plan sponsor's actual claims experience is preferable, the actuary may use premium rates as the basis for initial per capita health care rates, with appropriate analysis and adjustment for the premium rate basis. The actuary who uses premium rates for this purpose should adjust them for changes in benefit levels, covered population, or program administration. The actuary should consider that the actual cost of health insurance varies by age (see section 3.4.7), but the premium rates paid by the plan sponsor may not. For example, the actuary may use a single unadjusted premium rate applicable to both active employees and non-Medicare-eligible retirees if the actuary has determined that the insurer would offer the same premium rate if only non-Medicare-eligible retirees were covered.

If, in the actuary's professional judgment, the unadjusted premium rate significantly understates or overstates the expected claim cost for retirees, the actuary should disclose this possibility in any communication regarding a measurement using an unadjusted premium rate as an initial per capita health care rate.

If premium rates, adjusted or unadjusted, are used as the basis for initial per capita rates in the measurement, the actuary should make an appropriate disclosure and consider the factors described in other sections of 3.4.

3.4.6 Impact of Medicare and Other Offsets—Where Medicare as the primary payer has a significant impact on the per capita health care rates, the actuary should develop separate rates for Medicare-eligible participants. Such rates should reflect the plan's Medicare integration approach or how the plan supplements Medicare. The actuary should also adjust for other offsets, such as workers' compensation and auto insurance, if their impact is considered to be significant.

The actuary should consider whether there is a significant inconsistency between the Medicare integration approach being applied by the claims administrator and the plan sponsor's representation to the actuary of the terms of the plan. See section 3.7 for further guidance.

Medicare and other governmental programs are subject to continual legislative revisions. The actuary should be aware of significant changes and make adjustments as necessary to fit the purposes of the measurement.

3.4.7 Age-Specific Claims Rates—The actuary should consider the variation in rates by age for the benefits being modeled and use appropriate age bands if the rates vary significantly. The age bands should not be overly broad, based on the expected rate variations within the bands. If rates vary significantly by age, it is inappropriate to assume a single per capita rate that does not vary by age. The relationship between the rates at various ages is an actuarial assumption that may be based on normative databases.

3.4.8 Adjustment for Plan Design Changes—The actuary should adjust the claims rates to reflect significant differences, if any, between the benefit plan designs in effect for the experience period and those in effect during the initial year of the measurement period.

3.4.9 Adjustment for Administrative Practices—Changes in plan administrative practices affect how costs emerge. The actuary should make appropriate provisions in the model for changes in administrative matters such as the following:

    a. Claims Adjudication—The actuary should consider how overall costs and utilization rates may be influenced by the method by which enrollees and providers submit claims (for example, provider electronic submission vs. enrollee paper submission of claims) and the manner in which claims are reviewed.

    b. Enrollment Practices—The actuary should consider the effect enrollment practices (for example, the ability of participants to drop in and out of the plan) have had on participation and health care costs.

3.4.10 Adjustment for Large Individual Claims—The actuary should recognize the significance that large claims may have with respect to claims experience and make appropriate adjustments. The actuary should review the frequency and size of large claims when data are available and consider whether the prevalence of large claims is expected to be significantly different in the future. Future periods may have a higher or lower incidence of such claims than past experience periods under examination. The actuary should review both stop-loss coverage and other large claims, as described below.

    a. Stop-Loss Coverage—The actuary should consider the financial impact of stop-loss insurance in all projections.

    b. Other Large Claims—The actuary should also consider large claims that may be below the stop-loss coverage level.

13

3.4.11 <u>Adjustment for Trend</u>—When adjusting earlier claim period experience to the initial year of the measurement, the actuary should reflect the effect of past trend. An adjustment of the initial per capita health care rate to reflect recent past trends may include experience from outside the plan.

The actuary should consider using separate historical trend rates for major cost components (for example, hospital, physician, drug costs, and plan administration).

3.4.12 <u>Adjustment When Plan Sponsor is Also a Provider</u>—The retiree group benefits plan sponsor may also be a provider under the plan, as may happen in cases where the plan sponsor is a hospital, medical office, clinic, or other health care provider. In these situations, the plan sponsor pays itself, in effect, for services it provides its own members. Therefore, the actuary should analyze the charges incurred and reimbursements received by the plan sponsor-provider and make appropriate adjustments in the measurement model to properly reflect the underlying transactions.

3.4.13 <u>Use of Other Modeling Techniques</u>—Health care costs may be modeled and projected using techniques in addition to those mentioned above. When using an alternative approach, the actuary should disclose the method used and comment on its applicability. Examples of alternative approaches include models that project a distribution of expected claims with an associated probability distribution and models that assign different claims costs for the last year of life.

3.4.14 <u>Administrative Expenses</u>—In addition to the cost of claims, the plan sponsor is usually responsible for the cost of administering the retiree group benefit plan. The actuary should consider administrative expenses when performing the measurement. The actuary may model administrative expenses in various ways. For example, administrative expenses may be included in claims rates or expressed on a per capita basis, as a percentage of claims, or as fixed amounts.

3.5 <u>Modeling the Cost of Death Benefits</u>—Death benefits may be provided directly by the plan sponsor upon the death of a retiree or may be paid by an insurance company through a life insurance program. The life insurance program may be either participating or nonparticipating with respect to policy dividends. The modeled death benefit cost should appropriately reflect the financial arrangement through which the benefits are provided, including dividends, retiree contributions, carrier administrative expenses, and risk charges.

When selecting assumptions and measurement methods regarding death benefits, the actuary should consider that the actual cost of life insurance varies by age, but the insurance rates paid by the plan sponsor may not. The actuary should reflect appropriate costs by age in the projection model.

3.6 Model Consistency and Data Quality—Before proceeding with the measurement, the actuary should review the modeled plan provisions, covered population, per capita health care rates, and death benefit costs as a whole to evaluate their consistency. The actuary should evaluate the relevancy of any data received and the significance of all data used for actuarial purposes. ASOP No. 23, *Data Quality*, provides guidance on selecting and reviewing data and making appropriate disclosures regarding the data. Additional data quality requirements that are particularly applicable to the retiree group benefit area are mentioned below.

3.6.1 Coverage and Classification Data—The actuary should consider the importance of coverage distinctions (such as HMO vs. indemnity plans) and classification distinctions (such as hourly vs. salaried, or benefits that vary among different groups of retirees) that result in variations in the benefit availability among participants. The actuary should consider whether such differences are significant enough to require further refinement of the model. The actuary should document the coverage and classification distinctions incorporated in the model.

3.6.2 Consistency—If the actuary finds data elements that appear to be significantly inconsistent with known plan provisions, other data elements, or data used for prior measurements, the actuary should take appropriate steps to address such apparent inconsistencies before proceeding with the measurement, as discussed below. To the extent that significant inconsistencies cannot be reconciled, the actuary should disclose them.

a. Plan Operations—The actuary should determine whether eligibility and payment data received conflict significantly with information received about known plan provisions or administration. See section 3.7 for further guidance. Examples of inconsistencies include the following:

1. Average claims costs that are secondary to Medicare are very high in relation to average costs that are primary. This might reveal that the carve-out method of integration with Medicare may not have been used, despite the sponsor's indication of that method, or that the classification of the covered spouse is based on the retiree's age.

2. Individual contribution amounts for participation before Medicare eligibility are so low as to make it unlikely that plan sponsor subsidies are as limited as the sponsor may indicate.

3. The ratio of spouses to retirees in total or for a subgroup (for instance, those who are not eligible for Medicare) is inconsistent with expectations. This might mean that it is unlikely sur-

viving spouse coverage is as stated, that coding of spouse ages is inaccurate, or that survivors were coded as "retirees."

4. Known plan provisions include benefit maximums, but the actuary's analysis of claims data indicates a likelihood that claims are in excess of the maximum.

b. Medicare-Related Data—Data concerning Medicare eligibility and age may be inaccurately and inconsistently coded for both claims and covered population. The actuary should make and document any appropriate adjustments in this regard.

c. Demographic Distinctions—The actuary should consider demographic breakdowns (such as age, gender, geography, and hourly/salaried classifications), which may reveal results that are inconsistent with prior data or the actuary's prior expectations.

d. Data for Spouses, Survivors, and Dependents—The actuary should scrutinize coverage and classification information for spouses and survivors and, if significant, for dependents, with as much care as for employees and retirees due to the significant impact they may have on the results of the measurement.

3.6.3 <u>Sources of Data</u>—The actuary should consider the various types and sources of data available for the covered population, for the coverage and classification of participants, and for benefit costs, as discussed below.

a. Census Data—In most cases, the plan sponsor or administrator will supply the eligibility and demographic information about participants in the plan. A participant census used for underwriting or pension purposes may contain useful information about the covered population. The actuary should determine whether these sources represent plan participation with sufficient accuracy (see sections 3.3.6 and 3.4.2) and, if not, seek more accurate census information.

b. Claims Payment Data—Various sources of data are available for establishing per capita rates, including normative claims databases and experience data specific to the plan sponsor. The actuary should review plan experience relative to normative ranges of value, but also recognize the legitimacy of plan sponsor experience, to the extent it is credible, and the limitations of applying normative data to an unrelated situation. ASOP No. 25 provides guidance in the assignment of credibility values to data.

    c.   Data Quality at Each Level of Usage—Data that may be of appropriate quality for determination of certain assumptions within a model may not be of appropriate quality for determination of other assumptions. When data are combined or separated, the actuary should review the data for suitability to the purpose. For example, data from an individual employer may be sufficient for setting an aggregate per capita health care rate, but not be of sufficient size to set per capita health care rates by location.

3.6.4   Reliance on Data Supplied by Others—ASOP No. 23 provides guidance regarding the use, review, and disclosure of reliance on data supplied by others.

3.7 Administrative Inconsistencies—In the course of performing the measurement, the actuary may find that the plan is being administered in a manner that is inconsistent with the plan documents, stated plan sponsor policies, or participant communications. Inconsistencies most often arise with respect to participant contribution determination (see section 3.2.1(c)(2)), claims payment practices (see section 3.2.2(a)), Medicare integration (see section 3.4.6), and plan operations (see section 3.6.2(a)). When the actuary becomes aware of a significant inconsistency between administrative practice and plan documents, stated plan sponsor policies, or participant communications, the actuary should do the following:

    a.   discuss the inconsistency with the plan sponsor or administrator;

    b.   adjust the model appropriately, consistent with the purposes of the measurement (in making these adjustments, the actuary may rely on the plan sponsor's representations);

    c.   document the resulting steps taken by the actuary in developing the model; and

    d.   disclose any significant unresolved inconsistency.

3.8 Projection Assumptions—In selecting projection assumptions, the actuary should consider the following:

3.8.1   Economic Assumptions—With respect to any particular measurement, each economic assumption selected by the actuary should be consistent with every other economic assumption selected by the actuary to be used over the measurement period. The actuary should reflect the same general economic inflation component in each of the economic assumptions selected by the actuary. The relationships among economic assumptions should be reasonable relative to the underlying economic conditions expected throughout the projection period.

The actuary should comply with the guidance contained in ASOP No. 27, *Selection of Economic Assumptions for Measuring Pension Obligations*, when selecting the inflation assumption, discount rate, investment return assumption, and compensation scale (when needed for benefits such as life insurance) to be used in measuring retiree group benefit obligations. In applying ASOP No. 27, the actuary should take into account the purpose and nature of the measurement, and the differences between the characteristics of retiree group benefit obligations and the characteristics of pension benefit obligations. For example, the discount rate selected for measuring pension benefit obligations for purposes of SFAS No. 87 (*Employers' Accounting for Pensions*) may not be appropriate for measuring retiree group benefit obligations for the purposes of SFAS No. 106, because the payment patterns may be different.

Economic assumptions not covered by ASOP No. 27 that are typically required for measuring retiree group benefit obligations include the following:

a. Health Care Cost Trend Rate—The health care cost trend rate reflects the change in per capita health claims rates over time due to factors such as medical inflation, utilization, plan design, and technology improvements. The actuary should consider separate trend rates for major cost components such as hospital, prescription drugs, other medical services, Medicare integration, and administrative expenses. Even if the actuary develops one aggregate trend rate, the actuary should consider these cost components when developing the rate. The actuary should consider the following key components in setting the health care cost trend rate: inflation, medical inflation, definition of covered charges, frequency of services, leveraging caused by plan design features not explicitly modeled, and plan participation. The actuary should not consider aging of the covered population when selecting the trend assumption for projecting future costs.

b. Other Cost Change Rates—The actuary should consider other costs that may change in the future, such as the cost of life insurance and long-term care insurance.

c. Participant Contribution Changes—Depending on the modeled plan, the measurement may require an assumption for the rate of change in participant contributions. For some plans, this may be a function of health care trend rate or other economic assumptions. For some other plans, there may be no contributions currently but plan limits and assumed trend rates may make it likely that contributions will be required in future years. In those cases, and depending upon the purposes of the measurement, the actuary should determine when contributions are expected to be required during the measurement period, and model subsequent increases accordingly.

    d.   Adverse Selection and Changing Participation—When a retiree group benefits plan requires a contribution as a condition of continued participation, those choosing to participate may have a higher average benefit cost than those not participating. When a retiree group benefits program requires a contribution or offers a choice of plans, it can be expected that, over time, the process of adverse selection will have an impact on plan costs.

The actuary should consider whether adverse selection will result from such items as decreasing participation. Because the impact of any adverse selection is very difficult to quantify over the long periods customary in a retiree group benefits measurement, this standard does not require the use of assumptions about adverse selection in measurement models. But if the measurement assumptions project a significant decrease in the proportion of eligible retirees who participate, the actuary should consider an upward adjustment for adverse selection in per capita health care rates, or, alternatively, moderate the assumed decrease in participants. The actuary should document any adjustments made for adverse selection.

3.8.2   <u>Demographic Assumptions</u>—With respect to any particular measurement, each demographic assumption the actuary selects should be consistent with the other demographic assumptions the actuary selects. For example, if the mortality assumption anticipates increasing life spans, the actuary should consider whether the retirement assumption should reflect the fact that individuals may choose to retire later because they are healthier or because they may not have sufficient accumulated savings to afford a lengthened retirement period.

The actuary should comply with ASOP No. 35, *Selection of Demographic and Other Noneconomic Assumptions for Measuring Pension Obligations*, when selecting the retirement, termination, mortality, and disability assumptions to be used in measuring retiree group benefit obligations. In applying ASOP No. 35, the actuary should take into account the purpose and nature of the measurement and the differences between the characteristics of retiree group benefit obligations and the characteristics of pension benefit obligations. More refined demographic assumptions may be required to appropriately measure retiree group benefit obligations than are required to measure pension obligations. In determining whether demographic assumptions developed primarily for pension benefit measurements are appropriate for retiree group benefit measurements, the actuary should consider the following:

a. Assumptions Based on Pension-Liability-Weighted Experience—Pension plan termination and retirement rates may have been developed based on pension-liability-weighted experience, which will reduce the effect of participants terminating or retiring with smaller pension benefits. The actuary should determine whether the pension plan termination and retirement assumptions are appropriate for retiree group benefit plans and, if not, modify the assumptions appropriately.

b. Disability—Assumptions regarding disability incidence, recovery, mortality, and eligibility for Social Security disability benefits should be consistent with the coverage provided to disabled participants under the plan. When the actuary considers disabled life coverage significant to the measurement, the actuary should select assumptions that appropriately reflect when benefits are payable to disabled participants, the definition of disability, and how the benefits are coordinated with other programs.

c. Retirement—The retirement assumption is critical in retiree health plan measurements because of the higher level of primary coverage a retiree receives prior to becoming eligible for Medicare. The actuary should select explicit age-related retirement rates. A single average retirement age is generally not appropriate.

d. Mortality—When the per capita health care rates are expected to increase during the projection period, the results of the measurement may be sensitive to the mortality assumption. Because of this sensitivity and the observation that life expectancies have increased significantly over the recent past, the actuary should consider reflecting future mortality improvements. Pension benefit measurements may use unisex mortality tables. Use of gender-specific mortality tables, however, may be more appropriate for retiree group benefit measurements, depending on the levels of retiree, spouse, and surviving spouse benefits as well as the demographic composition of the covered population.

3.8.3 Coverage Assumptions—In addition to covering eligible retirees, many plans also cover the spouse and dependents of retirees. Also, plans may offer some or all participants a choice of coverages such as HMOs, PPOs, and POS plans. The magnitude of the retiree group benefit obligation can vary significantly as a result of the coverage assumption. The actuary should therefore consider historical participation rates and trends in coverage rates when selecting the coverage assumptions.

a. Plan Participation—For plans that require some form of contribution to maintain coverage, some eligible individuals may not elect to be covered, particularly if they have other coverage available. Empirical data on plan participation, where available and credible, should be considered when selecting the participation assumption for future retirees. When developing the participation rates, the actuary should consider how plan eligibility rules, plan choices, or retiree contribution rates have changed over time. Furthermore, plan participation may be different in the future due to participants' response to changes in retiree contribution levels and plan choices (for example, Medicare+Choice). For plans that anticipate changes in retiree contributions the actuary should consider the appropriateness of participation rates that vary over the projection period for both current and future retirees. The actuary should consider plan eligibility rules governing dropping coverage and subsequent reenrollment when selecting participation rates.

b. Spouse and Dependent Coverage—The actuary should consider who is eligible for coverage under the plan and make appropriate assumptions regarding the coverage of spouses and dependents. The actuary should also consider the impact of plan rules governing changes in coverage after retirement, such as remarriage, if significant. The actuary should review historical data on spouse and dependent coverage rates when selecting the assumption to be used in the projection. If the gender mix of future retirees and retired plan participants differs, the actuary should consider developing separate spouse coverage rates for males and females.

c. Spouse and Dependent Age—Wherever practical, the actuary should use actual data for the age of the spouse and dependents of retired participants. If actual data is not available for all retired participants the actuary should review the empirical data and develop an appropriate assumption for the spouse age difference and dependents' ages. The spouse and dependents of an active employee today may not be the same spouse and dependents covered at retirement, therefore the actuary should generally select an assumed spouse age difference for purposes of projecting future spouse coverage and assumed dependents' ages for projecting dependent coverage.

3.8.4 Effect of Plan Changes on Assumptions—When selecting projection assumptions, the actuary should consider the impact of relevant plan design changes during the measurement period. Whenever a plan design change is being modeled, the actuary should consider whether or not assumptions, which in combination are appropriate for measuring overall plan costs, are also appropriate for valuing the element under study. For example, if a plan sponsor adds or advises the actuary of its intent to add HMO coverage for a portion of its retiree group, the actuary should consider how that affects the cost of current coverage, future cost trends, and participation (including changes in coverage between plans).

21

Assumptions selected for purposes of estimating short-term cost increases or decreases arising from a plan change may not be appropriate for developing the long-term cost implications. For example, a change to the contribution level may change participation in the plan, which may, in turn, have an impact on per capita health care rates due to adverse selection after the change. A change in benefits or cost-sharing may have a similar impact for a plan requiring participant contributions. The actuary should exercise professional judgment about the impact on long-term assumptions, but this standard does not require explicit assumptions about changing participation rates or adverse selection.

Many plan sponsors have reserved the right to unilaterally change or terminate their retiree welfare plans. When appropriate for the purpose of the measurement, the actuary may include assumptions in the measurement model that attempt to quantify the probability that the current plan will change significantly in the future, beyond the changes already included in the modeled plan. For example, the actuary might assume a probability of plan termination or assume a discount rate with an additional risk premium that implicitly reflects the participants' financial risk in receiving benefit coverage that is not guaranteed. The actuary should disclose that such an assumption has been used. Such assumptions are not appropriate for all measurement purposes. For example, SFAS No. 106 requires that the actuary assume that the substantive plan will continue indefinitely.

3.8.5 <u>Assumptions Considered Individually and in Relation to Other Assumptions</u>—The actuary should consider the reasonableness of each actuarial assumption independently on the basis of its own merits and its consistency with the other assumptions selected by the actuary. When selecting assumptions, the actuary should consider the degree of uncertainty, the potential for fluctuation, and the consequences of such fluctuation.

3.8.6 <u>Reviewing Assumptions</u>—The actuary is not required to do a complete assumption study at each measurement date. However, at each measurement date the actuary should consider whether the selected assumptions continue to be reasonable. If the actuary determines that one or more of the previously selected assumptions are no longer reasonable, the actuary should select reasonable new assumptions in accordance with this section.

3.8.7 <u>Changes in Assumptions</u>—Whenever a change in an assumption is considered, the actuary should review other assumptions to assess whether they remain consistent with the changed assumption. For example, if the actuary is anticipating more disabled participants due to recent experience, consideration should be given to the impact on plan costs of the health risk of this group.

3.9 Selecting a Cost Allocation Policy—When the measurement involves the allocation of an obligation to different time periods (including measurements that take into account plan assets, plan amendments, or actuarial gains and losses), the actuary should select a cost allocation policy, based on the following considerations:

    3.9.1 Criteria for Acceptable Actuarial Cost Methods—The actuary should select an actuarial cost method that meets the following requirements:

        a.   Limits on Allocation Period—The period over which the allocation is made for an active participant should begin no earlier than the date of employment and should not extend beyond the last assumed retirement age. This period may be determined for each participant individually or for the active participant group as a whole.

        b.   Reasonableness of Allocation Basis—The allocation basis should be reasonable and produce an orderly allocation of the actuarial present value of future plan benefit costs.

    3.9.2 Dedicated Assets—In measuring the unfunded obligation and allocating costs to time periods, the actuary should take into account dedicated plan assets, if any.

        a.   The actuary should collect data regarding the amounts and types of dedicated assets held.

        b.   In general, the actuary should value the dedicated assets using a method that takes into account market value, unless constrained to use an asset valuation method prescribed by law or regulation. Asset valuation methods include market value; market-related methods that smooth out the effects of short-term volatility in market value; and methods that discount the future cash flow of the underlying investments. The use of book or cost value may be prescribed for some specific purposes (for example, in determining tax on trust income under Section 512 of the Internal Revenue Code).

        c.   The actuary should obtain sufficient details regarding insurance policies held as dedicated assets to determine an appropriate value, reflecting the nature of the contractual obligations upon early termination of the policies, as well as the costs of continued maintenance of the policies. If the cash surrender value of the policies is not readily determinable, the actuary should rely on his or her professional judgment to develop an appropriate value, depending on the purpose of the measurement.

3.9.3 <u>Amortization Methods</u>—Unless already reflected in the actuarial cost method, the actuary should select a reasonable and systematic amortization method to recognize changes in plan obligations arising from plan amendments (including plan initiation), actuarial gains and losses, changes in assumptions, or changes in the actuarial cost method.

3.9.4 <u>Cash Flow Adequacy</u>—Absent regulatory or legal restrictions, where a cost allocation policy is used to determine funding requirements, the actuary should select a policy that accumulates assets such that, absent experience losses, adequate funds are on hand to pay benefits included in the measurement when due.

Notwithstanding the above criteria, the actuary may be required to use a prescribed cost allocation policy for a particular purpose (for example, for financial reporting purposes under SFAS No. 106 the actuary is required to use the Projected Unit Credit Cost Method and a defined approach to recognize changes in obligation arising from plan amendments and actuarial gains or losses (see section 3.11)).

3.10 <u>Use of Roll-Forward Techniques</u>—The actuary may determine that it is appropriate to use prior measurement results, using a roll-forward technique, rather than conduct a new measurement.

3.10.1 <u>Full and Partial Roll-Forward</u>—Roll-forward techniques include full roll-forwards of both claims and census data, as well as partial roll-forward techniques. For example, the actuary may use partial roll-forward techniques that use health care claim rates developed for the prior measurement trended forward to the current measurement date coupled with updated census data.

3.10.2 <u>Limitation</u>—The actuary may use roll-forward techniques to reduce the frequency of full measurements. In general, the actuary should not rely on prior measurement results if the measurement date is three or more years earlier than the current measurement date. For example, a January 1, 2000 measurement could be used to develop roll-forward results as of January 1, 2001 and 2002, but should not be relied upon for measurements or cost allocations after December 31 , 2002.

3.10.3 <u>Appropriateness</u>—Generally, the actuary should not use full roll-forward techniques when the population, plan design, or other key model component has changed significantly since the last full measurement.

3.10.4 <u>Disclosure</u>—Whenever the actuary uses a roll-forward technique, the actuary should disclose such use in the actuarial communication.

3.11 Prescribed Assumptions, Cost Allocation Policies, or Other Model Components—When the actuary uses assumptions, cost allocation policies, or other model components prescribed by the plan sponsor or other binding authority, the actuary's communication should state the source of the prescribed elements. Examples are the initial per capita health care rates prescribed by the plan sponsor and the discount rate basis and cost allocation policy prescribed by SFAS No. 106.

3.12 Reasonableness of Results—The actuary should review the measurement results for reasonableness. For example, the actuary could compare the overall measurement results to benchmarks such as measurement of similar plans, or could review the results for sample participants for reasonableness.

　　3.12.1 Modeled Cash Flows Compared to Recent Experience—The actuary should compare the expected claims produced by the model for the first year from the measurement date to actual claims over a recent period of years. If the expected and actual claims are significantly different, the actuary should consider the likely causes of such differences (for example, cost trends, large claims, a change in the demographics of the group, or the volatility of experience in small plans), and consider the impact of those differences on the reasonableness of the measurement results.

　　3.12.2 Results Compared to Last Measurement—The actuary should compare the overall results to the last measurement's results when available and applicable. If the results are significantly different from results the actuary expected based on the last measurement, the actuary should consider the likely causes of such differences. If another actuary performed the prior measurement, some allowance may be made for differences due to different actuarial techniques or modeling. The actuary should, if practicable, review the prior actuary's documentation and, if necessary, seek further information.

3.13 Sensitivity of Results to Chosen Assumptions—There can be a broad range of reasonable results when measuring the present value of retiree health benefit obligations because projected benefit payments are often uncertain and based on assumptions about future claims. The combination of different present value factors applied to projected future benefit payments produces wide variations in present values. For example, if a 1% change in the discount rate produces a 20% change in the present value, and a 20% change in initial per capita health care rates produces a 20% change in present value, then changing both assumptions could produce a 44% change in the present value, or a 4% change.

In light of the sensitivity of the results to key assumptions, the actuary should consider the purpose of the measurement and use professional judgment when advising the plan sponsor and presenting present values. In some instances the actuary may develop alternative results using a range of reasonable assumptions.

3.14 Reliance on a Collaborating Actuary—The various elements of a retiree group benefit measurement require expertise in the two different actuarial fields of health data analysis and long-term projections. In recognition of the complexities involved, two or more actuaries with complementary qualifications in the health and pension practice areas may collaborate on a project. While each actuary may concentrate on his or her area of expertise during the project, the actuary (or actuaries) issuing the actuarial opinion must take professional responsibility for the overall appropriateness of the analysis, assumptions, and results.

Section 4. Communications and Disclosures

4.1 Documentation—The actuary should maintain appropriate documentation regarding the analysis of the known plan provisions, covered population, and claims and expenses, as well as documenting the measurement model and the use of the model output. Documentation should demonstrate how the actuary has met the requirements of sections 3.2–3.14 above. The methodology and assumptions used in the measurement should be documented and, in some cases, made available for disclosure. In particular, ASOP No. 31 provides guidance on documenting the work of section 3.4 and 3.6–3.8 as applied to ratemaking.

4.2 Disclosure—The actuary's communication of the results of the measurement should identify the data, assumptions, and methods used in the measurement with sufficient clarity that another actuary qualified in this practice area could make an objective appraisal of the reasonableness of the actuary's work. In particular, this standard calls for disclosure of the following:
   a. information about known significant plan provisions, including anticipated future changes (section 3.2.1(f)), any combining of plans (section 3.3.7) for measurement purposes, and a description of any known significant plan provisions not reflected in the model;

   b. significant information about the covered population;

   c. the initial per capita health care rate assumptions (including the use of normative data or premium rates), assumed future trends, and all other significant projection assumptions;

   d. significant modeling techniques and methods, such as those mentioned in sections 3.4.12, 3.4.13, 3.8.4, and 3.10;

   e. identification, including the source, of any assumptions, methods, or other model components prescribed by the plan sponsor or other binding authority;

f.   significant and unresolved inconsistencies in data or administration, such as those mentioned in sections 3.6 and 3.7; and

g.   information significant to interpreting measurement results.

To the extent the disclosures identified above have been described in a previous actuarial communication available to the intended audience, such disclosures, if appropriate for the circumstances, may be incorporated by reference.

4.3   Prescribed Statement of Actuarial Opinion—This ASOP does not require a pre-scribed statement of actuarial opinion (PSAO) as described in the *Qualification Standards for Prescribed Statements of Actuarial Opinion* promulgated by the American Academy of Actuaries. However, law, regulation, or accounting re-quirements may also apply to an actuarial communication prepared under this standard, and as a result, such actuarial communication may be a PSAO.

4.4   Deviation from Standard—An actuary must be prepared to justify the use of any procedures that depart materially from those set forth in this standard and must include, in any actuarial communication disclosing the results of the procedures, an appropriate statement with respect to the nature, rationale, and effect of such departures.

Note: The following appendixes are provided for informational purposes, but are not part of the standard of practice.

Appendix 1

Background and Current Practices

Background

Actuarial Standard of Practice (ASOP) No. 6, originally titled *Measuring and Allocating Actuarial Present Values of Retiree Health Care and Death Benefits*, was adopted by the ASB in October 1988. Because measuring retiree health and death benefits was a new and emerging field and because it would become a new practice area for many actuaries, this standard was needed to provide guidelines regarding what was acceptable actuarial practice. The original ASOP No. 6, however, purposely provided a high degree of flexibility to allow for emerging understanding in this developing practice area.

In December 1990, the Financial Accounting Standards Board issued Statement of Financial Accounting Standards (SFAS) No. 106, *Employers' Accounting for Postretirement Benefits Other Than Pensions*. SFAS No. 106 generally requires plan sponsors to recognize the cost of providing retiree group benefits over an employee's service period. Before the implementation of SFAS No. 106, most plan sponsors accounted for retiree group benefits on a pay-as-you-go basis. Therefore, at the time SFAS No. 106 was implemented, few actuaries had any experience measuring retiree group benefit obligations and practices for performing such measurements were not consistent.

Actuarial Compliance Guideline No. 3, *For Statement of Financial Accounting Standards No. 106, Employers' Accounting for Postretirement Benefits Other Than Pensions,* was adopted in October 1992. ACG No. 3 was written with a great level of detail and with a high level of educational content for the same reasons as ASOP No. 6.

Since the adoption of ASOP No. 6, ACG No. 3, and SFAS No. 106, both the design of retiree group benefits and the actuarial practices for measuring retiree group benefit obligations have evolved. Faced with the recognition of large unfunded liabilities for retiree health care benefits, many plan sponsors have taken steps to reduce their retiree group benefit obligations. Often, this has meant introducing or increasing participant contributions (including placing fixed dollar limits on the average plan sponsor obligation per person, with the balance to be paid by participant contributions). Participant contributions have not always been implemented consistent with the plan sponsor's objectives. For example, participant contributions may, in practice, have been set based on combined active and retiree claims, resulting in "hidden" plan sponsor subsidies (see "Participant Contributions" in appendix 2 for more detail).

Other types of plan design changes intended to reduce plan sponsor obligations include restricting eligibility for plan benefits (including requiring preretirement contributions), reducing annual or lifetime benefit limits, and changing the way the plan integrates with Medicare. But here again, actual plan operation may not be fully consistent with the plan sponsor's intent. For example, the claims payer may not have the data or systems necessary to implement lifetime limits on plan benefits.

The actuary may be in the best position to identify such discrepancies between the plan sponsor's stated intent and actual plan operation. Often the plan sponsor has divided internal responsibility for administration of the retiree group benefit plan between different departments. The actuary may be the only person to have seen data elements and plan provisions as a whole. Plan sponsor policy may not have considered subsequent changes in future eligibility, cost levels, medical practice, health care delivery systems, or other plan elements that have a significant effect on financial obligations. Written provisions regarding aspects of dependent coverage, contribution levels required from participants, and integration with Medicare may be absent. As a result, data that the actuary receives may conflict significantly with information received about known plan provisions or administration.

Current Practices

Actuarial practices for measuring retiree group benefit obligations have evolved since SFAS No. 106 was implemented. As noted above, actuaries have recognized the importance of evaluating information about plan operations (including actual participant contribution levels, participation rates, and retiree claims data) as well as plan documents and plan sponsor policies to resolve any inconsistencies. As a result of the trend toward greater retiree cost-sharing, the modeling of participant contributions has become increasingly important. This includes appropriately reflecting the effect of increased participant contributions on plan participation and per capita health claims rates of those electing to participate.

Measuring retiree group benefit obligations generally requires expertise in both the development and projection of health care claims rates and the long-term projection of the covered population. Therefore, it is common for two actuaries with complementary qualifications (such as a pension actuary and a health care actuary) to collaborate on a measurement. In some cases, it may not be clear which actuary has taken professional responsibility for the overall appropriateness of the analysis, assumptions, and results.

The models used to value retiree health care benefit obligations have become increasingly sophisticated. Models commonly use age-specific initial per capita health care rates within the retired population (for example in individual age brackets). Some of these models are based on net incurred claims, while other models are based on gross expenses incurred reduced by amounts paid outside the plan or not covered by the plan. Some models project a distribution of expected claims with an associated probability distribution, while other models use separate age-specific per capita claim rates for the last year of life and for survivors.

Despite the development of these more sophisticated approaches, some actuaries continue to use highly simplified models. Examples include using pension census data as the basis for the measurement, using only two initial per capita health care rates (for Medicare eligible participants and for participants who are not yet eligible for Medicare), and developing initial per capita health care rates based solely on premiums or normative databases. Such simplified approaches may result in significantly understated or overstated retiree group benefit obligations for the following reasons:

1. Retiree group benefit eligibility requirements are often different from pension benefit eligibility requirements, so pension census data may not appropriately reflect retiree group benefit plan participation;

2. Significant discrepancies between the plan sponsor's stated policy and actual plan operation may not be identified and "hidden" subsidies may not be valued;

3. Normative databases may be applied inappropriately, or may be outdated;

4. The effects of aging of the retired population on future per capita claim rates may not be appropriately taken into account; or

5. The impact of expected future participant contribution increases on future participation and projected per capita claim rates of participants may not be appropriately reflected.

Appendix 2

Supplementary Information

Normative Databases

In the absence of credible plan experience, a normative database can provide support for assumptions about the probability of future events or likely relationships between variables. Examples of normative databases include published mortality and disability tables, proprietary rate manuals, and experience on similar retiree group benefit plans. However, normative databases also have limitations, including the following:

1. normative databases lose relevancy over time;

2. a normative database may not be appropriate for the particular situation at hand; and

3. many normative databases have not been subject to rigorous development and review.

Measurements Using Premium Rates

A premium is the price charged by a risk-bearing entity, such as an insurance or managed care company, to provide risk coverage. The premium usually has a basis in the expected value of future costs, but the premium will also be affected by other considerations, such as marketing and profit goals, competition, and legal restrictions. Because of these other considerations, a premium for a coverage period is not the same as the expected cost for the coverage period.

The demographics of the group for which the premium was intended may be different from the demographics of the group being valued. When these two groups are different, the premiums are unlikely to reflect the expected health care costs for the group being valued, even if it is a subset of the total group for which the premium was determined. In particular, the expected value of future costs for a group of retirees is unlikely to be the same as for a group consisting of actives and the same retirees. Examples of this are shown in the "Participant Contributions" section below.

This standard notes numerous ways the demographics of two groups can differ, but a difference that is quite likely to have an effect on rates is a difference in average age, or age distributions, of two groups. This, of course, is particularly likely to occur when one group contains retirees and active employees while a second group consists only of retirees. But differences can also be significant within a group made up entirely of retirees, even retirees who are all eligible for Medicare. When a rate applies over a broad age range, it may misrepresent the average cost at applicable ages much older or younger than the central age of the range to which the rate applies.

Consequently, many actuaries use a separate initial per capita health care rate assumption for each age within a range where there are wide variations, such as rates that differ for every age from 60 to 75 or from 55 to 80. (This also may have an effect on costs in future years and is addressed again below in the "Health Care Trend Rate" section.)

The term "premium rate" is used for both insured group plans and self-insured group plans. In the case of self-insured plans, the "premium rates" may also be referred to as "budget rates" or "phantom premiums." Future changes in insured premiums are frequently affected by the experience of the insured group. When they are not directly affected by the experience of any one group, but rather by experience of a community of groups, the plans are referred to as "community-rated." Further comments about these common types of retiree group benefit plan premiums follow:

1. Self-Insured Premiums—Some self-insured plans have expenditures that the plan sponsor refers to as "premium rates." These rates may reflect the experience of retirees, active employees, or both. Also, the rates may reflect only expected claims experience, or may include other adjustments (such as administrative expenses and stop-loss claims and premiums). Furthermore, the rates may reflect the effect of the plan sponsor's contribution or managed care strategy.

2. Community-Rated Premiums—In some regulatory jurisdictions, community-rated premium rates are required by statute for some fully insured plans. There is variation in the structure of community-rated premium rates. For example, retirees not eligible for Medicare may be included with active employees in a community-rated premium category, while retirees eligible for Medicare may be included in a separate community-rated premium category. There are also different community-rating methodologies, some incorporating group-specific characteristics. Note that a community-rated premium including both retirees not eligible for Medicare and active employees probably understates the expected claim cost for the retirees alone. If the insurer appears to be committed to continuing such subsidy for the retirees, there is some justification for valuing future retiree costs for the postretirement plan sponsor with the community rate as the basis, although the plan sponsor may want to know of the apparent subsidy and the possibility that it might not be available in the future. There is also some justification for valuing future retiree costs with the higher expected claim cost for retirees as the basis, since the subsidy may disappear.

3. Other Fully Insured Plans—In addition to community-rated plans, there are other types of fully insured plans and there can be some variation in how actual plan experience affects the premiums. The same comments mentioned above for self-insured premiums apply here.

Health Care Trend Rate

The health care trend rate reflects the change in per capita health claims cost over time. The trend rate may differ by major cost components such as hospital, prescription drugs, other medical services, Medicare offsets, and administrative expenses. The health care trend rate is affected by the following interdependent factors:

1. Inflation—General economic inflation defined as price changes over the whole economy.

2. Medical Inflation—Changes in the per-unit prices of medical supplies and services covered by the plan.

3. Covered Charges—The definition of charges that are covered by the plan will determine how inflation and medical inflation affect per capita health care claims cost. For example, if the plan pays benefits based on a fixed schedule of benefits, the cost of services is controlled by the plan's schedule. If the services on the schedule and the dollar amounts are not changed, the underlying cost inflation of the plan will be zero.

4. Utilization of Services—This factor considers the change in frequency of health care by type of services over time, as well as the nature of services due to changes in medical practice and technology.

5. Leveraging Caused by Plan Design Features—The net plan cost under health plan designs with fixed-dollar cost-sharing will increase faster than the total costs. For example, for a prescription drug costing $50 today and a plan design with a $20 copay per prescription, a 20% increase in the cost of the drug (from $50–$60) will increase the net plan cost by 33%, from $30 ($50–$20) to $40 ($60–$20).

6. Aging—The aging of the covered population may have contributed to historical health care cost changes. The use of age-graded per capita health care rates for projecting future health care costs removes this aging component from the future trend assumption.

7. Participation—If a lower percentage of eligible individuals elect coverage (for example, because of increasing participant contribution rates or competing plans such as HMOs), per capita health care claims costs may increase due to adverse selection.

Interaction Between Trend and Plan Provisions

Plan provisions and health care trend rates in combination impact the projected net per capita health care rates. Examples of the interaction of plan provisions and health care trend rates include the following:

33

1. Covered charges can be affected by limits on allowable provider fees and the plan's Medicare integration approach. Benefit plan provisions may help in identifying these limits, as well as what services are covered.

2. Health plan deductibles may or may not be set at a fixed-dollar amount. Health care trend will, over time, erode the relative value of a fixed-dollar deductible.

3. Coinsurance payments may be expressed as a percentage or fixed-dollar amount. Again, over time, trend will erode the relative value of a fixed-dollar coinsurance.

4. The Medicare program provides coverage for most U.S. retirees over age 65; however, the retiree group benefits plan may cover a different mix of services than Medicare. Trend rates may differ between Medicare-covered services and the retiree group benefit.

5. Other payments or offsets may exist, such as subrogation recoveries or plans other than Medicare. These payments or offsets may change in the future.

6. Lifetime and other maximum dollar limits also affect claims costs, and the effect can change over time.

Participant Contributions

Participant contributions are very important to the financial understanding of how retiree health plans work. Plan sponsors must advise participants and plan administrators as to the specific dollar amounts of currently required contributions. Plan sponsors usually have administrative policies for determining future contributions (formulas, subsidy limits, or overall contribution philosophy). Based on the required contributions, an individual will decide whether to participate, which may result in adverse selection.

Formulas, subsidy limits, and the contribution philosophy of the plan sponsor are subject to different interpretations about what data and techniques are to be used in deriving the current monthly contribution used in the measurements of retiree group benefit obligations. Here are two examples:

1. The plan sponsor's stated policy is that retirees who are not yet Medicare eligible will contribute 50% of the cost of their health care benefits. However, the plan sponsor determines a retiree contribution of $100 per month ($1,200 per year) based on average annual per capita health care claims of $2,400 for active employees and pre-Medicare retirees combined. When the actuary evaluates the claims experience of pre-Medicare retirees separately from that of the active employees, the actuary determines that the average annual claim per retiree is $4,000. So the plan sponsor subsidy is really $2,800 or 70%, not the stated 50%.

2. A "defined dollar benefit" plan sponsor will pay $2,000 annually toward retiree health care coverage for retirees who are not Medicare eligible. The plan sponsor determines an annual retiree contribution of $500 based on average per capita claims of $2,500 for active employees and pre-Medicare retirees combined. However, when the actuary evaluates the claims experience for pre-Medicare retirees, the average annual claims per retiree is determined to be $4,500. The actual plan sponsor subsidy is $4,000 ($4,500 average claims per retiree less $500 retiree contribution)—double the "defined dollar benefit" of $2,000.

Once the contribution is determined for the current year, future increases can then be incorporated into the model. The contribution increase assumption is often a function of the claims trend assumption. If the model assumes contributions increase at the same trend as assumed for age-specific claims rates, the projected contributions will not have a constant relationship to projected claims, due to the aging of the population.

Some plans impose conditions such that contributions will begin a certain pattern at some triggering point in the future. This can happen in a number of ways, but the most common may be the use of "cost caps," where the sponsor has limited its subsidy to an annual amount per capita that has not yet been reached. Participant contributions may or may not be required currently, but after the cap is reached participant contributions are to absorb all the additional costs. After the caps have been reached, this design is akin to the defined dollar approach, but before that point, the plan sponsor's costs will increase. The assumptions about future health care trend rates (interacting with the cost caps) will increase projected costs to a time when the caps are reached, and thereafter participant contributions will increase.

Finally, participation rates may be lower when contributions are required. Assumptions about lower participation rates can vary by small amounts and yet result in large differences in present values. Furthermore, lower participation may result in adverse selection on the part of participants. The combination of lower participation and adverse selection assumptions may or may not be significant in a measurement model.

Assets

Retiree group benefits are generally not subject to minimum funding requirements; however, a number of plan sponsors have, for various reasons, accumulated assets dedicated to fund the retiree group benefits. These assets provide some measure of financial security for the participants and reduce the plan sponsor's unfunded obligation, thereby reducing the future funding needs.

1. Dedicated Assets—Certain assets set aside to provide for the plan sponsor's modeled benefit may partially or completely offset the retiree group benefit obligation. Examples include the following:

    a.   whole life insurance policies held by the plan sponsor to cover some of the plan sponsor's retiree death benefits;

    b.   welfare benefit trusts (for example, VEBAs in the U.S.); and

    c.   section 401(h) accounts in a qualified pension plan in the U.S.

2.   <u>Non-Dedicated Assets</u>—Several plan sponsors have purchased life insurance policies (so called corporate-owned life insurance or COLI policies) with the intent that the proceeds of the policies will "fund" emerging retiree welfare benefits. Even though these policies may have been "earmarked" for funding retiree group benefits, they remain corporate assets and are not taken into account in measuring the plan sponsor's unfunded obligations.

<u>Compliance with Other Requirements</u>

The following provide guidance for the measurement of retiree group benefit obligations performed for specific purposes. The list represents rulemaking bodies and specific references as of the publication date of this standard, and is not intended to be exhaustive.

1.   Financial Accounting Standards Board (FASB)—Accounting for financial statements for companies that comply with U.S. generally accepted accounting principles (GAAP). Current standards applicable to retiree group benefits include SFAS Nos. 88, 106, 132, and 135.

2.   American Institute of Certified Public Accountants (AICPA)—The AICPA provides audit and accounting guidelines for its members. Current guidelines include the AICPA Audit and Accounting Guide, *Audits of Employee Benefit Plans,* and Statements of Position (SOP) 01-2, *Accounting and Reporting by Health and Welfare Plans*, and 94-6, *Disclosure of Certain Significant Risks and Uncertainties.*

3.   U.S. Internal Revenue Code (IRC)—Various sections of the IRC govern the funding of retiree group benefits, including sections 401(h), 404, 419, 419A, 420, and 512, and the regulations and other rulings that interpret the code.

4.   Cost Accounting Standards Board (CASB)—The CASB is responsible for developing accounting standards for U.S. government contracting. Current applicable standards are CAS 412, 413, 416, and the proposed CAS 419.

5.   Federal Acquisition Regulations (FAR)—The FAR are regulations governing the acceptability of costs for U.S. government contracts. FAR 31.205-6 provides guidance for retiree group benefit costs.

6. Government Accounting Standards Board (GASB)—The GASB promulgates accounting standards for state and municipal governments. GASB 26 provides rules for disclosure of retiree group benefit obligations.

7. National Association of Insurance Commissioners (NAIC)—The NAIC provides model regulations for insurance company accounting that individual states may use directly or modify for their particular circumstances. The NAIC has issued Statement of Statutory Accounting Principles No. 14 that addresses rules for insurance companies with retiree group benefits.

8. International Accounting Standards Committee (IASC)—The IASC issues international accounting standards that each country's accounting profession may use as its GAAP. IAS 19 provides guidelines for retiree group benefit plans.

Appendix 3

Comments on the Exposure Draft and Task Force Responses

The exposure draft of this actuarial standard of practice was issued in October 2000, with a comment deadline of March 31, 2001. (Copies of the exposure draft are available from the ASB office.) Twenty-two comment letters were received. The Task Force on Retiree Group Benefits of the ASB carefully considered all comments received. Summarized below are the significant issues and questions contained in the comment letters and the task force's responses.

GENERAL COMMENTS	
Comment	Some commentators requested the reorganization of various sections and appendixes.
Response	The task force incorporated some suggestions into the standard. Other suggestions were inconsistent with ASB standard format and thus not implemented.
Comment	Several commentators suggested slight changes to the wording in nearly all sections of the standard.
Response	The task force implemented such suggestions if they enhanced clarity and did not alter the intent of the section.
Comment	Some commentators requested language to deal with specific SFAS No. 106 or SOP 92-6 accounting issues.
Response	The task force directs all readers to the accounting profession for clarification of specific accounting issues.
TRANSMITTAL MEMORANDUM	
In the transmittal memorandum of the exposure draft, the task force solicited comments on the key issues contained in the draft. These comments and the task force's responses to them have been incorporated in the applicable sections below.	
Comment	Some commentators requested that ACG No. 3 not be replaced by this revision due to the perceived need for the material pertaining specifically to SFAS No. 106 that is not retained in this revision.
Response	The ASB's current policy is to avoid publishing as a standard any material that is largely educational in nature, such as ACG No. 3. Educational material is included where appropriate in the appendixes. The task force understands the commentators' concern and wants to encourage the further development of educational material related to all aspects of retiree group benefits; however, we agreed with the ASB that such material should not be codified as a professional standard.

SECTION 1. PURPOSE, SCOPE, CROSS REFERENCES, AND EFFECTIVE DATE	
Section 1.2, Scope	
Comment	One commentator asked whether plan design projects should be included in the standard's scope.
Response	The task force recognizes that not all plan design projects involve the measurement of obligations; those that do would be within the scope of this standard. Therefore, the task force modified section 1.2(d) to expand that part of the definitions to explicitly include plan design projects that are cost-based.

Section 1.4, Effective Date	
Comment	One commentator requested a later effective date; other commentators pointed to the need to clarify the effective date language.
Response	The task force clarified the language regarding the effective date of the standard; however, the primary effective date was not changed.
SECTION 2. DEFINITIONS	
Section 2.1, Actuarial Cost Method	
Comment	One commentator suggested the deletion of the "more than one" phrase.
Response	The task force agreed and modified the definition accordingly.
Section 2.2, Adverse Selection (previously titled "Antiselection")	
Comment	One commentator suggested that "Antiselection" was a misnomer and that it be replaced with "Adverse Selection."
Response	The task force agreed and modified the name.
Section 2.7, Dedicated Assets (previously section 2.4)	
Comment	One commentator stated that the definition should be expanded to include assets held in trust.
Response	The task force modified the definition to broaden the scope.
Section 2.11, Medicare-Eligible Participant (previously section 2.8)	
Comment	One commentator thought this definition had extraneous wording.
Response	The task force agreed and removed the extraneous wording.

Section 2.12, Medicare Integration (previously section 2.9)	
Comment	Two commentators suggested that Medicare Supplement Plans be included in this definition.
Response	The task force agreed that Medicare Supplement Plans are prevalent; however, these plans are a supplement to Medicare and do not integrate with Medicare.

Section 2.14, Participant (previously section 2.11)	
Comment	Several commentators suggested that the definition of participant was too broad.
Response	The task force agreed and modified the definition. The task force also added a sentence to section 3.3 to clarify that open group measurements are permitted but not required.

Section 2.15, Retiree Group Benefits (previously section 2.12)	
Comment	Two commentators suggested changes to this definition. One was concerned that the definition was not clear that death benefits paid from a retirement income plan are not retiree group benefits.
Response	The task force believed that the definition was sufficiently clear and made no modifications.
Comment	One commentator questioned whether a plan is a retiree group benefits plan if all it provides is that participants are allowed to self-pay for coverage from their retirement date until Medicare eligibility.
Response	The task force intended such a plan to be a retiree group benefits plan, covered broadly in the definition, and did not believe a change in the definition was needed to convey that intent.

Section 2.19, Trend (previously section 2.16)	
Comment	Several commentators were concerned that the definition did not exclude aging or age-related morbidity.
Response	The task force chose not to narrow the definition, although it recognizes that "trend" can be defined to include or exclude age-related morbidity. The task force shares the commentators' concern that demographic changes due to the changing makeup of a population should not be included in a trend factor used to project the future cost when age-specific rates are being projected. Section 3.8.1(a) states that for the purposes of projection assumptions, trend should not include the effects of aging. For the purposes of determining the initial per capita health care rate from claim experience (section 3.4), however, the effect of aging in past trend is difficult to separate from other factors. The task force did not believe this standard should mandate the use of age-specific trend factors in analyzing past experience.

SECTION 3. ANALYSIS OF ISSUES AND RECOMMENDED PRACTICES	
Section 3.2.1, Components of the Modeled Plan	
Comment	One commentator thought the list of major plan provisions should be expanded. Another thought that the list should not be included and that the actuary should determine the major plan provisions. A third commentator was concerned that the section contradicted the SFAS No. 106 requirement that no assumption with regard to future changes in government programs be made.
Response	The task force did not intend for the list to be all-inclusive; however, the task force believed that these are the minimum components that should always be modeled. In regard to the third commentator's concerns, the task force refers the commentator to section 3.2.1(f).
Comment	One commentator was concerned that section 3.2.1(a) required that a "gross claim" model be used.
Response	The task force modified the wording to remove such a requirement.
Comment	With respect to section 3.2.1(b), one commentator suggested that the standard should provide more discussion pertaining to the modeling of lifetime maximums.
Response	The task force believes that this is not a practice area where appropriate guidance has emerged.
Comment	One commentator expressed concern that section 3.2.1(c)(2) required the actuary to act as the auditor.
Response	The task force agreed and modified the section heading and wording accordingly.
Comment	With respect to section 3.2.1(c)(4), one commentator expressed concern about requiring the actuary to determine the year the limit is reached and the implications of reaching it.
Response	The task force disagreed with the commentator on the necessity of knowing when the limit will be reached. Such information is crucial to appropriately determining the obligation associated with such a cap. The task force, however, did agree that the "implications" wording was not clear and removed this language.
Comment	One commentator suggested that section 3.2.1(c)(5) be deleted since participation rates are covered in section 3.8.3(a).
Response	The task force agreed that participation rates are more appropriately addressed in the later section and deleted the paragraph.

Comment	With respect to section 3.2.1(f), two commentators stated that SFAS No. 106 allows for recognition of changes other than those that have been communicated.
Response	The task force agreed and modified the wording of this section to include changes that are the result of the continuation of a historical pattern.

Section 3.2.2, Historical Practices

Comment	One commentator thought that section 3.2.2(a) was too onerous and that the actuary needs to establish only "a reasonable level of comfort" that the benefits provided are consistent with major plan provisions. The task force agreed and modified the language.
Response	
Comment	With respect to section 3.2.2(c), one commentator stated, "[I] do not believe it is the actuary's responsibility to determine whether a past practice or a pattern of regular changes indicates a commitment by the plan sponsor to make future changes to the plan."
Response	The task force agreed that the actuary should not be responsible for determining the plan sponsor's "commitment." The actuary, however, may include the continuation of such past practices in the model.
Comment	One commentator thought that section 3.2.2(d) did not belong in the "Historical Practices" section.
Response	The task force believed that the language on "Government Programs" was appropriately placed in the "Historical Practices" section, but it clarified the language.

Section 3.3, Modeling the Covered Population

Comment	Several commentators noted that no mention was made of open group valuations, while others were concerned that the standard required the use of open group valuations.
Response	The task force revised the text to indicate that while the standard does not require the use of open group measurements, they may be used when appropriate.
Comment	A commentator suggested that the term "covered population" be included in the set of definitions.
Response	The task force agreed and added a definition.

Section 3.3.2, Employees Currently Not Accruing Benefits	
Comment	One commentator suggested section 3.3.2 be clarified to distinguish between employees who are not accruing service and never expected to do so, and those who, while not currently accruing service, are expected to do so in the future.
Response	The task force agreed and modified the language.

Section 3.3.3, Contingent Participants	
Comment	One commentator questioned the need to develop reentry assumptions when measuring contingent participants. The commentator suggested that the actuary should determine if any significant obligation exists and only when this is so should the obligation be reflected in the measurement. Otherwise, the actuary should disclose that reentry possibilities were left out of the measurement.
Response	The task force modified the language to clarify that appropriate measures should be taken when individuals may reasonably be expected to become participants. The task force believes that additional disclosures on this element of the model are not needed.

Section 3.3.4, Spouses and Survivors of Participants (previously titled "Spouses and Surviving Spouses of Participants")	
Comment	One commentator expressed concern about including spouses in the modeled population, when, based on the commentator's experience, these data often are not available.
Response	While the task force understands that complete information on spouses may not be available for all measurements, the importance of the spousal obligation to the measurement requires that the actuary model spouses and surviving spouses in the covered population. The task force believes the current language is sufficiently broad to allow the actuary to use both empirical data, where available, supplemented by reasonable assumptions where necessary.

Section 3.3.5, Dependents	
Comment	Several commentators found this section confusing.
Response	The task force redrafted the section to clarify the intent.

Section 3.3.6, Appropriateness of Pension Plan Data	
Comment	Several commentators suggested alternative language and additional examples of edits and adjustments to pension plan data to represent the retiree group plan covered population.
Response	The task force considered these suggestions and incorporated them in the revised text.

Section 3.3.7, Use of Grouping	
Comment	One commentator raised a concern about the requirement to disclose the use of grouping, which the commentator did not see as standard practice. Another commentator was concerned that the requirement to disclose the use of grouping techniques may be interpreted to imply that some imprecision results from grouping.
Response	The task force incorporated suggested text changes to clarify that grouping techniques may be appropriate when, in the actuary's judgment, this is not expected to unreasonably affect the measurement results.

Section 3.4, Modeling Initial Per Capita Health Care Rates	
Comment	One commentator suggested that the initial paragraph of section 3.4 include the word "credible" before "plan experience" in the third sentence.
Response	The task force made no change since it believes the last sentence of the paragraph appropriately addresses the issue of credibility.
Comment	Two commentators requested guidance on the use of plan experience for small plans. One commentator remarked that even if detailed claim information were available for small plans, it generally would not be credible.
Response	The task force did not revise the standard to address small plans specifically, but did expand the discussion of premium rates in appendix 2. The task force also notes that while plan experience for a small plan may not be fully credible, that does not mean the plan experience has no credibility. ASOP No. 25 is recommended for guidance in regards to assigning credibility to experience data.
Comment	One commentator noted that ASOP No. 31 also had relevance to ratemaking aspects of sections of the standard other than section 3.4.
Response	The task force agreed and modified that reference accordingly.
Comment	The task force received several comments regarding the development of the initial per capita health care rate and the actuary's responsibility to document that development.
Response	The task force addresses those comments below in relation to section 4.1. The task force believes development of per capita claim rates for measuring retiree health benefit obligations should be subject to a ratemaking process, whether the purpose is cost projections, financial reporting, or other actuarial work within the scope of this standard. The task force also notes that ASOP No. 31 is not a standard on ratemaking, but rather provides "guidance on documentation in the process of health benefit plan ratemaking."

Comment	One commentator suggested that the standard address situations where another person or organization gives the actuary the rates.
Response	The task force believes the standard addresses this by noting the handling of premium rates in section 3.4.5 and reliance on a collaborating actuary in section 3.12. The development of initial per capita health care rates for measuring retiree health obligations is an actuarial responsibility. Others will furnish information during the measurement process and tasks in the development process may be delegated to non-actuaries, but the professional judgment of an actuary is necessary in determining the initial per capita health care rates (section 3.4) and ensuring its consistency with the rest of the model (sections 3.6 and 3.12).
Comment	One commentator suggested that gender be added to the list of elements the actuary should consider. Another commented that spouse rates and disabled rates should be considered.
Response	The task force expanded the third paragraph to indicate examples of when multiple rates may be appropriate. The task force also notes that section 3.4.2 mentions gender.
Comment	One commentator suggested the section include material on expenses.
Response	The task force made no changes, noting that the first sentence mentions benefit costs rather than claim costs, and section 3.4.14 covers administrative costs.
Comment	One commentator disagreed that the second paragraph of section 3.4 outlined a process generally used, citing the use of actual-to-expected studies.
Response	The task force believes the standard accommodates other methods, which would include the use of normative databases and actual-to-expected studies, when plan experience is not sufficiently credible. The task force is aware there may be differences of opinion as to when, and to what extent, plan experience should be tempered with normative data. The task force believes this should be left to the actuary's judgment but that there should be a bias towards plan experience. Appendix 2 notes some of the limitations of normative databases. The second paragraph of section 3.4 was intended to outline the process, however, and not establish a requirement, so the task force deleted "the actuary should follow" from the opening sentence in this paragraph. Similarly, other wording in the first two paragraphs was modified to clarify the preference for credible historical plan claims experience and the use of alternative methods.

Section 3.4.1, Net Aggregate Claims Data	
Comment	Two commentators questioned whether the last sentence of section 3.4.1(a) implied that differences between paid claims and incurred claims for the same time period were always insignificant or that factors of trend and discount always offset each other.
Response	The task force believes the full paragraph adequately addresses the likely significance of the differences. The task force also recognizes that, while the usual objective of claims analysis is the development of an incurred rate, a valuation of future paid claims may be valid, since determination of the present value of long-term obligations is based on the principles of discounted cash flow. The standard guides the actuary reviewing past aggregate claims to acknowledge differences in paid and incurred claims, as well as the effects of trend and the time value of money, and make adjustments to enhance the ability to forecast likely future claims levels.
Comment	One commentator suggested the first sentence of section 3.4.1(b) was not clear.
Response	The task force clarified the language.
Comment	One commentator suggested that, "To the extent that net claims are used, the actuary should consider the effect of their use on other assumptions, (e.g., trend assumption)."
Response	The task force agrees that the actuary should consider the effect of trend assumption and other assumptions, regardless of whether the initial per capita health care rate is based on net or gross claims. The task force believes the issue is addressed in section 3.8, particularly in section 3.8.1(a), which mentions leveraging caused by plan design features that are not explicitly modeled.
Section 3.4.2, Exposure Data	
Comment	Three commentators suggested the need to compare exposure data and the census even though they are not expected to match exactly.
Response	The task force agreed and modified the language accordingly.
Section 3.4.3, Use of Multiple Claims Experience Periods	
Comment	Three commentators noted that more recent experience is not always more reliable.
Response	The task force agreed and modified the language accordingly.

Section 3.4.4, Credibility	
Comment	One commentator suggested that credibility adjustments should include those for differences in plan design.
Response	The task force agreed and modified the language accordingly.

Section 3.4.5, Use of Premium Rates	
Comment	One commentator noted that the second sentence of the section did not add clarifying value to the section.
Response	The task force agreed and combined the important elements of the sentence with the initial sentence.
Comment	One commentator suggested that section 3.4.5 pertain only to self-insured plans and that fully insured plans need not be subject to this section, particularly if they consist solely of reimbursing insurance premiums.
Response	The task force believes there is consensus among actuaries performing retiree group benefit measurements about the almost universal need for adjustments when using premiums as the basis for projected future cost, regardless of whether the plan is fully insured or self-insured. The "Measurements Using Premium Rates" section of Appendix 2 provides additional comments on this issue.
Comment	The same commentator suggested that the impact of aging is often effectively included in the trend rates.
Response	The task force believes that the future impact of aging on health care costs of a given population of actives and retirees does not have a strong enough correlation to trend to be effectively included in the trend assumption. The standard requires a separation of the impacts of age and trend through the use of age-specific per capita claims rates (see section 3.4.7).
Comment	Several comments were received about the second paragraph concerning community rates.
Response	The task force discontinued the use in the standard of the concept of community-rated premium after recognizing that the term was unlikely to have a satisfactory common definition. The task force modified the language concerning the use of premium rates as the basis for an initial per capita health care rate assumption to clarify the significance of age differences in determining rates and to exemplify the limited circumstances under which an unadjusted premium rate might be used and the disclosures appropriate for such use.

Comment	One commentator raised a question about a per capita rate that had been approved by an accounting firm.
Response	The task force notes that section 3.11 (previously section 3.8.8) and section 4.4 may be relevant to this question and that section 3.4.5 covers actuarial aspects of the use of premium rates.

Section 3.4.6, Impact of Medicare and Other Offsets

Comment	Several comments were received regarding the requirement to confirm the Medicare integration approach.
Response	The task force did not intend this to be an audit requirement and deleted the confirmation wording, believing that recognition of the Medicare integration approach and need for consistency in section 3.7 adequately address the issue.
Comment	A commentator noted that while section 3.4.6 urged adjustments if Medicare changed, it was not clear on the timing or purpose of adjustments.
Response	The task force believes that adjustments for scheduled or proposed changes in Medicare are somewhat contingent upon the purpose of the measurement and modified the standard accordingly, while leaving to the actuary's judgment whether to anticipate changes before they become law.
Comment	A commentator noted that the requirement to develop separate rates for Medicare eligible participants may apply to benefits unaffected by Medicare and to those eligible for Medicare before age 65 by reason of eligibility.
Response	The task force agreed and modified the language to recognize these differences.

Section 3.4.7, Age-Specific Claims Rates

Comment	Several commentators questioned the appropriateness of requiring, at a minimum, five-year age bands for claims rates. Most agreed with the general practice of age grading but some noted instances, such as dental care or medical benefits above age 90, where age grading was relatively flat and five-year age bands would not be appropriate.
Response	The task force withdrew the requirement that initial per capita health care rate assumptions use claims rates in age ranges not to exceed five years and substituted language requiring age bands that are appropriate and not overly broad.

Comment	Two commentators seemed to believe the standard required analysis of the specific claims experience to determine the rates at each age or age band.
Response	The task force clarified that the intent is not to subject claims experience to analysis by age bands but rather to ensure that rate projections account appropriately for the possibility of significant utilization and cost differences within small age bands. This will most likely be demonstrated by normative data.
Comment	Three commentators thought it was sufficient to have only two different claims rates, for non-Medicare eligible versus Medicare eligible ages, or for pre-age-65 and post-age-65 ages.
Response	The task force disagrees that a medical benefits model is likely to be sufficient with only two different claims rates for non-Medicare eligible versus Medicare eligible ages, or pre-age-65 and post-age-65 ages, since such wide bands would be overly broad for the likely age variation in claim rates for a retiree group with lifetime coverage.
Comment	One commentator thought that a defined dollar benefit would fall outside this requirement. Another believed that for a premium reimbursement plan only the premium rate experience would be relevant.
Response	The task force disagrees that this section will be irrelevant to the measurement process for these specific instances and notes that other sections, such as 3.2.1(c), 3.7, 3.8.1(c), and the "Participant Contributions" portion of appendix 2, offer guidance when sponsor financing has defined limits.

Section 3.4.8, Adjustment for Plan Design Changes

Comment	A commentator suggested that this section be expanded to include plan design changes effective in the future.
Response	The task force agreed that, for some purposes, adjustment for future changes might be appropriate, but made no changes to the requirements of this section, feeling the matter is covered adequately in section 3.2.1(f) and 3.8.4.

Section 3.4.9, Adjustment for Administrative Practices

Comment	Three commentators pointed out that these adjustments were most relevant when there had been changes in the administrative practice.
Response	The task force agreed that changes in administrative practice are the relevant concern for rate development, for both claims adjudication and enrollment practices, and changed the language accordingly.

Section 3.4.10, Adjustment for Large Individual Claims	
Comment	Three commentators were concerned about the plan sponsor's ability to supply large claim information, due to privacy concerns or other reasons, or whether the additional workload was justified by additional accuracy.
Response	The task force modified the language to clarify the actuary's duties but does not believe privacy laws will preclude the minimum duties.

Section 3.4.11, Adjustment for Trend	
Comment	A commentator noted that initial per capita claim rates were not always exactly congruent with the first year of the measurement period and suggested that language about trend adjustments should reflect that possibility.
Response	The task force agreed and modified the first sentence accordingly.
Comment	One commentator indicated the effect of trend on the plan's historic experience might not be credible.
Response	The task force agreed and clarified the language.

Section 3.4.12, Adjustment When Plan Sponsor is Also a Provider	
Comment	Three commentators asked for additional guidance on this topic.
Response	The task force believed this was not a part of the practice where appropriate guidance had emerged in succinct form, but did add consideration for reimbursements, such as Medicare, which might be received by the plan sponsor.

Section 3.5, Modeling the Cost of Death Benefits	
Comment	Two commentators pointed out that group term life premium rates often do not vary by age, which produces a reconciliation problem between accounting charges and the true cost of coverage.
Response	The task force believes that the model should still accurately measure true costs and that the accounting issues are not within the scope of this standard.

Section 3.6.1, Coverage and Classification Data	
Comment	One commentator suggested the phrase "merit further refinement" be changed to "require further refinement."
Response	The task force agreed and modified the language.

Section 3.6.2, Consistency	
Comment	Several commentators believed the requirement to "evaluate the operations of the plan" went well beyond the duties of the actuary, and that the actuary should be able to assume that the provisions are being properly administered unless data suggests otherwise.
Response	The task force did not intend the actuary to "audit" the plan operations, and has therefore amended the requirements on plan operations. The task force believes the actuary is in a unique position to observe the plan operations, and thus may discover inconsistencies in plan operations that affect the measurement. In such circumstances, the actuary is directed to section 3.7 for the appropriate actions.
Comment	One commentator suggested an additional example of situations where average claims costs that are secondary to Medicare are high in relation to average costs that are primary.
Response	The task force expanded the example to include the classification of covered spouses based on the retiree's age.
Comment	One commentator suggested the phrase "if significant" in section 3.6.2(d) should not apply just to dependents.
Response	The task force disagreed. While the obligation for spouses and surviving spouses can generally be expected to have a significant impact on the results, the obligation for dependents would do so only if the dependent coverage was extensive and dependents made up a significant proportion of the total covered population.
Section 3.7, Administrative Inconsistencies	
Comment	One commentator suggested that disclosure include "an illustration of the effects of recognizing such inconsistency on either the anticipated level of future claims or the determination of any special one-time cost."
Response	The task force did not believe this was a requirement for all measurements, although it may be appropriate for some.
Comment	One commentator suggested that section 3.7(c) be separated into two points.
Response	The task force agreed and modified the structure.

Comment	Four commentators were concerned that the language required an audit of the plan's administration.
Response	The task force agreed that was not its intent and modified the language of the first sentence to indicate that it addressed guidelines for an actuary who might come across administrative inconsistencies during the course of the measurement process.

Section 3.8.1, Economic Assumptions

Comment	One commentator stressed that the consistent use of a general inflation component in each of the economic assumptions is a necessary but not sufficient condition so as to have consistent overall economic assumptions.
Response	The task force agreed and modified the wording of the first paragraph accordingly.
Comment	Another commentator suggested that since most employers have a consistent discount rate assumption for their SFAS No. 87 and SFAS No. 106 measurements, the new standard should mandate the use of the same discount rate for the pension and retiree welfare valuations.
Response	The task force believes that such a mandate would be excessively stringent and that there are certainly cases where varying the discount rates is quite reasonable, taking into account differences in duration between pension benefits and retiree group benefits.
Comment	One commentator suggested that educational material pertaining to health care cost trend rates be added to this standard.
Response	Actuarial standards of practice typically do not include educational material in the body of the standard, the task force included material in appendix 2 that provides commonly used definitions and illustrations of the factors that can affect health care cost trend rates.
Comment	Three commentators suggested that practitioners be allowed to utilize a single composite trend rate assumption.
Response	The task force agreed and added the following sentence to section 3.8.1(a): "Even if the actuary develops one aggregate trend rate, the actuary should consider these cost components when developing the rate."

Comment	One commentator suggested that there be separate recognition in the actuarial model of the health care trend rate and the plan design elements that may modify the trend.
Response	The task force appreciates the commentator's concern, but believes that the leveraging caused by plan design features can be reflected in the health care cost trend rate if it is not explicitly modeled.
Comment	One commentator suggested that there were two opposing statements in section 3.8.1(d)—that "this standard does not require the use of explicit assumptions about antiselection" and that "the actuary should consider an upward adjustment for antiselection."
Response	The task force modified some of the wording, but stresses that the second sentence to which the commentator referred should be read in its entirety. The task force agrees that the standard should not require the use of specific assumptions for adverse selection. If the actuary changes assumptions for adverse selection such as the participation assumption, however, the actuary should be aware that other assumptions (per capita health care rates) should be modified appropriately.
Comment	Another commentator expressed concern that section 3.8.1(d) allows the actuary to reflect possible antiselection through an implicit assumption.
Response	The task force modified the wording of this section to remove any ambiguity about assumptions for adverse selection.

Section 3.8.2, Demographic Assumptions

Comment	One commentator suggested that it would be helpful to include some discussion about the potential interdependence of the various demographic assumptions. The commentator also suggested that discussion of the other factors that should be considered in choosing a retirement assumption be added.
Response	The task force agreed and modified sections 3.8.2 and 3.8.2(c).
Comment	One commentator questioned whether the ASB is mandating the use of disability assumptions.
Response	The task force directs the commentator to the second sentence of section 3.8.2(b), which states that the actuary should select disability assumptions if the actuary considers the disabled life coverage significant to the measurement.

Comment	One commentator believed that the definition of disability (and issues surrounding how it should be reflected) is amply handled in section 3.5.4(a) of ASOP No. 35.
Response	The task force agrees and notes that section 3.8.2 refers actuaries to ASOP No. 35 for guidance when selecting any of the demographic assumptions.
Comment	One commentator stated that the actuary may decide to use different mortality assumptions for medical (i.e., annuity) and life benefits.
Response	The task force agreed, but believed that no change was needed in section 3.8.2(d) to address this. The task force did, however, add wording to suggest that gender-specific mortality rates may be more appropriate for retiree group benefit obligation measurements rather than unisex mortality rates.
Comment	Another commentator suggested that projecting future mortality improvements could be overstating realistic expectations.
Response	The task force made no change since the second sentence of section 3.8.2(d) states "the actuary should consider." If, after consideration, the actuary determines that future mortality improvements are negligible, he or she should reflect this in the choice of mortality assumptions.

Section 3.8.3. Coverage Assumptions

Comment	One commentator suggested that the guidance could include some consideration of future availability of options, particularly the reduction in availability of Medicare Risk HMO options. This commentator also stated that the actuary could be directed to consider the impact of plan rules on whether a spouse or dependent could be added after retirement.
Response	The task force agreed with both comments and modified the section accordingly.
Comment	One commentator stated that section 3.8.3(a) seems to assume a large group with credible experience while in many cases this will not be the situation.
Response	The task force added wording to stress that group-specific data be used in selecting assumptions when such data are available and credible.

Comment	Another commentator suggested that variations in participation may occur after retirement and thus may affect current retirees as well as future retirees.
Response	The task force agreed and modified sections 3.8.3(a) and (b) accordingly.
Comment	One commentator questioned whether some of the material in this section should be covered in section 3.3.
Response	The task force believes that these assumptions are relevant to future years and are appropriately discussed here.
Comment	One commentator believed that section 3.8.3(a) should be clarified to state that participation can vary by type of coverage when more than one type are available.
Response	The task force agreed and modified the language accordingly.
Comment	Another commentator suggested that, in addition to appropriate age assumptions for covered spouses, appropriate age assumptions should be made for non-spouse dependents.
Response	The task force agreed and modified section 3.8.3(c) accordingly.

Section 3.8.4, Effect of Plan Changes on Assumptions

Comment	One commentator believed that the concept of the additional risk premium in the discount was not clear.
Response	The task force agreed and modified the language accordingly.
Comment	Another commentator expressed concern about the context in which the advice in this section is given.
Response	The task force agreed and modified the language of the second paragraph.
Comment	One commentator believed that the use of the term "professional judgment" in the second paragraph implies that actuaries should never allow anticipated plan change savings to continue into the future.
Response	The task force believes that the second sentence of the second paragraph does not restrict the actuary in recognizing plan change costs/savings in future years. The sentence does require the actuary to exercise judgment before making such a decision.

Comment	Two commentators questioned whether the assumption of the probability of plan termination is an acceptable practice.
Response	The task force believes that there are certain limited circumstances where the use of an assumption of the probability of plan termination should be permitted.

Section 3.8.6, Reviewing Assumptions

Comment	Two commentators stated that the setting of assumptions for the measurement of costs does not always rest with the actuary (for example, SFAS No. 106 measurements).
Response	The task force agrees and refers the commentators to section 3.11, Prescribed Assumptions, Methods, or Other Model Components.

Section 3.8.7, Changes in Assumptions

Comment	One commentator believed that this section should be modified to restrict consideration to other assumptions selected by the actuary, and that no such consideration is required for a change in assumptions not selected by the actuary.
Response	The task force believes that the actuary should review all assumptions, including client prescribed assumptions, where the actuary was asked to give advice, for continued reasonableness.

Section 3.9, Selecting a Cost Allocation Policy (previously titled "Selecting Actuarial Cost Methods")

Comment	Several commentators suggested the section heading should be changed, as the amortization of plan amendments and actuarial gains and losses are not necessarily part of the actuarial cost method.
Response	The task force agreed, modified the section heading and wording accordingly, and added a definition of "cost allocation policy" in section 2.
Comment	One commentator suggested that cash flow adequacy criteria for selecting an appropriate cost allocation policy should be limited to apply solely to situations where only the existing assets will be used to pay benefits.
Response	The task force disagreed.

Section 3.9.2, Dedicated Assets (previously section 3.9.3)

Comment	One commentator suggested that a different example be developed for section 3.9.2(b).
Response	The task force believes the example of a prescribed asset valuation method is relevant.

Section 3.10, Use of Roll-Forward Techniques (previously section 3.9.2)	
Comment	One commentator agreed with the limitation that roll-forwards should be limited to no more than two years after a prior measurement. Another questioned the selection of two years, and several commentators believed this was too restrictive, interpreting the standard to prohibit the use of a 1/1/2000 measurement for SFAS No. 106 12/31/2002 disclosures. A survey of one commentator's firm's clients found that, in addition to biennial re-measurements, triennial measurements were used for a fair number of clients. The survey did not find any situations where a measurement was performed less frequently than once every three years.
Response	The task force had intended the use of roll-forward techniques with triennial re-measurements and modified the text and example in section 3.10.2 (previously section 3.10(b)) to clarify this.
Comment	One commentator questioned the restriction on the length of the roll-forward period when the accounting standard to which the work applies has a requirement for an actuarial study that must, at a minimum, be updated every five years.
Response	The task force recognized that special circumstances could apply and modified the language accordingly.
Comment	One commentator interpreted the restriction on roll-forward techniques to imply that a complete experience analysis of every assumption and claim rate must be preformed at each re-measurement.
Response	The task force refers the commentator to section 3.8.6, which states, in part, that the actuary is not required to do a complete assumption study at each measurement date.
Comment	One commentator suggested the example in section 3.10.1 (previously section 3.10(a)) be clarified so that claim rates used at a prior measurement are trended forward.
Response	The task force agreed and modified the language accordingly.
Comment	One commentator noted that the term "significantly" in section 3.10.3 (previously section 3.10(c)) may cause debate among actuaries as to what is significant.
Response	The task force recognizes this issue, but did not modify the language, as it believes it is appropriate for the actuary to decide, based on professional judgment, whether a key model component has changed significantly since the last full measurement.

Section 3.11, Prescribed Assumptions, Cost Allocation Policies, or Other Model Components (previously Section 3.8.8, Prescribed Actuarial Assumptions)

Comment	One commentator stated that this section should discuss what implications the prescribed assumptions have on the need for the actuary to use consistent assumptions.
Response	The requirement to use consistent assumptions, set forth in section 3.8.5, applies only to assumptions selected by the actuary.
Comment	Another commentator was pleased with the elimination of the language regarding disclosure of exceptions (ACG No. 3, section 6.2) and suggested that this point be more emphatically stated.
Response	The task force believes that the issue is adequately addressed in the fourth paragraph of section 1.2.
Comment	One commentator noted that an actuary cannot be responsible for assumptions prescribed by others or be responsible for the overall appropriateness of results where the prescribed assumption might not be considered appropriate. This commentator cited section 3.8.8, Prescribed Actuarial Assumptions (now section 3.11, Prescribed Assumptions, Methods, or Other Model Components).
Response	The task force agreed that this may be an important distinction in some cases and modified this section to acknowledge exceptions due to section 3.11.

Section 3.12, Reasonableness of Results (previously section 3.10)

Comment	One commentator suggested the language regarding sample participants be clarified.
Response	The task force agreed and modified the language.
Comment	With respect to the requirement to compare expected claims with actual claims, several commentators believed that the requirement was excessive, that actual claims may not be credible, and that only significant differences should be evaluated.
Response	The task force agreed that the actuary should evaluate only significant differences, which may include the volatility of experience in small plans. In response to one commentator, the task force added the word "available."

Section 3.13, Sensitivity of Results to Chosen Assumptions (previously section 3.11)

Comment	Three commentators pointed out that a 20% increase plus a 20% decrease produces a 4% decrease, not 0%.
Response	The task force agreed and made the change.

Section 3.14, Reliance on a Collaborating Actuary (previously section 3.12)	
Comment	Three commentators questioned the implications of this section. One wanted a statement to the effect that each of two actuaries could issue an actuarial opinion with respect to the part of the valuation for which he or she was responsible. Another wanted a statement on the role of the non-actuary who might be qualified by the nature of his or her professional experience, education and training. A third said that the standard implied that one actuary must have expertise in all aspects of the project.
Response	The task force recognizes in section 3.14 that two or more actuaries may collaborate on a project. One may have an expertise in health data analysis and another in long-term projections. Nothing in the standard prevents each from issuing an actuarial opinion with respect to his or her responsibility. Each of these expertises, however, is an actuarial expertise. Neither the task force nor the ASB is aware of any other profession where a practitioner is qualified by the nature of his or her professional experience, education and training to perform the health data analysis or long-term projections that are key to the measurement of retiree group benefit obligations. For an actuary to issue a professional opinion on such measurement and meet this standard, that actuary must take responsibility that all significant aspects meet this standard or disclose the deviation from standard. The standard does not require that one of the actuaries must have expertise in each and every aspect of the measurement, but does require at least one of the actuaries to take responsibility that the results of the health data analysis used for initial rate and other health care assumptions mesh appropriately with the assumptions and model used for long-term projections.

SECTION 4. COMMUNICATIONS AND DISCLOSURES	
Section 4.1, Documentation	
Comment	The task force received several comments regarding documentation of health care rate development. A commentator questioned the applicability of ASOP No. 31 to retiree health benefits, particularly since there seems to be a specific exemption in ASOP No. 31 for work related to SFAS No. 106.
Response	The sentence referred to in ASOP No. 31 contains a contingent exemption. It states, "The standard does not apply to work done in connection with [SFAS No. 106] unless ASOPs pertaining to SFAS No. 106 specifically call for application of this standard." That sentence is followed by the statement, "A task force is being created to address issues related to SFAS 106."
	The task force that was created recommended the revision of ASOP No. 6 and also believed it was appropriate for ASOP No. 31 to apply to SFAS No. 106, as well as other retiree group benefit measurements. The current task force agrees that ASOP No. 31 should apply to SFAS No. 106. The ASB affirms that ASOP No. 31 does apply to work performed in connection with SFAS No. 106. The contingent exemption in ASOP No. 31 relating to SFAS No. 106 is now erased.
	Documentation is an essential component of actuarial practice. ASOP No. 31 provides guidance on important aspects of documenting health benefit plan ratemaking. Not every issue covered by ASOP No. 31, however, applies to every development of rates. The actuary developing or using rates for a retiree health valuation should comply with those aspects of ASOP No. 31 relevant to the case at hand.
Comment	A commentator suggested that claim rates used in retiree health valuations differ from other actuarially derived claim rates and are not subject to the same outside review as the ratemaking covered under ASOP No. 31.
Response	The task force believes this may be a misreading of the purpose of ASOP No. 31, which is not a standard on ratemaking, but rather provides "guidance on documentation in the process of health benefit plan ratemaking." The task force believes development of per capita claim rates for measuring retiree health benefit obligations clearly falls within the ratemaking process, whether the purpose is plan design, cost projections, or financial reporting. ASOP No. 31 also clearly states that it is not a standard on pricing, which may be subject to extensive regulatory review.

Comment	Another commentator suggested this standard should include a requirement that documentation regarding development of health care rates be made available to another actuary upon the client's request and that it not be withheld as proprietary.
Response	ASOP No. 31 states that "Documentation should be available to the actuary's client or employer, and it should be made available to other persons when the client or employer so requests and provided such availability is not otherwise improper." The task force believes this accurately states the actuary's need to cooperate with others who have an appropriate role in determining the rationale for a particular assumption about per capita health care rates. While there may be software that is proprietary, the actuary's cooperation should encompass source data and methods. Differences of opinion on what is proprietary might be referred to the Actuarial Board for Counseling and Discipline (ABCD).
Comment	One commentator noted that ASOP No. 31 also had relevance to ratemaking aspects of sections of the standard other than section 3.4.
Response	The task force agreed and modified that reference accordingly.
Comment	Several commentators objected to the documentation requirements of the standard as being "excessive," "inappropriate," "severe," or "burdensome." One commentator suggested that the proposed requirements were beyond the normal documentation requirements.
Response	Upon review, the task force believes that the extent of the documentation required by this standard is consistent with other, contemporaneous standards. In addition, the documentation required seems to be the minimum level necessary "so that another actuary qualified in the same field could assess the reasonableness of the work." Furthermore, the task force notes that some commentators appear to have confused documentation with disclosure requirements, which is the difference between one's work papers and the communication of one's work product.
Section 4.2, Disclosure	
Comment	One commentator questioned the meaning of the word "significant" throughout this section.
Response	The task force identified the items subject to disclosure, but leaves it to the professional judgment of the actuary to decide the appropriate extent of such disclosure, given the purpose of the measurement and the expected use of the disclosure material.

Comment	Two commentators requested a clarification of terms used in section 4.2(a).
Response	The task force added references to sections in the standard.
Comment	One commentator said that the last paragraph was too restricting, in that it limits external references to only actuarial communications.
Response	This paragraph is intended to reduce the repetition of previously disclosed actuarial material in a current document; it should not be seen as limiting any other external references to commonly available documents.

BIBLIOGRAPHY

[1]   2000 Technical Review Panel on the Medicare Trustees Reports, *Review of Assumptions and Methods of the Medicare Trustees' Financial Projections*, December 2000.

[2]   2004 Technical Review Panel on the Medicare Trustees Reports, *Review of Assumptions and Methods of the Medicare Trustees' Financial Projections*, December 2004.

[3]   Anderson, Arthur W. *Pension Mathematics for Actuaries*, The Windsor Press, Inc., 1985.

[4]   Board of Trustees, *2006 Annual Report of The Board of Trustees of the Federal Hospital Insurance and Federal Supplementary Medical Insurance Trust Funds*, May 2006.

[5]   Centers for Medicare and Medicaid Services, *Data Compendium*, 2003 Edition.

[6]   Centers for Medicare and Medicaid Services, *Enrolling in Medicare*, Department of Health & Human Services, Publication No. CMS-11036, June 2004

[7]   Centers for Medicare and Medicaid Services, *Medicare & You 2006*, Department of Health & Human Services, CMS Publication No. 10050, January 2006.

[8]   Chaikind, Hinda Ripps and Fran Larkins, *Health Insurance Coverage for Retirees*, Congressional Research Service, June 2005.

[9]   Congressional Budget Office, *CBO's Analysis of Regional Preferred Provider Organizations Under the Medicare Modernization Act*, October 2004.

[10]   Congressional Budget Office, *A Detailed Description of CBO's Cost Estimate for the Medicare Prescription Drug Benefit*, July 2004.

[11]   Dopkeen, Jonathon C., *Postretirement Health Benefits*, Pew Memorial Trust Policy Synthesis, Health Services Research 21:6, February 1987.

[12]   Employee Benefit Research Institute, *Retiree Health Benefits: What is the Promise?*, ERBI, 1989.

[13]   Feldman, Roger, Bryan Dowd, Marian Wrobel, *Risk Selection and Benefits in the Medicare+Choice Program*, Health Care Financing Review, Volume 25, Number 1, Fall 2003.

[14]   Financial Accounting Standards Board, *Statement No. 106, Employers' Accounting for Postretirement Benefits Other Than Pensions*, December 1990.

[15]   Fronstin, Paul, *The Impact of the Erosion of Retiree Health Benefits on Workers and Retirees*, Employee Benefit Research Institute, Issue Brief No. 279, March 2005.

[16]   Gabriel, Roeder, Smith & Company, *The GASB's Accounting Standards for Other Post-employment Benefits*, briefing paper, August 2004.

[17]   Governmental Accounting Standards Board, *Statement No. 43, Financial Reporting for Postemployment Benefit Plans Other Than Pension Plans*, April 2004.

[18]   Governmental Accounting Standards Board, *Statement No. 45, Accounting and Financial Reporting by Employers for Postemployment Benefits Other Than Pensions*, June 2004.

[19] Grossman, Robert J., *Holding Back Bankruptcy*, HR Magazine, May 2003.

[20] Guterman, Stuart, *Putting Medicare in Context: How Does the Balanced Budget Act Affect Hospitals,?* The Urban Institute, July 2000.

[21] Hoffman Jr., Earl D., Barbara S. Klees and Catherine A. Curtis, *Brief Summaries of Medicare & Medicaid, Centers for Medicare and Medicaid Services*, November 2005.

[22] Ingber, Melvin J., "Implementation of Risk Adjustment in Medicare," *Health Care Financing Review*, Volume 21, Number 3, Spring 2000.

[23] Jeweler, Robin, *Employment-Related Issues in Bankruptcy*, Congressional Research Service, November 2005.

[24] Jordan, Chester W., *Life Contingencies*, Society of Actuaries, 1971.

[25] Kaiser Family Foundation, *Medicare Fact Sheet—Medicare Spending and Financing*, April 2005.

[26] Kaiser Family Foundation, *Medicare Fact Sheet—Medicare Advantage*, September 2005.

[27] Kaiser Family Foundation and Health Research and Educational Trust, *Employer Health Benefits—2005 Annual Survey,* 2005.

[28] Kaiser Family Foundation and Hewitt Associates, *Prospects for Retiree Health Benefits as Medicare Prescription Drug Coverage Begins*, December 2005.

[29] Moran, Anne E., *No Good Deed Goes Unpunished—Employers' Attempts to Modify Retiree Health Plans,* Steptoe & Johnson, September 2002.

[30] O'Sullivan, Jennifer, Chaikind, Tilson, Boulanger, Morgan, *Overview of the Medicare Prescription Drug and Reform Conference Agreement, H.R. 1*, Congressional Research Service, December 2003.

[31] Paul, Robert D. and Diane M. Disney, *The Sourcebook on Postretirement Health Care Benefits, Panel Publishers, Inc.*, 1988.

[32] Petertil, Jeffrey P., "Measuring Terminable Postretirement Obligations", *North American Actuarial Journal*, Volume 9, Number 1, 2005.

[33] Petertil, Jeffrey P., "Aging Curves for Health Care Cost in Retirement," *North American Actuarial Journal*, Volume 9, Number 3, 2005.

[34] Pope, Gregory C., Kautter, Ellis, Ash, Ayanian, Iezzoni, Ingber, Levy and Robst, *Risk Adjustment of Medicare Capitation Payments Using the CMS-HCC Model, Health Care Financing Review*, Volume 25, Number 4, Summer 2004.

[35] Reese, Adam J., "Development of the Last-Year-of-Life Valuation Model for Retiree Medical Plans," *North American Actuarial Journal*, Volume 4, Number 2, 2000.

[36] Rizzo, James J., *OPEB News You Can Use*, Florida Governmental Finance Officers Association newsletter, October/November 2005.

[37] Silverblatt, Howard and Dave Guarino, *S&P 500 2005: Pensions and Other Post Employment Benefits,* Standard & Poor's Report, June 6, 2006.

[38] U.S. General Accounting Office, *Retiree Health Benefits—Employer-Sponsored Benefits May Be Vulnerable to Further Erosion*, May 2001.

[39] Winklevoss, Howard J., *Pension Mathematics With Numerical Illustrations*, Pension Research Council Publications, 1993.

[40] Yamamoto, Dale H., *A Guide to FASB Statement No. 106*, Pension and Profit Sharing Section 2, Bulletin 50, Research Institute of America, March 1991.

[41] Yamamoto, Dale H., *Design and Funding of Other Post-Employment Benefits*, Society of Actuaries, Study Note 8R-115-00, 2000.

[42] Yamamoto, Dale H., *FAS 106 and 112*, Society of Actuaries, Study Note 8R-220-00, 2000.

[43] Yamamoto, Dale H., What Comes After the Retiree Drug Subsidy?," *Benefits Quarterly*, 3rd Quarter 2006.

INDEX